THE MIND'S FATE

THE
MIND'S
FATE
ROBERT
COLES

A PSYCHIATRIST LOOKS

AT HIS PROFESSION—THIRTY

YEARS OF WRITINGS

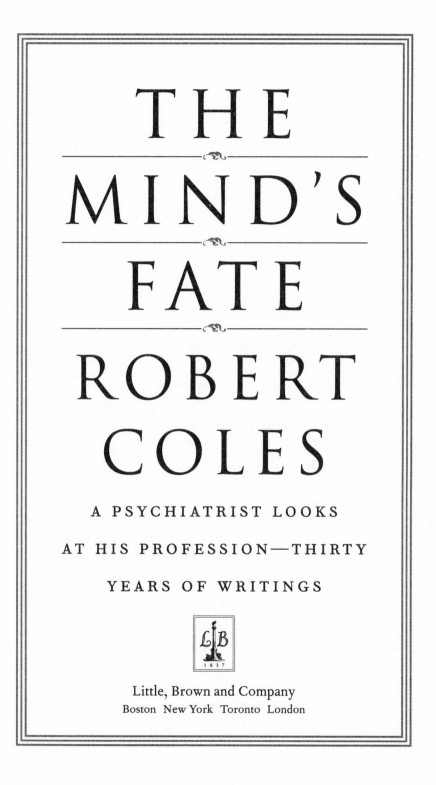

Little, Brown and Company

Boston New York Toronto London

SECOND EDITION

"Clinical & Human: Interpersonal Psychoanalysis" © 1965 by The New York Times Company.
Reprinted by permission. "The Way of the Transgressor," "Still and Quiet Consciences," "Hell on
Earth," and "The Stranger" were previously published in *The New Yorker*. "The Inner and Outer
World" reprinted from *The Infant at Risk*, Symposia Specialists, P.O. Box 610397, Miami, Florida.

Library of Congress Cataloging-in-Publication Data
Coles, Robert.
    The mind's fate: a psychiatrist looks at his profession: thirty
years of writings/Robert Coles. — 2nd ed.
        p.   cm.
    Contains articles reprinted from various sources.
    Includes bibliographical references and index.
    ISBN 0-316-15164-5
    1. Psychiatry.   2. Psychoanalysis.   3. Coles, Robert.   I. Title.
    [DNLM: 1. Psychiatry — collected works.   2. Psychoanalysis —
collected works.   WM 7 C693mb 1995]
    RC458.C54   1995
    616.89 — dc20

                                                        95-12028

                10 9 8 7 6 5 4 3 2 1

                        HAD

Published simultaneously in Canada by Little, Brown & Company (Canada) Limited

Printed in the United States of America

TO ANNA FREUD
AND TO JOHN WESTERN

"The mind's fate is, after all, a person's fate. We are drawn along by our private visions, but beyond them stretch almost infinitely for each of us the vast and compelling mysteries of chance and circumstance."

GEORGES BERNANOS

CONTENTS

Contents

INTRODUCTION

TO THE SECOND EDITION

In the summer of 1961, when the first essay of this collection appeared in *The Atlantic,* I was thirty-one years old. I had gone to medical school with the intention of becoming a pediatrician; had taken post-graduate training in order to become one; had decided to become a child psychiatrist, instead, after working with boys and girls who were sick with leukemia and polio, and who wanted so very much not only to be "treated" by a doctor, but to talk with him, ask questions of him, try with him to figure out what mattered much, what mattered little, and why; had done my required two-year stint in the military in Biloxi, Mississippi (where I worked in an air force neuropsychiatric hospital), and simultaneously had begun psychoanalytic training in the nearby New Orleans Psychoanalytic Institute. At the time, no matter all those years given over to training and more training, to seemingly endless "supervisory sessions," to the study of pediatrics and psychiatry and child psychiatry and psychoanalysis and child psychoanalysis, I was increasingly unsure of my life's direction. I knew that I wanted to work with children; knew that I had been learning more and more about how their bodies, their minds,

worked. I was living then in the South, a consequence of the fatefulness of a particular assignment, and I also knew that a great struggle
was taking place there: the onset of the civil rights movement. I had
myself, also by chance, witnessed a significant moment in that growing struggle: the entrance by Ruby Bridges into the first grade of the
Frantz Elementary School. The result would be a complete boycott
of that school by its white population. I was on my way to a psychiatric conference at Tulane Medical School the day Ruby started her
school life, and because the police had blocked traffic on the streets I
usually used, I found myself witnessing a mob at work: shouts and
screams, threats and curses, meant to tell a black child that she was
utterly worthless, and that she would soon enough die if she (and her
family, of course) didn't have some serious second thoughts about
obeying the federal judge J. Skelly Wright, who had ordered her, and
her alone, to desegregate a Louisiana school six years after the
Supreme Court had knocked down the "separate but equal" ruling
that had given sanction to generations of segregated education in the
South.

I still remember, actually, what crossed my mind as I listened to a
mob's rising rage and watched a little girl, escorted by federal marshals, climb the steps of a schoolhouse, her jeopardy, her vulnerability, so visible to any of us living in that old, cosmopolitan port city
who cared to pay attention. I was to be a "respondent" at a clinical
conference that day, and now I would not be there. What would
"they" think, my psychiatric colleagues? I fear that I also can recall,
even now, the capacity of my mind to anticipate what might be said,
the direction that a certain kind of reasoning might elicit: Did he have
some "problem" that prompted this absence? Was he "working something out"? If such thoughts now seem foolish, even laughable, they
at least tell of an occupational hazard that has, in the past, confronted
some of us in the so-called mental health professions, one that, I suspect, will even today strike some young psychiatrists in training as not
unfamiliar. It is a peculiar version of George Eliot's "unreflecting
egoism," which ignores social reality in exclusive favor of an omnipotent psychology, as if everything we do or don't do, everything that
happens to us or doesn't take place in our lives, everything we become
or don't end up being, has to do only with what takes place in our
mind. It is easy, in that regard, to caricature such an attitude, such a

way of seeing things — the pitiably cloistered psychiatrist or psychologist who won't allow for luck or chance or circumstance, who funnels relentlessly all human experience into the workings of a particular theoretical scheme. Yet, even now I remember those questions posed in response to one or another incident in a person's life: Why did you go there, or do this, and even if you couldn't avoid that situation or turn of events, why do you let it bother you so? In the 1960s, such a hermetic psychology, turned in on itself, and at a radical remove from the cultural and political world, began to crumble as more than just the Frantz School was asked to take stock of itself, change its assumptions, about what (and who) matters. The psychiatry I knew in the North during the late 1950s, in the South during the early 1960s, awaited its own kind of desegregation — applicants of color, yes, of course, but also the shift in perspective that comes when diversity challenges an entrenched insularity.

Not that Freud, or those gifted conceptualists who picked up his mantle, hadn't foreseen the perils of orthodoxy, maybe its inevitable ascendancy — which, just as inevitably, would someday, somehow be challenged. Freud was constantly revising his ideas, and in some of his later writing, responding to the dramatic changes that took place in Europe during his lifetime, he was anything but the possessive theorist or ideologue, anxious to enforce the compliance of unquestioning faith from his followers. He knew well that his own discoveries would be followed by those of others; that psychology has to contend with its two great antagonists, biology on the one hand, and on the other, that flow of human affairs that gets called history. He knew, put differently, that a new social or political reality can have a major impact on the way children think and feel, on the way members of families manage their time together, on the way people behave — and too, he understood that a new biochemical and physiological knowledge can make a difference in what is possible for psychiatrists to do for their patients. We live in particular neighborhoods and nations, and at a particular time; we also live in a body that has its various rhythms, its possibilities and its limitations. The mind belongs to the neurochemistry that is the brain, as the young Freud who experimented with psychotropic drugs well realized, and as the aging Freud, ever the dreamer, also realized when he foresaw a biological psychiatry as a partial successor of sorts to psychoanalysis — a new means of understanding how we human beings think and, as well, how we go wrong in our thinking, become prey to various apprehensions and terrors.

A founder's breadth and depth of vision is not, however, always granted to or adopted by his followers. As early as 1936 (in *The Ego and the Mechanisms of Defense*), Anna Freud was worrying publicly that her father's bold surmises and conjectures, ever subject to his own visionary revision, were becoming a matter of creedal compliance by all too many. She went further, contrasted the pioneers who created a new science raw, wrested it out of their own marginality, their own personal hurt and suffering, with those who came to psychoanalytic psychiatry for its established authority, influence, and yes, for the privileges it offers: influence, money, respect. Her most distinguished analysand, Erik H. Erikson, only seven years her junior and also among the founding fathers (and mothers!) of child psychoanalysis, was also worried (by the middle and late 1940s) about a kind of orthodoxy that had befallen, ironically, a field of study meant to give those who understood it more, not less, intellectual and emotional leeway. In his epilogue to *Childhood and Society* (the very title a challenge, an insistence), Erikson warned of the dangers that go with a didactic literalism. He himself dared to go learn from native American children (the Sioux, the Yurok) — left the upper-bourgeois world that predominantly constitutes psychoanalytic practice, for quite another human environment. In so doing, he began to see that Freud's chronological depiction of childhood (the well-known oral, anal, phallic "stages") was but one of many ways of considering the passage of the young through time and through the family and community experiences that significantly give shape even to the first years of life, never mind those spent in school.

"I spent a good part of my writing life trying to amplify psychoanalytic ideas in accordance with observations I made outside my clinical office," Erikson said in 1971 as he retrospectively contemplated his research, his efforts to describe it. Then, he spoke an instructive afterthought: "It's not always easy to add a footnote here, a reservation or amplification there, to a body of work that is for some becoming set in stone — but that is what one generation can do for another, our children helping us to see what we, for understandable reasons, didn't notice. The issue is not 'right' or 'wrong,' 'good' or 'bad' — those unfortunately moralistic polarizations that take place in science as well as religion or metaphysics. The issue is more historical, what we get to see over time. Even our notion of what a 'cure' means will vary, depending on who we are and when and where we are living. This is a 'pure common sense,' but we all lose some of that as we get caught up in one kind of struggle or another!"

In his own tactful way he was posing a vigorous, critical challenge to others. The psychoanalysis he knew so well, practiced, used as an instrument of research at the middle of the twentieth century, had given its mostly Western and well-to-do adherents a penetrating look, indeed, at the bedroom, the nursery, the parlor — all that happens in the home life of families. Still, as he well knew, those homes are but part of the story: they carry mortgages, for instance, and into them come all sorts of powerful, affecting stimuli, through radio and television, newspapers and magazines. Our dreams tell us about our mothers and fathers, our brothers and sisters, our husbands and wives and friends and lovers; but they also tell us about race, class, nationality, occupation, the anxieties and fears, the worries and worse that they, too, can generate in our minds, in our consciousness and in the unconscious alike. It was Erikson's distinctive and important achievement to point that out, to make the case for an enlargement of psychoanalytic theory that did not, however, diminish the enormous scope of its pioneering founder, that "first psychoanalyst," and his colleagues.

As I look at the essays that follow, I realize, in retrospect, their overall intent: to help document through resort to what James Agee called "human actuality" the kinds of connections Erikson suggested as important — how, for instance, a six-year-old black child fighting her way past a mob of heckling, threatening adults comes to terms both cognitively and emotionally with such a moment in both her life and that of her country. Before I "met" that child, saw her on a New Orleans street, I had been asked to write about my experiences as a hospital resident for a proposed issue of *The Atlantic* to be devoted to psychiatry in American life. I struggled hard with that essay — anxious to say what was on my mind, but also a little afraid to do so. I well remember the encouragement I received from my own psychoanalyst, whose position as president of a psychoanalytic institute did not prevent him from appreciating the risks that might accompany even a carefully worded critique of a profession that, as Erikson once put it (speaking of careful wording), had become "perhaps too consolidated institutionally." For Dr. Kenneth Beach, that appraisal was, perhaps, not sufficiently admonishing in nature. Once, back from a psychoanalytic meeting up north, he described what he regarded as "ideological rancor" — a sad disappointment to someone who very much valued the essence of his profession, its emphasis on the exploration of human relatedness.

I have to say that Ruby's example made a big difference to me as I finished the writing of that piece — as did my wife Jane's constant encouragement. As she once put it for me: "If Ruby can walk past that mob, you can raise your voice just a little." Fearful and self-absorbed, I said no. She not only insisted, but wrote several of the more critical paragraphs, determined that we try to suggest a direction for "young psychiatrists" to pursue, to try to give expression to a mix of appreciation, gratitude (all that a given profession can enable in its practitioners, in their patients), and a discontent (a certain narrowness of availability, a growing inclination to impose theoretical speculation upon human complexity, to the point that what, finally, are reifications become taken for reality). I worried silently then (I still worry) that the conceptualizations and generalizations of social science don't do justice to the human scene, to the ironies and ambiguities, the inconsistencies and contradictions and paradoxes that continually inform our everyday lives — which, after all, don't necessarily unfold in the linear direction dictated by this or that paradigm, but respond to accident and incident, to the unforeseen, the unpredictable, to luck, good and bad. I suppose, even back then, as is certainly the case now, I was turning toward novelists and short story writers for a kind of psychology and psychiatry that responds with an unashamed wonder and bemusement to life's surprises, its fateful turns. Still, as Erikson once pointed out to a group of us anxious to celebrate the psychological capaciousness of, say, *Middlemarch* or *War and Peace*, "novelists don't have office hours for patients" — and then, from him, a reminder that "theory is a jab at the unknown" and is best regarded as such. "You may be disenchanted lovers," he went on to observe — and then the explanation: we had once expected more of theory than it could possibly deliver, and now were overlooking our own former idolatry by hitting hard at that of others. All of that was offered in a spirit of good humor (and autobiographical candor), a contrast with the chastising psychological reductionism that can be used to silence all dissent by turning it into an occasion for vented, accusatory psychopathology.

Today's psychiatry is, naturally, far less preoccupied with the value or the flaws of psychoanalytic theory. Today's psychiatry is heavily biological in nature, making a concerted effort to influence human behavior through psychopharmacology. Now, an assortment of medications promises a growing degree of control over psychotic behavior, an expanding influence even on the everyday difficulties several generations have learned to consider relatively "normal": the anxieties and fears that go with living. Now, pediatricians give growing numbers of children ritalin for a diagnostic entity called "attention deficit disorder." I hear some of them wondering exactly what that "syndrome" is, and why, suddenly, so *many* children (once considered a bit unruly, maybe, or to be going through a spell of recalcitrance or truculence) are now to be regarded as "sick" and in need of a neurochemical course of treatment. "I have five children out of twenty-three with 'attention deficit syndrome' and on ritalin," a fourth-grade teacher tells me, as if my past clinical training qualifies me as the proper respondent to her more than implicit perplexity, her quizzical sense that something is awry, all right, but something not entirely "medical" in nature. On another occasion, she is more candidly forthcoming, moves from a terse statistical comment to a more plaintive cry of alarm: "I've been teaching all these years [twenty-two at the time she spoke], and I thought I knew something about children — most of all, I thought I knew the ones in real trouble, and the ones just growing up, in their own ways [the difference between the two]. Over the years, I've called up some parents, only a few, and told them I'm concerned, that's how I start out. The long and short of it, maybe they'll take stock and see where they might go [to talk with their son or their daughter, to go see the pediatrician, maybe, or the psychiatrist]. You know, sometimes that call from me is all it would take: the parents would be put on notice, and they'd try to figure out what they should do.

"These days, though, it's something else, again, as my daughter says. Now, I'll be quite happy with the way it's going in school for this child or that one, and the next thing you know, *I'm* being called by parents (it's the other way around!), and the parents have gone to the doctor, and he's said, she's said, well, the child is 'hyperactive,' or 'borderline-hyperactive' — that's the one I hear [about] all the time, the 'borderline' case — and either the child should go on a 'trial' of the drug, or we should 'reevaluate' in a couple of months. Oh, I think to myself, this is an all-right kid, that's what I'd *like* to say, but I dare not! No one wants to have a long talk with me — or with the child, either! You talk about 'attention deficit' — that's what a lot of kids in the crowded day-care centers experience: a lack of individual concern, a hunger for their parents, who aren't with them enough. The kid has done something that has the mother worried, or, more likely, the day-care people, the folks who look after the children until the parents get home, they're worried, and the next thing you know, the doctor is brought into it, and it isn't as if they're having these long talks with him, and he's having long talks with the child. I've heard the story again and again — they'll [the parents] tell the symptoms, and he'll ask some questions, and the next thing you know, there's this 'diagnosis,' or maybe there might well be something wrong, so a diagnosis is around the corner, and then it's pills. Of course, some of our teachers here are on them, too — pills, but a different kind. They'd deny it, but they are [on medication], I know, because I'm the 'mother confessor.' They'll call me, they'll tell me, and so I hear it all. And I think to myself, what about the time when we had our troubles, and they'd get us down, and if we didn't snap out of it, we'd go see a minister, or we'd talk with our friends, or, all right, we went to the doctor, and we talked with him, and if it was real bad, we'd go see a psychiatrist — I've known that to happen. But now you have teachers on pills, a lot of them, and I'll tell you, the school nurse of our children, she's taking pills, and how many of their parents, I don't know, but a lot; and I *do* know, because the kids will make a mistake and say something, and then I know. Anyway, if you want my opinion about *some* of these kids taking ritalin — they're children who haven't had enough attention paid to them, and now they don't know how to pay attention to others: they have *that* kind of [attention deficit] problem!"

I offer this edited excerpt from a long conversation with a New England schoolteacher who works in a fairly well-to-do suburban town because, even though I didn't agree with all she said, in her own manner this earnest woman of long experience was addressing a matter of great contemporary consequence to psychiatry: how to regard the troubles of those who come to us. Are the patients we see most likely to be in need of many and long conversations, in the expectation or hope that the source of their worries and fears will be discovered, that the origins of those worries and fears in childhood and family experiences will be traced, that their self-protective (if exhausting, unnerving, trouble-making) maneuvers of the mind ("defenses") will be exposed? Are we to regard those patients more sociologically, to emphasize their occupations, their income, their skin color, their background with respect to nationality or region as crucial in their lives, in the formation of their sense of who they are, of what is possible (and impossible) for them, and why? Or are those same patients to be viewed as being in biochemical or neurophysiological jeopardy, with part of their brain in one or another kind of "imbalance," with this or that substance lacking altogether, in short supply, or, indeed, all too much present? The one safe answer to those three questions, of course, is to say, loud and clear, *all of the above,* and to mean it, to insist upon a personal and familial scrutiny, a socially sensitive evaluation that looks at the neighborhood, the school, the values transmitted by a particular community, and to consider the symptoms presented as possible clues to the brain's function, its biology and chemistry, both.

Nevertheless, the various decades impose their particular stamps of considerable approval, or relative lack of interest. I was trained at the height of psychoanalytic ascendance, as it were. Later on, I spent a good part of my professional working life trying to learn how factors such as race, class, ethnicity, religion, and politics can in their everyday implications for children and their parents alike have substantial psychological, even psychiatric import. Now, as I become, at the very least, eligible to write an essay titled "A Far-from-Young Psychiatrist Looks at His Profession," I realize that I'm very much with the teacher quoted above in mind, in spirit, as I wonder what to make of the working lives, for example, of the young psychiatrists whose hospital and clinic work I supervise. They tell me of their "drug rounds," meaning ten minutes to each patient to make sure he or she is doing well on this or that drug. They tell me that fewer and fewer of their patients are on no medication — that, often enough, all of their patients have been or soon enough are to be on this or that drug. They tell me that *thereafter,* once the best dosage is ascertained, conversations about "the emotions" can be begun to some effective purpose: pharmacology as a decided prelude to psychology — and indeed, not rarely, the former as the essential mainstay of today's psychiatry, with interpretive, "psychodynamic" exchanges far reduced in number, as compared to past years.

I listen, and again, like the teacher, wonder what to think, how to integrate in my own mind (let alone share with others through writing) what I have recently heard, seen, learned, with what I have experienced these past thirty-five years (that is to say, heard, seen, learned from those many patients who teach all of us so very much). These days, more and more, psychiatrists think of their patients as neurochemically unbalanced in one way or another, as challenges, therefore, to a gradual process of drug initiation and titration. A growing number of patients spend little or no time talking with their doctors about their everyday difficulties in getting through life; rather, they hope for a kind of calm to settle on them, courtesy of a pill that will do its work, cast its magic spell by dint of its effect on the brain's circuitry. (Not that substantial numbers of people won't respond favorably even to a pill made up of sugar — as psychopharmacologists know, when they talk of "the placebo effect.") Under such circumstances, patients expect from their doctors not so much understanding of their various difficulties as relief from the symptoms (anxiety, moodiness, fearfulness) those difficulties prompt. A medical student of mine, at twenty-eight "on medication" (Paxil), tells me, "I feel good now," whereas before he felt "crummy all the time." I ask him why he used to feel like that, and he tells me he doesn't really know. He saw a psychiatrist, who prescribed a medicine, and now a patient is quite pleased. I wonder, at this point, why I am so concerned. Perhaps I have an old-fashioned sense that this young man, in fact, had good reason to feel some anxiety, some moments of sadness. His brother is mortally ill, and he himself is on the verge of making two major decisions about his future: whether he'll marry a longtime girlfriend, and which branch of medicine he'll pursue in a residency. Still, he is glad to be rid of the symptoms that brought him to a psychiatrist (a tightness at his throat, insomnia, spells of panic that seemingly came out of nowhere), glad to be feeling "fine" — even as I wonder whether, were I in his shoes, I'd really want to be immune to anxiety, to a heaviness of heart that surely qualifies as melancholy: no anxiety in the face of danger here or there, no sadness, no down times in the face of an imminent death of a loved one or the times of aloneness that follow such a loss? Another medical student, on Prozac since her college years, speaks of that drug as if it offers entrance to the New Jerusalem, provides a constant means of steadying her nerves, everyone else's nerves, and is a harbinger of happiness for millions of psychologically needy people. I wonder, as I hear her talk, what has happened to her natural skepticism, her otherwise robust scientific skepticism. Yes, Prozac has helped her and so many others, but she speaks of it the way, well, some of us forty years ago spoke of psychoanalysis: as an answer to anyone's problems with anything.

I remember working with alcoholics in the Massachusetts General Hospital during my adult psychiatry residency. The year was 1959, and the alcoholism clinic was run by Alfred O. Ludwig, a psychoanalyst who had once been an internist. Several of my patients were not only charming, as certain alcoholics can notoriously be, but dangerously convincing to the rather innocent and gullible (and, yes, all too optimistic) doctor I then was. They kept telling me that they loved to drink; that they felt so much better when they "had a few belts" in them; that *if,* if only there weren't all those consequences, those side effects, the hangovers and worse. Dr. Ludwig listened as I recited such a line of argument, a little persuaded (seduced) myself. Together we listened to some interviews he had done (and taped) with alcoholics — listened to them celebrating the near euphoria they felt for a while, followed, alas, by the descent into nausea, incoordination, headache, and general malaise. I can still hear one patient urgently addressing rhetorically not only one doctor, but an entire profession (addressing, in fact, the future) by asking whether, one day, someday, a drug would come along that enabled the high of drinking, without its debilitating postlude. Dr. Ludwig smiled, sitting beside me, even as we together heard him address his patient on that score, ask her whether she'd really want to live all the time on the kind of highs she was extolling. Of course, her answer was an emphatic yes, and the doctor listening to her was not, then, ready to disagree; only to pay her close heed, learn, wait for another time to discuss that particular matter. But for us residents he had more than enough time and inclination to remind us of the issue at stake: here was a mind-altering drug that brought big changes in outlook to many who used it — at a price. What would we think (what would happen) if the price were lowered, significantly lowered: if there could be a sustained alteration of attitude and mood, with no crippling downside afterward? Moreover, what would *our* job then be? To pursue such folks, figuratively, with our grim reminders that they aren't facing up to this life's quite evident, quite troubling and disheartening realities?

To be sure, some who use today's psychotropic drugs are enabled to resort to one or another version of Freud's "talking cure" — that is, to take advantage of tension subdued, of apprehension allayed, in order to speak with a doctor about what ails them, frightens them, sends them into fits of alarm or gloom. Still, even among my medical and teaching colleagues, I know of men and women who "maintain" themselves on a given drug, with the help of brief and increasingly occasional visits for "monitoring." Is this a new, more effective kind of psychiatric care, or an evasion of this life's psychological reality by dint of "drugs," albeit ones made by pharmaceutical companies rather than distilleries or farmers of the third world? Unquestionably, there are specific psychiatric disorders (manic-depressive psychosis, for instance) that respond with seeming precision to one or another drug. But complaints such as anxiety or fearfulness or gloom obviously connect with what happens in the world, which so often accounts for, even justifies an emotional response, sometimes a quite profound and upsetting one — hence the recent concern by some that psychopharmacology in some hands has become an instrument of evasion or "denial" not unlike that of alcohol or narcotics.

For all the changes taking place in the psychiatry of these last years of the twentieth century; for all the discussion over the role of psychopharmacology in clinical practice; for all the tensions between the various schools of therapy, of psychoanalysis; for all the tugs between theorists and their prideful property, ideas and concepts, the ultimate mission of those who are doctors of the mind remains solidly that of the attentive listener first, who has learned how to make sense of the remarks made by his or her patients — the inside cry for a knowing assistance that is at the heart of a person's decision to visit a physician. We human beings are creatures of awareness, of language, of long and articulated memory — and also, creatures whose special skills and triumphs live side by side with a special capacity for tragedy. Our losses, our vulnerabilities, our weak spots and soft spots, our ultimate destiny of disappearance from this planet are known to us, as they are not to all other forms of life on this earth. Through words, whether spoken to others or silently put to ourselves, we constantly struggle to make sense of things, even as we try (if we can) to prepare ourselves for the worst: hunker or huddle down, reach out, whistle in the dark, while trembling mightily within ourselves. Not rarely, at such moments, we have learned in this century to seek the counsel of psychiatrists, men and women presumed to understand our many possible predicaments, our wild or loony sides, our lapses into incoherence or rage, into lusts and times of darkness that threaten our reliability, our stability, our very lives (or those of others). To be sought out, to be asked to attend such a cry, such a call from others, is no small honor and privilege, and ought to be regarded as such by us, even in this day of a medicine increasingly bureaucratized, commercialized.

Of course, even if we commonly know how to figure others out, in the end what counts most heavily of all is what we *do* with what we have come to know: how we respond to those who sit opposite us, lie on couches before us. Civility, tact, respect, a willingness to put ourselves in the situation of others, see ourselves as, finally, their kin, because they are fellow human beings, no matter the differences between any of us and any of them — all of those qualities of mind, heart, and soul are still the utter bedrock of our professional competence. When all the strategies and breakthrough developments and innovations are taken into consideration, we are still the singular human beings we have spent our lives becoming, and therein may be our greatest challenge and opportunity: to figure out how to use our inevitably flawed lives, the character and personality that have emerged from it, in the service of others — their distress turned into our chance to take on, with another person, a measure of this world's pain in hopes of diminishing it, and thereby feel ourselves of some use in our time's scheme of things. "Our patients are constantly educating us — and constantly enabling us to do our work, and thereby they are healing us," Dr. Ludwig kept reminding us residents as we worried about where we were going, and why, in the course of our work. Yes, that is it, we only slowly learned: that we "hand one another along" in this life, in our many ways, as the novelist Walker Percy put it at the end of *The Moviegoer,* and as (one hopes and prays) both doctors and patients keep realizing all the time in those offices, those clinics, those hospital wards.

March 1995

INTRODUCTION

TO THE FIRST EDITION

When I was finishing a residency in child psychiatry at the Children's Hospital in Boston, a supervisor of my work, a child psychoanalyst, suggested that I write an essay about my chosen profession. We had for a year been discussing the difficulties that various children face — and as well, those special difficulties that present themselves to a doctor who finds himself at once glad to be in a position (sometimes) to help children, but also rather troubled at the state of his profession. The result was an essay published in *The Atlantic* [in 1961], the first one in this book. My supervisor knew that I had only by accident (or so it seemed) become a psychiatrist. I had come to medicine because I wanted to work with children as a pediatrician and had received some training in that field, only to find myself, one day, attending a lecture of Anna Freud's. I was enormously stirred by what she said — and, too, I have to say, at her manner; so unassuming and modest, so thoughtful and learned, yet so wondrously plainspoken. She was trying to tell a group of pediatric physicians what psychoanalysis had to offer them, and I was more than persuaded. Indeed, as I listened to her, I remembered a remark I had heard from William Carlos Williams years earlier: "If I had it over, I might try psychiatry." He was quick to reverse himself, to say he didn't think he had the patience, the "knack," he put it, for such a specialty; but he was vastly interested. At the time I was far more interested in Dr. Williams's poetry (about which I wrote my undergraduate thesis) than psychiatry; if I eventually chose one of his two professions, I had scant information, when I did so, of following his advice. (The remark about what *he* might do if another medical life were permitted him was, I now realize, offered me as tactful advice.) Suddenly, that day in 1955, Miss Freud's message, her way of seeing things and putting things, had made me realize that I might give Dr. Williams's recommendation a try.

So began my experience of what must be the longest and most carefully watched over professional training known to Western man — except, perhaps, for that undertaken by Jesuits. When I was finally finished with all those years of psychiatry, child psychiatry and personal psychoanalysis, I was, for a while, at a loss to know what to do: surely there must be yet another period of training or supervised introspection. But in no time, it seemed, I was off to the South, called up to Air Force duty. What I saw there absorbed me in what has turned out to be a lifetime of study. Still, I was never willing to put aside an interest in psychiatry and psychoanalysis, however involved I was in the rural South and Appalachia with black and white children, or more recently, in the Southwest, with Indian and Chicano children. I left hospitals, clinics, and the possibility of private practice because I wanted to see, firsthand, how children I might not otherwise get to know managed the particular stresses that poverty and racism generate. I left, also, because I was a little annoyed by the various rigidities and orthodoxies of a given profession. But I did not lose interest in the clinical side of psychiatry; I have continued to see patients, when it has been possible — and I have never stopped taking a strong interest in what certain psychiatrists and psychoanalysts have had to say, and as well, in the vexing questions which confront a field perhaps too quickly and too uncritically embraced in my country. So, the essays have continued to appear over the years, in a variety of journals, magazines and reviews, as well as inside books, as introductions, or by themselves as monographs. When, however, the same psychoanalyst who suggested I begin writing about our work recently suggested that I pull together some of the writing I have done on the subject these past years, I was more reluctant than I had been the first time around. Why add yet another book to an already cluttered market? Still, my first venture in a collection of essays, *Farewell to the South,* had somehow been of use to a number of people; and an invitation from Miss Freud in 1974 to visit the Hampstead Clinic where she works to present some of my ideas, moved me farther along. She and I had been in correspondence for a number of years, and I had been fortunate enough to meet her in New Haven during one of her American visits. She had now asked me to present my views on a variety of issues of mutual concern, and I found that in order to do so, in order, really, to find out what I felt and believed important about my profession, I had to review what I had been writing — a sort of analysis through reading of one's persistent if not consistent preoccupations. The result is this book.

I have tried hard to include here only those essays which I believe merit a second chance at publication. I have wanted to keep this book from becoming an amorphous collection of vaguely related or indeed unrelated pieces: evidence, alas, of a particular writer's unremitting volubility. I have arbitrarily excluded all essays written for medical, pediatric, psychiatric and psychoanalytic journals, because the subject matter almost invariably was technical, and unfortunately the writing, often enough, responded to the occasion. I have also, for reasons of space, kept out a long involvement with the drug controversy, pursued in a number of periodicals (*Partisan Review, Yale Review, New England Journal of Medicine, American Journal of Orthopsychiatry,* and so on). I have already gone into the various dilemmas that the use of drugs presents to my profession in another book *(Drugs and Youth),* so republication of the many essays devoted to the subject, however much they concern themselves with psychiatry, and however controversial they were when published, is perhaps unnecessary.

I suppose that it is possible to boil down what follows, make a few categorical generalizations about one's "position" — in a "field," as it is called, all too prone toward ideological splits and antagonisms, if not outright internecine war. The various essays speak for themselves, I trust, but I would especially recommend as a general statement of my viewpoint the last section, with its two fairly long pieces, one originally presented to a psychoanalytic society, the other to a university audience at a formal convocation. Gradually, over the years, I have developed, in the words of the psychoanalyst mentioned above, "a way of seeing psychiatry and psychoanalysis," hence the book's subtitle. And so, in general I have kept to a chronological order. I have mostly kept the titles given pieces by editors, though in one or two cases I have felt it wise to retain my own title. And of course, I have tried to catch the errors that sometimes occur on the pages of magazines, even as their editors have not rarely succeeded in catching mine. I have divided the book a bit arbitrarily into sections; though I think the thread of continuing concern with certain themes justifies the arrangement. Before each set of essays I include a short descriptive and analytic statement.

In one rather long essay I declare my overall indebtedness to Anna Freud; her way of regarding children has been, for me, by far the most satisfactory. Her emphasis on "direct observation," accompanied by theoretical restraint and a certain narrative simplicity, I find quite worthy of emulation. Out of deep respect and admiration I dedicate this book to her — the second time, actually, I have done so. (The first was a short book called *The Wages of Neglect*, meant to reach those who work with nursery school children.) I also dedicate this book to a young countryman of Miss Freud's, an Englishman who has studied sociology in America and whom I met in South Africa. John Western has traveled far and wide on this planet, trying to understand how many different kinds of its people live and make do. He has also given of himself generously and impressively — working alongside the suffering and near starving black people of Africa's Burundi, and among the hard pressed "colored" people of South Africa. His ability to mix scholarly study with commitment to social change, his quiet idealism, his inclination to view the people of the world as one community, I find encouraging and admirable. One turns to the wisdom of an eighty-year-old woman and the compassionate activism of a youthful school scientist with thanks and in some hope — despite all the spoken and printed banality or worse that impinge upon our ears and eyes, not to mention the gross and awful injustice abroad in this world of ours. And one also acknowledges the wisdom one is lucky enough to have rather constantly available — the advice of an intelligent, thoughtful editor, Peter Davison, and the advice of a wife who knows how, and is willing, patiently and against certain obstacles, to teach another the difference between appreciation of a given profession's possibilities and literal-minded idolatry.

I
SOCIAL
AND CLINICAL
COMMENT

ஃ *The essays in this section have to do with both clinical and social comment. I am interested in the way psychiatrists regard themselves and are regarded in America and elsewhere. Put differently, I try to show that psychiatrists are very much influenced in their offices as well as outside, by their own situation as members of a given society, and as persons alive at a particular moment in history. In several pieces I try to show how hard it is for the poor to get proper medical and psychiatric care. They are shunted to the wretched back wards of nondescript and inadequately staffed psychiatric hospitals. There are other outcasts and victims, too: prisoners, conscientious objectors, and even those who have no psychiatric problems whatsoever; hence the essays on Karl Menninger's efforts for the sake of prisoners, and on Willard Gaylin's work with conscientious objectors. I keep coming back to the intersection between American culture in general and my own profession. Even Michael Wechsler's private torment had a larger context, as his father made abundantly clear when he wrote about the various, and alas, mostly unsatisfactory meetings his son had with a succession of psychiatrists. There are also essays of social comment — such as "American Amok," "The Letter Killeth," "Racism and Populism," "Hope and Despair in the Very Young," and "Madness in Films"; in them I try to look at some of the more troubled or hateful or violent corners of American life, with, I hope, a certain discretion. At times one is compelled to regard the very essay being written as ironic — one more occasion in which a social scientist is asked to make sweeping generalizations. Here, and elsewhere in this book (in the essays on Piaget and "Psychoanalysis and Religion," for instance), I call attention to the thinly disguised secular religion that in some quarters goes under the name of psychia-*

try, or psychoanalysis — or, alas, educational reform. In the essay "Medical Ethics and Living a Life" I try to attend a matter that ought to haunt all of us, including those of us who are doctors, or teachers, or indeed, writers — how one brings this life into some reasonable accord with one's moral pronouncements, so that "ethics" is not only something studied or argued or analyzed, but exemplified in one's daily actions, a notion so obvious and simple as to be, alas, utterly daunting for so many of us!

I

A YOUNG PSYCHIATRIST

LOOKS AT HIS PROFESSION

Recently, in the emergency ward of the Children's Hospital in Boston, an eight-year-old girl walked in and asked to talk to a psychiatrist about her "worries." I was called to the ward, and when we ended our conversation I was awake with sorrow and hope for this young girl, but also astonished at her coming. As a child psychiatrist, I was certainly accustomed to the troubled mother who brings her child to a hospital for any one of a wide variety of emotional problems. It was the child's initiative in coming which surprised me. I recalled a story my wife had told me. She was teaching a ninth-grade English class, and they were starting to read the Sophoclean tragedy of *Oedipus*. A worldly thirteen-year-old asked the first question: "What is an Oedipus complex?" Somehow, in our time, psychiatrists have become the heirs of those who hear the worried and see the curious. I wondered, then, what other children in other times did with their troubles and how they talked of the Greeks. I wondered, too, about my own profession, its position and its problems, and about the answers we might have for ourselves as psychiatrists.

We appear in cartoons, on television serials, and in the movies. We are "applied" by Madison Avenue, and we "influence" writers. Acting techniques, even schools of painting are supposed to be derived from our insights, and Freud has become what Auden calls "a whole climate of opinion." Since children respond so fully to what is most at hand in the adult world, there should have been no reason for my surprise in that emergency ward. But this quick acceptance of us by children and adults alike is ironic, tells us something about this world, and is dangerous.

The irony is that we no longer resemble the small band of outcasts upon whom epithets were hurled for years. One forgets today just how rebellious Freud and his contemporaries were. They studied archaelogy and mythology, were versed in the ancient languages, wrote well, and were a bit fiery, a bit eccentric, a bit troublesome, even for one another. Opinionated, determined, oblivious of easy welcome, they were fighters for their beliefs, and their ideas fought much of what the world then thought.

This is a different world. People today are frightened by the memory of concentration camps, by the possibility of atomic war, by the breakdown of old empires and old ways of living and believing. Each person shares the hopes and terrors peculiar to this age, not an age of reason or of enlightenment, but an age of fear and trembling. Every year brings problems undreamed of only a decade ago in New York or Vienna. Cultures change radically, values are different, even diseases change. For instance, cases of hysteria, so beautifully described by Freud, are rarely found today. A kind of innocence is lost; people now are less suggestible, less naive, more devious. They look for help from many sources, and chief among them, psychiatrists. Erich Fromm, in honor of Paul Tillich's seventy-fifth birthday, remarked: "Modern man is lonely, frightened, and hardly capable of love. He wants to be close to his neighbor, and yet he is too unrelated and distant to be able to be close. . . . In search for closeness he craves knowledge; and in search for knowledge he finds psychology. Psychology becomes a substitute for love, for intimacy. . . ."

Now Freud and his knights are dead. Their long fight has won acclaim and increasing protection from a once reluctant society, and perhaps we should expect this ebb tide. Our very acclaim makes us more rigid and querulous. We are rent by rivalries, and early angers or stubborn idiosyncrasies have hardened into a variety of schools with conflicting ideas. We use proper names of early psychiatrists — Jung, Rank, Horney — to describe the slightest differences of emphasis or theory. The public is interested, but understandably confused. If it is any comfort to the public, so are psychiatrists, at times. Most of us can recall our moments of arrogance, only thinly disguised by words which daily become more like shibboleths, sound hollow, and are almost cant.

Ideas need the backing of institutions and firm social approval if they are to result in practical application. Yet I see pharisaic temples being built everywhere in psychiatry; pick up our journals and you will see meetings listed almost every week of the year and pages filled with the abstracts of papers presented at them. These demand precious time in attendance and reading, and such time is squandered all too readily these days. Who of us, even scanting sleep, can keep up with this monthly tidal wave of minute or repetitive studies? And who among us doesn't smile or shrug, as he skims the pages, and suddenly leap with hunger at the lonely monograph that really says something? As psychiatrists we need to be in touch not only with our patients but with the entire range of human activity. We need time to see a play or read a poem, yet daily we sit tied to our chairs, listening and talking for hours on end. While this is surely a problem for all professions, it is particularly deadening for one which deals so intimately with people and which requires that its members themselves be alive and alert.

It seems to me that psychiatric institutions and societies too soon become bureaucracies, emphasizing form, detail and compliance. They also breed the idea that legislation or grants of money for expansion of laboratories and buildings will provide answers where true knowledge is lacking. Whereas we desperately need more money for facilities and training for treatment programs, there can be a vicious circle of more dollars for more specialized projects producing more articles about less and less, and it may be that some projects are contrived to attract money and expand institutions rather than to form any spontaneous intellectual drive. We argue longer and harder about incidentals, such as whether our patients should sit up or lie down; whether we should accept or reject their gifts or answer their letters; how our offices should be decorated; or how we should talk to patients when they arrive or leave. We debate for hours about the difference between psychoanalysis and psychotherapy; about the advantages of seeing a person twice a week or three times a week; about whether we should give medications to people, and if so, in what way. For the plain fact is that, as we draw near the bureaucratic and the institutionalized, we draw near quibbling. Maybe it is too late, and much of this cannot be stopped. But it may be pleasantly nostalgic, if not instructive, to recall Darwin sailing on the *Beagle*, or Freud writing spirited letters of discovery to a close friend, or Sir Alexander Fleming stumbling upon a model of penicillin in his laboratory — all in so simple and creative a fashion, and all with so little red tape and money.

If some of psychiatry's problems come from its position in the kind of society we have, other troubles are rooted in the very nature of our job. We labor with people who have troubled thoughts and feelings, who go awry in bed or in the office or with friends. Though we talk a great deal about our scientific interests, man's thoughts and feelings cannot be as easily understood or manipulated as atoms. The brain is where we think and receive impressions of the world, and it is in some ultimate sense an aggregate of atoms and molecules. In time we will know more about how to control and transform all cellular life, and at some point the cells of the brain will be known in all their intricate functions. What we now call "ego" or "unconscious" will be understood in terms of cellular action or biochemical and biophysical activity. The logic of the nature of all matter predicts that someday we will be able to arrange and rearrange ideas and feelings. Among the greatest mysteries before us are the unmarked pathways running from the peripheral nervous system to the thinking areas in the brain. The future is even now heralded by machines which think and by drugs which stimulate emotional states or affect specific moods, like depressions. Until these roads are thoroughly surveyed and the brain is completely understood, psychiatry will be as pragmatic or empirical as medicine.

Social scientists have taught us a great deal about how men think and how they get along with one another and develop from infancy to full age. We have learned ways of reaching people with certain problems and can offer much help to some of them. Often we can understand illnesses that we cannot so readily treat. With medicines, we can soften the lacerations of nervousness and fear, producing no solutions, but affording some peace and allowing the mind to seek further aid. Some hospitals now offer carefully planned communities where new friendships can arise, refuges where the unhappy receive individual medical and psychiatric attention. Clinics, though harried by small staffs and increasing requests, offer daily help for a variety of mental illnesses. Children come to centers devoted to the study and treatment of early emotional difficulties. If the etiologies are still elusive, the results of treatment are often considerable. Failures are glaring, but the thousands of desperate people who are helped are sometimes overlooked because of their very recovery. Indeed, it is possible that our present problems may give way to worse ones as we get to know more. The enormous difficulties of finding out about the neurophysiology of emotional life may ultimately yield to the Orwellian dilemma of a society in which physicists of the mind can change thoughts and control feelings at their will.

However, right now I think our most pressing concern is less the matter of our work than the manner of ourselves. For the individual psychiatrist, the institutional rigidities affect his thoughts and attitudes, taint his words and feelings, and thereby his ability to treat patients. We become victims of what we most dread; our sensibilities die, and we no longer care or notice. We dread death of the heart — any heart under any moon. Yet I see Organization Men in psychiatry, with all the problems of deathlike conformity. Independent thinking by the adventurous has declined; psychiatric training has become more formal, more preoccupied with certificates and diplomas, more hierarchical. Some of the finest people in early dynamic psychiatry were artists, like Erik Erikson, schoolteachers, like August Aichhorn, or those, like Anna Freud, who had no formal training or occupation but motivations as personal as those of a brilliant and loyal daughter. Today we are obsessed with accreditation, recognition, levels of training, with status as scientists. These are the preoccupations of young psychiatrists. There are more lectures, more supervision, more examinations for specialty status, and thus the profession soon attracts people who take to these practices. Once there were the curious and bold; now there are the carefully well-adjusted and certified.

When the heart dies, we slip into wordy and doctrinaire caricatures of life. Our journals, our habits of talk become cluttered with jargon or the trivial. There are negative cathects, libido quanta, "presymbiotic, normal-autistic phases of mother-infant unity," and "a hierarchically stratified, firmly cathected organization of self-representations." Such dross is excused as a short cut to understanding a complicated message by those versed in the trade; its practitioners call on the authority of symbolic communication in the sciences. But the real test is whether we best understand by this strange proliferation of language the worries, fears, or loves in individual people. As the words grow longer and the concepts more intricate and tedious, human sorrows and temptations disappear, loves move away, envies and jealousies, revenge and terror dissolve. Gone are strong, sensible words with good meaning and the flavor of the real. Freud called Dostoevski the greatest psychologist of all time, and long ago Euripides described in *Medea* the hurt of the mentally ill. Perhaps we cannot expect to describe our patients with the touching accuracy and poetry used for Lady Macbeth or Hamlet or King Lear, but surely there are sparks to be kindled, cries to be heard, from people who are individuals.

If we become cold, and our language frosty, then our estrangement is complete. Living in an unreliable world, often lonely, and for this reason attracted to psychiatry as a job with human contacts, we embrace icy reasoning and abstractions, a desperate shadow of the real friendships which we once desired. Estrangement may, indeed, thread through the entire fabric of our professional lives in America. Cartoons show us pre-empted by the wealthy. A recent study from Yale by Doctor Redlich shows how few people are reached by psychiatrists, how much a part of the class and caste system in America we are. Separated from us are all the troubled people in villages and farms from Winesburg to Yoknapatawpha. Away from us are the wretched drunks and the youthful gangs in the wilderness of our cities. Removed from us are most of the poor, the criminal, the drug addicts. Though there are some low-cost clinics, their waiting lists are long and we are all too easily and too often available to the select few of certain streets and certain neighborhoods.

Whereas in Europe the theologian or artist shares intimately with psychiatrists, we stand apart from them, afraid to recognize our common heritage. European psychiatry mingles with philosophers; produces Karl Jaspers, a psychiatrist who is a theologian, or Sartre, a novelist and philosopher who writes freely and profoundly about psychiatry. After four years of psychiatric training in a not uncultured city, I begin to wonder whether young psychiatrists in America are becoming isolated by an arbitrary definition of what is, in fact, our work. Our work is the human condition, and we might do well to talk with Reinhold Niebuhr about the "nature and destiny of man," or with J. D. Salinger about our Holden Caulfields. Perhaps we are too frightened and too insecure to recognize our very brothers. This is a symptom of the estranged.

In some way our hearts must live. If we truly live, we will talk clearly and avoid the solitary trek. In some way we must manage to blend poetic insight with a craft and unite intimately the rational and the intuitive, the aloof stance of the scholar with the passion and affection of the friend who cares and is moved. It seems to me that this is the oldest summons in the history of Western civilization. We can answer this request only with some capacity for risk, dare, and whim. Thwarting us at every turn of life is the ageless fear of uncertainty; it is hard to risk the unknown. If we see a patient who puzzles us, we can avoid the mystery and challenge of the unique through readily available diagnostic categories. There is no end to classifications and terminologies, but the real end for us may be the soul of man, lost in these words: "Name it and it's so, or call it and it's real." This is the language of children faced with a confusion of the real and unreal, and it is ironic, if human, to see so much of this same habit still among psychiatrists.

Perhaps, if we dared to be free, more would be revealed than we care to admit. I sometimes wonder why we do not have a journal in our profession which publishes anonymous contributions. We might then hear and feel more of the real give-and-take in all those closed offices, get a fuller flavor of the encounter between the two people, patient and psychiatrist, who are in and of themselves what we call psychotherapy. The answer to the skeptic who questions the worth of psychotherapy is neither the withdrawn posture of the adherent of a closed system who dismisses all inquiry as suspect, nor an eruption of pseudoscientific verbal pyrotechnics. Problems will not be solved by professional arrogance or more guilds and rituals. For it is more by being than by doing that the meaningful and deeply felt communion between us and our patients will emerge. This demands as much honesty and freedom from us as it does from our patients, and as much trust on our part as we would someday hope to receive from them.

If the patient brings problems that may be understood as similar to those in many others, that may be conceptualized and abstracted, he is still in the midst of a life which is in some ways different from all others. We bring only ourselves; and so each morning in our long working day is different, and our methods of treatment will differ in many subtle ways from those of all of our colleagues. When so much of the world faces the anthill of totalitarian living, it is important for us to affirm proudly the preciously individual in each human being and in ourselves as doctors. When we see patients, the knowledge and wisdom of many intellectual ancestors are in our brains, and, we hope, some life and affection in our hearts. The heart must carry the reasoning across those inches or feet of office room. The psychiatrist, too, has his life and loves, his sorrows and angers. We know that we receive from our patients many of the irrational, misplaced, distorted thoughts and feelings once directed at parents, teachers, brothers, and sisters. We also know that our patients attempt to elicit from us many of the attitudes and responses of these earlier figures. But we must strive for some neutrality, particularly in the beginning of treatment, so that our patients may be offered, through us and their already charged feelings toward us, some idea of past passions presently lived. Yet, so often this neutrality becomes our signal for complete anonymity. We try to hide behind our couches, hide ourselves from our patients. In so doing we prolong the very isolation often responsible for our patients' troubles, and if we persist, they will derive from the experience many interpretations, but little warmth and trust.

I think that our own lives and problems are part of the therapeutic process. Our feelings, our own disorders and early sorrows are for us in some fashion what the surgeon's skilled hands are for his work. His hands are the trained instruments of knowledge, lectures, traditions. Yet they are, even in surgery, responsive to the artistry, the creative and sensitive intuition of the surgeon as a man. The psychiatrist's hands are himself, his life. We are educated and prepared, able to see and interpret. But we see, talk, and listen through our minds, our memories, our persons. It is through our emotions that the hands of our healing flex and function, reach out, and finally touch.

We cannot solve many problems, and there are the world and the stars to dwarf us and give us some humor about ourselves. But we can hope that, with some of the feeling of what Martin Buber calls "I-Thou" quietly and lovingly nurtured in some of our patients, there may be more friendliness about us. This would be no small happening, and it is for this that we must work. Alert against dryness and the stale, smiling with others and occasionally at ourselves, we can read and study; but maybe wince, shout, cry, and love, too. Really, there is much less to say than to affirm by living. I would hope that we would dare to accept ourselves fully and offer ourselves freely to a quizzical and apprehensive time and to uneasy and restless people.

The Atlantic, 1961

2

AMERICAN AMOK

This summer private madness briefly managed to push aside the wars, riots and strikes that bedevil us. Pictures and stories cut a swath through the front pages of the newspapers, showing and telling a horrified and confused nation that merely unfortunate or even exemplary men can become in a flash murderers, striking out of nowhere at anyone for reasons that never quite measure up to what they presume to explain. We learned that a "bewildered" Richard Speck, pictured looking just that, was declared by his lawyer not guilty of recently strangling and stabbing eight nurses to death in Chicago. We learned also that Charles Whitman, initially described as a model citizen and student, had the day before gone wild on the University of Texas campus, shooting and killing in all directions from the top of an observation tower, and in the end establishing something of a record for himself in the annals of what might be called American *amok*.

A few days after that, an eighteen-year-old school dropout told Texas police about the murders of two schoolboys and a schoolgirl he said his twenty-year-old companion had shot and strangled. All over the world, those who needed additional evidence that America is a violent, murderous nation had it; and those who did not need it but wanted it for their own purposes also had it. The extent to which political commentators use events — of almost any character or incidence — to lend weight to one or another ideological persuasion perhaps goes unnoticed until the theories suddenly emerge, apparently ready-made and waiting for their chance. We were once again proven a savage, uncontrollable, unpredictable, gun-ridden and murderous people, with our pilots showering upon Asians the same brutal iron a Texan youth blasted down on his classmates in Austin.

Another category of observers heard from were those whose interests center not on nations but individuals. We learned that the message on Richard Speck's tattooed arm — "born to raise hell" — showed the long-standing and so to speak ingrained character of his violence. (I suppose thousands of men are now wondering what *their* tattoos forebode.) The man was described as a drifter, though a cunning psychopathic one who could successfully calm and persuade a room full of girls to comply with his wishes. A number of outraged people see the kind of justice our Supreme Court has now demanded as threatening that the murdered nurses (and the rest of us) go unavenged.

We had no reason to worry about having Charles Whitman's head, but we were particularly anxious about what had gone on inside it. If Speck was the obvious (and reassuring) marginal man, Whitman at first seemed little more than the good American everyman, as we quickly found out. His credentials were imposing: a former Eagle Scout, a former Marine, a Scoutmaster, a good student, the handsome and eminently likable husband of an attractive woman. What else could we do but somehow find him secretly but decisively flawed?

In the effort no one was spared — members of the family, friends and experts, both willing and reluctant. Within hours of the tragedy Whitman's father stood before the hungry, prying and poking devices of men who wanted to capture his looks and get him to speak his story. What did he know? How could he account for it all? Since the police had armed the interviewers with a précis of Whitman's last, disordered notes protesting father-hate, it seemed only appropriate to rush to his father, confront him with the facts and ask him all about the family's bad blood — particularly when the two *women* closest to the "child" were slain, along with another dozen people aimed at from a college building, and more than likely to be age-mates, classmates, and thus contemporary competitors. If Whitman had ever feared asking his father anything, he died making sure others would have the chance he missed.

Meanwhile there was an autopsy and a discovery, both of which provided information enough to keep everybody curious rather than fatalistically resigned. A small tumor was found near the brainstem, and for a while neurologists all over the country were asked whether wildly multiplying cells could produce wild and unintended behavior. Slowly that possibility diminished. The growth was far away from the brain's "thinking area," and it turned out to be slow-growing and benign. In any event, what of those thousands whose nervous systems have been riddled with cancer? Every day they live and die among us, their suffering kept to themselves or shared only with sympathetic loved ones. The pathologist appeared to take that fact into consideration when he made his diagnosis: "an anti-social psychopath." He added that "they are the worst kind," and of course by definition he was right.

For a fleeting second there was the specter of drugs: a number of dexedrines were found in Whitman's pockets. Might he have been excited and driven mad by pills? A less likely or compelling answer from the start, its worth soon faded. A sample of the dead man's blood revealed not a trace of that or any other drug. Naturally, the same logic that had to be applied to the first guess would apply to the second: even more people work themselves up with dexedrine than fall sick to brain tumors, yet Whitman's *deed* was unparalleled in its outcome, and its purpose had only a handful of recorded precedents in our recent history.

From the beginning the psychiatrists seemed the best if not the only hope; moreover, there was information — quickly made public — to support the conviction that underneath it all Whitman was already disturbed months earlier, and in the long run a product of a home whose peculiar troubles in some fashion would produce a sick mind if not a violently mad one. He had consulted a psychiatrist, in the South and West (except for California) not something to be taken for granted. Furthermore, his parents had just been separated, with the mother recently arrived in Texas to be near her son. In interviews with reporters the father called himself a "fanatic about guns"; they were said to hang in every room of his home in Florida. If the father was quickly found to be odd or "fanatic," he was sure his son was a "sick boy." Certainly he was "not the boy I loved and who loved his father." Yes, he had been a strict father, but he had been raised an orphan and in poverty. Indeed, the more he told of himself the more typical (even archetypical) his life became. He had fought his way up with little education and through hard, muscular work to a position of money and respect. In the home he was an admitted bully, but a loyal, loving and generous one — the kind we all know, from top to bottom. To his neighbors he was the head of a stable, and by no means eccentric, family. Still, in Florida, the father said his son was ill, though nobody knew what made him *that* ill.

In Texas a psychiatrist might be able to tell. I do not know why the officials in the university infirmary decided to violate the utter confidentiality of medical records. A summary statement could have been issued, and certainly the doctor interviewed; but for a patient's entire psychiatric record to have been instantly made available for no explicit medical reason seems to me at least a panicky reaction to a stressful situation. In any event the report had one distinct surprise to it. There was hostility; there was a history of family tension; there was a problem with study; but amid all that rather common clinical information there was one "vivid reference" made by the patient which the doctor quotes directly. He thought about "going up on the tower with a deer rifle and start shooting people."

There it is, the deed predicted by the patient and the prediction written down by the doctor. Might it all have been prevented? Yet, as the psychiatrist left off reading his notes to comment on them and put them in the context of his daily work — and the experience of other psychiatrists — what seemed like the substance of welcome reason rapidly turned into the essence of bewildering ambiguity. It seems that many students bring a variety of suicidal and even homicidal fantasies to college psychiatrists, and in the University of Texas those fantasies often center on or involve the tower. To Charles Whitman's psychiatrist — his, only by virtue of one visit — the patient's story was coherent, unalarming, not exceptionally remarkable, but definitely an indication that help was needed, as with many others. Come back next week, the student was told. I would imagine that most psychiatrists read of their colleague's sudden predicament both nervously and sympathetically — as well they should. There is every reason to believe Whitman presented himself to the doctor exactly as described: sane and possessed of rather prosaic difficulties that were destined to be transient.

We were left, then, with nothing substantial to "explain" a terrible crime, the obvious rampage of a madman. With each of his friends, acquaintances or teachers questioned, Whitman became steadily more ordinary. True, there were signs that he was on occasion tense; there were signs that he was almost too good; there were signs that he might have had something troublesome "going on" inside him; there was meager hearsay of occasional moodiness or mild, commonplace wrongdoing, such as gambling and even, in 1961, poaching. What it all ironically confirmed was that Charles Whitman was a fallible human being.

What is to be said — and done? Two men in rapid succession have once again reminded us of two enormously vexing problems that face, among others, any psychiatrist willing to look even a short distance outside his office. For one thing, we know much more about the way people think and dream than we know about their actions — about what they do or will do. For another, we face terribly complicated issues when we try to go from an individual's illness to the various disorders that plague the masses of individuals we call a society or a nation.

We *now* can rummage over the lives of Richard Speck and Charles Whitman and raise our eyebrows knowingly over this and that detail, but to little avail. There are fiercely suspicious and sullen people whose minds are commonly worked up by hate and rage, whose thoughts in a second can be determined insane, whose parents may or may not have exceeded Speck's or Whitman's in roughness, toughness, or worse — yet by the thousands they walk the streets a danger to no one but themselves. We simply do not know right now what specifically makes for the way people choose to act or find themselves acting, for the good or the bad. We can throw psychiatric labels around here and there. We can connect crimes to complexes and trace the gifted man's productions all the way back to his own mother's womb. In doing so we only appease our own craving for an-

swers and explanations. For every quiet, apparently harmless individual who becomes a criminal are there not dozens of manifestly angry and even crazy people who not only commit no crimes, but live extremely useful lives? Do not many so-called "ordinary" people share whatever we find in a gifted person's personality? These are yet riddles, not ones to shame any profession, but not ones to go unacknowledged, or be buried in a display of wordy and dogmatic psychiatric interpretations.

Equally puzzling is the matter of what to recommend for a society startled by these recent atrocities and presumably anxious to prevent their recurrence. As we were in 1963 after President Kennedy was shot, we are again reminded how readily guns can be obtained, not just rifles for hunting, but pistols and automatic guns for human slaughter. The figures are appalling: Americans are killed by fatal shootings at the rate of 17,000 a year, or nearly 50 a day. In this century alone over 750,000 of our citizens have died from gun wounds "at home," as against a total of about 530,000 killed in *all* of our wars, from the Revolutionary War to the present one in Vietnam. Nevertheless, Senator Dodd's fight to place even modest controls on the sale of weapons has failed. There is a powerful rifle lobby that watches our legislators from impressive headquarters in Washington, and it is more than a match for any support Senator Dodd may gain from the general (unorganized) public.

An Oswald or a Whitman calls attention to the millions of guns about, but only temporarily. People say it is dreadful, what has happened; then they ask whether a law restricting access to guns might have prevented the tragedy. The answer is that of course a determined murderer can get around any bill Congress is even remotely apt to pass and find his weapon. That is not the issue. Every psychiatrist has treated patients who were thankful that guns were not handy at one or another time in their lives. Temper tantrums, fits, seizures, hysterical episodes all make the presence of guns an additional and possibly mortal danger. In this country today children can obtain guns by mail-order. I have treated delinquents who have grown up with them, not toy guns but real ones. We cannot prevent insanity in adults or violent and delinquent urges in many children by curbing guns, but we can certainly make the translation of crazy or vicious impulses into pulled triggers less likely and less possible. It is as simple as that, though many politicians refuse out of fear to let it be as simple as that.

There is, finally, the need we feel to make larger sense of individual behavior. Curiously enough, it is easier to deal with a mass murderer such as Whitman than with the concentration camps and battlefields this century has witnessed. We can call one man a lunatic (for what he has done, if not for what doctors can discover in him). That is, we can understand why he may have *felt* violent (and violated) even if we still do not comprehend why those feelings prompted in him the particular action he took. In contrast, what can we say about those many thousands who a few years ago killed millions in gas ovens or through bombing? The further we get from a particular person's words or deeds, the more haunting and nightmarish is the whole business of man's continuing murder of his fellow man. We say Hitler was an exception, a maniac become dictator. Yet, historians, political scientists and psychiatrists will discuss and argue the relationship between Hitler and his times, Hitler and Germany, Hitler and Wall Street or Hitler and the Communists until the end of time without providing what really cannot be provided: a tidy statement that demonstrates how countless people — large segments of whole nations — came to be murdered by the ordinary citizens of a supposedly civilized continent. Accidents, misfortunes, the crafty genius of individuals, complicated historical and political forces combine as "factors" to make any explanation of wars and institutionalized murder incredibly harder than the task facing us with even so puzzling a phenomenon as Charles Whitman.

On the very day Whitman killed sixteen, about the same number of Klansmen denied before a federal court in Mississippi that they killed one Negro man. If they are guilty, how do we explain *their* actions, *their* minds? What do we say about the mind of a man who wants to be governor of California, and is said to have suggested that North Vietnam be "turned into a parking lot"? How do we analyze the thinking of inscrutable leaders who would sacrifice a country's entire generation to forced labor, prisons and hunger in the name of abstraction like "dialectical materialism," an ideology whose meaning and purposes cannot really be debated in such countries save by a very few? While "primitive" people have given something like *amok* a cultural form (among the Malay, Iban and Moslem groups of Borneo and elsewhere), mighty and "civilized" nations threaten to destroy everyone alive on this planet. This mind shudders before the prospect of looking at it all, the awful carnage of which man is capable. We turn away in disbelief, or we use every device to justify the unjustifiable. For a second the Whitmans of this world catch us by surprise and make us wonder — but not for much longer than that second, and not to any effect.

The New Republic, 1966

3

STILL AND QUIET

CONSCIENCES

History tells us that the United States of America came into being because unconventional, scorned, rebellious people were willing to risk suffering and death in order to live as they believed it right to live. Some of our first settlers had been jailed or threatened with jail in England because their ideals offended the government, if not the dominant majority. And over the centuries this "new world" has attracted millions of people who felt despised and persecuted or exceedingly vulnerable to all sorts of arbitrary political force.

It is too early to know what future history will say about the kind of country the United States became in the second half of the twentieth century, but those who choose to read Dr. Willard Gaylin's *In the Service of Their Country: War Resisters in Prison* (Viking) may well conclude that we are no longer a sanctuary for the hunted, the proudly different, the stubbornly independent, but that we, like George III and many others more recent, regard dissenters, however thoughtful and peaceful and sincere and earnest, as people to be punished, to be treated as castoffs rather than citizens. Perhaps later history will note the irony: men fight and die so that they and their descendants can say what they think, believe as they will, live as their consciences tell them they must, and then, gradually but relentlessly, under the banner of "defending freedom" abroad, lose the freedom to speak out against their government, its laws, its practices, its purposes, and the freedom to say that this loss is a violation of a law higher than any that a particular congress has enacted and a particular President (God save his endangered soul) has set out to enforce. It is arguable that we have come so far from our professed ideals as a democracy that we have nearly betrayed our own revolution. How does one know, though? Sometimes events are dramatic and clear-cut. Yet things can change slowly enough to confuse but not frighten us, not make us stop and think. We merely discuss these matters, too often abstractly, rhetorically, with self-justifying pieties and simple-minded slogans. And, indeed, no antipollution law will clear the air of all the hysteria, the abusive words, the apocalyptic warnings, the sly appeals to hate, the open calls for violence; as long as we remain free, our ears will suffer the noise of wily and banal propagandists.

Meanwhile, dozens of citizens are in jail because they have refused to fight in Vietnam and by no means are all these young men leftists or members of "extremist" groups. Some of them voted for Goldwater and consider themselves staunch conservatives; some have had no political involvement at all. What they do have in common is an opposition to the war we are waging, an inability (according to their draft boards) to qualify as "conscientious objectors," and a refusal to flee the country, or to claim a wide range of medical and psychiatric deferments, or to declare themselves drug addicts or homosexuals. Simply, directly, these young men have said they are conscience-bound not to help our war in Vietnam. They have resorted to no violence, they have invaded no draft board headquarters, they have shouted no obscenities, they have not taken jobs that enable deferments, they have not enrolled in an academic program that helps them stay out of the army. Stubbornly, they have pushed themselves and their draft boards and perhaps all of us to the legal and moral limit. And thus they may help the nation decide some of the large political, philosophical, and historical issues so many of us are thinking about, and with concern.

Dr. Gaylin, an experienced psychoanalyst, teaches — at the Columbia-Presbyterian Medical Center — young psychiatrists who want to become analysts. He also teaches at the Union Theological Seminary. He embarked upon the research he describes in his book not because he was politically active against the government and wanted to use war resisters as a basis for a critique of America's foreign policy; in point of fact, his research began when he was asked by a friend to see his only son. The son, a graduate student, had been deferred, but the urgency of the war had ended that deferment. He was not a religious objector or a pacifist, and he did not wish to leave the country. The father knew his son would go to jail if, against a background of good health and a reasonably sound mind, he persisted in refusing to heed the demand that he put on a uniform. Both father and son thought it was wise to talk the issue over with an analyst. Analysts have that famous "distance"; they can try to sort out the rational from the irrational, weigh alternatives, ponder difficulties, stresses, and strains. Dr. Gaylin heard out the troubled son's very real dilemma, and one gathers that the doctor himself became troubled and confused, and began to wonder about the war resisters who went to prison. Who were they, and why did they voluntarily let such a fate befall them? How did they manage — these idealistic youths, so different from others behind bars? He went through the "literature" available, but he found no answer. He asked the federal Bureau of Prisons if any research was going on that might provide answers. No, there was not even an effort to determine the number of imprisoned who were resisters, or what proportion of the nation's draftable population they were, or what their racial and religious backgrounds were, or why they chose prison.

No doubt by then the doctor was, as it is put in his profession, "involved." (There is danger in that word; it is as if psychiatrists ought to maintain a fine impartiality, a scrupulous neutrality toward everyone and everything.) The question was what to do with that "involvement." Analyze it? Forget it? Hope someone else would turn in a report? Do one of those "research proposals" that Dr. Gaylin says are almost invariably "half promise, half puff, and all pitch"? He decided that he would go it alone, without help from even the more imaginative foundations; as for the federal government and its largesse, the doctor reasoned that "the preparation and processing of a proposal for the National Institutes of Health has been known to take longer than the performance of the proposed research." He did, though, petition the government for permission to visit its prisons. He feared his project would become entangled in the delays that the National Institutes of Health force applicants to endure, but he was greeted with respect, interest, and cooperation at the Bureau of Prisons, though at the prisons themselves the situation was different. Yet at least he could spend hour after hour with war resisters in two prisons. He describes his attempt to make sure he saw a wide range of youths, and the obstacles put in his way by nervous, suspicious, and not always intelligent prison bureaucrats who wanted only that routine be followed to the letter. He describes the quiet, patient, almost plodding way a psychoanalyst does his work, the prisons he visited, the things he looked and listened for as he brought his watchful eye, his trained ear to bear on over two dozen young men. And then he offers some conclusions; he describes the values, hopes, and fears of those men, and their responses to prolonged confinement.

The subject matter of this book and the author's thoughtful, dedicated way of setting down his observations in themselves justify respect and interest. But Dr. Gaylin wishes to tell us more, for he is a careful and methodical psychoanalytic investigator, a tactful and kind observer, a warm and giving person, able to keep his silence and to prompt things from others, a man sympathetic and responsive, a man outraged in the presence of the stupid, degrading side of prison life. And he is a writer; each of the young men becomes a person, not a bundle of "neurotic problems" or a tormented youth who needs years of "treatment." Yet "whenever I have discussed this group in the psychoanalytic community I have encountered a bias that assumes in advance a high degree of psychopathology." Yes, indeed; one can hear the words he heard over and over about these young men: they are masochists, they have a deep-rooted guilt, they are psychotic. The doctor tries to understand his colleagues, but one can feel his impatience, his wry amusement, his barely concealed annoyance as he writes, " 'To the pathologist all is pathology' is a favorite axiom of medicine — and the psychopathologist is no different," pointing up the narrow-mindedness and condescension of our psychiatric and psychoanalytic "community." Perhaps this book will be read widely in that community and have an effect. In any event, a much larger community — a whole nation — needs to know what happens when a young American citizen quietly follows his conscience and is jailed.

We find out what happens by reading Dr. Gaylin. He does not give us "case histories" or the conventional biographies. He manages to make each youth not just himself but a stand-in for many who would never let themselves go to jail yet who certainly have taken notice of the hypocrisy and deceit that flourish not only in Washington but all over the world. Slowly, with muted irony and humor, with lean and precise prose, Dr. Gaylin brings these prisoners to us, and there is about his writing a novelist's ability to unfold a story compellingly, to bring alive its implications, its drama, its significance. Of one of the young men he says:

> I was particularly concerned about this deterioration because, while there was good psychological evidence to anticipate it, I had not expected it to occur so rapidly. At no time during the course of this research have I experienced the frustration of a psychoanalytic investigator to the degree I did at this moment. As an investigator one sees all the pathology that is available to the therapist, yet with none of the opportunities to reverse it, and with only minimum capacity to alleviate the suffering. It is particularly distressing with a group so innately attractive.

Of another, he says:

> Toward the end of this session, which was our second last, Matthew asked when I would be coming back. I asked him why, and with some embarrassment he said he was wondering if he would see me before his discharge. I indicated that I would try to, and he told me how much he looked forward to meeting with me and added with great embarrassment that he liked me.

One can understand Matthew's getting to like Dr. Gaylin — a development not to be taken for granted. These were men hounded for a long time before they were sent to jail. Once locked up, they were constantly being ordered about, reprimanded, herded. They lived in sight of gun turrets. Every moment, every move was controlled. Their letters were opened. They had few, and carefully regulated, visitors. They were surrounded by robbers and arsonists, and the danger of homosexual rape. Something would have been wrong indeed had such youths not been fearful of a man with a tape recorder who wanted to know, in the psychoanalyst's wide-ranging way, whatever came to mind. But they must have felt something in the doctor that was not an abstract effort to become "aligned with the subject," as it is put in certain clinical conferences — something suggested by words like "grace" and "decency." "Sentences," says Dr. Gaylin, "were often left unfinished, like the phrases of a bop solo, with the implication that the point was made halfway through and there was no sense in killing it with obviousness." And here is a passage from one "research project": "And as our time ran out, I became aware that this time I was reluctant to see the meeting come to an end, for with John it was not just the end of the interview but in all probability the end of a relationship. Despite all the training and discipline, this comes hard to a psychiatrist, too."

To extract such remarks from a book is to risk distorting the nature of an author's work. Before John and Dr. Gaylin could feel free with one another, there were the hours when observer and observed probed at and kept their distance from each other. It can be dangerously easy for us — no doubt a little guilty and more than a little sympathetic — to become ecstatic over both those young men and the doctor whose tenacity and imagination made such a study possible; when, therefore, we come across evidence, and plenty of it, that the imprisoned men are largely intelligent and honorable and admirable human beings, we are saddened by what has happened to them (and to our country, because it has done what it has done to them), and we are impressed by and grateful to Dr. Gaylin for what *he* has done. His account of his talks is quite unsentimental. The youths are prone to self-criticism and a hard-headed, undeluded characterization of their motives and their predicament. They are quick to see the martyr in themselves surface. They know the struggle they must wage if they are not to become arrogant, self-righteous social critics. They do not come across to us as ideologues, so they have waged a successful struggle. They do not rant. Many of them possess a profoundly religious sensibility. They know that, and know their imperfections (which admittedly makes for a degree of saintliness), and so does their observer.

> He then went on to mention a few of the men who annoyed him. He particularly resented those few who seemed eager for martyrdom or those who were the most polemic. These were characteristically the newer inmates. It was generally true that the men who had served a longer time had little patience with what they saw as the jingoism and pomposity of many newly arrived prisoners.

Whatever their faults, and however they acted or spoke when they arrived in jail, these were not youths prepared by their lives for imprisonment. Talking about Hank, a black man, at twenty-one a veteran of many a civil rights demonstration, a sullen and angry youth who could at the same time be restrained, introspective, and gentle, Dr. Gaylin notes, "I wanted to be sure, to comfort him, to reassure him, but our relationship was beyond lies, deeper than reassurance. I merely shrugged." He shrugged because he could not answer Hank's civilized question "Are you still so sure I'm not capable of violence?" And how could he be sure? Had he not seen that in prisons a small number of armed men obtain the fearful compliance of a large number of men by separating them, isolating them, curbing them, encouraging passivity, lethargy, undermining self-confidence, pride, manliness, and individuality? Men are not rehabilitated that way; instead, the idea of future violence is planted.

Dr. Gaylin starts out with war resisters, but he ends with yet another critique of our outrageous prisons. Like Warren Burger, he sees our jails as self-defeating institutions; the criminal becomes more of a criminal, at huge expense to all of us. The war resisters did not become the thieves and killers they never could have been, but they, too, had to pay — with bitterness and hurt and self-doubt. Even in the last pages of his book, Dr. Gaylin gives us no cause for joy. True, they will all get out, maybe in a year or two, or five. But they will be a particularly sensitive and impressionable group of men, unlikely to forget what they have experienced.

In living up to their difficult ideals, imprisoned war resisters are not, in general, political activists. Most do not even think in political

terms. They are, in the main, Christian pacifists. They "are a different population from the college radicals," Dr. Gaylin says. "They
are not for the most part organizers, and when they attempt such activity often fail." Rather than exhort their fellowman, they "believe
in action by example and witness," and so make themselves vulnerable and lend themselves to all sorts of exploitation. Prison wardens,
like political leaders, and maybe even draft boards and judges, know
who has a "constituency" and can stir up a storm of protest, and who
is utterly alone. For all the pain these war resisters have known, will
continue to know, Dr. Gaylin seems to have found in them what
Shakespeare called "a peace above all dignities, a still and quiet conscience." I fear that most of us crave quite other dignities, and that
we know rather well how to silence whatever noise our consciences
make in those occasional moments of honesty we have with ourselves.

The New Yorker, 1970

4

THE WAY OF

THE TRANSGRESSOR

In March of 1528, John Calvin left Paris for Orléans where he would study law under the great Pierre Taisan de l'Etoile. Calvin's father was a lowgrade lawyer — a "notary-apostolic," a "procurator-fiscal" — and he wanted his son to become a legal authority. Four centuries later, the wish is still being realized, because we still fall back on his son's brilliant mind, so adept at handing down laws for men and judgments about men, all in the name of God's will. To Calvin, God is our only hope. Without his nod, we are guilty and corrupt; Adam's fall is a disaster to be felt by man until time ends. After his fall, we became heir to malice and corruption, and because of that fall — i.e., man's fall — we all deserve to be condemned before God and sentenced to hell. Calvin spared no one. Unlike Luther, he was given neither to sentiment nor to bursts of passionate and merciful generosity. His mind was a logician's, a stern judge's. In the second book of his *Institutes of the Christian Religion,* even little children do not escape, for at the moment of birth we are already evil "and therefore infants themselves, as they bring their condemnation into the world with them, are rendered liable to punishment by their own sinfulness, not by the sinfulness of another. For though they have not yet produced the fruits of their iniquity, yet they have the seed of it within them; even their whole nature is as it were a seed of sin, and therefore cannot but be odious and abominable to God." Yet Calvin's icy logic and breathtaking gloom yield to Christ, though only partly. God became incarnate in order to redeem us. The man Jesus became a prophet, a king, a leader, but he died the death of an outlaw, only to be resurrected as the Christ, who now could be a redeemer because he had waged an earthly struggle, had sacrificed himself the mortal to become part of a mysterious, ineffable trinitarian Godhead. In a way, to Calvin, Christ was a man who was tested, who remained obedient and trusting, who earned God's forgiveness and his sanction to forgive others, but within limits, for God has predestined some to eternal life and some to eternal death, some to salvation and some to punishment. Calvin's unyielding fatalism survives today in the West's religious and philosophical tradition. Puritan England (and New England) took his teachings to heart, and even people who have little desire or claim to be called Calvinists have unwittingly felt the influence of a man who was not only a theologian but a determined lawgiver and a shrewd observer of men. (He makes what he calls "connections" between the knowledge we have of God and the knowledge we gain of ourselves, and, in doing this, manages to describe men and their motives with candor and subtlety.)

For Karl Menninger, the author of *The Crime of Punishment* (Viking), a discussion of Calvin's ideas and principles is no senseless indulgence. To Menninger, John Calvin is very much alive in contemporary America, however sectarian and antireligious our culture may appear. Underneath all the libertine gloss and shine, underneath the worship of the mind's knowledge and the body's comfort, we have remained loyal to our past — to John Calvin and John Knox and Cotton Mather and Jonathan Edwards, who, for all their differences, shared a view of the world perhaps best described by Perry Miller: "The Puritan mind was one of the toughest the world has ever had to deal with. It is inconceivable to conceive of a disillusioned Puritan; no matter what misfortune befell him, no matter how often or how tragically his fellowmen failed him, he would have been prepared for the worst, and would have expected no better." Yet, for all their uncompromising morality, the Puritans had a willingness to see in themselves what they condemned in others. They saw faith as elusive and never really won for keeps. They saw sin everywhere, in saints as in the most obvious criminals. But the Puritans were far more generous to their criminals than we are to ours. In Scotland and in the Massachusetts Bay Colony, they put liars and crooks in stocks and punished blasphemy with the pillory and the whip; they punished their neighbors — and, indeed, themselves — severely, but they never condemned anyone to a *life* of punishment. Swift pain, administered in public and accompanied by outright scorn, was followed by nervous forgiveness; the next man to be condemned might be a judge, a minister, an avowedly righteous man. The Puritans knew they were sinners, and a community like theirs can generate its own paradoxical democracy — the kind that ultimately rests on Christ's challenge to the scribes, to the Pharisees, and, indeed to all of us: "He that is without sin among you, let him first cast a stone at her."

In contrast, we set our outlaws apart in such a way that only a few ever return to live among us for very long. We punish and punish and punish them, and worry not that they continue in their wrongful ways. They are criminals — born to be, driven to be — and they deserve everything we give them: a sentence to the life our prisons offer, an existence thoroughly apart from us. They deserve confinement, without the sustained company of their wives, husbands, children, friends, neighbors, and lovers, and without privacy, good medical care, a chance to learn and be more than a member of a constantly guarded road gang. "We derive an innate depravity from our very birth," said Calvin, but for "we" and "our" we use "they" and "their" in dealing with criminals — to make it clear that they deserve *on this earth* a pitiless exile that might anger even the fevered Calvinists. It is one thing to use the whipping post, to rap knuckles and box ears, to apply the rack and the gallows; it is another to confine people, year after year, in the hope that they will become good citizens.

Fifteen hundred years ago, Justinian I, the Roman emperor who codified Roman law, insisted, even though he was a barbarian from the Balkans, that "a prison is for confinement, not for punishment." For centuries, high-court judges in England worked "to deliver the gaols" — to empty them, not fill them. In the Middle Ages, jails were meant only to hold prisoners awaiting trial. The tower of a castle, a gatehouse, the cellar of an inn would do until the prisoners had their day in court. At first, prisoners were simply fined. Later, capital punishment became popular for a number of "serious offenses," and after that came what to Menninger is the cruellest and most ironic hoax: extended committal — in the past to mines and kitchens and workhouses, in our time to jails — all to further "correction." It is as if "progress" meant a refinement of cruelty, an absolute distinction between those who more or less obey most laws and those who at one point or another don't. Though we consider ourselves more enlightened than our ancestors, many prisoners might gladly take their chances on Justinian, or even John Calvin, rather than on some of the men in charge of the Cook County jail or the prison farms of Arkansas — to mention two that gained notoriety recently.

The Crime of Punishment is an enlargement of three lectures by Dr. Menninger after he received the Isaac Ray Award, which is presented annually to a physician or a jurist whose concerns are of interest to students and teachers of both medicine and law. Menninger has given years of his life to the study of criminals (and judges and prosecutors and defense attorneys), so making the award — a distinguished one — to him was a logical move. The book is not a shrill one, and its argument is not a reckless one. The author marshals reason against irrationality, compassion against the spirit of vengeance, and pragmatism against what I suppose can be called legalism and a sort of moralistic absolutism. He reminds us that there are crimes and crimes, criminals and criminals. In 1967, a billion dollars was embezzled by employees so deftly that no one could even be accused, and "one hotel in New York lost over seventy-five thousand finger bowls, demitasse spoons, and other objects in its first ten months of operation." Then, there are income-tax statements that don't include everything. And "the Claims Bureau of the American Insurance Association estimates that seventy-five percent of all claims are dishonest in some respect, and the amount of overpayment [is] more than three hundred and fifty million dollars a year." Many of us go about our transgressions unnoticed, but most of those who are accused of crime are quickly convicted and punished. Ninety percent of all defendants plead guilty without a trial; of the other ten percent, more than half are convicted. People who worry about coddling and about "law and order" simply do not know those percentages. Nor do many of us know what prisons are like. Dr. Menninger presents an unnerving description of prison life in this country, though he has no hope that yet another account will bring an end to the awful things a twentieth-century democracy still permits, because exposés and investigations have not substantially changed conditions. We still put young first offenders beside hardened criminals. We still fail to sort out the dangerous and brutal and bloodthirsty from the confused and mentally retarded. We still mix ignorant and thoughtless men with confidence men. The "recidivists" are soon back in court, to be sentenced by judges who have little more choice than the prisoners:

> The judge undoubtedly hopes that the prisoner whom he is sentencing will undergo a change in his personality. But from what influences? No judge wants him changed in the direction of the features of prison life. How will the character structure of the offender, his particular strengths and weaknesses, be ascertained? And were this possible, let us say by some diagnostic setup, to what agencies will the judge refer the man for carrying out a program of induced change? Some judges do strive to accomplish these things in spite of the lack of facilities, the lack of time available to them, the lack of precedent in many jurisdictions.

The director of the Federal Bureau of Prisons, Myrl E. Alexander, remarked in an interview recently:

> Simply removing an offender to an institution as punishment often only compounds the problem of reintegrating him into the community as a law-abiding citizen. All too frequently it costs him his job, severs his family ties and pins on him a label that makes all of his problems more difficult to overcome. So, as a means of punishment and as an instrument with which to change criminal behavior, imprisonment is still a failure.

We persist in our ways, though. Mr. Alexander says that two-thirds of our prisoners could be paroled at once without making our streets any more dangerous. Dr. Menninger says that a prison brands a man as hopeless, as a leper, and destroys what good judgment and common sense and sanity he may have. Mr. Alexander says that prisons do not offer the education and training so many convicts need to become law-abiding. Dr. Menninger points out what prisons *do* offer: bitterness, loneliness, hate, vengeance, sexual frustration, sexual perversion, futility. But we build larger prisons; we continue to believe that we will secure order and justice by locking up more of the poor, the marginal, the badly educated, the sick, the weak and bewildered human beings — the majority of those who are caught and imprisoned. Meanwhile, crime flourishes, and will flourish if we build five hundred jails a year and fill them: "And while an army of men across the country tries to serve our interests and safety by turning the wheels of this infernal machine for the grinding up of a minority of the easily caught offenders and administering to them the futile ritual of punishment, a horde of known but immune predatory criminals grows fat and famous in front of our eyes." Those are the criminals — Menninger's "professional" ones — who have lawyers, who have money to spend on politicians, sheriffs, legislators, judges, and jurors. If such criminals ever go to jail, they go to the few "good" prisons, where they are still privileged and are soon released on parole or pardoned. Money influences the law, and so do the psychiatric experts who advise judges and juries about insanity, "mental status," and "motives." Dr. Menninger says that some of his colleagues use "obscurantist, pejorative designations" and "pompous fraternity jargon," and that the American Psychiatric Association holds "eighteenth- and nineteenth-century notions." He will have none of their labels. Psychiatrists, he declares, can be — to use an old-fashioned word — disedifying. They wrangle with one another, and use words like "sick" or "pathological" or "abnormal" with flagrant imprecision, with condescension, with malice; any disagreement with their findings is evidence of "sickness," for which, of course, the dissenter needs something called "treatment." In a way, psychiatrists can become bulwarks for the evils, the caprices, the irrationality of the law. There is always the psychiatric "out": the prisoner is "ill," therefore he must be sent for "observation." Some psychoanalysts, Dr. Menninger points out, have even come up with this kind of thinking: People "need" to see a certain number of criminals severely and arbitrarily punished; inside us, Nemesis lives and will not be denied; we believe in an eye for an eye. So psychiatric and psychoanalytic theory can be used to defend the status quo: what exists in a society expresses what is emotionally "needed." Implacable instinct is everything, and all the social, political, economic, cultural, and historical forces that shape our ideas and desires are mere reflections of the one great given, however variously and confusingly it is interpreted, that goes under the name of "human nature." But to Menninger people respond enormously to the world they live in. If they are poor and hungry, they turn on themselves, or they strike out at others and try to take things away from them. If they have been brutalized at home and at school and in their neighborhood, they feel brutal toward themselves and they go after others brutally. None of which means that crime and violence are inevitable. We learn by example, and Menninger says that the two great examples of violence are a nation's willingness to wage war abroad and at the same time to herd many of its own citizens together, give them wretched food, beat them, flog them, set up conditions that encourage them to assault, rape, kill.

We seem haunted by "crime on the streets," and many of us believe in longer sentences and more prisoners, so in a sense, Dr. Menninger's timing is poor. A large number of us don't want to hear his sane voice asking its unsettling questions, its tone of reason and compassion and forgiveness, of concern for both the violated and the violent, whose own sense of violation will not disappear, however solid and dark and bare and cold our dungeons are. What we presumably want to know, he says, is "how to identify, detect, and detain potentially dangerous citizens." Yet the best of our doctors can't be sure which of today's troubled (or, to all appearances, untroubled) children will be tomorrow's killers or thieves. Psychiatrists — and I am one of them — can offer a coherent and reasonable explanation of why a person is driven to break the law, but we cannot always do much to change him. There are only a few of us, and a good amount of our time is given over to (purchased by) people whose crimes are often imaginary. Moreover, as we keep saying in all those journals, even the most intact of personalities responds uncertainly to the best of psychiatric care. But the matter of crime does not give us reason only for gloom and despair. Prisoners (among others) do not have to be psychoanalyzed to be rehabilitated. The Bureau of Prisons, which runs far better programs than most of our state prisons, has achieved many notable successes. Myrl Alexander told his interviewer:

> Correction is a continuous and closely interwoven process, no one element of which can be successfully isolated from the others. Juvenile detention, the jail, the court, probation, halfway houses, juvenile institutions, penitentiaries, parole, work-release and pre-release programs, academic education, vocational training, group therapy — all are inseparable in their total impact on delinquent and criminal behavior.

We still do not know why one man falls sick and another stays reasonably well, why one person's violence becomes a disaster for all of us and another's can be channeled into useful forms of expression. In fact, the very way we define what is "normal" and "abnormal" and "good" and "bad" will continue to trouble us. (In the British psychoanalyst R. D. Laing's unforgettable words, "A man who prefers to be dead rather than Red is normal. A man who says he has lost his soul is mad. A man who says that men are machines may be a great scientist. A man who says he *is* a machine is 'depersonalized,' in psychiatric jargon.") What matters is that, despite all those riddles and dilemmas, men have always shown themselves capable of transformation, of growth, for reasons no social scientist may ever be able to specify. The ironic title of Dr. Menninger's book brings to mind Dostoevski. Raskolnikov and Sonia would hardly be considered good "treatment risks" by many of our psychiatrists, nor would many of us find much mercy in our hearts for them. To Dostoevski, however, punishment is absurd and worthless unless it leads to a new beginning:

> They wanted to speak, but could not; tears stood in their eyes. They were both pale and thin; but those sick, pale faces were bright with the dawn of a new future, of a full resurrection into a new life. They were renewed by love; the heart of each held infinite sources of life for the heart of the other.

I suppose such words can be dismissed as embarrassing sentiment, the prerogative of soft, muddleheaded visionaries — which brings to mind an added embarrassment. We are fast approaching the year 2000, which will again remind us how long ago it was that a child was born whom others eventually scorned, arraigned, and punished with the harshest penalty, only to find the man revealed as God Himself.

The New Yorker, 1970

5

RACISM AND POPULISM

As Hitler's hysterically racist version of fascism year by year strengthened itself in Germany and then spread all over Europe, a generation of intellectuals, not to mention millions of ordinary men and women, had to confront some unsettling questions. Could "it" (Nazism) happen here or there or, indeed, anywhere? How did the nation of Beethoven and Brahms, Goethe and Schiller and Gropius turn itself over to a bunch of thugs, murderers, and confidence men? Was there something special about such a turn of events, something rooted in the German "national character," in a particular people's history and culture? And anyway, why did the Führer's racial hate, directed at so many segments of the world's population, strike so many responsive chords: enthusiastic applause; discreet approval; sympathy; the embarrassed silence of those who suddenly heard spoken on a grand scale what hitherto had to be whispered or joked about in private?

Once the Nazis were beaten, many of us were glad to forget those issues, or leave them to theologians, moral philosophers (sometimes masked as novelists or playwrights), and, not least, social scientists.

Of the latter, some were traditional scholars: economists, political scientists, or historians, they had the task of sifting through the rubble of this century's destroyed dreams and realized nightmares — in the hope of finding answers to all sorts of persisting questions. How deliberate was Hitler's rise, how much the product of right-wing intrigue, left-wing myopia and ideological rigidity, popular indifference, rising unemployment, a long tradition of fear and hate that goes back, say, to Martin Luther's later years? How did Versailles lead to National Socialism — and if Hitler's particular leadership had not been available, might Germany never have embarked on the course that led to the Second World War? Indeed, could the Weimar Republic have survived and even flourished, given a reasonable measure of support from Germany's one-time enemies (and constant competitors), the capitalist democracies of Britain, France, and the United States?

Meanwhile others belonging to relatively young fields like psychology, psychoanalysis, sociology, and anthropology began to come up with a different way of looking at the appearance of the Nazis — as well as developments in Europe and the United States. In 1941, Erich Fromm's *Escape from Freedom* anticipated this new kind of inquiry; there and in *Man for Himself* (1947) the eternal struggle between good and evil obtained yet another kind of metaphorical expression. An exploitative and hoarding "character type" was contrasted with its opposite, a loving and gentle "character," and an "authoritarian" conscience was compared with the "humanistic" kind. Fromm has never been a naive, label-prone psychoanalyst or social psychologist. He repeatedly reminds his readers that he is not trying to look upon the rise of Hitler and his followers as a purely psychological problem: "Nazism is a psychological problem, but the psychological factors themselves have to be understood as molded by socioeconomic factors."

Still, the Nazis progressively claimed the obedience, loyalty, and passion of the German people, and in Fromm's mind did so for reasons that a certain kind of psychologist is especially trained to understand: insecure, fearful, narrow-minded, and blindly submissive parents, themselves hurt and stifled by the kinds of lives they have to live, turn on their children and make of them the kind of putty that shrewd demagogues can almost infinitely, it seems, shape and use.

Fromm does not hesitate to make generalizations. He speaks of the "lower strata of the [German] middle class, composed of small shop-keepers, artisans, and white collar workers." He refers to their love of the strong and hatred of the weak; their pettiness and pervasive hostility; their thriftiness with feelings as well as with money; and essentially their asceticism, hence susceptibility to a leader who knows how to sanction mass hysteria. Unsure of their jobs or income they feel unsure of themselves, turn on outsiders and strangers with a vengeance, become envious of all sorts of people, and convert that envy into a curious (and dangerous) kind of moral indignation, which ambitious politicians have no trouble taking advantage of.

Needless to say, Erich Fromm did not claim that he had spent among German workers the amount of time analysts offer to their upper-middle-class patients. He does indicate in a footnote[1] that the "view" he is presenting of German workers, and by extension others in the industrial nations of the West, "is based on the results of an unpublished study of the 'Character of German Workers and Employees in 1929/30.'" In that study, interestingly enough, "the responses of six hundred persons to a detailed questionnaire showed that a minority of the respondents exhibited the authoritarian character, that with about the same number the quest for freedom and independence was prevalent, while the great majority exhibited a less clear-cut mixture of different traits." Fromm studied the responses of that group of people to certain questions, then tried to make a series of formulations that would be suggestive and clarifying — just as a poet or dramatist hopes with a metaphor to make connections hitherto unnoticed.

In the late 1940s and early 1950s, Fromm's line of thinking was pursued with great thoroughness by Theodor Adorno and others in this country. The result was a vast study, *The Authoritarian Personality,* which extended and strengthened Fromm's views. On the basis of questionnaires, psychological tests, and interviews, certain men and women were found to possess what was called an "authoritarian personality": that is, they seemed rigid, conformist, somewhat self-righteous, not particularly introspective, rather deferential to those considered their superiors, and unable to tolerate life's ambiguities.

---

[1] *Escape from Freedom* (Holt, Rinehart & Winston, 1941), p. 42.

Such people were far more likely to be prejudiced and, as the book's title suggests, those same people can be considered potential recruits for a totalitarian movement.

While Adorno and others were trying to distinguish between various "groups" of people by asking them questions and giving them tests, without getting to know them over the months, let alone years, of their lives, psychiatrists and psychoanalysts were also speculating at great length on the forces that compel particular individuals to fear and hate others. Robert Waelder (1960) connected the totalitarian mentality to a "paranoid system." Ernst Simmel (1946) and Rudolph Loewenstein (1947) emphasized the prejudiced person's need to find scapegoats, to attribute his or her own greed, envy, hate, or lust to others.

As one goes through the articles and books by these and other analysts, the mind's deviousness and complexity once again become clear — even as they do when a particular patient's "psychodynamics" are discussed by the kind of doctor who treasures the subtlety and ingeniousness of a person's thinking. Sibling rivalry, parricide, incest — themes familiar to Greek tragedians as well as to a white Southern novelist like William Faulkner — come up repeatedly in the psychiatric literature on racism, and if sometimes the formulations are extravagant or awkwardly stated, there can be solid and luminous moments, too.

The more tentative and modest efforts hold up today as the best. When, for example, the analyst Rudolph Loewenstein writes about anti-Semitism he draws upon his clinical work with both Christians and Jews, and carefully refrains from sweeping sociological or historical generalizations. Consequently, the reader gets a sense of depth: he has been taken deep into the confines of a concentration camp, helped to understand how the men there feel; but he is not allowed to forget that he will have to turn elsewhere if he would know when and by whom such a place was first developed, or what people now run and profit from it, and if indeed he would determine the spirit that, finally, obtains among the prisoners, hard-pressed and endangered as they are.

Still, as one analyst has commented, "Members of hate groups are not prone to subject themselves to psychological investigation.

Therefore, any observation of such individuals, no matter how brief and incomplete, deserves to be communicated." The analyst who wrote those words, Terry Rodgers, had seen one white man in analysis for five months and in so doing observed "the evolution of an active anti-Negro racist."[2] The man had come to the doctor with serious symptoms and as one reads the clinical discussion, one can only sympathize with both analyst and patient and be impressed with the unwillingness of the former to use his experience with the latter in order to characterize millions of other white people.

Another analyst, Dr. Joel Kovel, is more audacious and ambitious. In *White Racism* (1970) Dr. Rodgers's brief and abruptly terminated clinical experience is called upon for good reason: the author has no firsthand clinical observations of his own to report, not to mention reports of interviews with any of the "white racists" he is convinced constitute the largest group of this nation's population:

> A really deep survey of white Americans would doubtlessly reveal a great mixture of racial patterns in everyone, but it might be predicted that the substantial majority continue to reserve their most intense feelings for the hallowed racial patterns of yore; that is, they hold to a mixture of dominative and aversive racist beliefs, according, one would expect, to their authoritarianism and the degree to which their superego has internalized aggression.

Dr. Kovel mentions the strong influence that Herbert Marcuse's writing has had on his own thinking; both men have in common a bold and imaginative approach to the West's social and political problems. Neither of the two is much given to optimism: Dr. Kovel says that only a "minority, who are in the vanguard of history," are free enough of racism to offer any hope at all that things will basically change, and in *One Dimensional Man* Professor Herbert Marcuse sees most Western men and women rendered utterly inert and compliant by the power of what he calls "advanced industrial culture." Those who dissent are in one way or another appeased, pla-

---

[2] *The Psychoanalytic Study of Society*, Vol. 1 (International Universities Press, 1960) pp. 237-347.

cated, deterred, assimilated. We are systematically indoctrinated with false needs, which are "superimposed upon the individual by particular social interests in his repression."

The result is that our "universe of discourse is populated by self-validating hypotheses which, incessantly and monopolistically repeated, become hypnotic definitions, or dictations." As for Marcuse himself, he and no doubt a few others, too, have somehow struggled away from such "hypnotic definitions"; and if one happens to wonder how he can be so sure that millions of Americans haven't likewise done so, the answer is to be found in his book: the newspapers, radio, and television every day express what is on just about everyone's mind, hence how corrupted and enslaved we all have become — except, of course, for a few social critics, like the author of *One Dimensional Man*.

Meanwhile millions of American men and women live and work and try to make do as best they can; and they, unlike the racist patient Dr. Rodgers writes about, do not find their way to the buildings where psychiatrists practice or, for that matter, to the academic offices of those social or political theorists who write so persistently and surely about what is happening to this or that "majority." For over ten years I have been trying to find out how some of those American men and women (they are white-collar and blue-collar working people) think and feel about — well, about many things: black people, the bosses who own or run the nation's factories and stores, the politicians who come and go, the radio or television programs that Professor Marcuse mentions watching and Dr. Kovel considers part of a culture which "generates racism for the benefit of a false whiteness."

No doubt about it, at times I can only be grateful for what I have read in the various books I have just mentioned and a number of others like them. I sit in the living room of a man who works in an automobile factory, or a policeman or a fireman, or a store clerk, and I hear "the authoritarian personality" giving vent to itself, and "white racism" coming forth in one awful word or phrase after another, and "one-dimensional man" affirming proudly what he and his neighbors have come to. On such occasions a theorist's ideas about what is happening in a society, like a good psychiatrist's interpretations, rightly timed and sensibly worded, help one to pull together what seems otherwise chaotic or frightening, or both.

Yet there are other moments, and they are not so infrequent either. Here is a man speaking who works in a General Electric factory outside Boston — and I have to emphasize as strongly as I can that I have known him and his coworkers and neighbors for five years, spent that length of time with them and their families and neighbors:

"The country is in bad trouble, that's how I see it. We're paying for all the wrong things we've done; I'd say that. We had no business getting into Vietnam in the first place; they're a bunch of crooks and thieves and liars, the people in the government we're supporting. Look at some of the countries we're pouring money into all over the world — dictators and generals run them, and there are a small bunch of rich, and most of the people are so poor you can't even imagine how they live, like animals they live. Here in this country you have the highest standard of living in the world, but it's still the same: there are the rich and there are the poor, and then there are people like us — we work day and night to keep up with the expenses. (I don't know how I'd make it if I didn't have a second job on the weekend.)

"I get sick and tired of welfare cheaters and worse are the hippies, who sit around doing nothing — but they call up Daddy if they run into trouble; and the niggers, always pushing, pushing. But what the hell, who really is in charge of this country, who is calling the shots, who is raking in the money? Not the poor colored people, I'll tell you, it's not them. What have they got for themselves out of this country, for all the damn back-breaking work they've done since they got picked up in Africa by guys with guns and sent over here like cattle? What does the ordinary worker get out of this economy, that he doesn't have to fight for every year or two? Nixon freezes wages, he freezes prices, but the bankers and the stock market people (gamblers, that's all they are, nothing else), those guys just keep pulling it in, profits and more profits. Some of them have these high price lawyers and accountants and they fix the tax forms up so that a millionaire can end up paying practically nothing compared to the hunk they deduct from my check every week. (And if they run into real trouble, there's always the lobbyists in Washington who can go see congressmen and senators and get the tax laws changed.)

"Sometimes I wonder what to tell my kids. They ask you these whys: why one man has so much money that he owns five houses and buys a painting for a million dollars, and meanwhile children are hungry and there's no work for thousands and thousands — right in this country. I tell them that it was always like that: even Jesus Christ couldn't beat the big boys, the rich boys; they got rid of him, plenty quick. So, what can a guy like me do? I tell my kids not to try and make sense out of this country; it's like with people, there's a lot of bad and a lot of good. If you ask me, I think in the long run the working people of this country will have to realize that it's their sweat that produces the wealth, and that means we should have the same rights as the stockholders. No man should have to beg, and no child should go hungry, and no board of directors of a big company should be allowed to sit and make decisions as if it's the stock market people, always buying and selling their shares, who turn out those cars and all the other things our factories produce.

"I can't figure out how to make things more honest and fair in this country; I'm no big brain. But I'll see some of those big brains talk on television, and I've seen them on the streets protesting, and a lot of them are damn fools, that's right, and in love with hearing their own voices. They write about one scheme and then another (they get paid for doing it) and they're against everything that they haven't come up with themselves, and they hit you every place; they make you feel ashamed of everything in your life: your country, the schools your kids go to, the factories where you work and the things you help make, the union you belong to, the dreams you have — that your kids go to college and get good jobs.

"I notice, mind you, that the people who criticize this country most, they're not doing so bad. They call America all kinds of names, but just look at them: they live the good life; they look pretty prosperous to me; no one's stopping them from saying anything they want. I'd sure like to let off some steam every once in a while the way they do — and maybe pick up a few bucks for doing it, and get cheered; but no, I have to clock in at eight, and I'm no sooner home than it's time to eat and say good night to my kids and go to bed myself. Before I get there, though, I'll hear on a program or I'll read in the paper that I'm a bigot, people like me, because I'm not fair in my mind to the colored — or to youth, they're called, not kids, or to the women and the fairies. Everyone wants liberation; that's what you hear, liberation this and liberation that, liberation for everyone — yes, everyone except families like mine, and we're the majority, only that Nixon is mistaken if he thinks we're always going to be so damned silent. All we want is to get by this week and go into the next one without drowning in bills.

"Maybe all of us who just work and don't bellyache ought to start demanding liberation for *us*. I mean, we could quit showing up at the factories and start calling a lot of other people names. Soon there'd be no food in the stores and nothing to buy, and the planes wouldn't work, and the TV would stop and the newspapers, and we'd all be shut up. Then maybe we could start over again. You see injustice in this world, and you think sometimes that we *should* — start it all over, and make the country better, make it more like the people said it should be, the people who wrote the Declaration of Independence. I still remember some of the words in it, even now — about men being created equal; it's a shame they're only words."

The longer I know this man, the more I hear him talk, the harder it is for me to call him this or that, and in so doing feel halfway responsive to the ironies and ambiguities and inconsistencies that I hear in his words and, more important, see expressed in his everyday deeds, his situation in life. He speaks at times about blacks and students and college professors with more anger and contempt than this excerpt indicates. He can be irrational, mean, narrow-minded; and he can work himself up into a spell of mixed racism and jingoism that would only please some of the very people he chooses to attack later on: the rich and powerful, the "vested interests," an expression he learned from Harry Truman and uses over and over again.

He can also be seen working beside black men, talking easily and warmly with them, sharing food with them, offering advice to them and taking advice from them — on what kind of gas to buy, where to get a household item, a gadget, an article of clothing. One day, sometimes one minute, I hear him waving the flag frantically, or treating the struggles of all kinds of people with a nervous scorn that does nothing to reassure him about his own worries and fears. The next day, if not the next minute, he is a strong social critic, a populist, an independent-minded citizen who sees through all sorts of sham and cant and hypocrisy, as spoken and practiced by people he will often collectively refer to as "the powers that be." A white racist, a one-dimensional man, a male chauvinist, an American imperialist, an authoritarian person, he is a far cry from the noble, unblemished proletarian hero some radicals have praised to high heaven — and sought to lead.

Maybe there never was such a proletarian man, at any time in history, in any country; I have no way of knowing. I have enough trouble with my own reactions to what I observe. I become annoyed, saddened, frightened, outraged. I also feel admiration, respect, affection — and a measure of shame. Some of this man's barbs hit home, bring me up short, and make me wonder why it has been, why it continues to be, that in my mind's way of thinking I can't quite do justice to the complexity of his life, let alone the "problem" that arises when someone like me spends time with him and with others more or less like him.

In a way, when I met these white American working men and their families, I was as ill-prepared to comprehend them as I was to make sense of the black people I first worked with in the South and later met up North. I had heard about *them*, too, from psychological and sociological theorists — about the "mark of oppression," about the "basic Negro personality," with all its weaknesses and failures and "disadvantages." Yet, year after year I saw enormous strength and resiliency as well as liveliness and resourcefulness in people who were (*also*, it has to be immediately added) capable of being moody, tired, worn-down, and quick to express anger against themselves as well as against a white visitor and his kind.

Perhaps I should have known all along that only a certain kind of novelist or moral philosopher or social historian can do proper justice to the lives of human beings as they are lived in such flagrant disregard for the needs and insecurities and ambitions that various theory-prone social scientists or ideologues happen to have. So one belatedly turns away from one kind of social observer and searches out another: James Agee in Alabama; George Orwell in Wigan; Simone Weil among France's workers and peasants; C. Vann Woodward trying to fathom the life of Tom Watson — only to find that for them, too, it has been hard, and sometimes impossible, to avoid one or another pitfall.

When he sat down to write up his experiences, Agee had a hard time commenting upon the darker, less generous side of the Alabama tenant farmers he grew to love so much. (In 1941 liberal intellectuals could only be moved to compassion by Agee's words and those honest and powerful photographs of Walker Evans; yet I know from my own work in Alabama how "racist" such people can be — and no doubt in 1965 the road between Selma and Montgomery was lined by people not unlike Agee's friends.) When George Orwell wrote about England's coal miners he also shifted back and forth; at one moment they are fine and decent and honorable, but at other times he realizes that the grim and uncertain lives they live affect their temperaments and the way they react to others, especially strangers. Likewise Simone Weil goes back and forth, now stressing the dignity she would see expressed in the course of her work in factories near Paris and among the peasants of Bourges, now emphasizing the "workman's woes" she encountered, and the effect they had on the spirit of the people she tried so hard to be with and feel close to.

If all three of those extraordinary social observers tried to reconcile for themselves and their readers what seemed almost irreconcilable in the people they went out of their way to meet, there is something else each of them couldn't seem to stop doing when they wrote: scold the intellectuals. In *Let Us Now Praise Famous Men, The Road to Wigan Pier,* and *The Need for Roots* one can detect the following sequence: sympathy and concern for people hurt, cheated, brutalized; outrage at the society that permits and sanctions such a state of affairs — accompanied by expressions of disapproval, disrespect, or outright contempt directed at the intellectuals, toward whom Orwell can become almost violent, Agee sarcastic, and Simone Weil impatient. (In *The Need for Roots* she says: "A condition of any working-class culture is the mingling of what are called intellectuals — an awful name, but at present they scarcely deserve a better one — with the workers. It is difficult to make something real out of such a mingling.")

Often I wonder whether those three somewhat tormented souls have not unwittingly used their annoyance with intellectuals as a means of acknowledging the impossibility of the task they as observers and writers have set out for themselves. True, plenty of intellectuals can be smug, condescending, narrow-minded, arrogant, cruel, noisy, self-serving, full of empty-headed postures and prejudices. But intellectuals are also an exceedingly convenient target, especially for their own kind. Maybe they are easier to take after and ridicule than those bankers and board chairmen and municipal bond lawyers turned public officials who keep their mouths shut, put very little down on paper, but pull strings to their own enormous satisfaction and profit.

The closer Agee, Orwell, and Simone Weil came to the people they wanted to understand, the more confused and outraged each of those three rather sensitive intellectuals must have felt. In no time confusion and outrage can turn to hate; and hate directed at people who are familiar or highly visible is easier than hate turned upon a whole social and economic system, and those who benefit handsomely from it. So the worker I quoted above shouts loudest at blacks when he is most angry at those "vested interests" he keeps on mentioning — and not necessarily because his "personality" is rigid or "authoritarian." I suspect that for Agee or Orwell or Mlle. Weil a similar process took place, with the intellectuals filling in for the factory workers' blacks — the more so because a good number of intellectuals, in contrast to the vulnerable poor of our ghettos or rural areas, actually do make up an influential and parochial and by no means impoverished "vested interest."

In any event, I believe the fourth person I mentioned, C. Vann Woodward, once went through a bit of what the other three did; but perhaps because he was not out there in what anthropologists call "the field," but rather at work on a political biography, the experience was less tortured and easier to put in perspective. Even so, Professor Woodward worried that he would be accused of being too sympathetic with so notorious a racist as Tom Watson turned out to be. Nor could he resist saying this: "When a liberal journal fastens upon Watson the responsibility for the sinister forces of intolerance, superstition, prejudice, religious jingoism, and mobism, it is indulging in half-truths as surely as does the veriest demagogue it denounces."

Woodward's *Tom Watson* concretely and quietly offers a shrewd and subtle examination of what we now call "white racism." As a young man Watson demonstrated his decency, generosity, kindness; a poor and honest idealist, he struggled for years against Georgia's railroad companies, utilities, and growing corporations, as well as their dependable allies, the newspapers. He was repeatedly tricked, abused, slandered, made to realize the futility of his efforts — and eventually he certainly did give up and in despair and rage and hate turn on just about everyone. The analogy between his predicament and that of millions of ordinary working-class men and women is by no means a farfetched one. He and they might have come to be different, might at any point in their lives have changed, found new loyalties, sympathies, affiliations — if the economic and political system had asked them in a significant way to do so.

In 1960 I watched white mobs harass black children as they tried to enter previously all-white schools in New Orleans. The anger I heard, the obscenities and threats, sounded crazier than anything I'd heard when I worked in mental hospitals. When I went to psychiatric meetings I was constantly asked why, in God's name, people do and say such things. Were they all psychotic? Did they need psychiatric "help," perhaps some exposure to "sensitivity groups"? Yet, in 1961 Atlanta had no mobs, no violence, not because that city's population has a higher degree of "mental health" (whatever that is) but because a city, a state, and the federal government had in effect decided that school desegregation had to begin — quietly and without interruption.

Historical change was taking place, and in millions of minds, in ids and egos and superegos all over the South, that development was noticed and had its effect. In 1960 I heard this from a member of the Ku Klux Klan, Louisiana branch: "Let them try putting those nigger kids in our schools. We'll boycott them. If necessary, we'll sacrifice our lives to defend our schools, keep them white." In 1961 I heard this from a member of the Ku Klux Klan, Georgia branch: "It's a bad thing, this school desegregation, but it'll never amount to much, even if it spreads. The main work we have is to keep the white people proud of their race, and let the niggers know that some of us aren't going to sell out to them for their votes. We are teachers, the Klan is, that's right." Even on the extreme borders of fanaticism and racism assumptions change, and rather more quickly than some of "us" (richer, more powerful) might grant or, for that matter, find it in ourselves to manage.

Even when such progress does take place, maybe most of us continue to be, in Dr. Kovel's term, "meta-racists" — people who, he says, "acquiesce in the larger cultural order which continues the work of racism." A definition like that possesses a staggering inclusiveness which one takes for granted from certain evangelical ministers, but not from a physician concerned with the complexities of the human mind. There is a showy kind of pessimism that psychoanalytic social critics have always had, mingled with a strain of moralistic self-righteousness and arrogance that sets off a small "us" from millions and millions of "them."

One wonders, anyway, whether both Dr. Kovel and Professor Marcuse don't in countless respects join the rest of us (breadwinners and homeowners) who "acquiesce in the larger cultural order," as do twenty million blacks, six million of whom — a good deal more than belong to the NAACP, let alone the Black Panthers — are glad and proud to say that they belong to the Baptist Church. Day after day I have heard from ordinary blacks or Chicanos what they, like America's working-class white people, have in mind: work, more money, a higher standard of living for themselves and their children.

> We want in, we want to live like other Americans, we want the good things of life for our children. Let the hippies laugh at money and good clothes. Let college students say America is no good, and our schools are no good, and we should go live in communes. I want to finish high school and be an electrician, and I'd like to live in my own house and have good furniture in it and a new car and all the rest.

Black, poor, a serious student, the youth who practically shouted those words at me, or the white youths I know who speak in a similar vein and work in steel mills or automobile factories, deserve to be described with a vocabulary that does not dismiss them all as brainwashed dupes, but takes into consideration their ability to look into their minds analytically and examine their own society critically, even as our intellectuals claim to be able to do.

Here is the black youth just quoted doing precisely that:

I think a lot of white people are prejudiced; but the same goes for black people. We'll call each other racist names, and we call white people a lot of names, too. But my uncle just got a job, a construction job, and he says he's had some good talks with the honky-whites. He says you can't just write them off; you can't write anyone off, not if you're on the bottom side of the world, and you want it to change. You have to keep pushing, and it's like my grandmother says: she's lived to see so many changes in this country, changes she never believed would happen. The rich people, the well-off white people, they can wring their hands; it doesn't cost them any money to do so. I can't afford to think that way. The way I see it, there's a lot wrong with the country, but there's a lot right with it, and I'd like to be nice and comfortable, with a good job and plenty in the bank, then I could sit back and do my criticizing — maybe I could go to college and get paid for doing it.

A particular element of class consciousness is to be found in much of what I hear from such youths, black or white: while they must work hard for relatively little, and keep their mouths shut, and hope to get more of what they need, others live well, call themselves "liberals" or "radicals" or whatever, come up with one idea after another, have the freedom to do so, and the time, too — even get paid for doing so. And some of those ideas, those elaborate if not overwrought theories, have about them, as they filter down to "them," the impersonal objects of description and formulation, an air of unreality if not comic absurdity.

For instance, a former factory worker now become a union official says this:

"Look, I'm not perfect, and the men in our union aren't. Who said we were, anyway? I've heard some of these radicals talk — they say the worker would be so wonderful, if it wasn't for the capitalist system, or the kids would be so wonderful, if it wasn't for bad parents and bad teachers, and the black people, they would be so wonderful, if it wasn't for all the white racists. Who can swallow that stuff? People are good and bad, all of them. That's no news, but I'll tell you there are some people who won't stop until they make life so complicated that it's a miracle we're still around and kicking, us plain, dumb, ordinary people who keep everything running while the professors write about us and call us everything — God knows what, and I wonder sometimes if He could understand some of the talk you hear these days.

"I went to a meeting last week; they called it a 'workshop,' and we were told that it's 'white racism,' that's the cause of all the trouble in our cities, and unless we change these 'white racial attitudes,' we're going to explode, this country. They were all wringing their hands, and confessing that it's true, it's true, we're no good, all of us, we're white racists. Well, I didn't say anything. I thought to myself: go ahead, do your confessing; go ahead, meet every week and look inside yourselves, as they said they were doing.

"Sure, the Kerner Commission Report they read to us from was right; sure there's been racism in this country since it was founded. But the slaves weren't brought over here because white racists wanted them nearby to shout at, and the colored weren't kept on those plantations for that reason, and they're not sweeping floors and working in kitchens or any other place for that reason. They were *labor*, labor when they were brought over here, and they are labor now — a pool of cheap labor, and that's what the big boys who own plantations or corporations (or a big house they need kept clean) have always wanted: plenty of people desperate enough to do mean, tough, unpleasant work for cheap wages, or no wages at all.

"The more I hear people shout at me and my men, and call us 'white racists,' the more I realize that the people who shout the loudest know us the least — but you can be sure of this, they get paid plenty for writing, and telling the Kerner people our 'racial attitudes' are the 'basic cause.' The people who call me a 'white racist' are bragging, they're saying that they're the best people, they've looked into their souls, and changed their personalities, and got rid of *their* 'white racism,' and they're no longer bigots and all that, and taken in by the 'false values,' they call them, of this country. Of course these professors come here from all over the world to live; you bet they do — where else can they sound off as much as they want, and say all they do, and get a lot of money for doing it, and have a flock of those half-witted, gullible students rushing after them, one after the other, and calling them God?

"I'd sure as hell like to let off steam about a lot of things, and so would my men; but people like us are keeping the electric company going, and the gas company, and the telephone company, and the production lines — we're too busy trying to earn enough not to go broke, so we just have to live with our 'racism' and all the rest. But you go look for yourself: you'll see my men, black and white, doing their job. I wonder how much time these people that write all these things about us spend with black people — or with anyone except themselves. We're supposed to say yes to what they say about us — but just let us say a word or two about them, and we're called ignorant and pigs and racists and all the rest."

I suppose some of his anger and resentment is bound to rub off — another reason perhaps for the "defensiveness" or "anti-intellectualism" in the writings of Agee and Orwell. On the other hand, we have a right to expect from the well-to-do intellectuals who write about subjects like "the authoritarian personality" and "white racism" (for the government, foundations, or editors) a measure of concreteness and common sense, not to mention some evidence that what is handed down as virtual law has somehow been tried out in the world "out there" — tested against the social, political, and economic realities and, yes, the psychological ones, too, which the overwhelming majority of people live out rather than try to fit into theories or prophesies.

I have no wish to say that many of the factory workers I have come to know these recent years are not (in varying degrees and at particular moments) "white racists," and many other "bad" things, too. I suppose I have enough firsthand data to justify utter despair — the conviction that we are headed for the rubbish heap of history. Still, there are about us the examples of Cesar Chavez and Andrew Young, John Lewis and Ralph Nader, Dorothy Day and Saul Alinsky, and dozens of white and black political organizers I have been privileged to know this past decade — I think of Bob Zellner, once of SNCC and now in Louisiana and Mississippi trying to be of service to poor and working-class whites, and of Jim Branscome fighting the strip miners and big coal and oil interests through Save Our Kentucky, or of Charles Sherrod among rural Georgia's blacks.

A while back Julian Bond refused to be satisfied with a label like "white racist" even when applied to an obvious one, Lester Maddox. Mr. Bond took pains to emphasize that Maddox's struggles as a youth with bitter poverty require us to look at the Georgia Power Company, at the owners of textile mills, at the way the city of Atlanta and the state of Georgia are run — by whom, for whom, at whose overall expense. Quaint, those American populists — and infinitely shrewd about politics, economics, and, just as well, matters of the mind and heart.

None of the people I have just mentioned as sources of hope and promise has any new or ingenious answers for us; some of them are proud to say that they have never written a word, let alone constructed a theory or written a book, and some have written tentatively, yet also with a tough insistence, that there are all sorts of things that can be done and that they themselves are every day trying to do. And they know that they are exceptional, often isolated figures, up against more cynical and powerful leaders who long ago were willing to manipulate and sell out the working people who counted on them.

It may be that never in our lifetime or in anybody's lifetime will Americans rid themselves of "white racism" or "meta-racism," stop being "one-dimensional" and instead become two- or three-dimensional, shed themselves of the "authoritarianism" (and God knows what else) that lurks in their dreams and fantasies. But perhaps we can, many of us, black and white, intellectuals and workers, fight hard and politically so that children are well-fed, so that their parents can find work and get good pay for that work — and most important, in the words a young welder once directed at me, so that "the working people of this country have more and more say about what goes on in this country." A Southerner, the man's father belonged to the Klan:

Once my daddy when he was old, and just before he died, told me this: he said that if our country had been a better one, he'd have had a good job and lived a better life, and not been pushed around all the time and had the money from his crops go to big landowners and the banks, and then he'd have been a better person.

The poor, depressed, benighted, self-pitying, white racist old father could have done worse as a psychiatrist, a political scientist, or a social theorist.

The New York Review of Books, 1971

6

THE CASE OF

MICHAEL WECHSLER

❧

Recovered psychiatric patients don't usually write about their experiences in and out of the hospital, but enough of them have done so to make a tradition of sorts. One thinks of *A Mind That Found Itself,* written by Clifford Beers in 1907; or *Fight Against Fears,* Lucy Freeman's dramatic account of her troubles — a best-seller in the middle 1940s, when psychiatry was catching hold among the middle and upper American bourgeoisie; or more recently, Barbara Field Benziger's *The Prison of My Mind,* from which the reader learns how the rich can be hoodwinked and devastated by the seamier side of medicine and its various specialties — all those "rest homes" and "sanatoria" with their pretty names, set up to fleece patrons, whom they insult and humiliate, then quickly discharge when cash runs out or suspicions (no doubt labeled "paranoia") get dangerously active.

Then there are those who don't recover. They start out with something that is called "anxiety" or a "phobia" by the family doctor. With his help they struggle against their symptoms for a time, only to feel worse and worse. If they are reasonably well-to-do and educated they are likely to take themselves to a private psychiatrist.

If they have little money but are students or young professional men or women they may go to a clinic, where their youth and "promise" earn them favored status — "individual psychotherapy." If they are poor or their parents are working people — mechanics, gas station attendants, waitresses, switchboard operators — the chances are that "medication" will be prescribed, infrequent and brief "follow-up" visits recommended, and maybe, under the best of circumstances, some "group therapy" made available.

In 1958 August Hollingshead and Frederick Redlich, in their study *Social Class and Mental Illness,* concluded that money commands attention from psychiatrists, among others; those who are relatively poor or uneducated (meaning millions and millions of ordinary working people, who can barely pay the baby doctor for the routine childhood illnesses that come up, let alone bills for psychotherapy) are commonly treated in ways that require much less of the doctor's time. In the fourteen years since their book appeared, nothing has happened to change their description.

Yet here, as in so many other respects, psychiatry has to be distinguished from other branches of medicine. Nowhere in this country, or in any other country, do the rich and powerful fail to get better "care" than the poor. Hospitals vary, as does nursing care or the quality and quantity of medical attention, according to the patients' pocketbooks or positions in society. (Since Hippocrates, the call for another, more equalitarian approach has been given unremitting lip service.) Yet whether a patient is rich or poor, penicillin is prescribed for bacterial pneumonia, surgery for an inflamed appendix; class barriers have nothing to do with the way children are protected from polio or tetanus — the same vaccine is used throughout the country.

In contrast, psychiatrists talk about various "modalities of treatment," supposedly a rational response to separate "clinical entities," whereas in fact different patients, possessed of the very same "difficulties" (or "illnesses" as they are mainly called, an arguable use of medical imagery), receive thoroughly different kinds of "therapy" (in psychiatry, where irony and mystery if not mystification abound, quotes around words are not a temptation, but a necessity). One patient with the diagnosis of a severe "phobic disorder" or, perhaps more ominous, "borderline schizophrenia," is called "treatable," seen two or three times a week with what some of Freud's patients called "the talking cure." Another patient, similarly diagnosed, is pronounced "a poor treatment case," maybe especially "resistant" to intervention, or "unmotivated," an "undesirable candidate for psychotherapy" — to draw upon a phrase that I used to hear over and over again when I was a resident and, damn fool that I was in those calm Eisenhower years, never once thought to question.

Psychiatric terms, apparently so clear-cut and emphatic, have extraordinarily versatile lives: they come and go, blend into one another, are used by one doctor, scorned by another. More dangerously, they can have subtle and not so subtle moral or pejorative implications. "Good" patients, liked by their doctors, are described one way, "bad" patients, whose mannerisms (maybe just plain manners) or "attitude" or deeds are found to be unattractive, or described differently.

The difference is one of tone, emphasis, and, always, choice of words, many of them as portentous as they are slippery. This youth is "obsessive," but much of his behavior is "egosyntonic," and his primary struggle is "oedipal," even if his "defenses" are by no means adequate, and sometimes shaky indeed. Another youth is also "obsessive," but underneath are serious "pre-oedipal" conflicts. Furthermore, his defenses are "primitive," and he may well be a "borderline case." With additional exploration we might even discover an "underlying psychotic process."

Needless to say, the very same youth can be seen by one psychiatrist, then another, and on and on, with a similar divergence of opinion. X-rays do not affect the diagnosis. Blood tests cannot establish without doubt what has to be done. We are in a world of feeling, the doctor's as much as the patient's, so no amount of training or credentials or reputation can remove the hazards of such a world: inclinations of various kinds, outright biases, blind spots. I do not deny the enormous value that a personal psychoanalysis has for a future psychiatrist, or the effect years of supervision can also have. By the time most psychiatrists have finished their long apprenticeship they do indeed tend to know what kind of patient they work well with, what kind of patient they ought to avoid, and most important, what their vulnerabilities are.

Still, such awareness isn't always translated into wise clinical decisions. Patients are accepted who ought to be referred. Patients are treated one way, when perhaps another tack might make things a lot easier for both them and their doctors. And even when in a particular case things do begin to work well, "life" is always to be reckoned with. Not everyone can keep at therapy or analysis for those months that have a way of becoming years. There is a job to hold, and it might require a move. There is the draft. There are unavoidable accidents or emergencies that come up from time to time.

From the other side, a similar range of disruptions may arise: the doctor decides to move, or is in training, and so leaves one clinic or hospital for another; he may decide to switch from "practice" to more teaching and research; he finds that his private patient no longer can afford his fees, hence is to be referred to a clinic. It is no doubt painful for many of us to think very long about that last "factor," but it is not an uncommon one, and is yet another reminder about the nature of our society — psychiatrists make themselves available to those whose position in the world enables the purchase of the special kind of intimacy provided by the doctor-patient relationship.

Nor can the implications of such an arrangement be completely forgotten, by either the one who pays or the one who receives the money. Expectations and, later on, demands are backed up by expenditures, and payments establish for the man or woman who receives them their own mandate — while week after week two individuals are talking about the most extraordinarily personal matters and developing between themselves honest and, it is hoped, sustaining exchanges. As well as those "transferences" and "countertransferences" that measure our unfailing ability to find targets for our irrational strivings in those we meet and spend time with (and also, at one remove, in the books we read and the authors we occasionally lavish with praise or feel ourselves inexplicably turning against).

Obviously some of these issues are almost infinitely complicated; they have to do with how various human beings get on and, just as important, the subtleties of class and even caste (some would insist, thinking of patients in mental hospitals) as they affect the lives of both psychiatrists and patients. Once in a while, though, generalities and difficult arguments come into especially clear view for both psychiatrists and patients through the medium of a particular, concrete event.

James Wechsler's *In a Darkness* provides such an occasion. The reader knows from the beginning that unlike Clifford Beers, Lucy Freeman, or Barbara Benziger, Michael Wechsler, son of James and Nancy Wechsler and brother of Sally Karpf, committed suicide at age twenty-six, after a long and stormy series of involvements with no fewer than eight therapists, whose offices are scattered over Boston and New York, which, incidentally, contain the heaviest concentration of psychiatrists in the world.

Mr. Wechsler is a well-known journalist; he is now editorial page editor of the New York *Post*. He has written his book with the help of his wife and daughter. They have wanted to look back and ask themselves questions which they know ought to be asked, not because they are laboring under a "grief reaction" and need "catharsis," but out of respect to their rights as intelligent and sensitive human beings who have gone through a saddening, at times harrowing, experience. They do not want to leave unexamined the many circumstances, moments of crisis, tragic as they turned out, which they and their son went through from the spring of 1960, when the boy, then in the Fieldstone School at Riverdale, New York, first felt the need to see a psychiatrist, until the spring of 1969, when his parents found him in bed and without a pulse, and rushed him to a nearby hospital, where he was pronounced dead, a victim of an overdose of barbiturates.

The book is short and unpretentious. Mr. Wechsler wastes no time in eulogies, nor has he any desire to use his considerable skill as a writer in order to achieve the kind of self-justification it would be only human for him to want. Rather his effort is to describe, from his and his family's point of view, a certain progression in the short life of a bright, sensitive, gifted youth, whose parents' emotional, social, economic, and political resources, however substantial, were in the end not enough to save his life — and when one says that, one must immediately make it clear that Mr. Wechsler has been moved to write this book and give it the title he has because he does not know to this day what *would* have been enough, what *was* needed to save his son's life.

Still faced with "darkness," the mystery and confusion that he as the father of a severely troubled psychiatric patient could never somehow escape from, Mr. Wechsler has written a book of great narrative power which will doubtless unnerve his readers (notably the educated lay public, but, I would hope, also the psychiatric profession itself).

Michael Wechsler was apparently a "normal" boy and youth until he was seventeen and a senior in high school. That is to say, he got along reasonably well with his family, was a first-rate student, had a number of good friends and a fairly active social life. He had presented no real problems to his parents as he grew up, and so they were taken aback when he asked them for the money to see a psychiatrist. Why? For what "problem"?

They would not easily find out, not then and, to some extent, not ever. They agreed to pay the bills, beginning with Doctor First. (Mr. Wechsler calls the doctors Dr. First, Dr. Second, and so on up to the last one, Dr. Eighth, which serves to dramatize the disruptive and bewildering aspects of the experience for both the patient and his family. Names like "Brightlawn," "Fairhope," "Grace Hills" are given to the five institutions in which Michael Wechsler spent a total of twenty-six months, which further evokes the kind of bitter irony and enigmatic fatefulness that Kafka felt drawn to.)

So it began, an awful journey for the young man and no less so for his family. At first things went reasonably well, even if there was considerable trouble between Dr. First and Michael's parents. When Michael was accepted by Harvard, the psychiatrist pronounced himself worried about his patient, but said that there had been progress, and certainly there was no need for the young man to hesitate about going up to Cambridge. In no time Michael was seeing Dr. Second in Cambridge, and because they didn't get on well, Dr. Third was brought in, with the blessings of Dr. First, to whom Michael had been quite attached.

The first year at Harvard is hard for many of the bright, earnest students who come there, with so much talent and so much self-consciousness about their supposed superiority. On the other hand, some strong and ambitious students quickly see the college as a place whose opportunities ought to be seized. Michael set to work, tried to keep up with the fast pace around him, and in time developed a strong interest in psychology — the experimental kind, meaning the possibilities in pigeons rather than the unconscious dynamics of human beings. He mainly kept to himself. He was shy and rather nervous, though certainly in that respect not much different from many of his classmates. Nor were his visits to the two psychiatrists at all remarkable; the Harvard University Health Services operate a much visited psychiatric department, staffed with a dozen or so doctors, and nearby are the private offices of more such doctors, some of whom spend most of their time with students.

The first year at Harvard went by, and the second, without too much difficulty. The Wechslers knew Michael was in trouble, but they kept hoping, as parents do, that somehow the turmoil and moodiness would go away. Instead, things began to get worse. Michael fell asleep at the wheel, was declared "accident-prone." Then he got a motor bike, and was nearly killed when he collided with a bus. In fact, the bus driver would eventually insist that the fault was his, he had suddenly taken a wrong turn.

But by then both Michael and his parents were well down a road all too many people have traveled; their every move was subjected (by them and by the doctors, one after the other) to a scrutiny so close that at times it became utterly self-defeating, because what was intended to clarify became a new source of anxiety and despair. When everything is so closely watched, when events are turned over and over, so that their "significance" can be appreciated, when psychological "meaning" is attributed to everything a person does, then awkwardness and self-consciousness become a fact of life — become life itself. A bus driver's mistake is taken as evidence of a patient's deterioration and his parents' negligence, if not outright wrongdoing, because they paid for the bike.

Anyway, Michael's condition did not substantially improve, in spite of the "help" he was getting. Young patients often simply outgrow the kind of self-centeredness that prompts psychiatric treatment — if they don't they are likely to be headed for a long stretch indeed with the doctor. Michael grew more and more inward, cut off from friends and family. He continued at Harvard, had some good moments, but by his junior year was in worse shape than ever before; he flunked his examination in psychology and soon thereafter was admitted to the university infirmary because he had swallowed a large number of pills.

The next step was a mental hospital, the first of six such episodes in the course of the following five years. At that point, in the chapter called "The First Mental Hospital," Mr. Wechsler's book gains momentum. The earlier uncertainties are now gone, and the author is free to show the reader directly how things went — downhill all the way. Everything is there: the rituals that a mental patient and his visitors have to go through in the hospital; the inscrutable faces, the rudeness and vulgarity, and occasional stupidity, of some doctors; the warmth, decency, and intelligence of other doctors; the banalities that psychiatrists, psychologists, and social workers use — not necessarily out of malice, but because they, too, are in the dark, and so find refuge in clichés and a certain calculated impassivity, the more insulting and harmful because they are clearly meant to stifle questions, let alone objections.

There are also the disagreements — between one psychiatrist and another, between the hospitals, the first one in Massachusetts, the others in New York; and the grim and sad life in Manhattan's East Village, where drugs overwhelm already vulnerable young people, no small number of them just out of or just ready to enter mental hospitals. Finally both patient and family get desperate as bad becomes worse, as doctors are given up for yet more doctors, as new "therapies" are suggested, tried, found wanting — so that all too soon hope recedes for good and everyone is content to hold on for dear life, knowing that the outcome of even such a day-to-day struggle can by no means be taken for granted.

Psychiatrists and the institutions they run are no less susceptible to sham than other professional men and other institutions, and Wechsler has a sharp eye for their hypocrisies. Anyone who has gone through psychiatric training in the Northeast will have little trouble recognizing the hospitals described and, for that matter, the not unrepresentative array of doctors presented. So will many patients with Michael Wechsler's upper-middle-class background and education. The author is sometimes unfair to his son's doctors, some of whom were and no doubt are as desperate as he was and is for the answers that might spare future young people and their parents the "darkness" this book documents. But his is a thoroughly restrained and thoughtful analysis, not without its moments of grim humor:

As we pursued this inquiry, we heard many favorable comments about another state hospital that had the incidental but appealing advantage of being located in the borough in which we lived. When we proposed it to the resident, his response was enthusiastic but he warned that it was extremely difficult to gain admission. Its prestige, however, was a major asset in convincing Michael of its desirability — he, too, had heard respectful comment about it through the patient grapevine. With his acquiescence assured, we exerted all available influence and we hailed the news that he had been accepted with some of the same delight we had felt when Harvard opened its doors to him.

Mr. Wechsler also describes the social workers who say, without expression, only "How do you *feel?*" or "What are your *feelings* about that?" One wants, at the very least, to tell them to come off it. To do so, however, would be to exhibit "hostility," just as a patient has to watch out, too, lest he or she be accused of "acting out." There are good reasons for social workers to keep in close touch with the relatives of hospitalized psychiatric patients, and beyond any doubt the intense feelings that psychotherapy can generate do indeed spill over from the doctor's office to the home, the job, and, in this instance, to the hospital ward.

Nevertheless, what Mr. Wechsler objects to and satirizes is something else — the heavy self-righteousness that the parents of a troubled child are especially apt to experience at the hands of certain "mental health professionals," as they sometimes call themselves. It comes across as a mixture of rhetorical phrases, thinly veiled accusations, and galling (because inappropriate) self-confidence. They seem to be telling one in a manner of almost absolute cool (one never gets excited, that is "neurotic") how everything must be: you've made your mistakes, let's face it, and even today you are compelled to repeat them, we know it, so we are the ones to take over now; and meanwhile, don't get in our way, don't go beyond the limits we in our knowledge (if not wisdom) will set, and let us do *this* and *that* — after all, he or she is without question suffering from X, maybe with a touch of Y.

Before he died Michael Wechsler saw psychoanalysts, psychotherapists, men-doctors, women-doctors; he received insulin, drugs, electric shock treatments; he had occupational therapy, a good deal of it; he was seen in private offices, on hospital wards, in clinics associated with important and well-known hospitals. Beyond question he came under the care of first-rate physicians, well-trained (even well-known) analysts; and he was a patient in America's "best" (teaching) hospitals. To add to the complexity of his case, he clearly was not as disturbed and overwhelmed as other "schizophrenic" (the diagnosis he eventually got) patients become in the course of what is one of the cruelest and most enigmatic states of mind or being man can fall prey to.

I refer to a "state of mind" because even though Mr. Wechsler keeps on calling his son "sick" and "ill," and even though the president of the National Association for Mental Health has told him that his son Michael's affliction is the "number one health problem in the world today," there are good reasons to hold off using that kind of medical imagery. Schizophrenia may indeed have its origins in faulty genes, in some neurophysiological or biochemical disorder we have yet to understand. But right now we know that it is a word meant to describe the way some people have come to live with themselves and others — they think and feel and often enough act in ways that to some degree distinguish them from the rest of us.

Why do they do so? How has it come about that they do so? For precisely what psychological (let alone genetic or somatic) reasons? These are questions best acknowledged as unanswered. Why does one youth, brought up by decent, kind, and attentive parents, become schizophrenic, whereas another who grows up among narrow-minded, stingy, even brutish parents pays a price for it but never goes crazy, never sets foot in a mental hospital, has no desire to commit suicide, is called "normal" by the rest of us — and by no means has to turn into a replica of his or her parents?

Psychiatric formulations can help to clarify what happened to those "in trouble" — else why have they gone to the doctor? In *retrospect* those doctors come forth with explanations, but child psychiatrists know how hard it is to single out exactly what is truly pathological and apt to remain so, as opposed to a particular child's way of growing up and coming to terms with himself or herself. They are correctly loath to predict the psychological future even of the upset children they do see, never mind those millions and millions who have no reason to go near a child guidance clinic.

When things go wrong with a grown-up or a child, everything that has happened or been said becomes potentially significant, as engrossed doctors labor hard to understand what they see and hear; and often the pieces just can't be picked up and put together — just as, when things are working well in a person's mind, no one notices the dozens of idiosyncrasies and blind spots ("neurotic character traits," some psychiatrists would call them) that we all have and that assume such importance only when we begin to get into "emotional trouble." In the face of such uncertainties and ambiguities, modesty on the part of psychiatrists and a certain hesitation to talk about "diseases" and their "causes," as other doctors are wont to do, might even be "therapeutic" for beleaguered patients and their relatives, who deserve more than nervously authoritative fiats, and for those clinicians who have to contend with what are, finally, life's complexities.

Mr. Wechsler explains why he was moved to write *In a Darkness:*

> Indeed, if there is a single message in these pages, it is that those who see in Michael some resemblance to someone they love resist being intimidated by professional counsel and place some faith in their own instincts. This is not to derogate the need for such counsel — too many are denied it for lack of private means or public resources — but, rather, to warn that it may often be conflicting, confusing, and stifling.

He does not repeat that assertion, but rather lets his account make the case: the changes from one doctor to another, one hospital to another, none of them initiated by the Wechslers; the assertions and counter-assertions handed down; the conflicting philosophies of treatment recommended; and perhaps most unsettling, the snide remarks made about each other by professional men and women. Nevertheless, the author seems to know that however justifiable the resentment he and his wife have felt, the real tragedy was a condition, a state of affairs in which they were each one of them caught up — not only Michael Wechsler and his parents, but also the long succession of doctors and nurses and fellow patients to whom the young man turned and from whom he drifted away.

Perhaps no one could have "saved" Michael Wechsler, which means helped him to shake off the suffocating grip his moody, self-lacerating side had gained. Yet, even though I do not fault the author's right to be severely disappointed with several of the doctors his son saw (the words and phrases reported ring completely true to my ear), I found myself thinking of what we *do* know, what many dedicated therapists *have* been able to accomplish over the years since psychiatry has become such a prominent part of American life.

One of the hardest things about being a psychiatrist is the terrible discrepancy between what is understood and what can be done. I really do think that several of those eight psychiatrists knew a lot more about Michael, understood him far better, than they could possibly reveal to his parents even if they had had the time or wanted to. They were doubtless haunted as any clinician is by their task: how to translate analytic vision into therapeutic action that works. Maybe the dogmatism, the gratuitous self-assurance, the rigid insistence on rules of conduct or treatment reflect not so much the anxiety doctors feel when they know deep down how much they don't know, but the despair a clinician feels when he realizes how much needs to be done and how hard it is to do — how uncharted, sometimes unsatisfactory, and occasionally hopeless therapy can be.

Maybe, too, several of those eight doctors were haunted by an awareness of the extraordinarily impressive example analysts like Harry Stack Sullivan, Frieda Fromm-Reichman, Harold Searles, and Gertrud Schwing have set for the rest of us. Anyone who has read Sullivan's *Schizophrenia as a Human Process*[1] or Fromm-Reichman's *Principles of Intensive Psychotherapy*[2] or Searles's brilliant and unashamedly self-scrutinizing *Collected Papers on Schizophrenia and Related Subjects*[3] or Schwing's *A Way to the Soul of the Mentally Ill*[4] can only realize the demanding and exhausting nature of the work such therapists do — but *do* do, day in, day out, and sometimes with astonishing results. Years of patience and persistence are required,

---

[1] Norton, 1962.
[2] University of Chicago, 1950.
[3] International Universities Press, 1966.
[4] International Universities Press, 1954.

and a special temperament. Many doctors simply cannot take to such work, or stay with it, managing the delicate balance of firmness and flexibility, of openness and self-containment that seem so welcome and healing to the kind of patient Michael Wechsler was.

We will never know what actually happened between Michael and the eight doctors he saw, but especially in Harold Searles's book (which is written for his colleagues rather than the general public) one learns how men and women far more disturbed than Michael Wechsler ever was were treated — and with eventual success. The patients' families were not told to stay away or regarded as outcasts. Nor were the patients themselves asked to endure the doctor's studied aloofness or silence, his "neutrality," his unwillingness to talk about himself, about his own worries and fears, and even his "needs" — including those that made him become a psychiatrist in the first place. If bitterness and resentment and various disappointments were seen as "problems" for those Dr. Searles worked with, then love, too, was acknowledged and appreciated as well as "analyzed" — including not only those childhood love affairs we all have experienced but also the respect and affection that may take place between a doctor and a patient, by no means all of it "irrational" or "neurotic" or adequately conveyed by the use of clinical terms like "transference" or "countertransference."

I write this aware that it is no solace at all to mention those books, those especially resourceful therapists — who, tough as they have to be, seem virtually inspired, graced with miraculous qualities of mind and heart. *If only,* one is saying, and *if only,* James and Nancy Wechsler must continue to think. Still, they themselves wanted to share their experience so that others might be spared needless suffering, even as Frieda Fromm-Reichman tried over and over again to tell her colleagues to take a stand against various rigid attitudes and policies, all in the hope that patients once shunned or wrongly approached would no longer be so condemned.

One can only keep on hoping that every young psychiatrist-in-training will read carefully what James and Nancy Wechsler saw and felt, and never forget the lessons they have suffered to learn. Were at least some of those doctors to do so, I believe Michael Wechsler's fine, compassionate spirit, which continues to press itself on his parents and comes across so movingly in his poems and letters, would find itself significantly affirmed — and that particular kind of re-demption, unostentatious but given expression day after day in the lives of others, may be all many of us on this earth can ever find for ourselves, no matter how long we happen to live.

The New York Review of Books, 1972

7

MADNESS IN FILM

Three recent and popular films have asked moviegoers to think twice
about the nature of mental illness and about those doctors whose
work it is, supposedly, to help patients in the midst of agony that is
primarily emotional rather than physical. *Equus* is a faithful film
adaptation of Peter Shaffer's successful Broadway play about a
young man (Peter Firth) murderously preoccupied with horses.
Eventually he blinds six of them in an assaultive orgy. His psychiatrist (Richard Burton) presumably aims to find out why such peculiar
and violent behavior has taken place, in the hope of preventing a recurrence and enabling the youth to achieve some lasting control over
his feverishly moody personality. But in a not unusual theatrical re-
versal, the doctor becomes the patient. He begins to worry about the
meaning of existence and shows signs of self-doubt, sadness, despair. He regards his life as one characterized by caution, compliance — the measured phrase, the guarded viewpoint. He has died
spiritually, or so he suspects, contrasting his self-containment with
the youth's outpouring of passion. We are asked to follow in Nietzsche's steps, to compare critically (if not with utter contempt) the

apollonian sanity of a bourgeois psychiatrist with the dionysian energy of a youth undeterred by convention and seething with a desire to unleash his impulses — at the expense, minimally, of defenseless animals.

Outrageous is a low-budget Canadian film that has found thousands of eager, attentive viewers, some of whom return a second and third time. In Cambridge, Massachusetts, I saw them line up at the movie house — students, of course, but also young, "with it" professionals and, interestingly, apparently conventional suburban, middle-aged couples. They came, I heard them say, to witness the way "two lost souls help each other," or how "two courageous people snub the conventional world and prove their worth."

In the movie a male homosexual (Craig Russell) who dresses in drag and impersonates famous female entertainers lives with a young woman (Hollis McLaren) who has run away from a mental hospital, where she has been diagnosed and treated as a schizophrenic — a serious illness indeed, involving hallucinations, delusions, disordered thinking, and emotional liability. These two wayward souls show affection and trust for each other. We are asked to consider their "relationship" (that 20th-century word of words) a haven of sorts; linked together, the hurt, the humiliated, the ostracized grow more secure and feel more in possession of their selves. As for the rest of the world, its crudities and grotesqueries form a grim background to the idyllic platonic love of the "crazy" and the "queer." Among the "better adjusted" are a vulgar, thoughtless, pill-pushing psychiatrist; an autocratic nurse; and scores of lost, dreary men and women who walk the streets of our cities or seek refuge in bars, in nightclubs where drag queens perform, and, not least, in movie houses.

The film *I Never Promised You a Rose Garden* brings a touching, lyrical, and autobiographical novel relatively intact to the viewer. The novel's message was clear and is implicit in the title: madness is a tough, unyielding, and if necessary seductive opponent, whose grip on a patient only slowly gives way, even with the help of the most dedicated and intelligent of therapists. In a mental hospital we meet one of these — Dr. Fried, sensitively played by Bibi Andersson. She manages well the balance of compassion and detachment that psychiatrists must achieve for the sake of their patients, and for their own sakes, too. Her antagonist (and every patient is, to a degree, an antagonist for every doctor) is equally well acted by Kathleen Quinlan, playing Deborah, a 16-year-old schizophrenic.

Their struggle with each other provides the central dramatic thrust of the movie. The girl's growing attachment to the doctor becomes apparent but is not made melodramatic. When the doctor goes on vacation, the patient begins to fall apart, as often happens — a covert acknowledgment of affection and dependence. The psychiatrist who covers for Dr. Fried turns out to be cold, arrogant, inconsiderate, and self-centered. We are, through him, reminded of how lucky a patient is to have a therapist like Dr. Fried and of how chancy psychotherapy can be. No outright cure is offered; the film's conclusion reveals a young woman psychologically on the upswing but still in the hospital. We have already seen how quickly apparent progress can give way to a setback.

There seems to be a common message in these three movies and in others that have come our way in recent years — *One Flew over the Cuckoo's Nest*, for instance, with its constant satirical thrusts at those who work in mental hospitals. Generalizations are always risky, yet I think films such as *Equus* or *Outrageous* would have been unimaginable a generation ago, not only because the moral climate then was more punitive toward explicit deviance, but because the movies were busy discovering the virtues of psychiatry. Casting the psychiatrist as a madman (*The Cabinet of Dr. Caligari*, 1919) had given way to portraying him as a person of patience, tact, decency, intelligence, and, not least, competence. Film therapists of the 1940s and 1950s had the ability to change human behavior, to heal through clarification and interpretation. In *Spellbound* (1945), for example, one psychiatrist (Ingrid Bergman) had the difficult challenge of unraveling the psychopathology of another (Gregory Peck), but she persisted and won a victory over his fears. (In the bargain, they solved a crime.) We were given to believe, by Alfred Hitchcock, no less, that mental life is indeed mysterious and confusing but that there were people who had penetrated a once bizarre or inscrutable world and found answers to significant questions: What makes us think, act, dream as we do? What prompts some to behave strangely or go berserk? What provokes even "normal" people to feel anxious?

Hollywood has always had a shrewd eye out for America's sectarian solutions — capitalizing on those ideas or values we find appealing now that so many of us have lost faith in God and old-fashioned pieties. For influential members of the *haute bourgeoisie* in the 1940s and 1950s psychoanalysis was decidedly in favor. Those taken up with Freudianism, even if by virtue of a passing fancy, learned a lot about themselves; thousands who had been in mental turmoil found psychoanalysis not only helpful but often life-saving, or to use a religious term, redemptive.

Yet fads give way to new fads, and sometimes to counterfads. In recent years an antipsychiatry attitude has spread, a glorification of the odd, the exceptional, and even, alas, the crazy; a cult of madness — as if losing one's mind is the way to come to one's senses. The British psychiatrist R. D. Laing has in some, but only some, of his writings lent intellectual assistance to such a trend. The counterculture has thrived on turning everything upside-down, defying customs, shaking a fist at conventions. And excessive expectations of psychiatry, along with fatuous claims for it, not surprisingly have been followed by disappointments, a progressive sense of disenchantment.

Yet Freud never promised us a rose garden; he was a stoic, and only wanted to understand more clearly what he and others were about, in the hope that we would be less at the mercy of what we have "forgotten" or repressed. For moviemakers and moviegoers to turn on psychoanalytic psychiatry as if it is a monstrous lie or part of an inhumane instrument of mind control; to picture psychiatrists in general as oppressive or deadened, or lacking in imagination and intelligence, or craven and mean-spirited; to find truth in or to exalt as a desirable life style the pain and sadness and terrible confusion of madness — all of that is to reveal how reactive we of this century can be, how lost in the shifting sands of the chic.

True, there are idiot shrinks, cruel or narrow-minded ones, as is the case in every profession. True, some seriously deranged people can also have luminous moments of insight. But mental hospitals are hardly bristling with ignored poets, novelists, artists, composers. Mainly they harbor people whose anguish deserves the compassion rather than the silly, ecstatic approval, the cheap hurrahs, of those lucky enough to be living on the outside with some degree of mental coherence.

It is, yes, *outrageous* to romanticize a severely psychotic woman and a shrill, hyped-up transvestite, to see them not as they are — nor even as disturbed as they acknowledge themselves to be — but instead as reflections of ourselves. The two characters in the film are indeed lost souls. When suburban couples or university students or young city professionals come out of *Outrageous* full of a self-centered identification with them, they cheapen the characters as well as themselves.

"We're all lonely and a little peculiar," I heard a Cambridge viewer say upon leaving the theater. There is arrogance and greed in such an assertion — an assumption that no one's experience is beyond such a person's demanding, assimilative reach; a damning of the lousy shrinks who (with what might be called common sense) insist that there *are* differences between people, between those whose heads are relatively sound and those in psychological disarray. How convenient to make the shrink a fool, or a witch, or a storm trooper; or an aging, self-doubting man mesmerized by a youth who viciously assaults animals and who may, for all we know (and we ought to be asked to contemplate the distinct possibility), next turn his murderous wrath on human beings.

Of these movies, only *I Never Promised You a Rose Garden* grants us a measured, honorable look at what psychiatry can do, given the time and the personal commitments of a decent doctor and a patient who decides to be helped. One can only hope that such a view of psychiatry, at once tempered and informed by the experience and respect earned every day in hospitals, offices, and clinics, will survive the flashy, indulgent excesses of other films. We deserve to be in touch with good judgment, a sense of proportion, and an awareness of complexity when considering madness or any other aspect of human life.

Horizon, 1978

8

MEDICAL ETHICS AND

LIVING A LIFE

A black woman in Mississippi's Delta told me in 1969, as I went from home to home with other doctors trying to understand how it went for extremely poor and hard-pressed people:

> We don't have it good here. It's no good at all. I turn and ask the Lord, a lot of times, why it's so — the unfairness in this world. But I'll never get an answer. My daddy told me: "Don't expect answers to the really big questions — not from anyone. We're put here, and we don't know why, and we try to figure out why while we're here, and we fight to stay around as long as we can, and the next thing we know, it's slipping away from us, and we're wondering where we're going, if we're going any place." If I was a doctor, I guess I'd wonder every day what it's all about, this life. A lot of times my children ask me these questions, ask me why people behave so bad toward other people, and why there's so much greed in the world, and when will God get angry and stop all the people who don't care about anything but themselves. I have to say I don't have the answers. Does anyone? If you go to college,

my oldest girl said, you learn the answers. She's twelve. She thinks that the more education you get, the more you know about how to be good and live a good life. But I'll tell you, I'm not so sure. I think you can have a lot of diplomas to your credit, and not be the best person in the world. You can be a fool, actually, and have a lot of people calling you professor, lawyer, even doctor.

That "even" — a measure of hesitation, of lingering awe, of qualified respect. She had experienced her "rough times" with doctors — not only segregated facilities, but poor care and more insults than she cared to remember. A self-described "uppity nigger," she had finally spoken up to a doctor, had an argument with him. She remembered the critical essence of their confrontation this way:

I heard him saying bad, bad words about my people on the phone, and then he came into the waiting room and he gave me the nod. He never is polite to us, the way he can be with his white patients, and the more money they have, the bigger the smile they get out of him, and he's as eager to please as he can be. But with us, it's different; we get one sour look after the other. That day he told me to "shake a leg." I guess I wasn't walking into his office fast enough. Then he started talking about all "the welfare people," and saying, "Why didn't they go get themselves work?" Then, as he poked my belly, he gave me lecture on eating and my diabetes — how I should "shape up and eat better."

That's when I forgot myself. I told him he should look to himself sometimes and stop making cracks at others. I told him he wasn't being much of a credit to his people and his profession, the way he was making these wisecracks about us poor folks. I told him he should know better, that there wasn't the jobs, and only now are we getting the right to vote, and the schools we've had weren't like the ones he could go to. I told him I expected more of him. Isn't he a doctor? If he can lord it over people, being a doctor, then he ought to remember how our Lord, Jesus Christ behaved. He was the Son of God, but did He go around showing how big and important He was, and calling people bad names, and making wisecracks, and sidling up to the rich and looking down

His nose at the poor? Jesus was a doctor; He healed the sick, and He tended after the lame, the halt and the blind, like our minister says. I told our doctor he ought to read the Bible more. I told him that instead of saying bad things about the poor people and us colored people, he should take a hard look at himself and see if he's living the best life he can — the kind of life a doctor should live — if he's going to preach to the rest of us, and be looked up to as if he's the best of the best.

She didn't get very far with such words, although, to his credit, the doctor not only heard her out but smiled and thanked her for the obvious courage (in the year 1967) that she had displayed. And it may be all too easy now, as it has surely been in past years, to call upon such an incident, the South being once again a convenient scapegoat for the rest of us. In fact, there aren't too many places in America, one suspects, where such a candid encounter could take place. How many of us in medicine have been asked by anyone — patient, friend, relative, student, colleague — to connect our professional position with the kind of life we live, the way we get on with those we attend in an office, clinic, ward? That woman, who today would be categorized as "culturally deprived" or "culturally disadvantaged" (the dreary banality of such language!), had managed to put her finger on an important issue, indeed — one that philosophers, theologians and novelists have struggled for a long time to comprehend: How does one live a decent and honorable life, and is it right to separate, in that regard, a person's "private life" from his or her working life?

In a sense, too, that woman was struggling with the issue of medical ethics: How broad and deep ought such a subject cut — to the bone of the doctor's life? Without question, we need to examine the ethical matters that press on us every day in the course of our work. Recently, such matters have gained increasing attention and have been worked into the curricula of our medical schools. The traditions and resources of analytic philosophy have been extremely helpful, as we wonder when life ends or contemplate priorities so far as scarce (or experimental) technology and medicine go. It is utterly necessary for us to confront our values (or lack of them) as, for example, we work with patients too young or too old or too sick to be able to speak for themselves. And the dying patient has, of course, by and large benefited from the recent attention given that final stretch of earthly time, though one hastens to wonder whether a certain kind of psychological self-consciousness has not had its own dangers: all those "stages" and the prescriptive arrogance that can accompany "reform." Aren't there some people who have a "right" to "denial," not to mention a belief in the Good News? When does psychological analysis become a kind of normative judgment, if not smug, self-righteousness? Sometimes, as I read the "literature" on "death and dying," I get the feeling that agnostic psychological moralists have the complete run of the field, with all too many ministers worrying all too much about something called "pastoral counseling," when a few old-fashioned prayers might be in order for the sake of the patient, the attending clergyman, and the rest of us as well.

Be that as it may, the woman just quoted from the outer precincts of Clarksdale, Mississippi, was aware in her own way that there have been, all along, two philosophical traditions — the analytic and the existential. The former allows us to ponder a host of variables and to make a specific (for the doctor, medical) decision. But the latter tradition urges us to go along with Kierkegaard, who surveyed Hegel's analytic abstractions with a certain awe but managed to remind himself and his readers that a man who had scrutinized all history and come up with a comprehensive theoretical explanation of anything and everything that had happened or would take place nevertheless had not much to tell us about how we ought to live our lives — we, who ask such a question and know that we have only so much time to find an answer. The existentialists (I don't like the glib, trendy use of the word, but what can one do these days with any word?) have stressed the particulars of everyday life — hence their interest (Buber, Marcel, Camus, Sartre and the father of them all, that at once high-spirited and gloomy Dane, Kierkegaard) in short stories, novels, plays and essays concerned with specific, concrete matters, as opposed to large-scale theoretical formulations meant to explain whatever comes in sight and then some.

It is the everyday life that clinicians also contend with — the unique nature of each human being. Since no patient is quite like any other, the doctor has to step from well learned abstractions to the individual person at hand — an important move, indeed. Novelists as well are wedded to the specific, the everyday; their job is to conjure up details for us, examples for us — the magic of art. And, as our black woman friend pointed out, everyday life has its own ethical conflicts. No wonder novelists do so well examining the trials and temptations that intervene, say, in a doctor's life. The point of a medical humanities course devoted to literature is ethical reflection, not a bit of culture polish here, a touch of story enjoyment there. There is an utter methodologic precision to the aim taken by George Eliot in *Middlemarch*, F. Scott Fitzgerald in *Tender Is the Night*, Sinclair Lewis in *Arrowsmith*, Walker Percy in *Love in the Ruins*. They are interested in exploring a kind of medical ethics that has to do with the quality of a lived life.

In *Middlemarch* Dr. Lydgate, a young doctor with high ideals, gradually must contend with a world of money and power. His marriage, his friendships, his everyday attitudes and commitments are revealed to weigh heavily, in the end, on the nature of his work. When he leaves Middlemarch for his excellent practice "between London and a Continental bathing place," he is not only abandoning a promising research career; he has changed so imperceptibly that he has no notion of real change. The ethical implications of his change of career are rendered with great subtlety. This greatest of English novelists knew better than to indulge in melodrama — the high-minded doctor come to naught through bad luck or a bad marriage or the bad faith of a particular banker. She makes it clear that to the outer world Lydgate is never a failure; he becomes, rather, more and more successful, as judged by the (corrupt and ignorant, we now know) standards of his time and place. The measure of his failure is his own early and well muscled ethical resolve. He had wanted to combat typhus and cholera — aware of the social as well as personal devastation those diseases wrought. He had wanted to take issue with the "principalities and powers" in his own profession. He ends up writing a treatise on gout. No doubt, gout, too, imposes suffering on people. And who is to decide what each of us ought to do — in any profession? But Lydgate had, indeed, made a series of decisions for himself and had hoped to see certain hopes and ambitions realized.

Middlemarch provides a chronicle of disenchantment. A steady series of minor accommodations, rationalizations, mistakes of judgment contribute to a change of purpose, if not of heart. A doctor's character is proved wanting, and the result is his professional success by the standards of the time. Such a devastating irony leaves the reader in hopes, no doubt, that a bit on contemplation will take place: a person's work is part of a person's life, and the two combined as lifework must be seen as constantly responsive to the moral decisions that we never stop making, day in and day out. What George Eliot probed was character, a quality of mind and heart sadly ignored in today's all-too-numerous psychological analyses.

Similarly in *Arrowsmith,* a novel that many of us, arguably, read and take seriously at the wrong time in our lives — as high-schoolers, rather than during medical school and the years of hospital training. Sinclair Lewis was no George Eliot; he had a ruder, more polemical nature as a writer. And he lacked her gifts of narration. But he knew how professional lives become threatened, cheapened, betrayed. And he knew that such developments take place gradually, almost innocently — the small moments in the long haul, or the seemingly irrelevant big moments, such as a decision to live with one or another person and in this or that setting. His novel offered a powerful indictment of the larger society (always Lewis' intent) that exerts its sway on medicine, even research medicine, which is supposedly insulated from the vulgar world of cash and politics. But, of course, nothing is completely removed from that world — not doctors and not writers and not church people either. *Arrowsmith* is a novel that confronts the reader with a doctor's repeated ethical choices, a novel that makes it clear that such choices not only have to do with procedures (to do or not to do) or plugs (to pull or not to pull) but with the fateful decisions of everyday life that we are constantly making.

Such decisions are the stuff of each person's life. Once made, such decisions shadow us to the last breath. That is why Dick Diver haunts us in *Tender Is the Night,* and that is why Thomas More of Walker Percy's sad, funny and compelling novel, *Love in the Ruins,* makes us so uneasy with his shrewd, satirical observations about himself and his fellow human beings. Those two physicians, the reader knows, have asked important questions about life — how to live it honorably, decently. They have also stumbled badly, and their "fall" troubles us. We want to know why. But the reasons, the explanations, are not the categorical ones of modern psychology — some emotional hang-up. Those two principal characters speak for novelists who know how seamless a web life is, how significantly each physician's career connects with his or her moral values. It is a truism that one takes a risk by isolating the various moments of one's time on earth; yet we commonly strain to do so, and we are even allowed, if not taught, to do so, in our colleges and graduate schools and postgraduate training.

Every day, for instance, I see undergraduates not only working fiercely in courses such as organic chemistry but showing evidence of malevolent, destructive competitiveness. I have talked with some of those who teach such courses — heard the horror stories, the accounts of spite and meanness and outright dishonesty. Yet, again and again one listens to it asked: What can we do? And the students tell themselves, and we tell ourselves — we, who have gone through the maze ourselves — that it is something "inevitable" and, once over, forgotten. But these bothersome novelists tell us that we don't forget, and Lord knows Freud managed to make that point rather tellingly during his lifetime. We may appear to forget; we may convince ourselves that we do, but the small compromises, evasions, surrenderings of principle have their place in the unconscious, an element of geography yet to be done justice to by psychological theorists — the way we "repress" our moral sensibility, accommodate to various situations and die in the way George Eliot indicates.

Each year I receive respectful letters from ministers, bishops and church officials of one kind or another; I am asked to pass judgment psychologically on candidates for the ministry. Once my wife, in a moment of mischief and perhaps common sense, wondered what would have happened to all of us, historically, had Rorschach tests, Thematic Apperception Tests, or, yes, psychiatric interviews, been given to St. Francis of Assisi, St. Teresa of Avila, Martin Luther or Gandhi, not to mention the Old Testament prophets or Jesus Christ. Would they have "passed" those psychiatric interviews — they with their anger at the injustices of this world and their extraordinary willingness to suffer on behalf of all of us? One shudders at the psychiatric words that might have been sent their way. For that matter, she also wondered: Would Freud be given a grant from the National Institute of Mental Health today and would he even be willing to fill out those idiotic forms, one after the other? But setting that detour of my wife's aside, one is still left with the "spectacle" (to use a word that St. Paul favored at a critical moment in the affirmation of his faith) of religious authorities relying rather eagerly on the judgment of my ilk regarding the selection of candidates — as if psychiatrists were especially successful in finding for themselves, never mind others, how it is possible to live a principled life.

In psychiatry and medicine, as in other walks of life, we might ask for a few letters ourselves — not only appraisals of "mental function" but judgments about the ethical qualities of our various candidates. Do we often enough ask for such judgments? Do we ask ourselves and our students the kind of questions that George Eliot had in mind when she gave us, forever, one hopes, Dr. Lydgate, who would soon enough realize that there are prices to be paid for not asking certain questions? Dr. Lydgate forgot to inquire about what it would mean to him to become financially dependent on the philanthropist Bulstrode. Dr. Arrowsmith saw again and again the way doctors, like others, fall in line, knuckle under to various authorities who curb and confine independent thinking, never mind research. What those novelists move us to pursue is moral inquiry of a wide-ranging kind, in the tradition of Socrates or the Augustinian *Confessions* or Pascal's *Pensées,* or again, the best of our novelists: intense scrutiny of one's assumptions, one's expectations, one's values, one's life as it is being lived or as one hopes to live it. The pivotal questions are, of course, obvious. How much money is too much money? Who commands one's time, and who does not? What balance is there to one's commitment of energy? And, from another standpoint, when do reformers start succumbing to the very arrogance or cruelty that they claim to fight? How ought we to resist various intrusions on our freedom, on our privacy as persons and as doctors — the bureaucratic statism that no one, however anxious for various governmental programs, should dismiss as being of little consequence, not after this century's testimony? And so on. Is there room to teach that kind of medical ethics, that kind of program of medical humanities in our medical schools? Is there any better way to do so than through the important stories and character portrayals of novelists who have moved close to the heart of the matter — the continuing tension between idealism and so-called "practicality" in all our lives?

New England Journal of Medicine, 1979

9

UNREFLECTING EGOISM

We are not doing well at all, the historian Christopher Lasch tells us in his latest book, "The Culture of Narcissism." He links his psychological title to a sociological subtitle: "American Life in an Age of Diminishing Expectations." He wants to show us how the latter is connected to the development of the former. He is a strong-minded cultural theorist, eager to reveal us to ourselves — an ironic effort, he must know, because if many of us have turned into the narcissists he describes, then it is narcissism itself, and not the desire for psychological insight, that will prompt an excited rush on our part to glimpse even this severely disapproving picture of our mental habits. His argument draws its ammunition from a growing psychoanalytic literature, which, in turn, is a response to the everyday clinical work of psychiatrists, who have for years recognized the usefulness and importance of the concept of narcissism. As early as 1914, Freud observed that certain patients, much hurt in various ways at an early age, had essentially given up as far as love for others was concerned.

A child who is often rebuffed or who has to face constant irrational shifts in the emotional behavior of a mother or a father may learn to be exceedingly guarded toward people. The child also feels sorely aggrieved, hence resentful. Since the outside world is so untrustworthy, so unreliable (seductively there one moment, achingly absent the next), the child falls back on himself or herself with a certain vengeance. Rather than take emotional risks and quite possibly end up losing, the mind concludes that it would do best to stick with itself, so to speak. The result is what George Eliot called "unreflecting egoism" — a driven kind of self-centeredness that dominates a person's mental life. Today's psychiatrists refer to "the narcissistic character disorder" — the affliction of one whose central, controlling ways of getting on give evidence of a strong avoidance of lasting attachments to other people, accompanied often by a hunger for just such human bonds, and, in the realm of feeling, by an anger (whose severity may not be recognized) at one's fate. There may be, too, a hard-to-shake sadness and a feeling of emptiness, of being lost, with no real hope of being found — by anyone.

Of course, we have all had our psychologically doubtful and threatening moments — in infancy, later childhood, youth, and beyond. Everyone has learned to fall back on his or her own resources, ideas, daydreams. Few of us have failed to experience moments when just about no one seems worth counting on — except the self, as a body that needs care, a mind that needs its satisfactions. As is always the case in psychiatry, the issue is quantitative — the extent of a particular person's self-preoccupation, and the effect it has on the way he or she lives. But Lasch insists that the issue today is also historical and cultural. He wants to make a connection between what he calls "the clinical aspects of the narcissistic syndrome" and "certain characteristic patterns of contemporary culture, such as the intense fear of old age and death, altered sense of time, fascination with celebrity, fear of competition, decline of the play spirit, deteriorating relations between men and women." His book is really a collection of essays meant to show that the so-called rugged individualism of the American past has given way to a collective narcissism, which suits the purposes of an economic system geared not simply to its own growth (as was the case in the past) but to a cultivated consumerism.

The first, and most devastating, critique is devoted to "the awareness movement." By now, we are rather accustomed to the dreary social stupidity generated by that movement, but the author is a historian, and he wants us to look back a little and be reminded of what went on recently in the name of "personal liberation." He goes directly to the sources — those who took part in the events of the last decade or so and decided to describe what they experienced. Here is Jerry Rubin talking about a stretch of twentieth-century time: "In five years, from 1971 to 1975, I directly experienced est, gestalt therapy, bioenergetics, rolfing, massage, jogging, health foods, tai chi, Esalen, hypnotism, modern dance, meditation, Silva Mind Control, Arica, acupuncture, sex therapy, Reichian therapy, and More House — a smorgasbord course in New Consciousness." I suppose such a list will make some laugh, and with good reason. But what kind of craziness, what kind of inner emptiness, what kind of blinded, rudderless personal condition has prompted many of us to join one, then another, then still another of these movements? They are, needless to say, quasi-religious in nature: an effort on the part of the lost to find something half believable and at least a tiny bit transcendent. But the thrust of all those activities is eminently, if not obscenely, narcissistic — a glorification of the mind and body of the individual member or participant, for whom, most likely, God is dead and patriotism a joke. Once, most Americans committed themselves without qualification to religious passion; in some parts of the world people still do. In the early years of this century, the nation-state received the devotion formerly reserved for God. But in our time the flag, the military, the political leadership of countries such as ours have excited the loyalty and enthusiasm of fewer and fewer citizens. What is left for them but themselves? Their narcissism, it can be argued, is a response to grim memories and terrible prospects. As Lasch puts it, "the Nazi holocaust, the threat of nuclear annihilation, the depletion of natural resources, well-founded predictions of ecological disaster have fulfilled poetic prophecy, giving concrete historical substance to the nightmare, or death wish, that avant-garde artists were the first to express."

Under such circumstances, why look back or think very far ahead? That is the question many men and women have asked; it represents a "waning of the sense of historical time," as the author calls this aspect of contemporary self-absorption. We want for the here and now "satisfying interpersonal relationships," "group skills." We want to own what is trendy to wear, to sit or sleep on; we aim to do what is chic, or go "where the action is." When a sense of the past or the future is either attenuated or lost, what is left but an endless series of fads? For every one of them, moreover, there seems to be a book that can command the dollars of thousands: *I'm OK — You're OK, Looking Out for #1, Your Erroneous Zones, Pulling Your Own Strings, Power!, Success!, How to Be Your Own Best Friend,* and many others. There are even some that are saturated with undisguised pornography or sadism. All are banal, and are sold to the reader as an aid to his or her self-promotion and self-enhancement. The encouragement of greedy, combative self-assertion appeals, perhaps, to those who can no longer go to a frontier and explore it, conquer it, and plunder it, and who (after Vietnam and Watergate) can't work themselves up to nationalist truculence or self-righteousness. Why not learn how to win more limited victories, over anyone who happens to come in sight or get in the way?

Psychoanalysts have wisely hesitated to make sweeping sociological statements on the basis of their direct observations in the doctor's office or in mental hospitals. But they do acknowledge that "changes in cultural patterns can affect family structure," and it is Lasch's chosen task to show how today's American culture does precisely that — intrudes upon the manner in which we act as parents, thereby decisively influencing the way our children grow up. In chapters on our schools, our sports, our treatment of the elderly, and our various secular "experts," he argues that we have been taught the importance of conformity — hence the importance of "adjustment," and the acquiescence that characterizes much of our educational and working lives. Once, there were families in which children saw their parents work and saw what that work meant — crops planted and harvested, or products made. But with industrialization home life and work became separated, and the nature of the latter is such that few people get any real sense of achievement from it. Assembly lines and vast bureaucratic offices are often places of confinement, boredom, and despair — time clocked in. Meanwhile, children have to be taught that such is their future life. Parents who are not exactly sure what they dare to want for themselves or their children (besides the various objects incessantly paraded before them with wicked cleverness on the television screen or in newspapers and magazines) turn eagerly to psychologists and psychiatrists, members of the so-called "helping professions," for advice; and they get it, in profusion. Even as parents have left the home to work in factories and offices, their children have had to come to quick terms with the outside world, because of the significant surrender of parental authority over them.

The author refers at one point to "the evil of psychologizing," but he must be one of very few who have the detachment and moral self-assurance to use such a phrase. Millions of us are caught up in the pretentious jargon of child-rearing guides, manuals, books. All that talk of "parenting." All those psychological explanations, not only naïve and sometimes absurd but ephemeral as well — replaced by new guides or contradictory ones: psychology as an instance of consumerism. Is it the first five years that really count, or the first three? And how you handle your child immediately after he or she is born? In one terse, sad quotation from a scholarly paper by Gilbert J. Rose, Lasch indicates what too many of us assume: "The naïve idea that sickness accounts for badness and that badness necessarily results from being misunderstood is the prejudice of a therapeutic morality." We want to "analyze" everything, including our children's behavior, and at the same time we have convinced ourselves that we lack the authority to take a firm stand on much of anything — with respect to their lives or our own. A large crew of hustlers has gleefully moved into this moral vacuum, talking "child development" and "human motivation." Why do parents rush toward these people, eager for their every pronouncement? What are the implicit promises made, if only one will obey all the rules handed down? We are obsessed with "techniques" in the home, as parents, for the same reason that we turn to the counsel of industrial sociologists, practitioners of "personal management," and "guidance counsellors." All these "experts" are disguised moralists, who want to give us answers and more answers, to put us in our place: Do this, don't do that, lest you be judged "maladjusted," "sick," or "abnormal." The covert nature of their preaching (backed up by considerable political and economic authority) is a measure of how uncomfortable we have learned to be with an open acknowledgment of any moral — never mind spiritual — concerns we may yet have, despite the age and its culture.

A number of writers, Lasch points out, have referred to "the de-cline of the superego." But he wisely emphasizes that it is not enough to stop there, or even to add, as he does, a cultural amplification — the obvious connection between psychological permissiveness and the hedonistic consumerism of advanced capitalist societies. To be sure, today's self-styled experts in "child care" don't encourage us to bring up thoroughly disciplined, proudly independent, morally con-cerned young men and women. ("Moral," for many, means "moralis-tic.") But Lasch goes on (backed, I would add, by plenty of evidence that has appeared in the literature of child psychiatry):

> The parents' failure to serve as models of disciplined self-restraint or to restrain the child does not mean that the child grows up with-out a superego. On the contrary, it encourages the development of a harsh and punitive superego based largely on archaic images of the parents, fused with grandiose self-images.

Put differently, if children don't learn how to control themselves as they grow up they will forever be at the mercy of the worries, fears, angers, and desires that characterize early life. Hence the out-bursts of wanton, senseless cruelty; the various binges of gratifica-tion (food, liquor, drugs, gadgets, travel); the spells of ferocious self-criticism that take the form of apathy, inertia, or the blues; a spurt of activity — motorcycles, cars — that is suicidal, and some-times homicidal, in nature; the self-abasement that expresses itself not only in some of the cults we have recently had cause to notice but in the phenomenon of celebrity, which Lasch examines rather closely.

Who are these "stars" (not only, nowadays, entertainers but ath-letes, politicians, and even scholars, writers, and artists), and what does the adoring response of their followers tell us about ourselves? If the famous are caught up in the narcissism that this book analyzes, so are the various crowds that attend them with such abdication of personal responsibility and such apostolic fervor. Among those who regard religion as a joke, as inconsequential, or as a mere ritual, and who have come to view many institutions as corrupt or exploitative, there can be, ironically, a flight to individuals: a suspension of skepticism with regard to them, an outright worship of them. A mind deprived of one kind of discipline will somehow find another. We revert to a childlike narcissism; celebrities become the heroes that boys and girls dream of being, of knowing, of following in causes or cheering on various playing fields. We model ourselves desperately after other people because we haven't really been taught to accept the limitations of life — not when advertisers offer us the moon and one or two of us actually get there, whereupon we conclude that in no time at all the rest of us will be following suit. It is a grandiosity that serves the interests of those who have things to sell. But it is a grandiosity that, finally, becomes infectious, and takes us all in — doctors who promise to "conquer" old age, engineers whose technology will supposedly subdue all of nature, and writers of futuristic stories, novels, screenplays, and essays who spin fantasies and more fantasies. Fantasies about what? About people sprung loose from themselves, on earth and in space — people who have become godlike. It is what Freud, in a paper ("On Narcissism"), once described with reference to the family:

> The child shall have a better time than his parents; he shall not be subject to the necessities which they have recognized as paramount in life. Illness, death, renunciation of enjoyment, restrictions on his own will, shall not touch him; the laws of nature and of society shall be abrogated in his favor; and he shall once more really be the centre and core of creation — "His Majesty the Baby," as we once fancied ourselves.

The trouble is, as this book convincingly demonstrates, such innocent and passing parental fantasies, as they once were, have become articles of faith for many of us. We possess no larger, compelling vision that is worth any commitment of energy and time. We are not inclined to settle for anything less than everything — all at once and at this very moment. What was once called "reality" has become for us a mere barrier, surely one day to be penetrated. We are good at getting things but unable to know where to start when it comes to facing the issues Freud referred to — the finite, complex nature of life itself. We shun the elderly, reminders of our own mortality. We worship super-athletes, promoted by endless and sometimes corrupt schemes. We cultivate postures — ironic cynicism, skeptical distance — meant to keep us from the inevitable difficulties of human involvement. We play it cool, play it fast, and, in the clutch, place our faith in lotions and powders and soaps and dyes and surgical procedures so that we can stay — we hope, we pray — in the game as long as possible, playing at life, because from the outside (society) we have every encouragement to do so and from the inside (family life) we have also learned that such a way of getting along is desirable.

Christopher Lasch has given us a short jeremiad. Perhaps, in his urge to bring us to our senses, he has overstated his case and forgotten to mention some of the nonsense that *other* ages found congenial to their purposes. Certainly he has no answers for our situation. He distrusts many who have answers. His viewpoint is that of one who has looked back hard and looked around keenly. In a summary statement, he observes that "in its pathological form, narcissism originates as a defense against feelings of helpless dependency in early life, which it tries to counter with 'blind optimism' and grandiose illusions of personal self-sufficiency." He adds this:

> Since modern society prolongs the experience of dependence into adult life, it encourages milder forms of narcissism in people who might otherwise come to terms with the inescapable limits on their personal freedom and power — limits inherent in the human condition — by developing competence as workers and parents. But at the same time that our society makes it more and more difficult to find satisfaction in love and work, it surrounds the individual with manufactured fantasies of total gratification.

That is a serious bind to be caught in, and one wonders how we will ever get out of it — short of a drastic reshaping of our society, and of ourselves as citizens of it. Meanwhile, our predicament would seem to resemble that of another civilization under extreme duress. When Aristophanes surveyed the Greek states caught up in the terrible destructiveness — personal, social, political — of the Peloponnesian War, he remarked, "Whirl is King, having driven out Zeus." It may give us some pleasure and yet be a blow to our narcissism as readers, writers, and social critics to know that in this "age of diminishing expectations" our doom is not as "different" as we like to think. The playwright's description still rings true, and the historical parallel is hardly reassuring. Even a widespread awareness of it would no doubt do nothing to lessen the narcissism among us.

The New Yorker, 1979

IO

CIVILITY AND PSYCHOLOGY

There was a time when the major discordance in American political and cultural life was regional; specifically, a matter of North and South — terms that represented not only two regions, but two ways of thinking about life and living it. The question of slavery dominated the argumentative discourse, needless to say, but even before our Constitution was ratified by the states of Colonial America, the great Virginia eccentric (and statesman and singularly shrewd social observer) John Randolph had prophesied the increasing polarization of a future nation: the pull of a strong central government, so convenient to urban manufacturing centers intent on getting resources and doing business, no matter the cost to this person or that community; as against the tug of a rural aristocracy, heavily slave-connected as well as dependent on a white yeomanry, but also devoted to ways of leisure and aspects of a cultural tradition (that of ancient Greece and Rome) at variance with the habits and interests of, say, the burghers of New England, New York, and Pennsylvania. William Taylor's felicitously stated polarity in *Cavalier and Yankee*[1] — the South as a repos-

---

[1] William Taylor, *Cavalier and Yankee* (New York: George Braziller, 1961).

itory of one set of apprehensions and aspirations, the North as a place where a rather different social and economic agenda predominated — was deeply embedded in our national life well into this century.

Even now, as the "New South" becomes, in fact, a *déjà vu* North ("commerce, everywhere commerce" we heard a member of Alabama's gentry say, with respect to Birmingham and Atlanta, in 1965), some of the distinctions Mr. Taylor emphasized haven't quite disappeared. The South's literary culture holds onto a distinct regional character — not only in Faulkner, dead less than twenty years, but in such recent or contemporary writers as Eudora Welty, Flannery O'Connor, Walker Percy, Shelby Foote, Reynolds Price, Tennessee Williams, Madison Jones, Alice Walker. These are writers who take no pleasure at all in what they regard as America's (increasingly, too, the South's) industrial ethic and its cultural overtones: a rootless, fast-moving cosmopolitanism. By the same token, Yankee critics have for some time seen the South as one large, amusing American heirloom: all those hard-to-fathom, or precious, or nostalgically satisfying, but strange, oh strange stories — a continuing collective melodrama which may please "us" in New York or Boston, but surely, as the cute Mr. Truman Capote once put it, tells us of "other places, other rooms" than the ones we know and inhabit.

If, as some would insist, there are still two principal opposites in American life, yet again they are grounded in geography; but today they are the East as against the West. There is, without question, a cultural tradition specifically and intimately Western. One thinks of Scott Momaday; the Pueblo oral tradition, now increasingly published — for example, *The Zunis: Self Portrayals*[2]; the literary and artistic accomplishments of the La Farges; indeed, a string of names, in painting and photography and the essay and the novel: Remington and Catlin, Horgan and Dobie, Ansel Adams and Wallace Stegner and Maynard Dixon, not to mention the strong documentary work of a woman for a while his wife, Dorothea Lange. When I was reading in preparation for my field work in New Mexico and Texas and Alaska, I was constantly surprised (a measure of a considerable provinciality) at the breadth, the richness, of particular, localist aspects of the

---

[2]The Zuni People, *The Zuni: Self Portrayals*, Alvina Quam (tr.) (Albuquerque: University of New Mexico Press, 1972).

West's cultural life — the words and the images, artistic or photographic, inspired by, for example, the Rio Grande Valley, its physical presence, its people. And without question, the West's political life these days lends itself to the speculation that there most certainly are a number of felt assumptions that set apart, at least to a degree, many of the people who live west of the Mississippi River: a preoccupation with land and, more subjectively, with a sense of space; a continuing apprehension about the availability of water; a feeling of distance from the federal city of Washington, and a desire to extend rather than shorten that distance. "Space is everything here — and movement, the right to pick up and go and be yourself and no one hassling you" — these are the words of a New Mexico cowboy we knew when living in the state. In contrast, we heard this from a Mississippi lawyer in the early spring of 1963: "Kin is what matters in the South — your people, in your town. If we lose that, we'll become just another bunch of American gypsies, going here and there and anywhere, because someone is singing the tune of cash."

Of course, both speakers, insistently regional, were connecting themselves to themes whose origin precedes the Revolutionary War by a century and more — the fierce, land-conscious independence of just about all our early settlers, and the intense sense of family and community to be found in the earliest American settlements of Massachusetts or New York as well as Virginia, the Carolinas, and Georgia. As with portraits of "national character," those meant to emphasize regional distinctions are best rendered tentatively, with proper qualification, and in a suggestive rather than categorical spirit. When I look at, say, the magazines *Rocky Mountain* or *New Mexico*, I see the West all right — but, God knows, the American West: our consumerism, our television culture, given the dubious relative permanence of pictures and words on paper. As Kevin Starr made quite clear in the title to (never mind the text of) his first-rate *Americans and the California Dream*,[3] even the farthest West is a place to which something was brought — culture as baggage of sorts, unselfconsciously worked into the lives of both those who stay put and those who travel a good distance in a strenuous search for a suppos-

---

[3]Kevin Starr, *Americans and the California Dream* (New York: Oxford University Press, 1973).

edly new or different life. Put differently, if the texture of our national life is changing, the supposedly more remote parts of the geographic entity will most decidedly feel the effect, especially in this age of the airplane, the television set, the telephone — as anyone knows who has landed in an Eskimo village way up the Arctic coast, or along the Kobuk River, and found pizzas, Coca-Cola, hi-fi sets, snowmobiles, pictures everywhere of the Grateful Dead.

But technology is not the only ingredient of our contemporary life that penetrates even our apparently inaccessible and forbidding territorial extremities. In the middle 1970s as my wife and sons and I visited one Indian reservation after another, one Eskimo community after another, we came upon (inevitably, we now realize) a number of what, I assume, some future archaeologist will call a species of North American artifacts, circa the twentieth century, late (?1970–1990). On a Hopi reservation (yes, *Hopi,* arguably the most persistent cultural critics this country has harbored within its midst) we found the following message, printed on a mimeographed handout: "Something on your mind? Don't be silent. We will meet to discuss a new Hope life. Come, and feel a lot better afterwards!" In Alaska's Kotzebue, and in Noorvik, not far away, we saw several copies of a book titled *Child and Baby Care,* by one Benjamin Spock. On the wall of a school in Kotzebue, this meeting was announced: "Weekly group to discuss teacher-student attitudes, Wednesday at 3." On a bulletin board in a town named Corrales, close by the Rio Grande River, north and west of Albuquerque, a pamphlet presented questions, and also some advice: "Unable to sleep? Overweight? Having Marriage Problems? Come talk about it! You'll feel better!" Then came the details (the place, the time) of a phenomenon surely not regional in nature: life's personal troubles as a subject for strangers (of course!) to mull over long and hard. One of my sons, wonderful with the camera, and with a keen anthropological eye for the strangeness of things, has made a habit of taking snapshots of such "moments" in our work. He was even allowed, indeed encouraged, to take pictures of a meeting in a small Utah town, where teachers were insisting to each other that they were "interacting" and "letting out" what they kept calling their "hostilities." The result would be "a more honest approach in the classroom." Such phrases belong, alas, to all of us in every region of

America; they are not merely handed down, out of memory, as part of one roaming family's "oral literature."

What about another kind of "literature," our national best-sellers; what is their cumulative, transparent message? An endless story, it seems of self-cultivation — what we can do for ourselves, say for ourselves, eat for ourselves. If we are "O.K.," everyone else is. If we consume X or Y or Z, we have our "health," and that is "everything." But, of course, it isn't; one must keep in mind other parts of the self — the sexual organs, say, or the appearance we give, or the "relationships" we have. And those relationships, Lord spare us — they determine whether we'll really get where we ought naturally want to be: "number one" in our minds, "best friends" to ourselves, knowing "where we're coming from," hence possessed of "mental health." I don't think there is a great need for an extended analysis of, or argument about, the collective impact of such a line of thinking. All the books on psychology, food, exercise, sex; all the sermons on how to win friends, on the importance of releasing tensions, on how to "cope," on how to "rear" children so they won't have "conflicts" or "problems," as if that were either possible or desirable — there is a high mound of evidence, in print, of what we are like culturally. The heart of the matter, I fear, is psychology, though not the kind fairly often taught in college and university courses (a scholarly discipline conveyed as such), and not the kind taught under the name of this kind of psychoanalysis:

... at the time when psychoanalysis laid great emphasis on the seductive influence of sharing the parents' bed and the traumatic consequences of witnessing parental intercourse, parents were warned against bodily intimacy with their children and against performing the sexual act in the presence of even their youngest infants. When it was proved in the analyses of adults that the withholding of sexual knowledge was responsible for many intellectual inhibitions, full sexual enlightenment at an early age was advocated. When hysterical symptoms, frigidity, impotence, etc., were traced back to prohibitions and the subsequent repressions of sex in childhood, psychoanalytic upbringing put on its program a lenient and permissive attitude toward the manifestations of infantile, pregenital sexuality. When the new instinct theory gave aggression the status of a basic drive, tolerance was extended also to the child's early and violent hostilities, his death wishes against parents and siblings, etc. When anxiety was recognized as playing a central part in symptom formation, every effort was made to lessen the children's fear of parental authority. When guilt was shown to correspond to the tension between the inner agencies, this was followed by the ban on all educational measures likely to produce a severe super-ego. When the new structural view of the personality placed the onus for maintaining an inner equilibrium on the ego, this was translated into the need to foster in the child the development of ego forces strong enough to hold their own against the pressure of the drives. Finally, in our time, when analytic investigations have turned to earliest events in the first year of life and highlighted their importance, these specific insights are being translated into new and in some respects revolutionary techniques of infant care.[4]

The author of those words, Anna Freud, takes note, a bit further on, of the intense hope and great (messianic) faith, if not sadly instructive and desperate gullibility, involved in all this: "In the unceasing search for pathogenic agents and preventive measures, it seemed always the latest analytic discovery which promised a better and more final solution of the problem." But then, the disappointment: "Above all, to rid the child of anxiety proved an impossible task. Parents did their best to reduce the children's fear of them, merely to find that they were increasing guilt feelings, i.e., fears of the child's own conscience. Where in its turn, the severity of the super-ego was reduced, children produced the deepest of all anxieties, i.e., the fear of human beings who feel unprotected against the pressure of their drives." And too, the discovery that yet another fantasied perfectionism had been tried, been found wanting: "It is true that the children who grew up under its influence were in some respects different from earlier generations; but they were not freer from anxiety or from conflicts, and therefore not less exposed to neurotic and other mental illnesses."

But Anna Freud was not only addressing her psychoanalytic colleagues with such penetrating and ironic remarks. She wrote as a social historian; and the tale she was telling has by no means come to an

---

[4]Anna Freud, *Normality and Pathology in Childhood* (New York: International Universities Press, 1965).

end. It is a story that has to do with widespread notions — in sum, psychology as a dominant theme, if not an obsession, in our national life: among those belonging to the higher realms, whom Miss Freud is gently educating, if not, ever so tactfully, reprimanding for a certain self-important and self-centered variety of fatuity; among those so-called ordinary people who see the best-sellers on the counters of stores located in each of our fifty states — including, I've noticed, the markets of obscure villages of the West or the South, where few know of or pay heed to the "important" (national) newspapers or magazines. Psychology, in this instance, means a concentration, persistent, if not feverish, upon one's thoughts, feelings, wishes, worries — bordering on, if not embracing, solipsism: the self as the only or main form of (existential) reality. Our two regional informants above, poor backward souls from New Mexico and Mississippi, talked about "kin" or "land" as of transcendent importance (even as God and later the nation-state once were held in such commanding esteem). Today it is "groups" that matter, people who know how to talk and talk and talk.

The hallmark of our time⁵ seems to be lots of psychological chatter, lots of self-consciousness, lots of "interpretations." As the saying goes, "Let it all hang out," and then we'll "talk about it." Soren Kierkegaard in *The Present Age*, written in 1846, makes George Orwell seem like a mere tyro — the difference between a leap of thirty or so years (from the late 1940's to 1984) and one of over 125 years: "What is *talkativeness?* It is the result of doing away with the vital distinction between talking and keeping silent." Imagine that, a notion that it is important, often enough, to keep one's mouth shut — rather than, for instance, to say something about someone's "behav-

---

⁵There are several theoretical ways to approach this question of twentieth century "psychological man." Philip Rieff has done so through a critique of psychoanalysis as a social phenomenon in *Freud: The Mind of the Moralist* (Chicago: University of Chicago Press, 1979). Richard Sennett has done so historically in *The Fall of Public Man* (New York: Alfred A. Knopf, 1977). Christopher Lasch has done so, brilliantly, by using narcissism as an angle of approach to the contemporary American social scene in *The Culture of Narcissism* (New York: W. W. Norton, 1978). In my work with children of well-to-do families I have had to comment repeatedly on the self-centeredness one finds, the "narcissistic entitlement" — see Robert Coles, *Privileged Ones*, vol. 5 of *Children of Crisis* (Boston: Atlantic-Little, Brown, 1978).

ior" or "motives" or "problems." At one point Kierkegaard even insisted that "silence is the essence of inwardness, of the inner life." Such an observation tells us today exactly what Kierkegaard meant it to tell his Copenhagen neighbors almost a century and a half ago — how far we've gone in a given direction.

Here is Kierkegaard again, also in *The Present Age,* letting us know that at least one nineteenth century observer was able to prophesy our time of "cool" — a time in which a crude kind of popularized psychology has become the moral standard many, many people rely upon: "A father no longer curses his son in anger, using all his parental authority, nor does a son defy his father, a conflict which might end in the inwardness of forgiveness; on the contrary, their relationship is irreproachable, for it is really in process of ceasing to exist, since they are no longer related to one another within the relationship; in fact it has become a problem in which the two partners observe each other as in a game, instead of having any relation to each other, and they note down each other's remarks instead of showing a firm devotion." And he could take the next step, to see the self becoming our moral *ne plus ultra.* No longer are we as persons subordinate to Yaweh or Christ, to a particular flag and all it stands for, to explicitly avowed and handed-down ethical principles which one tries desperately to live by, if necessary to die for. The self is our guide, our standard — those psychological "needs" we experience, those psychological "passages" through which we journey, those "emotions" we boastfully proclaim to each other. "Now everyone can have an opinion," Kierkegaard observed, and then added, "but they have to band together numerically in order to have one. Twenty-five signatures make the most frightful stupidity into an opinion, and the considered opinion of a first-class mind is only a paradox." If the self must at all costs put its banal cards on the table, then subjective universals (exactly who is without "hostility," "anxiety," and all the rest?) become a public phenomenon (Kierkegaard's "Opinion"), and "group psychology" becomes a major aspect of social reality (as in so-called encounter groups, T-groups, Esalen groups, EST groups — the lot of them).

"I want my say," I heard a child insist in one of the first desegregated classrooms I observed, in Clinton, Tennessee, late in 1958. My wife, a schoolteacher, was there, too; afterwards she wrote this, in her notes: "An impertinent, demanding boy pushed himself upon the class's attention, and the teacher, full of a lot of psychological talk she'd picked up in a university course called 'Mental Health and the Classroom,' didn't tell the child to sit down and shut up. The two black children were more shocked than anyone else — the nerve to do that, without so much as raising his hand! Little do they know what they're being 'integrated' into!" Maybe she was being, like Soren Kierkegaard, a bit too caustic — or maybe, more farsighted than I, certainly, was able to be.

In the third volume of *Children of Crisis, The South Goes North*, I tried to indicate how it felt for a conscientious, dedicated white woman from North Carolina, a teacher in a proudly "progressive" suburban high school, to go her own way — to be a wonderfully strong and inspiring person and educator both for black children bussed to the school and white children there by neighborhood right. But she was not left to her own resources (Kierkegaard's "first-class mind"). She was ordered to attend weekly group meetings, all of which were recorded forever by an elaborate audiovisual apparatus, so that what was said could be scrupulously gone over — and over and over:

> They say we've got to have "empathy," and we have to look inside ourselves and find our "prejudices." They say we should read these books on "the psychology of prejudice." We're all supposed to "talk up." I went for three months, every week, and I'll tell you, it was the oddest thing I've ever seen. Everyone was watching everyone else. You said something, and they told you *why* you said it. One poor woman didn't talk for the first few weeks, and they all jumped on her: *why?* If you spoke, they told you about your "problems." If you kept silent, they still told you about your "problems." All I heard was talk of "motives," and talk of "body language," and talk — about talk! "I hear you," they'd say; or "I hear where you're coming from." I decided I heard them, alright, and where they were coming from — a zoo! I told them no more; I want to *teach*, and I want my children to *learn*, and I don't mind hollering, and I don't mind being the boss of that room, and I don't mind running a tight ship. I don't care what my "needs" are, and why I "behave" like I do. Whose business is it? Why should I

be compelled to sit in such a "group," and be part of that "process"? God save you, if you criticize them: you have your "neurotic conflicts," and your "resistance." It's like communism: if you're down on it, you're a "capitalist pig"!

I told them, the last time I went, that I thought they were making more trouble than they were preventing. They get so nasty to each other, and about each other, and everyone else, and then we're supposed to walk out of that room and get along with each other half civilly. But we don't. You don't forget what's been said. They don't, I don't. Isn't there a time to hold your tongue, and try to get on with it — our *work?* What do they come up with, for all their psychological sophistication? They come up with what my mother used to tell me: "Sin is everywhere." Oh, catch them using the word "sin"! They've got *their* word: neurosis is everywhere! Big deal! "If neurosis is everywhere," I told them, finally, "we all cancel each other out, and let's go home!" Why do you say that, they kept asking. Well, I said: Why do you say *that* — the same old question, again and again: "Why do you say that?" There are my "problems," and then there are the "problems" they have which make them ask me what my problems are — it's like being on a merry-go-round. Well, not as pleasant as that! You know, the last thing I said? I pleaded with them: let's behave with each other, let's be civil.[6]

She kept coming back to that last word. She was not self-righteous, she was not "uptight," as it is so often put now. The children adored her and worked hard for her. I have already described her special and widely acknowledged ability to teach black children with compelling assertiveness and contagious enthusiasm. Yet, for all her personal vigor, her outspokenness and warmth when it came to asking for the children's attention and giving the same qualities of mind and heart back to them, she had a manner that radiated what she wanted to offer from herself to others: civility. A Southerner up North, she might well have been an Easterner gone West, or vice-

---

[6]Robert Coles, *The South Goes North*, vol. 3 of *Children of Crisis* (Boston: Atlantic-Little, Brown, 1972).

versa on either count, so far as the issue of civility is concerned, and she knew it. She was, that is, in distinct jeopardy of being called utterly "irrelevant" when she urged all of us, in her words, to act "half civilly" with each other. Those "Living" pages of our newspapers, even the supposedly "best," read by the "brightest," are saturated with psychological and confessional talk. Mother's Day, we were told in 1980 on one such page, is a "guilt trip," another piety to scorn — as if "guilt" need deter one from showing respect, and being glad for an occasion to join the company of others in so doing. Psychological candor as cant.

Even a modest consideration of civility brings us into territory smack in between psychology and politics. When John Milton reminded his fellow citizens of seventeenth century England how important it is "to inbreed and cherish in a great people the seeds of virtue, and public civility," he was making an important connection between educational principles and a nation's political life. Civility for him had to do with citizenship, membership in a particular national community — not a T-group or a single "cause" or a neighborhood or even a collection of them, called a region. He understood that a given social order was only as strong as the commitment to it of the men and women who, in their sum, make up that order. For him, politeness was no superficial attribute of human behavior, something to be stripped away in the interest of a supposed verbal bluntness that turns out to be, so often, an exercise in truculence, rudeness, self-display, if not a mix of self-promotion and self-indulgence — "fancy, glorified name-calling," as the teacher quoted above once called it after school, a little whiskey in her. Civility has to do with allegiance — a sense that one's behavior ought to be, under a range of circumstances, responsive to, and respectful of, certain standards: historically, they have been state-connected; more recently, they have tended increasingly to be social or conventional (in the nonpejorative sense of that last word). Now we have moved to the standard of the intensely private — ironically, a public phenomenon. Citizens show earnest, even exclusive respect for the autobiographical disclosures of other citizens, no matter that they might be pronouncements of an agitated or even ailing mind. The entire point is to "communicate." (It is, by the way, quite possible to find civility on the wards of mental hospitals — maybe more of it than in certain other places where an absence of civility, to turn Milton's advice round on its head, has become a virtue.)

When a culture begins to turn its back on civility, ought it be called "civilized"? One is not just playing with cognate words here, Latin roots. "Without politeness, without a tight lid on our big mouths at certain critical moments, it's a quick plunge into the old swamp we once called home" — the words of William Carlos Williams, as he contemplated the ornery, sticky, frustrating, galling side of the urban life he knew so well and worked so hard to improve as a doctor who climbed tenement house stairs every day. Maybe he needed a little of that "help" we're all told to go get. Or is it we who need "help" — because we've got so much of it, we've forgotten what else we have to do in this world besides keep getting more of it: live honorable lives in a big and complicated country which has so many problems that have little to do with psychology.

Is it making too brash a leap to say that there is a connection between, on the one hand, the insistent emphasis on self, buttressed by reductionist psychology as a secular, philosophical *raison d'être*, along with a consumerism fueled significantly by an "applied psychology" that tells us what's "in it" for ourselves; and on the other hand, the proliferation of single-issue political activity, whereby one gives one's all to what one feels most strongly about, and the devil with any notion of a larger personal, never mind social, responsibility? A long question, but I've heard it reduced all too readily to a terse statement, indeed: "I'm in this struggle because it means a lot to me; it's where I'm at." I'm afraid I can't describe the person as a poorly educated fool, so for that reason full of the usual encounter-group gibberish one learns to wince at or, if one can, ignore. A graduate of an Ivy League college and law school, a dedicated, hardworking environmentalist, he had the above justification for what amounted to a political yardstick. "They're with me or they're against me," he kept saying. All right, he lived in New Mexico, and had good reason to worry about the land, so stunning in its beauty, yet so vulnerable; the water, so necessary, yet so precarious in supply; the air, so clear and bracing, yet so thin and fragile, and already violated cruelly in parts of the Southwest. Still, here was an American citizen, talking about a vote for an occupant of a seat in the U.S.

Senate, and nothing else mattered — *to him,* he frankly admitted. And if he and all the rest of us are told all the time that what matters is what matters to us personally, and that what happens to matter to us must at all costs be spoken, then why not grab on for dear life and with all one's passion to one or another cause, movement, issue? The point is to fulfill *your* potential, do *your* thing, live and act in a way *you* wish and find comfortable — sexually, with friends, with respect to a career. Why not politically, too? True, millions can't find the kind of leeway ("liberation") a collection of newspaper columnists, book writers, and psychological experts, if not hustlers, tells them they require. But the cultural standards are there, the courts of last appeal: advice handed down in response to letters addressed to newspaper columnists; articles on what to do in just about every "psychologically significant" situation; and always that inquiry as to how one *feels* about something, anything.

Civility means all of us subordinating our feelings to certain shared imperatives; and in politics it means choosing candidates on the basis of not only one's personal tastes and inclinations but the entire country's requirements. If the country itself, however, has been very much taken by the notion that the overriding requirement is that each person follow his or her emotional dictates, respond to initiatives that he or she has found *within* (an examination not of political and economic and social reality, but of the mind's and/or the body's rhythms), then we surely are at a decisive point in American history. When the self becomes our transcendence, politics becomes, along with everything else, a matter of impulse, whim, fancy, exuberant indulgence, bored indifference, outright angry rejection. A political analogue to "doing one's own thing" is a one-issue politics. Civility is meant to guard diversity — because the unifying object of transcendence is something, by definition, above and beyond personal taste or inclination: a loyalty to constitutional principles and obligations, to a process meant to mediate, arbitrate, adjudicate, and yes, promulgate (laws, administrative decisions, acts of policy carried out). It is true that our Constitution explicitly refers to an "inalienable right" we have for "the pursuit of happiness"; but that is connected, immediately, to other issues (life itself, and liberty) and it is part of a long statement, with all sorts of provisions, cautions, reminders, denials, and prohibitions. Moreover, it is a *pursuit* that is mentioned — the task of sifting and sorting, saying yes, but also saying no. And if one person's "happiness" becomes another's pain and sorrow — by God, the Constitution and its Bill of Rights (a clear bill of responsibilities) makes quite clear a particular "civilized" bias, an inclination toward, an insistence upon, actually, civility: the checks and balances, the elaborate political courtesies, hesitations, curbs, second guesses, nay-saying prerogatives of a government, a national authority set up, finally, to make decisions, to govern. At some point, such an activity demands more than the responsive listening of duly elected authorities. It demands a commitment from us — not us as persons, "whole" or otherwise, but us as citizens. A surrender has to be made — not of values and principles, and not of the right to fight for one's (chief) cause or collection of ideas and ideals (ideology, or general political convictions), but of one's right to hoard allegiances — give them only as the property of a particular mind, a certain emotional life.

In losing we gain, in giving up we receive; the old Biblical paradoxes are built into what is called a republic, a civilization. Civility means losing a chance to have one's emotional, wordy say, giving up impulse. For what? For the sake of procedure, order, restraint; for the sake of a thankful absence of the other person's torrent of emotional impulses, visited on oneself and those near at hand. As Anna Freud has pointed out in a quotation above, nothing can be more fearful and disintegrating than being "unprotected against the pressure of [our] drives." The gift for the act of renunciation (civility) is, of course, civilization. Yes, with Freud's "discontents," but that is a small price to pay for sparing ourselves thousands, indeed millions, of breast-beating, fist-clenching, constantly jabbering and self-scrutinizing I's, with their haunting, unsettling refrain of recent years: *I* am all right; *I* have figured myself out; *I* know what *I* want — and that's all that counts. The sad paradox of a collective egoism.

Daedalus, Summer 1980

I I

TRENDS AND FADS

IN PSYCHOANALYSIS

When I was in medical school I used to visit William Carlos Williams, a person whose words and way of living a life had meant a lot to me all during college. I wrote a long essay on him as an undergraduate, sent it to him at the suggestion of my college advisor, and thereby got an invitation to visit the Rutherford, New Jersey, physician, poet, novelist, and social historian. I have never forgotten his mood one day. He had been sent a copy of a book about writers and their problems, written by a psychoanalyst, Edmund Bergler. Williams had read the book. He had thought about its import. He knew I was considering psychiatry for a career. Would I read the book? Yes, I would — and did. No inkling from old Doc Williams of his reaction. I was forthcoming with mine: a brilliant job. I was asked why. I don't remember my intellectual reasons — but I remember the fascination, then, that psychoanalytic psychology had for me: a way of understanding just about everyone and everything! I had read Freud on Leonardo, Freud on Moses. I had some of Erikson's biographical vignettes in Childhood and Society, which came out when I was a college student. As a medical student I was beginning to hear the name Franz Alexander; I was beginning to understand that diseases such as ulcers or ulcerative colitis were, in their essence, psychological. And so was the work of the writer, the artist — naturally: did not they, all the time, use their minds in ways that bespeak their struggles, their conflicts? Weren't we close, that is, to a great secret or two — the nature of creativity, not to mention, in certain instances, the chain of consequences that results in disease?

William Carlos Williams was a writer, and I suppose he had every reason to defend himself against what I now realize to be the overwrought, arrogant, presumptuous, and rather mean-spirited assaults of one Edmund Bergler. (Anna Freud, in one psychologically succinct phrase got to the heart of the matter: "the universally envied gift of creative energy.") But my older friend eventually spoke to me as a physician rather than as someone threatened by a psychoanalyst living across the Hudson — a psychoanalyst who, ironically, kept writing book after book about the various neuroses that characterized novelists or poets or essayists! "The trouble with this," Williams said, pointing at one of Bergler's books. I waited. Nothing. "The trouble with this . . ." He didn't finish. He asked me if I had any idea what might be wrong. No. In fact, I was quite sure that the analytic discoveries were badly needed ones. Williams became grumpy: "Professions try to prove themselves. They try to show how big their muscles are. They want to hold up the world. And they know the public is waiting eagerly."

There was more, much more; by the time Williams was through I'd been given a dose, and then some, of common sense. I'd been made to understand that a particular theorist, and with him, lots of readers, myself included, had become swept up, uncritically, in yet another self important, messianic moment; and too, had lost all sense of proportion and judgment, not to mention skepticism. And I'd been made to think not only about Bergler's heavy-handed diatribes, but about that conveniently anonymous "audience" out there: a readership. I'd been made to wonder about my own gullibility. Nor was Williams self-righteous. He was wonderfully humorous, wry, and self-critical. He reminded me that poets had fads, so did novelists, doctors, and certainly, various kinds of scholars: "It's what we do — out of our willfulness, our boredom, our desperation, or all three."

I've thought often of that last observation — not meant to be a world-shaking pronouncement, as are so many of today's social science theories. Just an aging doc's wisdom, handed over to a young friend full of the heady dreams of youth. It is in our nature, Williams was suggesting to me, that we try, through language, through ideas, to leave our mark on the world (show our willfulness); and it is in our nature to try to free ourselves from the humdrum everyday life (boredom) in some dramatic, prophetic way — lest we be merely another reflexively bound animal creature; and not least, it is in our nature to try to find an answer to the mysteries which surround this finite life we live (desperation). That being the case, we grasp at what we can find — and don't hesitate to invest our "discoveries" with the largest possible aura of hope. Even Freud, stoic that he was, and no stranger to pessimism, had all sorts of fantasies about the new kind of human being that psychoanalysis would enable (New Introductory Lectures). Meanwhile, he was slugging it out with rivals, bad-mouthing a few enemies, and in general, showing himself (brilliant and learned man that he was) to be — what? Yet another human being.

We all know now that Bergler was exceedingly wrong-headed; what he was describing was by no means confined to writers — or psychoanalysts. We all know now that there is no one "psychological type" of person who gets ulcers or asthma — but rather that there are all types of elements, having to do with inheritance, circumstances, the environment, and yes, a person's psychology, which together in some individuals (but not all) combine to give us X or Y syndrome. That is to say, we have yielded, in some respects, our deterministic fantasies. But they crop up elsewhere; and maybe because that is what we are, as the existentialist philosophers would put it — the creature, again, who isn't content to go along, to let nature take its course, so to speak, but who wants to know what Gauguin once asked: "Where do we come from? What are we? Where are we going?" Both the Bible, through the notion of "original sin," and the Greek tragedians, through the idea of "hubris," understood this inclination in us. I don't see us, in psychoanalytic psychiatry, free from that inclination — an aspect of our humanity.

And so, as I read about narcissism, say, in the literature, and see so very much connected to it, I have to realize that those who write about narcissism, and find it here or there, are themselves, too, struggling with it, showing evidence of it, and maybe, overstating its significance, as do we all, narcissistically, when we make our various points, stake out our positions, not to mention write our "opinion" pieces or critical essays. And I have to realize, as well, that there is no end likely to such exuberance, such heady moments of self-assertion. The universe is infinite, it seems; there is no likelihood, really, that any of us will transcend our limitations, and become the gods we are, nevertheless, able to imagine ourselves being. But that is the point: we are the ones who use language, who summon symbols, who are given by "destiny" (our inherited neuro-psychological makeup) the ability and inclination for imaginative leaps. No wonder, then, we view ourselves as reaching higher and higher, intellectually. No wonder we call out to our families, to our neighbors and friends, to our colleagues: this is what I think; here is what I see; that is what I believe. Others preceded us, had their chance to think, see, believe. Others will follow us, and demand a similar chance. We are here now, and by God, we have our opinions; and the fads (of theory as well as practice, of customs and habits and attitudes) tell us, well, that we are alive, I suppose, and are being, once again, ourselves. We are the creature whose fists get shaken insistently at the inscrutable universe — so a writing doctor once tried to explain to me, but not too insistently. Why his restraint? Because (I now understand) he realized full well that each generation requires its own time to get a bit of distance on its hunger, its greed, its lofty expectations; on itself, as yet another segment of the human parade — "world without end," as the Book of Common Prayer told us, though these days, given the nuclear madness about us, one wonders.

Journal of the Academy of Psychoanalysis,
1980

12

PSYCHIATRIC STATIONS

OF THE CROSS

Some months ago I visited a medical school classmate of mine in a first-rate Boston teaching hospital. He was (is still) seriously ill. Cancer will eventually take him, he knows. He has always been a rather quiet and thoughtful person — a stoic temperamentally. But he is also a deeply religious man; he attends a suburban Catholic church every Sunday, and on certain weekdays tries to set aside an hour or so for one of the Masses offered in a downtown chapel. When I came to see him he would have no part, from the very start, of any usual conversation. He was angry, and quite ready to tell me why. A priest had just come by, and indicated a strong interest in how the doctor/patient was managing to "cope." My friend said he was doing "fine" the way (he assumed) any of us has the right to say "fine." That is, he meant to indicate he was getting along reasonably well, given a particular predicament; *and* he had no great wish, at that moment, to elaborate on the matter in any detail.

For the visiting clergyman, however, such asserted poise and reticence were not to be accepted at face value. The priest persisted in asking questions which, in sum, amounted to a relentless kind of psychological inquiry. How was the patient "feeling"? How was his "spirit"? (These days, alas, such a word has lost its religious significance for all too many of us.) How was he "managing," in view of the "stress" he had to "confront"? Did he want to "talk about" what was happening? Were there any "thoughts" he might want to "bring up for discussion"?

The priest no doubt believed himself to be tactful, respectful, and considerate, but my friend was annoyed at the time of the visit, and a few hours later, quite enraged. He had wanted to talk with the priest about God and His ways, about Christ's life and death, about the Gospel of Luke (a particular favorite), about Heaven and Hell — only to be approached repeatedly with psychological words and phrases. In their entirety those words and phrases constituted a statement, an insinuation: you are in psychological jeopardy, and that is what I, an ordained priest of the Holy Roman Catholic Church, have learned to consider more important than anything else, when in the presence of a person such as you.

To the patient such an attitude, such a *faith*, really, put into practice, was an outrageously gratuitous and arrogant affront: "He comes here with a Roman collar, and offers me psychological banalities as God's word!" I tried to be a bit "understanding," as it is put, tried to say that the priest meant well. But my friend was not about to let *that*, of all remarks, go by unchallenged. The priest certainly didn't "mean well," I was told. The priest was a "fool," was yet another apostate from the Christian religion. The priest was mesmerized by the mind and its commonplace workings — when he was supposed to be a man of The Book, alert to matters *sub specie aeternitatis*.

Our conversation on this vexing subject lengthened. I found myself remembering all the letters I've written, over the years, to bishops in the Catholic Church or the Episcopal Church — certifying one person's or another's "mental stability" or "normality" or "psychological health." Had I ever known my fellow psychiatrists to ask the clergymen what they thought of the character, the moral make-up of this or that would-be doctor or psychiatric trainee? Put differently, why is it that psychiatry now has so much intellectual, and yes, moral authority among the clergy? Why are so many of us uncritical with regard to the endless willingness of so many in our society to use psychiatric concepts in a normative, if not self-righteous and moralistic manner? If one likes the person and his or her "behavior," one compliments him or her psychologically: "adaptive defense mechanisms," or a "healthy" way of "handling the problem." If one is not so friendly to a person, there are all sorts of names to hurl about: "sick," of course, or "pathological" or "disturbed," and dozens of others.

I do not mean to deny the value of clinical terms, only to indicate that they have become quite something else: a moral code strongly compelling not only to the laity, but the clergy — as in "pastoral counseling," which for all too many of us has become a religious calling, with the Bible and its various messages as anecdotal adjuncts, quaint leftovers from an earlier era. I recently read a description of the background and qualifications of an Episcopal parish's newly-appointed minister and, I swear, almost all the statements pertained to his various secular interests and experience — in schools and hospital clinics and various social or political causes. I wish to emphasize that I do not have anything against a minister (or anyone else) choosing to devote time and effort to the sick and the poorly educated, or to a given set of community, not to mention national, concerns. The issue is something else — a matter, one speculates, for some at least, of self-respect: the priest happy and fulfilled as a psychologist or a social worker or a political activist, with his religious duties — his wonderful sacramental responsibilities! — turned into mere habits or social routines.

My doctor friend, unfortunately, lacked compassion for the particular priest mentioned above — or so he told me. Indeed, he had his Bible ready for the next priestly visit: "I'll wait for him to do his song and dance about my 'feelings' — and I'll watch him as he thinks to himself how smart he is, slowly probing and nudging me toward the discussion he is determined to have, at all costs! Suddenly, I interrupt him, pick up the Bible from the night table, and ask him to read from it — any part he wishes. He looks surprised and confused. He asks me if there is anything more I want to 'talk about.' I say no. I say I only want him to read from our Lord's Book. He does. He opens up the Bible and begins reading. He doesn't select a page, he just reads from the page that happens to be there: Psalm 69. Then he leaves, without saying much except he hopes I do well."

One soon enough reads Psalm 69: "Save me, O God; for the waters are come into my soul. I sink in deep mire, where there is no standing: I am come into deprivation, where the floods overflow me." There are, of course, many kinds of burdens in this life. I wonder whether the deepest mire, the deepest waters, for many of America's clergy, not to mention us laymen, may be found in the dreary solipsistic world so many of us have learned to find so interesting: the mind's moods, the various "stages" and "phases" of "human development" or of "dying," all dwelt upon (God save us!) as if Stations of the Cross.

New Oxford Review, 1982

13

WHY FOLLOW FREUD?

Time and again that question which titles this essay has been put to me by others, and in moments of irritation or anger by myself, as I have read particular statements the founder of psychoanalysis made in his various essays and books, not to mention his letters. An immediate and important response ought to be a strong denial that one is, actually, trying to "follow" Freud in any creedal way — a denial that the issue has to do with a commitment to his every word and idea.

He was *sometimes* a shrewd observer of himself and others, and even if he was also at times wrongheaded or arrogant or self-serving or plain foolish, his better, more edifying moments deserve simple respect, and even continuing gratitude. Unfortunately we all tend to be undiscriminating at various moments and in various ways. Even as Freud anointed his first followers with rings, and banished those who took significant issue with his ideas (thereby setting the stage, in the first decade of this century, for future psychoanalytic orthodoxy), the rest of us are all too revealingly on the hunt for a body of thought that promises to tell us almost everything about ourselves — our origins as individuals; our habits of thought; the nature of our affections; our interests; our likes and dislikes. For every demanding ideology there are, alas, all too many adherents, if not believers.

Sometimes, actually, a later wholesale renunciation of a given person's thinking tells a lot about our earlier commitment to that thinking. I have met psychiatrists whose present-day scorn for psychoanalysis has been preceded, years ago, by a zealously possessive interest in that discipline's tenets. In any event, today it is the biological side of psychiatry that entrances many of us (the promise of pills that address the brain's neurophysiology), and so the old emphasis on talking and listening, on dreams and fantasies (with their symbols, their condensations, their elliptical messages, their extravagant flights of fancy as a means of both revealing and dodging the down-home truths of everyday family living) seems old-fashioned and unpromising. Of course, some of us psychiatrists who are now in our doddering fifties, and can remember the almost messianic fervor with which we took to psychoanalysis, have occasionally had our memories jogged as we listen to certain young neurochemical enthusiasts tell us that there are few psychiatric problems under the sun that Merck and Upjohn and Smith, Kline, French won't be addressing and solving in the coming decade or two.   .

In fact, no drug will obliterate the vicissitudes of ordinary human relatedness — the ups and downs we all have with one another as we try to navigate our way from one shore (the early years of life) to another shore (the final moments of our particular spell of time on this planet). When the physician and poet William Carlos Williams was old and ailing (a stroke, heart disease, cancer) he had become depressed and was urged to see a psychiatrist. He had always been somewhat suspicious of psychiatry as a discipline, and of any number of practitioners in the field he'd met in the course of his own medical work. He resisted the suggestions of his family and friends — and ultimately managed to do some important writing, which he pronounced once to be his own "cure" of his own stretch of gloom. It was at that time, with death not far away, that he said the following to a friend:

> I'd have gone to talk with a psychiatrist years ago if I had some reason to do so, *and* if there was no one else for me to talk with

frankly, *and* if I found an analyst I liked and trusted. I'm not opposed to psychoanalysis, if by psychoanalysis is meant a very careful series of conversations, with each person watching the other as attentively as possible, and with both of them learning a hell of a lot! There will always be plenty of room for *that* in this world!

No doubt there is more to psychoanalysis than Dr. Williams's description suggests, as some of us know from our daily work, but he had cannily approached the utter essentials: that for certain people, having certain personal difficulties, a certain kind of person as a steady and thoughtful listener over a fairly long haul of months — indeed, years — can make a real difference with respect to what one knows about oneself and how one gets on with others. Williams also had been smart enough, back in the 1950s, when psychoanalysis was such a cultural and intellectual fad among the so-called intelligentsia of the United States, to spot a danger point — the inclination of all too many to confuse the problems this life poses for all of us with a particular person's idiosyncratic and by no means inevitable trials and tribulations. "I'm sad because I'm sick and dying," Williams would say quite bluntly — and then he added: "I'll bet Freud felt the same way at the end!" Such devilish humor was, of course, evidence of an old man's wisdom — and, as a matter of fact, his capacity to push aside that "depression" he was declared to have. Dr. Williams was also shrewd enough to mention other important "variables" — the inevitable subjectivity of psychoanalytic work, hence the right both of patients and doctors to try to match themselves. "I'll take a surgeon, *maybe*, whom I don't personally like," Williams said in the course of that fairly extended conversation with a young friend, "but *damn* it if I'd go see a psychiatrist whose smell turned off the dog in me!"

He was a great one for animal metaphors, and maybe he was underestimating the complexity of human preference — the reasons we like and dislike various others, and the need some of us may have to rid ourselves of such (possibly) misleading, if not blinding predispositions. Still, he was not about to ignore the utterly human side of psychoanalytic work — its dependence on a given person's manner of being. Put differently, what the analyst learns about the patient (and about himself or herself through his or her responses to the patient) depends on who the particular analyst is (different ones might pursue different lines of inquiry with the same patient). Moreover, any psychoanalytic knowledge has to be transmitted by a particular doctor's *personality at work* — and how different, with respect to personality, we all are, even those of us who have gone through the exceedingly long and transforming (and potentially narrowing, stultifying, yes, even stupefying) training that prepares one to practice psychoanalysis.

What Williams was trying to say has to do with human individuality — just the side of things psychoanalysis still is meant to help us understand. Freud was a particular individual who happened to be a sharp observer of himself, and a great storyteller. His greatest book was his first, *The Interpretation of Dreams* (1900); in it he gives an inspired, compelling account of what his mind struggled to say and comprehend at night. He also let his patients become his teachers, and such instruction was not wasted on their ambitious and eagerly literary physician. The result was an important series of articles and books — communications which continue to edify any number of readers. It is *that* Freud who is well worth "following" — the gifted, self-scrutinizing writer, the doctor determined to learn about the mind's many twists, turns, and tricks, and to convey what was discovered in decently available prose. Nor are his followers, or his profession, psychoanalysis ("his" in the sense that he was the founder, the first practitioner), unworthy of being "followed" — again, in the tradition of our pursuit, as human beings, of as much self-knowledge as we (and others!) can provide. It is quite another matter, however, to "follow" the Freud who became a cultural hero, a secular demigod, his every word (and blind spot and prejudice and ignorant or foolish preoccupation, and none of us is without such) slavishly attended.

We need to sift and sort in this life, embrace what matters, set aside what clearly doesn't — hoping for the Lord's help and inspiration in that task, as in all others.

New Oxford Review, 1985

14

HOPE AND DESPAIR IN THE VERY

YOUNG AMONG THE VERY POOR

Every once in a while, as I have worked among the so-called "poor" — Appalachians, Hondurans, the favelas of Rio de Janeiro, the black inhabitants of the shanty towns of South Africa outside of Johannesburg and Cape Town — I have stopped myself in the middle of my research tracks, so to speak, and gazed in wonder at a particular crowd of young boys and girls.

They are always nearby. They might be playing a game, or all engrossed by an adult's presence (mine, the stranger), or simply standing or sitting with an inertia or apathy that I have learned to recognize as a mix of (anemic) tiredness and (social and cultural) boredom.

They manage to get through one day, then another. But at what cost psychologically? The answer seems obvious, and makes me harken back in thought and grim embarrassment to my own distant world, even as I shudder at the sight a few feet away.

I think of the ample food, the adequate clothing, the quite suitable housing that millions of "our" people simply take for granted. Then my mind makes (yet again) an assessment of what millions and millions of families cannot — ever — take for granted.

I remember that physicians such as myself are kept busy in well-to-do suburbs and even inner cities. Lots of troubled children, whose fears and anxieties and worries, whose eating disorders and sleeping disorders, whose antisocial inclinations, and yes, whose spells and longer of despondency, are a continuing reminder: Money and privilege do not necessarily get translated into happy homes and happy children.

Nor have the desperately poor of Brazil's slums, for instance, failed to wonder about just this matter: whether the relatively rich people of their own country, or those abroad, have boys and girls who are not only stuffed with food and well-dressed and in possession of every toy a mind can imagine, but also endowed with good spirits, plenty of hopefulness, and a persisting soundness of mind.

I once heard a favelado, a woman of Rio de Janeiro who at 25 had four young children to attend with another on the way, and scant means to care for them, ask:

I have wondered how children grow up who don't live here, who have everything the world has to offer. I once asked the priest if God would ever do us a favor, even a small one. The priest said we can pray, and maybe He will.

Then the priest wanted to know what my prayer would be. I told him I've given up praying for food and for a good house. I'd just like a few days of escape from here. Maybe we could all be asked to live near someone rich and help do errands and chores.

Maybe my children could become friends with those children who are lucky, who have God as their friend. The priest became cross with me. He said I'm wrong to think that because children have rich parents, they are going to be cheerful and good. He had seen lots of children in Copacabana and Iponema (wealthy seaside sections of the city) who are real "little monsters."

Yes, I'm sure he's right. But I'll bet they laugh and whistle and have good times for themselves!

She was approaching in her casual remarks, and no matter her lack of education or even literacy, an extremely important psychological paradox. As the priest well knew to tell her, lots of children in swank or comfortable neighborhoods are indeed spoiled brats and "little monsters."

I have noticed they are often self-centered, truculently snotty, and mischievously preoccupied with their own whims and impulses, as that phrase "little monster" implies. Nor have I seen them to be buoyant and care-free. Their selfishness and hauteur could be described psychodynamically as a developmental "narcissism," perhaps a budding species of "character disorder."

That mother knows how weary her young children already are: how fretful they get, and fearful, and sad-looking, and all too "wild" (she calls them).

When I ask her to spell out the qualities that prompt her to use the word "wild," she has no hesitation: "They cry, and they kick each other, or they pick up something and throw it."

She would prefer that they be "quiet," that they listen to her and obey her, and cause her no continual apprehension or distraction. She has her own way of comprehending the "wild" moments among her children:

> They are not comfortable here. I don't have all the food they'd like. Their skin is covered with bites and sores. They hurt — that is what: They hurt all the time. They are wild with hurt — the pain in them. Their souls feel the pain — just as our Lord Jesus, He was in pain, and He cried out — My children cry out. But sometimes they forget their troubles. They laugh like children do. I remember laughing not so long ago. Even now, on a day when the warm sun is upon us, and we have a breeze, I feel clean and strong, and I'm ready to smile, and thank God for giving me some time here on this earth of His!

Again and again, whether the speaker is such a woman, or her priest, the terrible plight of countless small children is acknowledged and fit into larger "contexts" — while we physicians try to figure out what words such as "happy" or "sad" mean when connected to the lives of young children.

That mother will one day tell me her children are "very sad"; the next day, shrug her shoulders and say they're "not doing so bad";

and every once in a while she will dare say that this life has its rather pleasant moments, for her and her children, and, anyway, eternity awaits.

More skeptical or cynical parents tell me that it is death that awaits, nothing more, and take their satisfaction in the universality of that outcome, its leveling consequences for the wealthy and the mighty.

"Despair" means "without hope." Most young favelas children I've come to know (even four and five years old) are cognitively quite clear on "the score" — that there is practically no chance that they'll live a reasonably secure and comfortable life. In that sense, they do indeed despair — an ongoing state of recognition, an all too accurate awareness of "reality" (as some of us say).

On the other hand, a good number of those children don't slip into the steadfast, tight, intractable grip of despair in the conventional (emotional) sense of the word. They don't strike me as "depressed" in a clinical sense. They don't seem to be predominantly apathetic, or lost to a grim and tenacious melancholy. They have their irritable moments. They cry. They scream. But they seem more or less responsive to the gentle shift of wind, the sun's benevolence described by that mother. Smiles break out. Play is managed, active and absorbing. And Lord knows they have lusty appetites, no matter the disappointments with regard to food supply that each day brings. I have seen few, if any, picky or fussy eaters among them — or boys and girls with "eating disorders," or with phobic attitudes toward particular foods. They seem to sleep well, even if their beds are flimsy or nonexistent. To be sure, they have nightmares, during which mothers are awakened by a screaming child. What does the mother do?

"I wake up," the mother I've been calling as a witness once told me, "and I wait, and in a few seconds, there is silence, and the next thing, it is morning, and we're all opening our eyes and hoping for some food."

She uses that word "hope" and attributes it to herself as well as her little ones. Yes, she tells me, not all hope is lost. Despair there is, yet not total despair. Not "depressive" nihilism or loss of hope. Not loss of pleasures and interests. Life fights with death, as a Viennese metapsychologist once put it earlier in this century, as young mothers and young fathers and very young children among the world's very poor also know.

One is left to ponder another of this life's perplexing ironies: that despair may spread its way in nation after nation among the impoverished children who want so much, but that the pathology of childhood depression — and indeed other pathologies we physicians try to treat — are by no means epidemic among the poor, and may be just as common and conspicuous among the well-to-do who have so much and who want so much.

Journal of Child and Adolescent
Psychopharmacology, 1990

15

PSYCHOANALYSIS AND RELIGION

∾

I was trained to work with children medically and psychiatrically in the 1950s at the height of the psychoanalytic orthodoxy that Erik H. Erikson has described in his memorable epilogue to *Childhood and Society*. The girls and boys, men and women whom I met in hospitals and clinics all too often were turned into a reductive putty in my mind. Even today I recall sadly some of the thoughts I had and the words I used as I worked with children who had their own moral concerns, philosophical interests, and religious convictions. Yet, I too often focused relentlessly on their "psychodynamics."

In particular, I remember an eight-year-old girl, Connie, whom I treated at the Children's Hospital in Boston for two years. I suspect [Ana-Maria] Rizzuto [author of *The Birth of the Living God*] would have found this child to be a helpful colleague in her religious and psychoanalytic explorations. Connie was utterly accepting of the Catholic Church. What Connie lacked, I certainly at the time felt pressure to possess — a sharply fault-finding, even disparaging attitude toward her involvement with a certain parish's ongoing activities.

"The Church saves me," she once told me. I dutifully wrote down the assertion and naturally asked for details: how does it do so, and what is thereby "saved"? She told me she sensed "bad habits" in herself, and they were only confronted successfully, she claimed, by prayers in church and by talks with a priest who was a great friend of her parents.

When I first heard that expression "bad habits," I had a hunch it was a smoke screen for the sexual activity I presumed she both felt inclined to, or did, implement. As for my supervisor, he wondered in that regard about the thin remnant of doubt I seemed still to retain: "In a while she will talk with you about her sexual life, and all this religion talk will go away," he reasoned.

I wasn't about to disagree. On the contrary, I kept trying to bring about just such an outcome by asking questions and picking up on comments Connie made in such a way as to take us closer to the kind of "resolution" my supervisor envisioned.

Gradually I began to realize that a concrete struggle of viewpoints was taking place in this child. She had been referred to us in the child psychiatry unit at the hospital because she was unruly at school — fresh and surly with certain classmates, and finally, with a teacher who called her a "tense girl." A school psychologist had talked with Connie and suggested she would become "anti-social" or "delinquent" when she got older if she were not "treated" before then. Moreover, during her initial interview, as mentioned before, Connie agreed that she did have "bad habits."

She was far from willing, however, to convert to our way of regarding her — not that we spelled out with her what we surmised and discussed among ourselves. Rather, she took note of the way we kept asking for more information, while ignoring lots of ideas, thoughts and feelings she most emphatically did make known to us.

I still have in my memory some of our conversations. This devoutly Catholic girl had seen a rerun of the movie *Song of Bernadette*, a film about the woman Bernadette of Lourdes, who would ultimately be sanctified by the Catholic Church. She wanted so much to talk to me about it. I did not, of course, stop Connie from talking about the movie, but I also showed no evident interest in her remarks, at least no interest in their substance. For me, such discussion was essentially "defensive." I assumed she was hiding behind religious interests as a means of not coming to terms with her aggressive and sexual impulses — a subject I had in mind for us to examine as soon as possible. But for young Connie, the movie was an important event in her life that required reflection — as was the matter of her "bad habits," and she willingly shared with me what her mind had concluded.

I thought I was at least being civil and courteous as I waited her out and listened patiently to both her religious speculations and her religious judgments upon herself. However, one day Connie became forthright and critical toward me in a surprising way never before shown. First, she asked me if I was "an atheist or a believer." Astonished, I quickly threw the question back to her (was I not "trained"?), all the while wondering what had prompted a question both personal and by implication negative in tone. (In Connie's neighborhood, even to ask such a question of people was a statement in itself!)

When I asked her why she asked me that question she said, "because," and then fell silent. I was about to inquire why she had answered that way when she let me know all right. I had no tape recorder going in those days, but I can offer the gist of her remarks.

Doctor, I was told, you're not interested in my religion, only my "problems." But without my religion I'd be much worse off, don't you see? How about *encouraging* me to talk about that movie, about what I experience when I go to church, instead of sitting here, bored, waiting for God to pass from this scene? How about trying to learn what I've learned as a child at home, at church, at Sunday school, so that you will be able to respond to me in my particularity and complexity, rather than with some abstract, formulaic, reductionist paradigm — of which my mind and its workings seem to be a mere illustrative instance for you?

I need not add that Connie put the matter in her own blunt, earthy, child's language. Some of the above she didn't so much say as convey with a look. ("Our patients can tell us everything with a glance, and let us add the words," Anna Freud once observed.) Some of the above she condensed into her original skeptical question. And yet some of what she said was spoken loud and clear: "I'd like to be like Bernadette was in the movie, but you don't believe me!"

How well I still recall that moment, both confessional and accusatory in nature! She was dead wrong, actually. I *did* "believe" her, in the sense that I knew she meant what she said — or that she *thought* she did. That self-serving afterthought is, of course, the heart of the matter for me and my kind. It is our conviction that there is an ultimate or bed-rock psychological reality to whose depths and contours we are especially privy. I wasn't letting Connie tell me about an important part of her life. Instead, I was telling her to hurry up and let me get to the truth underneath, disguised in this child's life by a Catholic fastidiousness.

Thank God (if I may) for Erik H. Erikson's *Young Man Luther*, which had just been released, and for one of my supervisors who had been analyzed by him. By suggesting I read the book, she gave me permission to connect psychoanalysis to religion as Erikson had done in his biographical effort at understanding part of Luther's life. Even though she was not supervising my work with Connie, I felt free to speculate with her on what was happening with the child. From her, I received suggestions which I can paraphrase this way: take her religious life seriously and see where you both go by doing so. What have you got to lose?

That question, word for word, gave me strength, as did the smile and shrug that went with it. Here was a shrewd and relaxed clinician telling a novice to ramble a bit, let the path meander, and, who knows, there might be a breakthrough.

No miracles of the secular kind happened as Connie's therapy progressed, but we continued and began to have fairly earnest and extended conversations. We talked abut her "bad habits," about her interest in Bernadette of Lourdes and other Catholic saints whose lives she had heard celebrated at home and in Sunday school.

She told me that one of her "bad habits" was "pride" — and I wondered aloud if she (a mere child of eight!) might explain herself further.

She explained that "pride" is "the sin of sins," and it has to do with being "stuck on yourself." I was surprised and intrigued by her way of putting things. Even today, as I look over the notes I took on her (and used when I "presented" her at a "grand rounds"), I am reminded how idiosyncratic this child was, how thoroughly she had integrated a body of religious imagery and various spiritual assumptions into her young life and vocabulary.

She did not want to become "a religious" she told me one afternoon. When she saw that the adjectival word, turned by her into a noun, had me puzzled, she explained that it's a way some Catholics refer to a person who becomes a priest or a nun. Then she told me why a nunnery would not be suitable for her; she did not want to miss out on a good time in life. Some people, she declared, even children her age, were "more religious than the priests and nuns."

I wanted examples. The one she gave was a "too nice person." She had already made her break from that ideal and had even spoken a bit freshly to a nun. At the public elementary school she attended, she was considered "picture perfect" one day, as one teacher had offered, and "a real trouble-maker" the next.

All this about Connie I began to understand both psychologically and religiously with her help. She let me know that the rebellious side of Jesus had not escaped her notice, and that in Bernadette of Lourdes and Joan of Arc she had examples of young Catholic women whose virtues and impatient spiritual lives were not at all instantly evident to established Catholic authorities — hence a justification of her own righteous outbursts. Most important, she let me know that her religious life was far more subtle and complex than I had been prepared to admit. She showed me that there was a personal, spiritual life in her that was by no means to be equated with her religious life, or regarded as a mere aspect or an expression of it.

It is this evolving distinction that became a critical issue in my work with Connie. I can still hear and see my child analyst supervisor, Abraham Fineman, and me going over my notes, trying to figure out this bright, troublesome girl who could one minute delight her teachers and others, and the next, drive them to distraction. As Fineman and I went back and forth, commenting on Connie's "ego strengths" and noting her "acting out," we tried to hold on to our mission at the hospital — to "treat" a child who could get moody and sullen enough to worry adults, hence her referral to us.

At one point, I was attempting a fairly ambitious psychoanalytic formulation in a discussion of Connie's "narcissism," when Fineman interrupted to ask me what I then thought was the most irrelevant question imaginable: "Do you think she has her own religious ideas?"

I had no idea. I sat silently. Fineman began explaining his line of reasoning: Here is a bright child who is intensely involved in Catholicism. She is also having enough psychological trouble —

truculence at school and in the neighborhood — to warrant visits to us (no small step for a working-class, culturally conservative, Irish Catholic family to permit in the late 1950s, I realize now, although at the time my mind wasn't interested in *that* kind of analysis). Now, I was trying to get her to speak our language — the psychological words and images we find useful, congenial. Instead she brought me lots of religious stories, themes, and metaphors. I responded with indifference — my own kind of tactful, ever so modulated "hostility." But she hadn't budged — there we were trying to calculate how to work with her, how to make inroads on a neurosis, how to win her over, really, to a commitment toward therapy. (I had been telling him that Connie often came late, and could be "argumentative" with me over small and not so small details: where she was to sit, the kind of paper she wished to use for the drawings I asked her to do.)

Dr. Fineman began to ask questions for both of us to consider. Why not shift tactics? Why not become seriously involved in her religious discussions? Why not let her educate *us* about her church, and also about her? No doubt she would offer some trite remarks, some memorized cliches — but who doesn't, and psychiatry (and medicine) as well as religion can generate them. She seems to have her own slant on things and this defiant individualism, the source of some of her school troubles, also seems to influence significantly her religious life. She makes it *hers*, rather than a mere rote replication of church truisms and slogans.

To end his exposition, Fineman posed this to me and to himself: "She's an *un*conventionally religious child. There's a spirituality at work in her, and we might explore her spiritual psychology."

What in the world did he mean? "Look," he tried to explain, "we're not getting very far with this girl and her family, and perhaps we need a change of tack." He was not arguing for a therapeutic compromise, or a surrender. Very importantly, he was not being condescending to Connie and her family. Fineman's attitude was quite different. His was a truly humble one I began to realize, and one displayed at a time when such modesty was not the predominant mode of behavior chosen by specialists of our kind.

Decades later I find myself hearing gratefully his exhortation that "we try to learn from this girl," that "we let her teach us her psychology." But I still had no idea what he meant by his use of that last phrase, and I told him so with a polite question — only to hear that he was as perplexed and uncertain as I was, though obviously far more sure of himself than I, hence ready for a gamble.

Soon thereafter, at wit's end, I changed directions in my work with this young patient. For the first time in my short-lived, inevitably anxious and striving career as a hospital resident, learning day to day to practice an exceedingly elusive mix of science and art, I told a patient that I wanted some "advice."

My discussion went something like this: "Connie, it would be a great help to me if you'd let me know how *you* see your life going, and what *you* think we here at the hospital can do to be of help. I know I've said this to you before, but I really do need your advice. I've discussed this with a wise, older doctor who has worked with children for many years and he agrees. He, too, thinks I need your guidance as to how our meetings might be designed to be of better use to you in whatever difficulties you're now experiencing." I gulp on those words now as I write them. Even back then, I'd begun to notice their ingratiating smoothness, if not slipperiness, and their faint air of patronization.

She listened carefully. She was not impressed, I later realized, with yet more of my clinical mannerisms, if not ploys, but she did take note of my reference to my psychoanalytic supervisor. "Oh, you've got someone watching over you, too?" she asked. I scarcely knew what to do with that comment. I managed a self-conscious smile, but she managed something else, an analogy.

As she saw it, and explained it to me, she had her God, and I had my supervisor. I fell silent. She continued by pointing out to me, in a reassuring way, how satisfying it can be to have "someone looking over you." Even now I can feel her words getting to me — and at a psychological truth. I had been reluctant to pull back from my hitherto relentless psychiatric pursuit. Though she had not intended to allude to that — she had in mind her God and my supervisor as a pair of sorts! — she had managed to make me feel cranky rather than give me pause, or even offer me cause for the enjoyment of an irony.

We got over that hurdle, though, and eventually Connie began telling me a lot about her religious life. She also began to share with me some of her private moments of awe, wonder, alarm, and apprehension as she sat in church with her parents, or in Sunday school, and listened to an imposing nun warn, lecture, promise salvation, and threaten the scourges of eternal hell.

After a month or two we were having rather intense conversations and I was, indeed, learning a kind of spiritual psychology, as Fineman (who did have a god-like role in my work) had predicted might happen. I learned how this girl felt as she contemplated heaven (the worry about not being with all her friends rather than the pleasant anticipation of good days ahead) and how she felt about going to hell (the curiosity about the place as well as the dread of it).

I learned about this child's "talks with Jesus." She spoke of her great devotion to Him, but also the anxiety that devotion caused her: "I worry that I'm asking for too much of His time." She was referring to her long spells of prayer, which comforted her, but also got her wondering in directions that made her nearly panic at times. How did *He* feel toward her? Did He have His favorites? If she slipped, made mistakes, did He not only become disappointed, but fall into a rage? (Hadn't the nun described Jesus as "very angry" when He walked into the temple to denounce various hypocrites and wrong-doers toward the end of His life?)

What was Heaven really like? The nun said, "You spend all your time with Jesus." What about hell? The nun said, "The devil gets you and he'll never let go of you." In the privacy of her thoughts, Connie felt terror, but also intrigue at the thought of such lasting possessiveness. Once she asked me, memorably: "How can He [God] have so many people in His grip, and never let go even once? I wonder."

These were not concerns easily shared, I realized, and they indicated a trust that had been slow in coming, perhaps because it had not for some time been earned. But those concerns also told me a good deal not only about Connie's spiritual life, but her ordinary, every-day one — family troubles that worked their way into her sense of who Jesus was, and what she might expect of Him, or fear about Him. Not that, thanks to Fineman, I pushed those connections into explicitly avowed "interpretations" on my part.

Essentially, I stayed on the spiritual side of things, as Connie seemed to wish, but I also discussed psychological matters with her. Yes, Jesus could be angry, though He was also forgiving. No, I hadn't the slightest idea how Jesus or the devil ran things in their respective realms, but I doubted they acted as we human beings do — doubted they literally spoke to people or held on to them in some physical way.

She listened carefully, and I knew we were, at those moments, skirting her personal life, her strong bond with her father, her dread at his tantrums. She had turned her father, I knew, into a larger-than-life figure. (I am *not* charging here that the essence of her religious life was that she moved non-stop in her mind from her father to Jesus or the devil.) When she contemplated spiritual questions and larger-than-life spiritual figures, she had difficulties not unlike those she faced at home and at school — as she herself began to recognize. That recognition, I gradually realized, was therapeutic pay-dirt. Her rebelliousness was the result of a fierce attachment to a parent. Her worry that Jesus might overlook her attested to a similar sense of jeopardy and precariousness with respect to important attachments.

None of the above psychological difficulties are all that unique and surprising in a child, but I fear I'd never have been able to recognize them and their consequences had I not learned of them in some detail as Connie talked about her personal way of being a devout Catholic, and also, a musing, speculative one who dared wonder, as theologians and philosophers have, about what it is such words as "heaven" and "hell," "grace" and "damnation" come to mean in human, practical terms. Of course, those words may not mean anything in such terms. The steps from the truths of psychology to those of spirituality may end in a disastrous free-fall — at least for some of us who attempt to make it intellectually. But for Connie, as she explained to me one day, "Heaven is right here, and so is hell, because we're choosing when we smile or we have that bad look on our face."

At first I tended to be dismissive and cynical as I considered the implications of that assertion, which I'd written down and duly presented to Fineman. So, that's what it all comes to — a big smile or a surly glare! But Fineman was more interested in the first part of Connie's statement — the earthiness of it, the insistence that the far-off, the metaphysical, the utterly mysterious and speculative, be tethered to this concrete life in each day's passing. Moreover, he pointed out that a girl scarcely a decade old had given herself a demanding, daily responsibility to choose with each move or gesture where she was going. No wonder she could be so sensitive, prickly, and quick on the draw emotionally. The stakes for her were exceedingly high under circumstances many of us would dismiss as trivial and inconsequential.

In the long run, I would learn to be more respectful of Connie's struggles and to see her symptoms as evidence not only of conflict, but of aspirations and yearnings inevitably undercut by particular moments in life, yet also sustained by a persistent vision of what might be won and by what a loss would mean. We doctors kept mentioning this child's vigilant, even overbearing conscience as a source of so much that went wrong for her. She had tethered this "agency" of the mind, the super-ego, to an enormous task, the success or failure of which she had her own manner of pondering through prayer, and through what she called "stargazing," meaning: "I look to see whether it's God's eyes that are looking at me or the devil's."

For Fineman, all of this was not only psychopathology, pure if not so simple. "Look," he once told me, "she's trying very hard to control that tyrannical judge inside her, and she's enlisted not only parts of her own mind but a religion, and her version of a religion — fairly ingenious. I'm not sure the priests and nuns in her neighborhood would agree with the way she talks about heaven and hell, but she's breathed life into those ideas during the course of her own daily life."

We were getting at least some of our bearings with respect to a child's spiritual psychology. As I think back to the talks I had with Fineman about Connie, and with Connie about herself, and as I look at my old clinical notes, I realize that Fineman and I were attempting some second thoughts on Freud's *Future of an Illusion*, and by implication, an aspect of 20th century ideological orthodoxy, much like the case Rizzuto makes in her book. Instead of seeing Connie's religious and spiritual life as evidence of a disturbed mind, we tried to let that life be our guide and teacher. We also began to understand how that life had kept a child together psychologically.

"I see Jesus smiling, when everyone else is looking real mean, even me," this girl had told me many years ago. As I read *The Birth of the Living God* in the early 1980s, my mind went back to that comment of Connie's, because Fineman, long a Boston colleague of

Rizzuto's, had anticipated her sense of things when he wrote this in a supervisor's summary: "This girl has begun to settle down in treatment. Her use of her Catholic faith has been both a stumbling block and an opportunity for her doctor and me. We have stopped trying to take on her faith clinically! She has built her own version of that faith, and we have let her tell us all about it, and learned more about her. For her, God is quite alive; He's a big part of her life. We're hoping He'll be of further help to her — and to us too."

I have always cherished those words. They gave a young doctor some encouragement toward a less polemical or confrontational relationship between a child's spirituality and her doctor's therapeutic energy.

Harvard Medical Alumni Bulletin, 1990

II

THE WORK OF

INDIVIDUALS

੩❧ *One looks to individuals in a discipline which, after all, hopes to explore systematically the way one person has grown up through a sustained, scrutinizing, open encounter with another person. Though Freud tried hard to formulate large-scale generalizations, he could become ironic about his own hard-won achievement, referring once to his "mythological theory of instincts" — this from a man who knew how much he wanted (and needed, in keeping with the spirit of his times) to be known as a rigorous scientist, a man of biology, chemistry and physics. He knew, however, that his ideas were meant to be suggestive rather than the basis for a legalistic orthodoxy. If at times he was indeed possessive about what he had come to believe in, it is rather obvious that succeeding generations of psychoanalysts have not been reluctant to make known their particular way of seeing the work and study they do.*

I have devoted a whole book to the life of Erik H. Erikson and, to use the subtitle, "the growth of his work," but I think the essay on him in this section offers the most pointed evaluation I have made of his significance as a thinker — and in addition, tells a thing or two about my own reasons for being associated with and close to him. (I helped him for several years teach his course at Harvard.) Then there are relatively brief comments on Clara Thompson, on Harry Stack Sullivan, on Margaret Lawrence, psychoanalysts who had the courage to pursue their own line of thinking, and who have inspired many others to follow suit.

I mentioned in the Introduction the strong bias I have in favor of Anna Freud's approach to children and to the discipline of psychoanalysis. I spell out my views in the essay on her "achievement." I have also repeatedly returned to the various achievements of William James —

his work was constantly pressed upon me as an undergraduate by the late Professor Perry Miller at Harvard. I was glad to be able to do a "reconsideration" piece for the New Republic *on James's valuable* Varieties of Religious Experience — *a book still to be surpassed as a bridge between social scientists and theologians. I still feel that the implications of his work are well worth our consideration. As for R. D. Laing, I do not agree with (or even, at times, follow or understand) all his writing, but upon occasion he has peculiarly understood us twentieth-century psychiatrists, and as well, our patients, whom he regards as fellow sufferers of his — indeed, of all the doctors who go under the name of "psychiatrists," and who upon occasion forget the bonds that unite them to those they "see," even as, of course, there is for any therapist the utter importance of detachment and perspective. In general, the essays in this section draw their energy from a continuing student's continuing need to learn from others — those teachers who give sanction to us as we try, with their help and guidance, to find our own way, our own voice.*

16

THE ARTIST AS

PSYCHOANALYST

❧

. . . Not the intense moment
Isolated, with no before and after,
But a lifetime burning in every moment
And not the lifetime of one man only
But of old stones that cannot be deciphered.

Like Eliot, Erik Erikson has stood respectfully before the riddle of
Man and his History. In this century both men have seen some of
those old stones yield their secrets; and still the problems which confront us are as hard as ever. One of those problems is the relationship
of our present knowledge to its wise and humane use. That insight
must embrace responsibility, that becoming aware has ethical implications if we are to turn ourselves to any account in this world, is this
book's central message. Not all scholars, doctors, or clergymen have
managed to see it that way, drawn as they often have been, to shades
of one or the other of these two concerns — the fervid pursuit of information or the insistent recital of duties.

Insight and Responsibility comprises six essays published before in scholarly and professional journals. Some of them have been revised for this book. However, this is more than a desultory collection assembled to feed our country's apparently insatiable appetite for books. It is an arresting series of pauses — to consider, wonder, and create — in the life's work of one of the world's great psychoanalysts. It is an important book and deserves every bit of our attention.

The work is a continuation of Erikson's earlier ones: *Childhood and Society* and *Young Man Luther*. No review of this sort can do justice to the richness of thinking or to the considerable beauty of style in any of these three books. One of the qualities that marks the author's work is its incredible variety, defying any of the quick and passing notices quite appropriate for much of the drab, pinched, not to mention incomprehensible stretches of words laid before us these days by some of our "social scientists."

The first essay is called "The First Psychoanalyst." It is a sketch of a lonely genius in his becoming. First delivered in Germany in 1956 as a lecture, it tells about the origins of psychoanalysis, drawing from the recently discovered early correspondence of Freud. The piece is at once an appreciation, a brilliant presentation of some of the historical and conceptual roots of psychoanalysis, and through it all a moving and sensitive discussion of the nature of the analyst's work, the demands placed upon him by that work, and the requirements which that work asks of him. In the way he discusses Freud's friendship with Fliess, and in the way he talks about the relevance of psychoanalysis to other fields, he emerges with a lucidity qualified only by its respectfulness not only to Freud but to all who seek after knowledge.

The second essay discusses the nature of clinical evidence. It begins with a review of the quality of medical healing, enabled as it is by the meeting of the doctor and his life's training and the patient with his particular distress. Erikson illustrates analytic work with dreams, and in so doing makes it clear that for him dreams are dreamed by human beings, and heard by analysts who are also human beings. (It is a shame that a remark like the foregoing, which may sound like the purest of clichés, has a tragic relevance for those of us who dig through some psychiatric and psychoanalytic journals and find ourselves thinking of dreams and lives as if they were mathematical symbols.)

The third lecture has the haunting title "Identity and Uprootedness in Our Time." Erikson is the author of our most significant literature on the subject of "identity" — such concerns, that is, as who we are, who we think we are, who we are not. We find in this piece some glimmers of what Erikson has elaborated at length elsewhere as well as some sharp comments on the peculiar tragedies and triumphs of our century as they affect the life of the mind — totalitarianism, the mass movement of frightened, seeking people, the development of an immensely proficient yet bewildering and, of course, potentially dangerous technological society. In comparison to some of the glib "existentialist" literature on this subject, it is a happy experience to find man's often ambiguous and complicated predicament explored rather than airily submitted to either an affirmative or negative outcry.

Next we come upon "Human Strength and the Cycle of Generations." Who else, I really wonder, on this confused planet is now writing about such matters as what makes for man's stamina and vitality, and how his qualities of mind and spirit are nourished and transmitted over the centuries? This essay, as daring a piece as one will find in this jargon-filled era, tries to develop against the background of our modern sensibilities the meaning of such "old" virtues as Hope, Will, Purpose, and Competence (arising out of childhood) or Fidelity (developing in adolescence) and, finally, Love, Care, and Wisdom (coming with adulthood). For some, such terms are the hackneyed soporifics of sermons. For others they are self-consciously or even militantly shunned in favor of ideas and words hardly as graceful and often simply a crying bore. To breathe new life into words like Love is no easy job in our sometimes perversely complicated intellectual climate. I suspect, and hope, that this essay will begin to grow into our culture as the first comprehensive placing of Freud's insights into the positive ideals of older civilizations.

The fifth essay is a very important one in modern psychiatric and psychoanalytic thought, and its influence, in only three years, has already been felt. Any psychoanalyst faces the understandable problem of how to view man as influenced both by his dynamic, individual past and the equally relevant and persuasive present, much of which is not only the present of the citizen's private world but the more public one of his society, or of the historical moment with all its fateful opportunities and risks. Perhaps more than any psychoanalyst since Freud himself, Erikson has tried to keep these two ways of looking at man's nature companionable rather than mutually ignored or even set against one another. This essay has special value not only to psychoanalysts but historians, because it is a definitive piece on the theoretical and practical connections between private lives and the momentum of history.

The final essay takes the Golden Rule and shows its essential bearing upon medical and psychiatric practice, and indeed upon the natural rhythm of life itself. Erikson has spent a good part of his own life describing the various currents which combine and shift one another about in the course of a life's flow. In this regard he has called his work the study of the "life cycle," and the term, like his use of "identity" is a contribution to a more reputable language for — as well as theory of — man's condition. He finds in our life cycle an essentially ethical basis — to be grasped, apart from logic or faith, by clinical observation (and its insights) of each person's capacity for a growing sense of conscience. This is the book's final message: that knowledge has its tasks, that a capacity, indeed a yearning, for kindness to one another is an integral part of human development, that man is less than God, but surely worthy of some quiet respect from his own kind.

The author came upon English as a grown man, yet he makes many of us born to the tongue feel shame. He is exceptionally attentive to language, aware of its possibilities and sensitive to its problems, all of which makes for his very unusual style, a mixture of German and English really: strong words, simple sentences which slowly grow longer, but always seem to stop to allow the reader respite before proceeding to a new try.

The book is a further consolidation of the author's joining of artistic feeling and clinical acuity. He has done it deftly but sturdily, yielding to no distortion or exclusiveness in either direction: the anti-intellectual abandon of the pseudo-artist or the cranky nihilism of the doctrinaire theorist. Perhaps because of this very balance, pursued and achieved, we find in all his writing an almost uncanny combination of confrontation and intimacy, as if we are met with the very stuff of how we grow up — and old — and how we fit into one another's life, contemporaneously and over the generations.

Since Freud's death there has been an aching lack of his kind of courageous knowledge from the living. Some who followed Freud mistook agreement with him for ritualized awe; others not only chose to reject his lead but allowed their disagreement to deteriorate into empty, pitiful rancor. Erikson has paid Freud the highest — and all too rare — honor of giving him the closest attention. Taking him seriously, he has *proceeded,* shaping his own ideas into his own vision, a Freudian one which draws not just on Freud, but on Freud the significant man, and one of many, in a long historical tradition.

Finally it should be acknowledged that since Erikson's first book appeared the better part of a generation of young psychiatrists has come to rely upon his distinctive wisdom. Tired of the dull and stale, they find freshness in his writing; tired of deadly glances, they meet in his words some honor for man's efforts; afraid of an imbalance which allows healthy suspicions about human motives to become an abiding, narrowing cynicism, they come upon a mind respectful of man's accomplishments precisely because of how hard won — and even shaky — they are. In sum he has given dignity to his work, and in so doing, to all of us. Scanning the landscape of much of the social sciences today, such an achievement must be declared mighty.

The New Republic, 1964

17

CLINICAL AND HUMAN:

Interpersonal Psychoanalysis

One of the hallmarks of genius is its contagious power to set in motion the imagination of others. Freud's achievement is all the greater because of what his work enabled others, coming after him, to see and do. One such gifted person was Clara M. Thompson; and just how valuable her influence was may be discovered by reading the first collection of her theoretical, clinical, and historical papers on psychoanalysis [*Interpersonal Psychoanalysis*].

In many ways this distinguished psychoanalyst's life can be viewed as a cameo, the figure of American practicality and hopefulness carved out on a somewhat contrasting background of European speculation often enough severe and theoretical in quality. Clara Thompson was born a New Englander in 1893 — Freud was then 37, and in that year published his studies on hysteria, the beginning, we now know, of his massive and lasting work. Her paternal grandfather was a rigger of whaling ships. Education itself did not come easy to her. She determined to go to college, to study medicine, to enter psychiatry, and, finally, to become a psychoanalyst. Only a willful and courageous woman could take on that series of challenges in the early decades of this century.

Opposition to psychoanalytic discovery at that time was powerful and fanatic, even in the leading universities. Freud's hard-won findings were just beginning to catch hold among American psychiatrists in the 1920s while Dr. Thompson was in training. It would take time before clinicians were to discard the old, dried ways of descriptive psychiatry (name the problem, then store the person away in often outrageous confinement) for the unafraid but unsettling view of the mind which psychoanalysis was offering. Today we may forget how much intelligence and even bravery must have been required to make the choice Clara Thompson made: she emerged in the 1930s one of the pioneers in American psychoanalysis, becoming the first president of the Washington-Baltimore Psychoanalytic Society.

In company with Harry Stack Sullivan, Frieda Fromm-Reichmann, Karen Horney, and Erich Fromm she also battled hard to adapt psychoanalytic concepts to the views of man's nature and predicament held by others — sociologists, cultural anthropologists, political scientists. With that effort went an attempt to apply its insights and therapeutic style to a more inclusive assortment of mental difficulties. Freud's work, for her, was too valuable to be confined to any particular kind of patient, or any rigidly defined interpretation. His work developed and changed, like life itself. His followers would have to know that. Some would; Clara Thompson was among them.

Her influence was thus secured in the historical context of a new and fast-growing profession. Under those circumstances any prominence would require flexibility, a capacity to share in the organizational life of psychoanalysis, while at the same time maintaining an alive interest in clinical problems and theoretical contemplation. Such many-sided interests were had in good measure by Clara Thompson, and just how successfully she blended them into a life's work (she died in 1958) is shown by this book.

The first section gathers together her written attempts to formulate the basis of psychoanalytic treatment. In so doing she not only gave her attention to what troubles patients, but at all times she was particularly concerned with the manner in which problems are variously handled by different patients, and what can be done in treatment once a symptom and its causes are identified. Some of these essays are rare specimens of clinical humility, abstaining as they do from grandiose categorizations and admitting as they so frequently and unabashedly do the stubborn and sometimes embarrassing refusal of human beings to submit to the rules and generalizations provided by those of us who observe and strive to treat them.

The second section provides us with her essays on Sándor Ferenczi, Sullivan, and Fromm, all of whom she knew well, respected, and commonly relied upon for the fellowship needed in the work of discovery. These papers aim to place those men in their proper relationship to the ideas of psychoanalysis as they unfolded. Many ideas first introduced or hinted at by Freud were pursued and modified by those three and others, often in the beginning with reluctant toleration at best from some colleagues. The writer constantly urges an open-minded attitude, and continually warns against the blight of dogmatic partisanship in a field which is in pursuit of truth rather than in full possession of it.

The next three sections take up clinical problems, especially those concerned with the role of women in our culture, its pressures upon them, and the general issue of how girls grow, develop psychologically, become (or fail to become) women in feeling as well as in body, and, all in all, get along with themselves, their husbands and children, their jobs, and their position in our society.

These papers, gathered together largely from professional journals, reveal a keen observer who at the same time does not lack warmth, humor, and a common sense that is precious indeed. The prose is lean and simple, the exposition refreshingly direct. Like Freud, she apparently never felt the need to slip into graceless, pretentious writing — where real disclosure and inscrutable shoptalk are dismally confused with one another. Agree with everything in the book or not, only a bold and steadfast mind could achieve both the knowing and the telling to be found in it; perhaps a kind of mind at a premium in any age and profession.

The New York Times Book Review, 1965

18

THE ACHIEVEMENT OF

ANNA FREUD

In the newsletter for June 1965 of the American Psychiatric Association, a brief announcement was made of Anna Freud's seventieth birthday, coming at the end of the year. It seems only a short while ago that she was seen beside her aged father, two Viennese exiles lucky to be standing in an English garden after the Anschluss of 1938. The old man had been ailing for a long time, but showed not a sign of it in the last photographs; his set face and piercing eyes hinted at the determination and fire in him to the last. He wrote until the end of his eighty-three years, starting the *Outline of Psychoanalysis* shortly after arriving in London and only fourteen months before his death — it was to be published posthumously — a brilliant, clear, up-to-date account of the heart of psychoanalytic work.

In his last years his daughter Anna did more than appear with him, holding his arm tactfully, smiling faintly while he looked ever serious (and defiant in the pain he constantly suffered). By 1926, at the age of thirty-one, she was a psychoanalyst specializing in child analysis. That year she gave a series of lectures, later published as *The Psychoanalytical Treatment of Children*, on the special requirements of therapeutic work with young boys and girls: earning their confidence, communicating with them in the absence of words, developing ways to explain their troubles to them, ensuring that what is won in treatment is not lost in the home or school. The following year, at the Tenth International Psychoanalytic Congress, held in Innsbruck, she read a paper rich in its theoretical discussion of the difference between analyzing adults and children. Adults know their suffering, and have developed characteristic styles of dealing with the various demands of the world, the devil, and the flesh. In contrast, children quite often have no idea that they are ill, want no help from an analyst, and are in the midst of growth, so that rather than presenting the fait accompli — that is, the neurosis which represents a "solution" to the various and conflicting demands of the mind — the child offers the challenge of his ongoing development (the symptom may go away in time anyway).

Moreover, the child's mind is much more public property than the adult's. What troubles the child is shared with his family, his teachers and school chums. That is to say, the child is going through the educational process of acquiring a "personality" (and, alas, neurosis) while the adult has likely forgotten all the trials — at home or outside — that contributed to the later pain or tension bringing him to analysis. Put differently, the adult is troubled but usually can't "remember" the exact sequence of events that are responsible for the trouble. The child often will describe quite readily what is happening about him, but may well not consider himself suffering or in danger — it is his parents or teachers who are concerned. In any event, he has a problem with the future as well as the past, since he must not only be helped to realize how he feels, but helped to grow, to think, feel, and act coherently and sensibly.

The differences between psychoanalysis of children and adults continued to occupy Anna Freud's thoughts in the next decade. In 1929, she gave a remarkable series of lectures to the Hort teachers in Vienna, later published as *Psychoanalysis for Teachers and Parents*. She was as much concerned with whom she spoke to, as with what she said. An account of the Hort says that it is "a kind of kindergarten, but particularly for children from six to fourteen years of age. The kindergarten itself takes only children up to six years or until school age. The children who come to the Hort are the children of parents who go out to work. They come daily and return to their parents in the evening. Here, in the Hort, they prepare their school homework, occupy themselves with light work or communal games, and are taken for outings by Hort workers."

The contents of this volume have had a sad time of it over the past thirty years. They have been widely and compulsively acknowledged yet by no means thoroughly understood. As a result, while Miss Freud's discussion of the Oedipus complex and the latency period in child development may seem quaintly old-fashioned, it is doubtful whether even now many readers truly realize the complicated nature of her final comments on the problems frequently encountered in raising children and for that matter teaching them in school. What Anna Freud said, she said firmly: no educational technique can really fill in for the absence of a solid, considerate relationship between parents and children; the character of the future citizen is established in his first years, the mother being the first law-giver; if parent or teacher does not appreciate the essentially understandable purposes and activities of the child they may both regulate and dominate him, but pay the price of his later illness or inadequacy.

While, again, none of that sounds very surprising today, the clinical cases used by the author to fasten down her abstractions are still as disquieting and pedagogically challenging as they ever were. One example after another tells parents and teacher alike not to mistake even psychoanalytic knowledge for the kind of emotional understanding and relationship it means to open up. The pain and conflict inevitable in all nurseries and classrooms are scrupulously illustrated in the hope that no one will walk away with a fixed set of principles, or ultimately worthless expectations, but rather a general willingness to see that the child's behavior *makes sense.* Once that is accomplished the child may rather flexibly be severely scolded or permitted liberty, depending upon the particular transgression at issue. (It is as if right then Anna Freud foresaw how, in the name of psychoanalysis, rigid indulgence would soon replace automatic harshness as the ruling order of the day.)

Her next labor was an enormously influential one, *The Ego and the Mechanisms of Defense,* published in 1937 by Leonard and Virginia Woolf at the Hogarth Press. It is safe to say that this book marked the most significant turn in psychoanalysis since the heightening of her father's interest in ego psychology twenty-five years earlier. In a real sense this one study conclusively divides two periods of psychoanalysis. At the beginning Freud saw and charted the instinctual segment of the unconscious, and psychoanalytic theory was all taken up with the energy (libido) of the drives and their many vicissitudes. Brill has described these pioneer concerns of Freud and his followers: "We made no scruples, for instance, of asking a man at table why he did not use his spoon in the proper way, or why he did such and such a thing in such and such a manner. . . . We had to explain why we whistled or hummed some particular tune or why we made some slip in talking or some mistake in writing. But we were glad to do this for no other reason than to learn to face 'the truth.' " By "truth" was meant the drive-bound promptings of the unconscious. Some still think so, not only in psychoanalysis but contemporary life in general, where uncovering the drives "deep down" in a person's mind is equated with "really" knowing him. Yet, how he comes to terms — both consciously and unconsciously — with those drives in his mind may well be the larger and more significant truth. In any event, it is the truth that eventually Freud, open-minded and willing to look hard at his own theories, came to seek toward the end of his life.

The workings of the ego, like those of the id, are in large measure unconscious. That is, not only what we think and dream may elude us, but how our minds make a habit of coping with those thoughts and dreams. Anxiety, fear, and a whole range of symptoms, come from the encounter of instincts with ego. Ego includes conscience (superego); and ego — as Anna Freud demonstrates — is no mere "window" between the impelling drives and the outside world, the kind of word for which "awareness" could be exchanged. The ego has a history. It is what has been learned at home and at school. It is the mind's intellect and skills, its social agent, its eyes and ears. The ego is an intricate style of being, a storehouse of implicit assumptions whose supplies keep us going, not to mention determining the land and distance we choose to travel. If in both nightmares and daydreams we are all mad, all wild and sometimes odd lovers, all murderers and anarchists, then what makes us different when awake is our native gifts, our upbringing, the time and place in which we live, and the manner we have somehow "chosen" (who can ever really settle the problem of free will?) to deal with ourselves.

The ways of the ego are numerous. One person habitually attributes the sources of his problems to others; another is exceedingly deft at converting sadness into joy, or vice versa. I may become fatigued and ache in my head or my stomach, while my neighbor turns *his* tension into a frenzy of rituals. Pride may mask despair, and shyness may call upon arrogance to give it expression. At the heart of these attitudes and postures, these "characteristics," and their attendant states of feeling, there are certain very specific irreducible "mechanisms" that deal with the instincts or drives. The activity of these mechanisms is as endless as the pressures the drives constantly exert. The imagery is either hydraulic or cloak and evil. Thus drives (and the behavior they urge) can be denied and pushed down whence they come; or they can be changed into their apparent opposites, or attributed elsewhere, to other people. They can be disengaged from their energy, the intellect thus presented with a bonus to use "thoughtfully," or they can be rendered weak by turning their original energy into complicated, hardworking so-called obsessions and compulsions that bind so relentlessly one or another aim. More ominously, drives can be otherwise handled, by being permitted to overwhelm the literally defenseless person's mind (psychosis) or compel his retreat (regression) into himself, his past, his very old ways of getting along.

There are names for all this life that goes on in the mind, and Miss Freud supplies them, but not without touching illustrations that enliven the meaning. Talking of the capacity adolescents have for "intellectualization" she observes the "wide and unfettered sweep of their thought ... the degree of empathy and understanding [they show]." She goes on to observe that the adolescent's "empathy into the mental processes of other people does not prevent him from displaying the most outrageous lack of consideration toward those nearest him. His lofty view of love and the obligations of a lover does not mitigate the infidelity and callousness of which he is repeatedly guilty in his various love affairs."

She saw it her task to demonstrate the consistency of our inconsistencies and to do so she did not shirk facing what are, finally, life's ironies. In the last pages of the book, when the ego lies before us in all its critical significance to our lives (and diagnostic importance to the psychoanalyst), we find comments like this: "In periods of calm in the instinctual life, where there is no danger, the individual can permit himself a degree of stupidity. In this respect instinctual anxiety has the familiar effect of objective anxiety. Objective danger and deprivation spur men on to intellectual feats and ingenious attempts to solve their difficulties, while objective security and superfluity tend to make them comfortably stupid."

So rich is the entire book it is possible to skip by comments like those as interesting but somewhat vague and oracular asides — until, that is, we seek explanation for the most upsetting dilemmas of our time. How, for instance, are we to comprehend many of the richest boys and girls in the richest nation in the world behaving like aimless delinquents? Or how do we account for the incredible survival managed by generations of Negro families in Mississippi, where brutality over the centuries seems to have produced people whose alertness, generosity, and integrity quite visibly bewildered those of us who spent the summer of 1964 there? All of us were so free, literate, well fed and clothed; yet confronted by the civilized, gentle endurance of the people we came to help, many of us wondered — out of no misty sentiment — what we lacked.

For Miss Freud such paradoxes are clearly to be expected, and she doubtless shares the confusion or surprise they generate in us. Indeed, shortly after her masterpiece on ego psychology was finished she herself was to experience unexpected hardship, and from it find the inspiration for a long time of hard and rewarding work.

When the Nazis came to Vienna they were still sensitive enough to world opinion to spare important people, though only after ransom was exacted. Freud thus escaped, to live on a bit over a year, even several weeks into World War II. Before his death he would see the madness he knew so much about given incredible political and institutional structure. Anna was not permitted leave from Austria with her father without a day's arrest and interrogation by the Gestapo, on March 22, 1938. "Anna bei Gestapo," Freud wrote in his diary. Until that day he had hesitated, at eighty-two, to leave a city he had lived in for seventy-nine years. Thereafter, he could not wait to get out.

Anna Freud's arrival in England, her continued stay in London, the enormous variety and productivity of her work there, all fit ironically into *her* earlier life. When the first World War broke out she was a youth of nineteen on a visit to England. It took some weeks for her to return to Austria — she came back with Austria-Hungary's ambassador to England via the long Mediterranean route rather than over a continent rendered impassable by war. A quarter of a century later she would return to England, this time by land, and just before that route would again be rendered impassable.

Nor did she return to England a stranger to its language or culture. She had learned English as a youth, and in 1920 — at twenty-five — used it fluently in an address to the Sixth International Congress of Psychoanalysis. In those years, the 20s and 30s, her initial profession, that of a schoolteacher, was not, properly speaking, abandoned, but joined to her interest in the analysis of children. When she talked to teachers about the psychological problems of schoolchildren she spoke not as the theoretician, or even clinician, come to deliver the "consultant's" wisdom, but as a comrade, all too aware of just how complicated a problem it is to teach, and for that matter, to give advice to teachers. "We must not demand too much from one another," was her way of beginning a lecture to teachers, or dampening even in the heady early 30s any inclination of the hungry for more than the lean truth.

Scarcely two years after meeting with the Gestapo she was noting under the title of "Further Observations" the reactions of children to the "big air attack on London on the night of Wednesday, 16 of April [1941]." She described it as follows: "Even for people who had gone through the period of the so-called Blitz in September and October 1940, the events of this night were surprising and alarming. There was more gunfire than ever before, the sound of falling bombs was continuous, the crackling of fires which had been started could be heard in the distance, and again all these sounds were drowned by the incessant droning of airplanes which flew over London, not in successive waves as in former raids, but in one uninterrupted stream from 9 P.M. until 5 A.M."

Her two books, *War and Children* and *Infants Without Families*, reveal the fate of children exposed to such conditions and their consequences — physical hurt, loss of home and parents, disruption of routine, constant moving about with exposure to all sorts of people and surroundings. With her friend and colleague, Dorothy Burlingham, she helped organize and run the Hampstead Nursery, three houses for children of different ages. It was one of many so-called "colonies" of The Foster Parents' Plan for War Children, Inc., which was started in 1936 when Spain's children faced bombardment. Throughout the war she worked in the nursery, dedicating herself to ordinary people up against terrible circumstances, caring for children and seeing to it that their emotional needs were as respected as their hunger and various injuries. During the war England was full of lonely, frightened, confused children; they often had a hard time making sense of a world of sudden explosions, arbitrary departures, shifting scenery, and inconstant grown-ups. Those who came upon Hampstead were fortunate.

Miss Freud's writings about these years turn careful, scientific scrutiny into poetry: "Children are, of course, afraid of air raids, but their fear is neither as universal nor as overwhelming as has been expected. An explanation is required as to why it is present in some cases, absent in others, comparatively mild in most, and rather violent in certain types of children." What others might call "case material" is offered as follows:

> One of our mothers, a comfortable and placid Irishwoman, the mother of eight children, when asked whether her rooms had been damaged by bombing, answered, with a beaming smile:
> "Oh, no, we were ever so lucky. We had only blast and my husband fixed the window frames again." Blast, which removes the window frames, not to mention the windowpanes, can be a very uncomfortable experience; but again, we can be certain that for the children of this mother the occurrence of the blast was not a very alarming incident. We had, on the other hand, the opportunity to observe very anxious mothers with very anxious children. There was John's mother. . . . She never went to bed while the alarm lasted, instead stood at the door trembling and insisted on the child not sleeping either. He, a boy of five, had to get dressed, to hold her hand and to stand next to her. He developed extreme nervousness and bed wetting.

Later on she notes that

> . . . the fear of air raids assumes completely different dimensions in those children who have lost their fathers as a result of bomb-

ing. In quiet times they turn away from their memories as much as possible and are gay and unconcerned in their play with other children . . . the recurrence of an air raid forces them to remember and repeat their former experience.

Summing up her thoughts about the reactions of children to evacuation (then thought the most humane thing to do for blitzed children) she asserts that

War acquires comparatively little significance for children so long as it only threatens their lives, disturbs their material comfort or cuts their food rations. It becomes enormously significant the moment it breaks up family life and uproots the first emotional attachments of the child within the family group. London children, therefore, were on the whole much less upset by bombing than by evacuation to the country as a protection against it.

It is hard to overestimate the worth of such information, supplied so quietly yet firmly. Incongruities are not feared, nor prevailing customs and sentiments left unchallenged. The psychoanalyst can at once see clearly, talk sensibly, and work with humor and kindness. It does not always happen that way.

After the war Anna Freud continued her very practical work with children and at the same time tried to fit whatever observations she thereby made into a coherent view of the mind's structure and function. Paper after paper appeared; they were usually short; they were all tightly written; and invariably they contained skillful, even elegant mixtures of the useful and the theoretical. Some of them appeared in scholarly annuals like the *Psychoanalytic Study of the Child,* while others could be found in journals dedicated to service, like *Child Study* or the *Health Education Journal.* The titles tell of her broad interests: "Nursery School Education — Its Uses and Dangers"; "Sublimation as a Factor in Upbringing"; "Sex in Childhood" and "Difficulties of Sex Enlightenment"; or "Certain Types and Stages of Social Maladjustment." Reading them I always feel her uncanny ability to put a fastidious mind to earthy subjects. Thus, in a classical paper on childhood feeding disturbances (1946) she covers an extremely broad and difficult subject in thirteen well organized pages. The coverage is both formal and categorical yet appropriately larded with descriptions of the "squashy and smeary foods" disliked by some children or the "sweets, biscuits and cakes" they may be drawn to. Characteristically, when she concludes, she is wary of the literal-minded reader: "The various types of eating disturbances, which have been separated off from each other in this paper for the purpose of theoretical evaluation, are invariably mixed and interrelated when observed clinically."

Now, in her seventieth year, Miss Freud has published a remarkable book, *Normality and Pathology in Childhood*. She has tried to fit together interests and ideas that have run through all her writings, not only the books and the score or so longer articles and lectures, but a number of briefer communications and monographs. She has also managed to provide a uniquely historical view of psychoanalysis as a changing field of inquiry. Someday a social historian will find this book indispensable as he studies psychoanalysis by tracing its emergence from a specific medical, intellectual, and social climate, showing the forces resisting it, those welcoming it, and even those uncritically entranced by it (a development Freud by no means overlooked). Such a history of psychoanalysis would naturally have to come to terms with Freud's mind — its action like a dazzling *pas de deux* between a pragmatic observer of the facts and a theory-bound metapsychologist. Beyond that, however, would be the larger historical task of describing the institutional development of psychoanalysis, its spread over the world, the different forms such geographic and cultural dispersal has given to it, and the reasons why.

Moreover, the concerns of analysts have been changing, not always harmoniously. The tug upon psychoanalysis from the doctors and the healers is matched by the pull of those who are much more interested in its intellectual promise, its possible contributions to psychobiography, to the social sciences and philosophy. Even in the clinical psychoanalytic study of children, as specialized a field as one can find in medicine or psychiatry, there are sharp differences in interests and in the interpretation of observations. More significant are the overall differences — they have become severe disagreements on occasion — in matters as basic as how to work with children, what use to make clinically of their day-to-day behavior, and where the actions of children may have relevance to a psychoanalytic theory of adult life. In most of these matters Anna Freud has quietly figured, taking her stand not by rhetoric but by the example of her work.

Her constant emphasis — in this book particularly and through her life — has been upon the importance of direct observation. For a long time psychoanalysts were quite naturally suspicious of what they saw, of the "surface" manifestations of the mind's life. They saw that after weeks and months of listening to a patient they found hidden truths about his feelings that nothing "observable" (his conversation, attitudes, interests, or manner) could reveal. As a consequence, any conscious expression, any kind of behavior that might simply be watched and noticed, seemed at worst an irrelevant distraction or disguise, and at best a mere pathway to a truth that is always hidden and deviously expressed.

In time, prodded by people like Miss Freud, drastic changes have occurred in the view many analysts have of what they can observe directly. The unconscious no longer has to be "proved," it can be seen in its everyday manifestations — slips, symptoms, patterns of thought or action — as well as in the office after a long course of treatment. The unconscious can also be seen in the way people respond to it, by the "mechanisms of defense" they adopt. What is more, in children it can be seen *developing*. Naturally, insofar as the analyst relies upon such observations, and draws conclusions very cautiously on the basis of those observations, his theoretical elbow room will be rather strictly limited. Whatever he postulates he will want to verify, either by checking on the observations of others, or making more of his own. Even among Freud's writings, he will tend to fall back upon those that grew out of clinical study rather than those that depended too exclusively on speculation. To such analysts the genius of Freud will be precisely those speculations that gave order to the considerable "clinical material" he encountered — and was both "free" and perceptive enough to notice. What he said about Moses, or Leonardo da Vinci, or the "death instinct" is fascinating and stimulating, but not in itself the basis for further psychoanalytic research. To those analysts the job ahead is not the further construction of theory — the edifice is already unwieldy, and some would say toppling — but further clinical study, further observations, in hospitals and clinics, in the society and across into other cultures, so that more "hard" facts can support whatever additional generalizations are to be made.

Children, particularly, demand watching. They are so individual, so diverse — not yet molded by society. Their constant activity, their spontaneity, their willingness to share unabashedly what thoughts, wishes, and fears they have, make them ideal candidates for the psychoanalytically trained observer. Since psychoanalysis itself has placed such emphasis on childhood, on its crucial events and enduring significance, one might have expected a rather extensive psychoanalytic child psychology to have developed — that is, a coherent view of normal child development which accounts for how emotional stability and "normal" behavior in infants, children, and youths are either enabled or thwarted.

In point of fact there was an ironic lag — it is only now being filled — between psychoanalytic *interest* in childhood and psychoanalytic *study* of childhood. What happened was that analysts took the observations they made in their office on neurotic adult patients and, in Miss Freud's delicately stated words, "ventured beyond the boundaries of fact finding and began to apply the new knowledge to the upbringing of children." Add to such efforts the inclinations of a nervous, affluent middle class, no longer interested in the Ten Commandments or the Sermon on the Mount — with enough time and success on its hands to believe that at last "happiness," that is "mental health," could be spelled out step by step for the child — and a social phenomenon was on its way.

A "psychoanalytic education" for children, one that would "prevent" neurosis, became a fervently sought goal. "The attempts to reach this aim," writes Anna Freud, "have never been abandoned, difficult and bewildering as their results turned out to be at times. When we look back over their history now, after a period of more than forty years, we see them as a long series of trials and errors."

She goes on to make a summary that may well be in itself a cultural document of this century:

> . . . at the time when psychoanalysis laid great emphasis on the seductive influence of sharing the parents' bed and the traumatic consequences of witnessing parental intercourse, parents were warned against bodily intimacy with their children and against

performing the sexual act in the presence of even their youngest infants. When it was proved in the analyses of adults that the withholding of sexual knowledge was responsible for many intellectual inhibitions, full sexual enlightenment at an early age was advocated. When hysterical symptoms, frigidity, impotence, etc., were traced back to prohibitions and the subsequent repressions of sex in childhood, psychoanalytic upbringing put on its program a lenient and permissive attitude toward the manifestations of infantile, pregenital sexuality. When the new instinct theory gave aggression the status of a basic drive, tolerance was extended to the child's early and violent hostilities, his death wishes against parents and siblings, etc. When anxiety was recognized as playing a central part in symptom formation, every effort was made to lessen the children's fear of parental authority. When guilt was shown to correspond to the tension between the inner agencies, this was followed by the ban on all educational measures likely to produce a severe superego. When the new structural view of the personality placed the onus for maintaining an inner equilibrium on the ego, this was translated into the need to foster in the child the development of ego forces strong enough to hold their own against the pressure of the drives. Finally, in our time, when analytic investigations have turned to earliest events in the first year of life and highlighted their importance, these specific insights are being translated into new and in some respects revolutionary techniques of infant care.

A little further on she takes note of the great hope and faith that was involved in all this: "In the unceasing search for pathogenic agents and preventive measures, it seemed always the latest analytic discovery which promised a better and more final solution of the problem."

In any event, some of the advice given to parents was useful, helping them to feel more open and relaxed with their children, and sparing their children a substantial variety of harsh and senseless practices. There were disappointments, too:

. . . Above all, to rid the child of anxiety proved an impossible task. Parents did their best to reduce the children's fear of them, merely to find that they were increasing guilt feelings, i.e., fears of the child's own conscience. Where in its turn, the severity of the superego was reduced, children produced the deepest of all anxieties, i.e., the fear of human beings who feel unprotected against the pressure of their drives.

All in all, what emerged were children to some extent unlike others before them, but nonetheless human: ". . . It is true that the children who grew up under its influence were in some respects different from earlier generations; but they were not freer from anxiety or from conflicts, and therefore not less exposed to neurotic and other mental illnesses."

Then she emphasizes that "this need not have come as a surprise if optimism and enthusiasm for preventive work had not triumphed with some authors over the strict application of psychoanalytic tenets." After all, she reminds the reader, conflict is built into life, into human development, into the complicated organization of the mind that characterizes "civilized" man. Somehow, to switch into a theological perspective she might not find congenial, the sin of pride permitted many people to forget this.

Even though Miss Freud might not take to such talk, she is clearly worried that the public will expect the impossible from analysis, and even more, that analysts will make unjustified assumptions about what they know and how they ought to do their work. In her new book she begins and ends with a reminder that not only do we lack the information needed to insure proper advice to the public on a number of matters connected with child rearing, but even more significant, the same situation holds for psychiatric and psychoanalytic work with children, our ability to *assess*, to appraise the child's behavior and decide what is pathological and what is a part of growth and development. "As our skill in assessment stands today," she concludes, ". . . accuracy of diagnostic judgment seems to me an ideal to be realized not in our present state of knowledge but in the distant future."

However, this book is neither pretentiously humble nor interested in conveying an impression of the widespread ignorance or incompetence of a scientific field of inquiry. On the contrary, it is probably one of the boldest, strongest — and definitely most original —

statements to come from an analyst in a long time, precisely because its author has the courage and intelligence to face squarely the really formidable and vexing problems in psychoanalysis. What, after all, is "normal?" Can we child psychiatrists predict the future adult's adjustment on the basis of what we see in him as a toddler or child of six or seven? And if so, can we prevent later illnesses by spotting them and immediately treating them? When, indeed, ought a child's emotional troubles be weighed serious enough for psychiatric evaluation? For that matter, what are the differences between the treatment of children and adults, and would it not be desirable for all children to have some exposure to therapy?

In many ways she demonstrates that the criteria for normality in childhood are topsy-turvy to those in the adult world, thereby giving us the clue that those criteria cannot simply be culled from evaluations made in the office or clinic, but involve social, developmental, and cultural influences — a fact that may be obvious to many outside both hospitals and psychiatric offices but forgotten by those inside who are under daily pressures to make diagnoses and afterwards embark upon various and decisively different courses of treatment. At what point does the "normally rebellious" adolescent become a "sick" one or an "antisocial" one? The medical disposition may vary depending upon which of those three labels are used. With children not yet adolescents food fads vary from culture to culture; and sleeping disturbances, clinging behavior, or temper tantrums may upset the parents or people in one neighborhood and not bother those in another. In any event they don't trouble the child: "Where the parents interfere (with such symptoms) their restraining action, not the symptom, is blamed by the child for causing distress." Moreover, it is eminently normal for children to be going through a continual series of trials: "In sharp contrast to former conventional beliefs, it is now well known that mental distress is an inevitable by-product of the child's dependency and of the normal developmental processes themselves."

What is normal for children thus varies with age, with culture, with the contemporary problems facing the child, with the relationship of his present troubles to his past achievements and the tasks about to face him, with his evident capacity (or lack of it) to resolve whatever problems confront him. To a large extent each child's strengths and weaknesses have to be evaluated on their own merits, and Miss Freud insists that there is a "wide range" even to the *variations* of normality. A child may be showing a temper or having trouble eating a certain food and be doing so quite appropriately — for his age some such development is understandable, reasonable, and common enough. Thus, a child will become anxious and petulant when left alone too long. If he doesn't, if his "patience" seems as plentiful as "ours," as the adult's, it is more, rather than less, likely that he is disturbed. Again, a child will go through periods of sleeplessness or insomnia that relate to his increasing awareness of the world, hence nervousness about it. When he gets older he will have more tension and misery as his mother, the first judge and referee he knows, sets limits on him. Of course, such *developmental* anxiety varies from family to family, and for that matter, from school situation to school situation. (Even more confusing, a child may be "good" at home and "bad" at school, depending upon a large number of possible considerations.)

Even with clearly disturbed children, there is no way right now to predict their psychological future. In 1951 Ernst Kris called the knowledge of the normal an "underdeveloped" or "distressed" area of psychoanalysis, though Anna Freud's effort to trace general *patterns* of growth has helped in that area. The same holds for the region of diagnostic prediction, even in adult work as well as with children. I can obtain similar clinical histories from two patients, yet find their current problems remarkably different. We daily see the parents of our sickest patients and wonder why *their* children. We meet only mildly troubled people and find their parents, their earlier lives, impossible. We wonder, as we hear of this or that complaint about the child and learn about his family life, how he might *ever* grow up, even with treatment, let alone without it. In a section dealing with "homosexuality as a diagnostic category in childhood disorders" Miss Freud speaks the facts bluntly as we now know them:

> . . . In other words, that certain childhood elements in given cases have led to a specific homosexual result does not exclude a different or even the opposite outcome in other instances. Obviously, what determines the direction of development are not the major infantile events and constellations in themselves, but a multitude

of accompanying circumstances, the consequences of which are difficult to judge both retrospectively in adult analysis and prognostically in the assessment of children. They include external and internal, qualitative factors.

The lesson is clear: human beings are thoroughly individual; and it is a risky business to categorize their complaints or to theorize smugly about their future.

Even the decision whether or not to treat a child is often a hard one to make. In some cases time will clearly "solve" the problem; in other cases there may indeed be a problem, but educational work with the parents and a brief kind of "fact-finding" work with the child may make therapy, or certainly analysis, unnecessary. Some problems classically need analysis, though they are not necessarily those manifesting the most open and troublesome symptoms. In other cases "the analyst is faced by nothing but enigmas, with no certainty about the therapeutic possibilities."

Finally, Miss Freud does not — as do some of her colleagues — recommend analysis for "normal" childhood conflicts: ". . . the child analyst cannot escape the feeling that here a therapeutic method is assigned a task which, by rights, should be carried out on the one hand by the ego and on the other by the parents of the child."

When Ernest Jones asked Anna Freud what she thought her father's most noteworthy characteristic was, she replied instantly: "his simplicity." He was indeed a man of simple personal habits. He wrote simple prose. He made an astonishing number of observations, and quite simply, quite stubbornly, fought for the intactness of their preservation, so that eventually they would survive over the generations and cross into every continent.

Anna Freud has remained fittingly loyal to her father by refusing to stand in useless awe of his accomplishments. She has gone forward where he left off, giving her life to children from unhappy homes, to children in the midst of the terrors of war, to normal children in their puzzling, inspiring variety. All the while she has written the clear, civilized prose of the confident scientist, the warm, good-humored prose of the kind and sensible human being. One can fairly glide along the pages of her latest book, even though it is obviously addressed to professionals. The most complicated idea emerges so effortlessly that it seems to be pure "common sense." She has never exploited her name or her profession. She has lived discreetly with her doubts, refusing to allow them to make her strident, pedantic, or doctrinaire. She, too, has achieved simplicity.

Massachusetts Review, 1966

19

PIAGET AS GOD

❦

Psychology and psychiatry continue to exert enormous influence on our unashamedly agnostic climate, our "upper-middle-class Western intellectual world," as it is sometimes called in one knowing swoop. There is nothing else, there can be nothing else, but *further* explorations deeper into the unconscious or higher into the sky or faster over land. We do not want salvation or redemption or seek to avoid damnation. We want "meaning"(better, "creative meaning"). *We*, of course, are the thousands of well-fed, well-educated, practical but sincere American citizens, who ponder issues, decide among "positions," and in general consider the world a difficult place, all right, but by no means an impossible one — to understand, to live in, to take very seriously, to change in all those ways, "significantly" or "basically" or "fundamentally." Perhaps Freud — so stubbornly and blindly unfriendly to religion — distrusted America because he knew that even he would not escape America's capacity (its "need" as it is put today) to make a religion out of almost anything, and most assuredly out of psychoanalytic psychiatry.

Unfortunately for them, secular religions don't last very long. One follows another, and each time the heady, exuberant period of discovery must give way to the inevitable disenchantment that comes when the next seer arrives on the scene. It makes no difference how "valid" and worthwhile the "old" ideas are. When knowledge becomes a sacred object, the man who has set the knowledge forth becomes a god; and perhaps Western intellectuals are still Jewish enough, still Christian enough, to be able to accept only one god at a time. Each of our seers has his moment. All eyes are on him. Criticism becomes strangely muted — sometimes (as in Christian history) after an initial period of public scorn and disbelief. Soon disciples appear: they have worked with the Man; they and they alone understand Him; He trained them; He was their friend, their "master," as Hans Sachs — a grown-up man — called Sigmund Freud.

In some cases institutions emerge, places where His thought is studied, where men assemble earnestly to do that study. In other instances the Man exerts His influence less formally but no less effectively. The ideas of other men are made to pass the muster of His name, whether those men wish it to happen or not, whether in fact they have read a word of His or not. They become Marxists, Leninists, Freudians, neo-Freudians, Jungians, Adlerians; or they become followers of Lévi-Strauss, members of Piaget's "school." And the followers and disciples fight one another with missionary passion and zeal. A particular truth is not something tentatively held, a vision that for the moment works, that for a while makes things clearer, lends them a certain order. A truth is considered *the* truth; it must be fiercely possessed, pitted against other truths, made an adversary, a combatant, a commanding source of loyalty. And I suppose it has to be asked: on a lonely planet, full of every conceivable kind of injustice, rampant with murder and hunger and brutality (the last evident among the well-educated and "civilized," too), why not worship this Man, that Idea? It is only a second we are here, and surely we deserve Someone near, Something tangible, concrete, specific, explicitly promising.

All of this I have to say before I discuss the work of Jean Piaget — whose ideas the interested American reader can now find presented in the book *Six Psychological Studies;* the essays in it are collected and published in English for the first time. I do so in no way to accuse Piaget, Freud, Jung or anyone else. No gifted thinker can escape the effects of what are in fact two universal, utterly common sins, the wish to be God, and failing that, the desire to make a God, find One that others don't yet know. For that matter, even if Freud and Piaget *were* gods, the idolatrous excesses of their worshippers could not be prevented, as anyone who has studied the history of the various religions well knows. In any event, neither Freud nor Piaget deserves the "treatment" he has received from the "public" — a treatment that in Piaget's case is perhaps on the ascendancy even as Freud's "influence" is said to be on the wane. (All of which may be a very good thing for Freud and his ideas, a very poor one for Piaget and his.)

Before we mention the various uses to which Piaget is now being put, we had best look at what the man has actually tried to do. Like Freud, he has been an incredibly prolific man, a brilliant observer and a leader around whom followers, themselves gifted, have gathered. He was born in Neuchâtel, Switzerland, some seventy miles northeast of Geneva, where he has lived and worked for many years. His first interest was in zoology — later extended to natural science and philosophy, in both of which he received doctorates. He has never really abandoned those interests, even though he is now best known by teachers and child psychologists. He considers himself an epistemologist of a certain kind. He has wanted to document the way man, a physical being, acquires knowledge, starting at birth and moving up the years. He has championed direct observation of children, rather than what some psychoanalysts (despite repeated warnings from Anna Freud and others) exclusively cling to: retrospective statements about childhood based on the fantasies and memories of adults who are patients. He has insisted upon a genetic and developmental view of knowledge: we learn about the world by having concrete experiences with it; and the more of those experiences we have, the more we know, the more "real" is our contact as individuals with the environment. He has been much concerned with the process of intellectual maturation, and with his associates has published some two hundred studies on the psychology of intelligence, including over twenty books and many monographs. The titles of his books give some clue to his interests: *The Language and Thought of the Child, Judgment and Reasoning in the Child, The Child's Conception of the World, The Child's Conception of Physical Causality, The Moral Judgment of the Child, The Origins of Intelligence in Children,* and his grand *L'Epistémologie Génétique.*

The six essays in Piaget's new book are meant to give a glimmer of what he has been trying to demonstrate. Despite the fact that, like all of his work, the essays seem preoccupied with children, learning and intelligence, it is safe to say that the "heart of the matter" is elsewhere, in the exquisite tension that a biologically-minded philosopher finds between the *inside* of man's thoughts or fantasies and the *outside* of man's physical surroundings and social atmosphere. In this sense Piaget is exactly like Freud — who also started out as a biologist, a neurophysiologist to be exact, and who also believed his later psychological interests to be part of a much wider and more ambitious pursuit (a philosophical one, even though he shunned the word because he wanted to be "scientific"). Neither man allowed himself to forget that the mind is part of the body — and if that seems like the purest and most evident kind of common sense, it is a common sense that many psychologists and psychiatrists have long since forgotten or, as it is put by some today, "transcended."

Freud views man as driven by inborn instincts. Piaget sees man from his first day on this earth as possessing "inborn reflex mechanisms" which progressively and relentlessly emerge and then become integrated, one to another, in the face of experience after experience. The baby encounters an object or an event or a person behaving in a particular way, and step-by-step the reflexes in the child come to terms with what happens outside him. The development of intelligence itself is a part of man's biological adaptation to the environment — though once man has actually become intelligent, has learned how to deal with objects, has learned about space and time and causality and logic, he has apparently set something else going: "Intelligence constitutes an organizing activity whose functioning extends that of the biological organization while surpassing it due to the elaboration of new structures."

The word "structures" leaps out at us today, even though Piaget wrote it in 1936. Suddenly Lévi-Strauss and Structuralism have become topical, influential, important. I suppose we can certainly call

Piaget a structuralist by the definition Lévi-Strauss offers: "Structuralism is the search for unsuspected harmonies. It is the discovery of a system of relations latent in a series of objects." More than that, structuralism asserts above all that man's actions are lawful; they can be comprehended precisely, given enough time, effort and intelligence; and they can be described or classified because they make sense, no matter how arbitrary, irrational, impulsive, wanton, inexplicable they seem.

Certainly Piaget has faith that a substantial part of man's thinking is constant and describable. More than that, he believes that some psychological events significantly transcend society, culture, history; they are events which unfold as part of our natural endowment, so to speak. That is, certain ideas held by the ancient Greeks or Chinese depend upon assumptions that modern children can also be observed learning for themselves — assumptions about density, space, and so on. Yes, Piaget sees the environment causing us to change (he calls it "accommodation") and he also sees us making changes in things as we deal with them ("assimilation"); but his chief concern is with processes that relatively ignore not only social, cultural or economic influences, but even emotional ones. Regardless of my endless hangups, I developed (from childhood into adolescence, in ways described by Piaget) certain approaches to "life" and its "challenges." I learned, for instance, that things thrown up fall down, that things of one size contain more (or less) than things of another size. Today I may know such "facts" so well that I don't stop and think about what I know, or don't even consider what I know to be "knowledge"; but so it is — as any mother knows who watches her children slowly and sometimes painfully learn answers, ask interminable "why's," and go on to "master" the playroom, the backyard, and finally one grade's work after another in school. (Piaget learned an enormous amount from "simply" watching his three children grow up.)

What have Piaget's ideas to do with the recent attention he has been receiving on this side of the Atlantic? His new book offers a good summary of his ideas about intelligence, about the mental development of the child, about the development of thinking and its relationship to language. To some, however, his ideas are a mere foil; they are meant to be used for quite other reasons than Piaget ever had in mind. Like Freud, he is being summoned and used as an ideo-logical spokesman (sometimes against Freud). If I find psychoanaly-sis too clinical, too preoccupied with the abnormal, too interested in the emotional, the unconscious, the "goings-on" between people, I can turn elsewhere. I can turn to Piaget and his emphasis on normal development, on the cognitive, on man the developing *thinker* rather than man the universal neurotic, on psychological events that take place as the child grows *older,* rather than as the child gets more and more intricately involved with his mother and his father. And if Freud is not the bothersome one, but rather Sartre, there is the struc-turalist side of Piaget to hurl against the existentialism that — like psychoanalysis — has after all, been around and dominant for a long time. Never mind that Freud also built his structures, "agencies" he called them, the id, ego, and superego. Never mind that Sartre's exis-tentialism is in search of the same "harmonies" and "laws" that both Lévi-Strauss and Piaget seek, though in comparison with them the "areas" Sartre chooses to examine and the methods he uses are in-deed different — from Freud's, from Lévi-Strauss's, from Piaget's.

The struggle goes on, as it always has, between logic and emotion, between men like Aquinas and men like Augustine, with all sorts of innocent "investigators" (like Freud and Piaget) becoming partici-pants — willingly or against their wills. Systems are hurled against systems, and even within a particular man's system, some ideas are emphasized and others totally ignored, to fit the needs of the person and the historical "time." We have an urge to simplify even the most complicated ideas; and even the most complicated of our thinkers are not above simple, direct insults and shouting matches in which their own ideas and the ideas of their enemies are given a bare, stark, polemical form — as in the contemporary conflict between Lévi-Strauss and Sartre, or the one worked up between various "follow-ers" of Freud and Piaget.

In Piaget's case one can be sure that he is rather indifferent to such developments, because his passion has been to understand how man attains, finally, the intellectual ability, the knowledge, that enables him to wage his ideological wars, to formulate laws and conceptual-ize "existentialist encounters" or "emotional conflicts," to become a Piaget or a Freud, to seek after God, and, alas, to confuse Him with a mirror image of man or with a given century's facts and technology.

Perhaps Piaget has a right to claim release from the wars which the rest of us cannot escape — even though many are trying to use him in their various struggles. After all, he is in a position to insist that he merely wants to know how we came to know — and he can be content to let those who claim to know Something or Somebody, continue their fighting and squabbling and wrangling, "world without end."

Commonweal, 1968

20

LIFE'S MADNESS

One of the ways psychiatrists have sorted themselves out in recent years has to do with the importance they give to concepts like "the normal," or "maturity" or "mental health." Some are dead serious about letting their patients and the public know what is abnormal or immature. On television they urge me to "fight mental illness," and though I am not exactly sure how to go about doing it, I am certainly left with the idea that there *is* such a thing as mental illness, that there is such a thing as its presumed opposite, mental health.

In contrast stand those psychiatrists who question the entire practice of calling one or another variation in human behavior "sick" or evidence of "disease." Thomas Szasz, in this country, has made his position quite clear by the title, let alone the content, of his book *The Myth of Mental Illness*. The English psychiatrist R. D. Laing has come to the issue from a somewhat different angle — he is less interested in legal problems than Szasz and is much more the philosopher. I have already quoted him in an earlier essay; I drew from *The Divided Self*, where he wrote as follows:

A man who prefers to be dead rather than Red is normal. A man who says he has lost his soul is mad. A man who says he is a machine is "depersonalized" in psychiatric jargon. A man who says that Negroes are an inferior race may be widely respected. A man who says his whiteness is a form of cancer is certifiable.

A little girl of seventeen in a mental hospital told me she was terrified because the Atom Bomb was inside her. That is a delusion. The statesmen of the world who boast and threaten that they have Doomsday weapons are far more dangerous, and far more estranged from "reality" than many of the people on whom the label "psychotic" is affixed.

That book and a later one *(The Self and Others)* demonstrated that Laing is a physician and psychoanalyst who can easily come to terms with the complicated thinking of Sartre, Heidegger and Binswanger. He has been trained to place people in psychiatric categories but he finds the practice worse than useless, in fact an insulting and gratuitous way of ignoring both the person, who is called a "patient," and his ideals or convictions, so easily dismissed as "delusions" or "problems." For Laing, as for other so-called "existential" analysts, what psychiatrists are busy classifying and labeling is actually a "false self," presented to the world by a man or woman who has learned from long-standing, nerve-racking experience the futility of anything but disguise, deception and escape. In contrast, somewhere in anyone who has managed to survive infancy, there resides what Laing calls the "inner self," the anxious, frightened person's sense of what he "really" is, what he wishes he might more solidly be, what he once thought he could be — alive, whole, secure, trusting, trusted, whatever. (The word is not the issue, and in any event words can only suggest the intricacies and ironies of experience.)

Laing would see the most angry, withdrawn or incomprehensible of psychotics as a person who is struggling to make his thoughts and feelings known to a disbelieving, unreliable and impassive world, more bent on demanding compliance than enabling each man to stumble upon and seek out his own kind of vision or faith. What do we do with the radical doubts of a man who distrusts the words and postures of his fellowmen, who uses a different syntax, carries himself in a different way, and finds in the sights and sounds of his private world a bit less of the cruelty and the cant that "we" take in our stride? Laing says we call him "crazy," call him "ill," fall back on our laws, and send him "away," where he stays until he learns to change his ways and abide by ours. ("The psychiatrist, as *ipso facto* sane, shows that the patient is out of contact with him. The fact that he is out of contact with the patient shows that there is something wrong with the patient, but not with the psychiatrist.")

Laing has now published a new book, *The Politics of Experience*, which contains a collection of essays published before in medical or philosophical journals and various quarterlies. As a psychiatrist I once again find his writing quite literally stunning. I am overpowered by the challenges he issues to what has become a rather conventional profession, very much the property of (and a source of solace to) the upper-middle-class American, this century's *civis Romanus*. To Laing, we psychiatrists are something else, too: willing custodians, who for good pay agree to do the bidding of society by keeping tabs on various "deviants," and in the clutch "taking care" of them — the double meaning of the verb being exactly to the point.

There seems to be something seriously wrong with Dr. Laing: he doesn't believe that the educated, literate and often enough psychoanalyzed Americans and Englishmen who read his books are without exception alert, vital and honest people. As a matter of fact he asserts that they commonly are the dead rather than the quick, well-behaved rather than alive. In a word, they do not experience — "life," one another, the ridiculous and the sublime that the world offers so freely.

Laing's new book is organized around a discussion of "experiences," whether they be called psychotherapeutic, schizophrenic, or transcendental. Even more, he asks the reader to experience this book, to grapple with the mind of R. D. Laing — a doctor, a writer, a human being trying to live enthusiastically and suffer honorably. What troubles Laing, however, is his conviction that he will fail, that deaf ears and blind eyes are everywhere, particularly among those who declare books "interesting" and those who "treat" what they call "syndromes." Intellectuals, he feels, turn the writer's passion into academic capital, ideas that come and go. Psychiatrists convert the experience of talking with another person, sweating it out with him, into one more icy, abstract "process."

We have, then, a psychiatrist who doesn't seem to distinguish between sanity and madness. On the contrary, he appears to be worried about *us*, the "well-adjusted" men and women whom society values so very much. He sees us educating our children "to lose themselves and to become absurd, and thus to be normal." Then he adds: "Normal men have killed perhaps 100,000,000 of their fellow normal men in the last fifty years." As I read the book I kept thinking of Auden's poem *The Unknown Citizen,* where the same painful message is spoken. Step by step, year by year, we make sure a child falls in line, so that when he becomes grown-up we call him "mature," meaning he will follow the leader, who in turn follows the polls. In Auden's words we will be able to say "he worked in a factory and never got fired," and he wasn't "odd in his views," and "our social psychology workers found that he was popular with his mates and liked a drink," and "his reactions to advertisements were normal in every way." Naturally, "when there was peace, he was for peace; when there was war, he went." At the end the poet asks: "Was he free? Was he happy? The question is absurd. Had anything been wrong, we should certainly have heard."

Laing also despairs, and tells why in this book. We are in the same sinking ship, oppressor and victim. Men of success live haunted and frightened by the climb they have made over the minds, bodies and rights of others. What they did to their neighbor can be done to them — and that goes for nations as well as individuals. As for the "failures," they have their "problems" too, everything from hunger to the sense of worthlessness "we" make sure "they" feel. Laing devotes a whole chapter to "us" and "them," to the ways we cut off others, deny them in desperate spite of the humanity we ourselves have lost. He also insists that psychiatrists have allowed themselves to be separated from their patients, to categorize them rather than learn from them and with them, to use "the economic metaphor" so that one hears physicians talk of emotions "invested" and "objects" gained or lost. In sum, because of their emphasis on "function," on getting people "going" or "adjusted" (to what?) Laing views his colleagues as captives of their own amoral pragmatism.

Dr. Laing is no glib and smart-aleck critic, masquerading as a psychiatrist. He has a good deal of clinical research to his credit, much of it done with schizophrenics and their families. (His work is described in two books, each written with a colleague: *Reason and Violence* and *The Families of Schizophrenics*.) He sees schizophrenia as a "special strategy that a person invents in order to live in an unlivable situation." He does not know why some people (rather than others) feel so utterly, decisively thwarted, but he wants insanity understood as an effort to reach out, to break out; and further, he wants it understood as potentially something more, something "transcendental." Madness is not only confusion and loss, an inner world of ideas, voices, shapes and impulses asserting itself as never before; madness is a radical departure, and Laing sees it as "potentially liberation and renewal."

It is refreshing to read his discussion of insanity, even if one does not accept his viewpoint completely. He is not out to blame anyone, or call people thinly disguised (psychiatric) names. He isn't hammering away at the weakness, the morbidity, the deviance of people. Nor does he glorify or romanticize madness; he wants to understand it, to see it for the universal and quite human condition that it is. He knows what many of his colleagues think, how they scan minds for "disorders of thinking" and sign commitment papers, one after another, so that patients — they are sick, sick, sick — will get "treatment." He asks what kind of treatment, and from whom? Will the psychiatrist under the best circumstances be someone highly trained but ultimately condescending, more interested in getting the patient to be like others than in finding out where he himself is going, and would like to go?

Yet, language itself fails us when we try to distinguish the "individual" from others, from the "social." On the first day of life a child begins to find out where and when he was born. The way he is handled, clothed and fed, the nature and amount of food he gets, his mother's moods, worries, fears — all that and more begins to affect him, and urge on him what I suppose could be called "conformity." Then he enters the backyard, and the neighborhood, and later the school — where he learns to accept this and forgo that. I know of no society where children are not "indoctrinated," "brought up," and in the course of things subjected to some kind of conformist restraint.

Since Dr. Laing realizes all that, the reader must ask why he as a psychiatrist objects so strenuously to what he knows to some extent is inevitable. As a matter of fact the book's real value stands or falls on whether the author stretches his criticisms to the point of irrelevance. Will we hear once again, and from a psychiatrist this time, that children are by nature *only* sensitive, kind or honorable, and destined to remain so were it not for the thieves and cheats who teach them and rule them, let alone bring them into the world? Are we to understand that things have to be pulled inside out, that madness is sanity and sanity the worst kind of madness? Are the sometimes murky existentialist words going to replace the dumb psychiatric ones — say "authenticity" for "mental health"? Do we have yet another author who tears down everything around with a certain vindictive relish but has not a damn thing to offer the millions who don't read him, who live outside of his coterie and whom he can only grant the scorn of his pity?

In my opinion, Laing comes off very well on such questions. He acknowledges the demonic and chaotic in man, and he does not try to make a religion out of psychosis ("Certain transcendental experiences . . . I am not saying, however, that psychotic experience necessarily contains this element more manifestly than sane experience.") In other words, he holds to the *reality* of madness, but insists upon its integrity — and so emerges as only a man, with precisely that "status," a knowing and searching human being rather than a self-important doctor.

Unquestionably, he is thoroughly dissatisfied with what twentieth-century industrial society does to the minds of people; and he is equally unhappy with the way psychiatrists generally manage to avoid facing sticky and controversial problems like that one. He will not have his profession used to "cure" those who dare question social or political absolutes, and even more radically, he is willing to find madness — in some cases — a necessary way station or a point of departure in a spiritual voyage all too few people care or dare to make, particularly since if they do the middle-class world will shun them, mock them and when they make enough "trouble," cart them off.

At the end of the book Laing demonstrates what he means by offering us first a "case history" and then in a chapter called "The Bird of Paradise," his own flight of fancy and terror. These last pages do not read easily, and at times I could not understand what was before me, which may be the author's point about me, you, and him — that in today's world we barely can hold on to the senses we are still permitted, let alone call them ours or convey their "meaning" to others. In any event the book as a whole presents an exceptionally courageous psychiatrist who is willing to plumb his own depths and challenge head-on the hypocrisy and duplicity of his own profession and the larger society of which it is so prominent a part. I can only hope that he will be heard and heard respectfully. I can only further hope that those who disagree will spare him and the rest of us those dishonest and contemptible *ad hominem* remarks that some psychiatrists reserve for any and all "opposition." (So-and-so has this kind of problem, Laing has that kind, and they need more analysis, more of a "going over.") Nor do I think Dr. Laing deserves the eager company of the psychoanalytically disenchanted, a growing minority in America today. It seems to me that he is trying to give the essence of Freud's journey a particular kind of historical, political and philosophical perspective. I do not think he means to deny the validity of the analytic method; quite the contrary, it has enabled much of his vision. The point anyway is not to pit views against one another, but find whatever coherence possible among them — without resort to ideological squabbles. Freud called himself a conquistador, and if the bookkeepers and bureaucrats have now descended upon the psychoanalytic "movement" in droves to claim his mantle, all the more reason for a man like Laing to stand fast as the psychoanalyst he is.

The New Republic, 1967

21

A HERO OF OUR TIME

There are men and women whose labor is exceptional in the very special sense that it takes place in professional territory that is ignored, scorned or most often feared. I assume that every profession has them, workers who are not good, or capable or productive, but literally inspiring and heroic in an old-fashioned religious or philosophical way. They cause their colleagues to see new things, go new places and most of all to feel less despair. Their achievement is singular enough to be called fateful by the more romantic. They themselves have no illusion that their deeds will earn the honest respect of their colleagues. What they win instead is the exile that sentimentality provides, the enshrined isolation that incompetent and timid people insist upon for those whose example they do not wish to follow. "He is outstanding," one hears — meaning his everyday honesty is simply too much for the rest of us, and must be declared so rare that it is irrelevant. "He must have had an unusual or strange life," one especially hears today — meaning the dignity of his work and its implications for everyone else's work are a threat indeed, and must be destroyed with whatever weapons are available, today's number one choice being the psychological observation dressed up in fancy language but nonetheless murderous.

In clinical psychiatric and psychoanalytic work there are a few such heroes, men and women whose intelligence, compassion and above all, candor illuminate their deeds, their words and the failures they inevitably suffer. I am thinking of the late Frieda Fromm-Reichmann and of Harold Searles. No one knows for sure what "causes" schizophrenia (or indeed, whether such a presumptuous medical word as *schizophrenia* is capable of describing so wide a range of human behavior), but anyone who has read how either of those two analysts have treated their patients will recognize himself in the presence of grace, even if it is the kind of grace one can only feel through the printed word. (By grace I do not mean treacly niceness, but the ability to be determined, tough and resilient against great odds.)

Certainly Bruno Bettelheim is another such hero, another clinician who has taken on the hardest imaginable challenges and done so with almost fierce pride — as if what is unknown must be discovered, and that is that. His latest effort, *The Empty Fortress*, stands as one more in an extraordinary series *(The Informed Heart, Love Is Not Enough, Truants from Life)*. Though its subject matter — the treatment and causes of infantile autism — commands relatively little general interest, I think the book is something more than the scholarly psychiatric and educational volume it purports to be. I want to say that it offers a glimpse of "damnation" or "redemption," but we have been trained to shun such words when considering the particular kind of human experience that psychiatrists and psychoanalysts know and write about. Even so, I do not think Bruno Bettelheim will mind if his readers have such a relapse — see his book to be a passionate description of *deliverance*, as it may be achieved for one child and denied to another.

Autistic children are alive, but keep utterly to themselves. Either they do not and will not talk at all, or the sounds they make, the words they speak are meant for no ears but their own. To the observer they often seem curiously set in their ways; they have habits, and they keep to them. They may cling to certain objects — a toy, a blanket, anything — as if life itself were at stake. While all children become devoted to playthings, autistic children seem exclusively absorbed with them, as if other human beings do not or should not exist.

It is not that such children are without enough intelligence; some are very bright. At first glance they may appear merely very shy and a bit odd — perhaps a welcome contrast to the insistent smilers and hand-shakers many parents make their children become. For some reason they frequently seem particularly thoughtful — when they are not wild and menacing. It is as if they are under a spell — as some fey adults appear to be — and waiting only for the "right" person to come along. Perhaps the word "limbo" serves to place them; only I fear in most cases the analogy has to be a rather literal one. They cannot be saved, or even given enough life to take an active part in shaping (with others) their own doom.

As might be expected when knowledge is lacking, clinicians have different explanations for what causes children to become so terribly alone or shut off. Perhaps one or more genes are at fault. Perhaps it is all something "constitutional" — a vague, nondescript word that means no one really has the answer to an awful, total puzzle. Again, it may be that the child's mind, responding to his daily experiences, has seen fit to accomplish this most decisive of renunciations. Who is to know the answer — when only a few really care to find out, and have in themselves the purpose, self-command and tenacity to do so?

Bruno Bettelheim has those qualities of mind; and in this book, as in his others, he is willing to share with us the experiences he has had (in the concentration camps) that consolidated what I assume to be a prior vitality and plasticity of temperament. The stresses he experienced at the hands of the Nazis made him forever after interested in how children face the worst that life offers — and not all persecution is done for political reasons. (It is interesting to learn, though, that he had already treated autistic children long before the Gestapo took him away.) Now, after many years of day-to-day work with dozens of these most isolated children he gives us a long, considered and at times haunting account of what he thinks happens to them that makes them act as they do.

The book is divided into three sections: an initial, general discussion of the child's developing mental life, done in the best and most sensitive psychoanalytic tradition; a lengthy report of how three autistic children fared at Bettelheim's famous Orthogenic School;

and a final review of the literature on autism, which includes a fascinating essay on so-called "wolf-children," whom the author convincingly pictures as autistic, and thus fearful enough to the rest of
us to require mythological treatment, in this case exile to the alleged
care (and responsibility) of animals.

A book like this one defies review. Perhaps even the writing up of
work like Bettelheim's is a near impossible task. How does one convey the continual energy, the care and thought that go into studying
and attempting to make real and useful contact with these children?
It is a round-the-clock job, and one that may well prove futile, as
Bettelheim does not shirk saying. On the other hand, there are successes, instances that tend to confirm what emerges as the author's
central proposition: until we have proof otherwise — from geneti-
cists or neurophysiologists — the autistic child can only be written
off by clinicians because in all honesty they do not have the time, interest or capacity to take on that kind of psychological problem.
None of the children whom Bettelheim describes failed to change
some. The incredibly dedicated people who live with them and try to
reach them do not work in vain. The child's parents may pose a
hopeless obstacle, or the child may have arrived too late, already too
late, already so old that no one and nothing can make enough difference to undo what years of extreme and unforgiving self-centeredness have established; but every child, however much to himself he is
in the beginning, notices and responds to the consistent effort that
Bettelheim and those working with him are willing to exert.

As a result, Bettelheim's research emerges as demanding and uncommon, but significant to the work of others, who confront less
difficult "problems," or study the way normal children grow and
learn. His clinical illustrations are impressive, but he does not fall
down as a theorist, either. He is modest, sensible and unpretentious
when he tries to specify the particulars that make for autism. Fate (he
is not ashamed of the word) in the form of the child's inheritance
meets up with the accidents, vicissitudes and fears of the mother's
life — all of which childbearing and child rearing make newly con-
sequential.

The book is free of muddled, densely abstract passages. Nor does
Bettelheim have any desire to use psychoanalytic concepts in that peculiarly moralistic, punitive and vulgar way one has come to expect

of any number of psychiatrists and psychiatric social workers. Here are autistic children — gravely apart from the rest of us, seriously "ill," if that is the word for their trouble. Yet, their mothers are not called "rejecting" or "schizophrenogenic"; their fathers are not called "aggressive" or "borderline." If a parent is fatally flawed in some respect, the author tells about it so that justice is done to the enormous complexity of the problem.

Put another way, the children are not used as pawns in a rude (at the very least) exercise of name-calling — which hurt, worried parents have come to accept as their due from so-called "trained professionals." For Bettelheim the mystery of autism — indeed of all mental illness — requires quite a different kind of analysis and action. He knows that what happens in families — and in the doctor's office — is hard enough to find out, and harder still to assign (not to mention blame) as the "cause" of anything. He knows that life's ironies and ambiguities demand from the psychiatric clinician every ounce of hard work, meticulous observation and modesty he can summon; that right now there are more questions than answers. Perhaps it is such knowledge, gained under baffling circumstances, that makes for the kind of quiet heroism he and his colleagues continue to demonstrate, day after day.

The New Republic, 1967

22

THE VARIETIES OF

RELIGIOUS EXPERIENCE

By the time William James delivered the Gifford Lectures in Edinburgh during the academic year 1901–1902 he was a man entering his sixties, a distinguished psychologist and philosopher, a forceful and influential Harvard professor. His *Principles of Psychology* (1890), despite its title, was no textbook, but rather a two-volume scientific effort worthy of the best European scholarship. Thoroughly versed in history, not without some of his younger brother's literary sensibility, able to feel at ease reading scientific treatises or working in a laboratory, James almost singlehandedly established psychology as a discipline respectable and sturdy enough to merit both teachers and students in more and more American colleges. Yet, for all his interest in physiology and psychology, he could not shake off an interest in more speculative matters, including theology and what was then called moral philosophy. For one thing, his father had been a Presbyterian minister, thoroughly versed in the writings of Emanuel Swedenborg, the Swedish scientist and religious philosopher, who had an uncanny ability to mix dramatic and sometimes apocalyptic speculation with dry, matter-of-fact, naturalistic observations. Moreover,

James was much influenced by what his Harvard contemporary George Santayana called "the genteel tradition," wherein ideas are developed and fashioned with great care and elegance, but not put to any great test in either the world of business or politics, or in the laboratory. Not that James feared down-to-earth experiments or involvement in the day-to-day issues of his time. He had graduated from Harvard Medical School, accompanied Louis Agassiz on an expedition to the Amazon, studied in Germany with hard-headed scientists like Helmholtz, Virchow and Bernard,. Still, he had about him, for all his intellectual energy, a certain frailty of mind and spirit. For several years he suffered from what was then known as neurasthenia; in his case the disease took the form of fearfulness, shyness, and episodes of exceedingly low morale. And like his novelist brother, he was a sharp but somewhat aloof observer who could fight hard for what he believed in, but was at the same time vulnerable and timid, an intensely private man, hard to know and even at times completely inaccessible, for all the wry wit that comes across in his writing and the charm he is reported to have possessed as a lecturer.

In 1902 *The Varieties of Religious Experience* was published, based upon the Gifford Lectures. For a decade before James went to Scotland, filled to the brim with information about saints and sinners and what they believe or ridicule as absurd, he had been expanding his psychological interests to include ethical and religious subjects. Though he looked upon himself as a skeptic and an empiricist, he dared talk about immortality and "life's ideals"; and he was very much taken with the notion of *will*. He believed us thoroughly willful, for all the constraints upon us. That is to say, neurophysiological impulses may exert their influence upon the mind, and the world around us may in many respects determine how we think and act, but for all of that, each of us is no mere bundle of reflexes, no social automaton — and yes, no "product" of whatever goes on within our unconscious minds. It may come as a surprise to some of us, but James in the 1890s knew rather a lot about the unconscious; he granted it power over much of our activities, and saw it as a clever, tricky, agile, and resourceful part of man's mental equipment, very much like the unconscious Sigmund Freud was in the same decade struggling to fathom. Of course Freud became much more preoccupied with the unconscious, and inevitably for a while gave the rest of the mind precious little margin over our destinies. Toward the end of his life, though, Freud was increasingly preoccupied with the play of forces in the mind, with the ego's ability to achieve for a given person a kind of limited but real mastery over the various urges and drives that push upon all of us without letup. More recently some of our most gifted American psychoanalysts, Allen Wheelis and Leslie Farber, for instance, have gone further — emphasized the coherence and self-sufficiency, the *intentionality* men in previous centuries called it, we more than occasionally muster, however buffeted by strong conflicts whose exact character so often eludes us. And when those analysts use the word "will," as they both do repeatedly, they are harking back to William James, who never forgot what I suppose a man of common sense wouldn't forget: that we not only have dreams and nightmares, and free or not-so-free "associations," and anxieties and phobias, but we (most of us) every day do things, act, make decisions, show ourselves to be competent, effective human beings, men and women going about the business of living with a thankful absence of self-consciousness.

For James *The Varieties of Religious Experience* was an occasion to summarize many of his ethical and philosophical views, but also an opportunity to show what he believed the human mind is all about, and not least, how psychologists and psychiatrists ought to think about their work. True, most of the book is taken up with presentations of, then commentary upon, the writings of various religious writers. Yet, even in this regard James quietly but persistently makes a point. He does not confine himself to the accepted Protestant and Catholic theologians, saints or prophets. He ranges wide and far, drawing upon religious documents held dear by Hindus, Buddhists and Mohammedans. He discusses yoga. He goes into the Hindu notion of "dhyana," their word for higher states of contemplation. He draws upon many obscure Western mystics, as well as the better known saints, like Augustine, Ignatius of Loyola, John of the Cross, or Teresa — though he also summons the words of men who would be more familiar to his audiences in Scotland or his readers in America: Jonathan Edwards, George Fox, Emerson and Thoreau, Cardinal Newman. Again and again in an offhand way he comes up with a remark like this — followed, needless to say, by a substantial excerpt from a book, a footnote that directs us elsewhere for more information, and finally a stretch of analysis: "We Christians know little of Sufism, for its secrets are disclosed only to those initiated. To give its existence a certain liveliness in our minds, I will quote a Moslem document, and pass away from the subject."

By no means is the cumulative effect one of pedantry and cleverness smugly displayed. James wants to show how self-centered any of us, from whatever background or society, can get — particularly when the stakes are as high as eternity itself. He has little patience with ecclesiastical arrogance, with the "absolutism and one-sided dogmatism by which both philosophy and religion have been infested." But he goes further than that; a Harvard professor, a scientist and a writer of books and essays, he notes at the beginning of his second in a series of twenty lectures that "the theorizing mind tends always to the oversimplification of its materials." Later on he takes note of the meanness and bigotry so often over the centuries resorted to in the name of Jesus Christ or Mohammed, but again supplies a larger view of such occurrences: "The plain fact is that men's minds are built, as has been often said, in water-tight compartments." The result is our ability to mouth pieties, then go on to climb over our neighbors and friends in pursuit of money, power, prestige, whatever — and in so doing let ourselves off the hook by calling all sorts of other people a variety of unfriendly names, thereby clearing our own slates quite thoroughly. Meanwhile, if anyone challenges us, tries to bring us up short, we can always dismiss him immediately as an outsider, or ignorant, or blind to truths we and we alone know. So, the bigotry one finds among churchmen, among others, has to be traced further, has to be seen as "chargeable to religion's wicked intellectual partner, the spirit of dogmatic dominion, the passion for laying down the law in the form of an absolutely closed-in theoretical system."

James wants very much to distinguish between church affiliation and attendance on the one hand and the experience of prayer, of communion with God, of self-transcendence. He wants to capture and convey the mind at work — appealing to higher powers, confessing its misgivings and hesitations, asking for yet another chance, demonstrating its awareness of God's gracious presence, indicating its willingness to subordinate all sorts of whims and fancies to a search whose outcome by no means can be taken for granted. Some silliness and wildness and marked confusion if not craziness does indeed come across in a few of the documents presented, but the man who analyzes them has no interest in showing us that in pursuit of faith men lose their senses. In fact they often enough gain something rare and impressive, a depth and breadth of feeling, a capacity to reflect seriously about things that matter, a sense of freedom — as if for a moment they have at last been sprung loose from the orthodoxies and banalities of the day.

At times the New England empiricist and pragmatist begins to sound like Dostoevski. He scoffs at "abstract definitions and systems of concentrated adjectives"; and he declares his impatience with "faculties of theology and their professors." What he stresses is "the complexity of the moral life, and the mysteriousness of the way in which facts and ideals are interwoven." For him there is something immensely powerful yet ineffable in "prayerful communion." The mind becomes more than it ordinarily is. He can't quite specify what he means, so he gropes for words; he speaks of a heightened and activated "centre of personal energy." He speaks of "regenerative effects unattainable in other ways." He even turns on himself as well as his colleagues, by pointing out that men like himself, who determine "the reigning intellectual tastes," can often be all too self-assured, and blind to "realities" other than those they happen to value and dwell upon. He gets a little awkward when he makes such a point, and sometimes he does so in a footnote — as if to say that he is aware many will consider, and maybe correctly (there seems no limit to his capacity for self-criticism) the swipes he levels at the influential theorists of his day to be rather gratuitous, or as it would have been put in the 1890s, an unedifying spectacle. He has to persist, though. The stakes are too high, he seems to feel. So, he goes ahead, and when he is through an aside has become a statement of purpose, a warning, and in a way a prediction of things to come: "Even the errors of fact may possibly turn out not to be as wholesale as the scientist assumes. We saw in Lecture IV how the religious conception of the universe seems to many mind-curers 'verified' from day to day by their experience of fact. 'Experience of fact' is a field with so many things in it that the sectarian scientist, methodically declining, as he does, to recognize such 'facts' as mind-curers and others like them experience, otherwise than by such rude heads of classification as 'bosh,' 'rot,' 'folly,' certainly leaves out a mass of raw fact which, save for the industrious interest of the religious in the more personal aspects of reality, would never have succeeded in getting itself recorded at all."

The point is that one generation's obvious truths become another generation's field of inquiry. James was no mystic himself, and when he writes about mystics and saints and healers and souls seized with lyrical revelations that defy description let alone quantification, he makes clear his own situation as an observer, a moderately sympathetic investigator, a man conscientiously responsive to those he is trying to comprehend. But he also cannot forget that the tone he gives to his lectures, the attitude he brings to those he is studying, can become terribly important. Are they all mad, in need of his clever and oh so definitive diagnosis, not to mention (if it were possible) his "help"? Are they gullible, or possessed of second-rate minds, hence worth a kind of analysis that makes us, who read or write or want to write books like *The Varieties of Religious Experience,* feel ever so pleased with ourselves — because surely we are not susceptible to hysteria, superstition, flights of self-deluding fantasy? In lecture after lecture the American psychologist resists blandishments he apparently knew only too well — and not because he was a shrewd observer of *other* people. Though nowhere in the book does he become autobiographical, one feels in many places the author struggling with intellectual competence and its not uncommon companion, a certain arrogance or *hauteur* which takes the form of impatience with all those lesser ones who try to make do as best they can in this world, and who even at times get grandiose enough to believe they have a few clues about life's meaning. Never is James condescending; nor does he reveal contempt with an outpouring of pity for those he quotes at such length. Perhaps he turns on "sectarian scientists" because he knows how tempted he himself is to dismiss people casually or even rudely. Perhaps a mixture of professional detachment and philosophical inclination permitted him to suffer gladly those he "really" believed to be fools. Yet, the quality of the book argues against such an interpretation; the lectures come across as serious and heartfelt, and the author at times intrigued, at times perplexed, but never bored or impatient.

Envious, at times the man is openly and unashamedly envious. He seems to know, and he has the courage to admit, that others after him will discover in their own way what others before him — again, in their own way — have already been impressed with and felt deeply, if not declared outright. Meanwhile he can only look at things in a certain manner and describe them with a vocabulary his particular moment in history permits. That is, he saw himself to be very much susceptible to the prejudices of his time, as does any sensitive man who has no fear of irony and knows the lessons of history; knows, that is, how endlessly repetitive so much we call "new" can turn out to be — repetitive, but also in certain respects different. So, James notes what yogis have done to control the physiological processes of their bodies, remarks upon how strangely and wondrously people can sense things and affect one another, comments upon the richness of the mind's "inner" life, so often appreciated and called upon by saints of old and "mystics" of every age — and rather wistfully writes this:

> Thus the divorce between scientific facts and religious facts may not necessarily be as eternal as it at first sight seems, nor the personalism and romanticism of the world, as they appeared to primitive thinking, be matters so irrevocably outgrown. The final human opinion may, in short, in some manner now impossible to foresee, revert to the more personal style, just as any path of progress may follow a spiral rather than a straight line. If this were so, the rigorously impersonal view of science might one day appear as having been a temporarily useful eccentricity rather than the definitively triumphant position which the sectarian scientist at present so confidently announces it to be.

James would not be surprised that in the summer of 1971 newspaper readers were told that "researchers at the Menninger Foundation are training migraine headache sufferers to relieve their own pains by taking conscious control of the internal processes causing them." He certainly would not be surprised by the strong and passionate interest many of our well-to-do young have in Christ's life, in yoga, in communal living, in a contemplative life that contrasts sharply with the commercial and industrial ethic that so many of us hardly think to question. His book is, therefore, a strangely contemporary one; but at the same time his manner of looking at things, and most especially at the values and preferences of others, is no more commonly emulated today than one suspects was the case some seventy years ago. He sought the heart's reasons, and like Pascal he knew such a pursuit can never satisfy the mind's uneasy need for certainty. What is more, the serious pursuit of the subjective requires a certain generosity of spirit and open-mindedness, lest the personal and private become shrill and fanatic slogans, pushed self-righteously upon everyone around — all of which, as James well knew, makes for *one* variety of religious experience.

I first read James's book while in college, at the behest of Perry Miller, who as professor of American literature was endlessly fascinated by those high principled, cranky and utterly compelling New England ministers and theologians, even the ones who tried to disguise themselves as essayists and novelists. At the time Mr. Miller had to be a little apologetic; it would have been far easier to suggest Freud's *The Future of an Illusion* or *The God That Failed* — the former a pitiless and severely limited analysis of what drives us to church, the latter a series of confessions by disappointed Communists. (Outside the universities Norman Vincent Peale's *The Power of Positive Thinking* was a best-seller.) This summer, as I was going through *The Varieties of Religious Experience* again, I found I could now understand Perry Miller's need to apologize for assigning and spending so much time on William James's book. Set in the margins beside the clear, forthright, unpretentious prose were my snide, unbelieving remarks, my clever psychological interpretations, my quick dismissal of this or that, my exclamation marks here and there, all of it meant to show how sophisticated we in the twentieth century have become. Poor Perry Miller: as recently as the 1950s he had nothing to go on but a sense of history, a keen imagination that made him see in certain eccentric and possessed men of the cloth the stuff of unforgettable tragedy and strange, unsettling comedy. And poor us, his one-time smart and voluble students — unaware that not only the religious-minded have had "illusions," that the Marxist kind of sectarianism was but the latest in a long series, world without end it seems, and that (of all things) "positive thinking" would turn out to be, years later, not unlike in a number of respects the ethic of militant self-assertion and stubborn self-reliance some members of a "counterculture" advocate. As for William James, he might not mind if a little of our self-pity rubbed off on him, also. It was his peculiar genius to understand that what he, what the rest of us, still happen to call "religious experience" inevitably has to do with our moments of vanity — our wish to persuade ourselves that we have once and for all fathomed the mysteries of the universe, our desire to make our mark during that moment of eternity in which we appear and disappear. No wonder, then, the great psychologist and philosopher was worried; he had to face the fact that he had tried to fathom a few mysteries, and had made his mark upon a certain age. One can practically feel him worrying about himself as he writes so brilliantly and convincingly; one can practically hear him reminding himself: "Vanity of vanities, saith the Preacher, vanity of vanities; all is vanity." But he need not have worried; humility and gentleness grace just about every page of *The Varieties of Religious Experience* — an outcome he knew enough (knew enough about himself, and maybe all of us) never to take for granted.

The New Republic, 1971

23

THE STRANGE, EPIC LIFE AND WORK

OF KNUT HAMSUN

More than most writers, Knut Hamsun lived a strange, epic life. He was born in the eastern part of central Norway; his parents were farm people. But when he was 4 the family moved way up to the so-called Nordland part of their country — long stretches of dark, an outburst of triumphant sunlight, then the shadows once more. Hamsun had little formal education. As a youth, he worked the land, apprenticed with a cobbler, set out for Oslo, tried writing, but to no success; he endured extreme poverty, took odd jobs, wandered from village to village. By the age of 23 (in 1882), he was in America, exploring territory long congenial to his countrymen, the small towns of Wisconsin and Minnesota. But tuberculosis claimed him, and soon enough he was back in Norway, seemingly moribund.

He recovered, though. He returned to Oslo and a marginal life. He again thought of himself as a writer, but was unproductive. In 1886 he was back in America, more restless than ever. In Chicago he was a streetcar conductor; in the Dakotas he harvested wheat. He tried being a barber. He had done a stint in Norway as a fisherman, and he dreamed of going to the Newfoundland Banks and settling in for a life on boats, interrupted by brief port-city respites. But severe, unrelenting homesickness, and a disgust for what he saw as America's growing materialism, compelled a return to Europe.

Now he could write freely. His first published novel, *Hunger* (Norwegian publication, 1890) earned him immediate notice and substantial acclaim. It was unguardedly autobiographical; the narrator means to confront Norway's bourgeoisie with the original, shrewd, iconoclastic musings of a half-starved man living at the extreme edge of things. The plot is minimal; the development of character of no evident interest to the author, who comes across as a moralist at once strenuously critical of the fake, the pretentious, yet artful in his ability to win over potentially unfriendly readers themselves (more than likely) connected to the world being so toughly regarded.

Other novels followed — *Mysteries* in 1893 and *New Ground* and *Editor Yuge* in 1894. In them, as in a number of short stories, poems and plays, Hamsun was tirelessly the scold, ever ready to fix his wide-eyed glare upon ambitious intellectuals, greedy businessmen and those who enter high-minded professions, only to reveal themselves extortionate burghers. Nor was Scandinavia the sole object of unqualified derision. In *The Cultural Life of Modern America* he mocked the life he'd seen here, including what he believed to be the preposterous optimism of our 19th-century transcendentalists. For Hamsun, life on this side of the Atlantic was a source of private, saturnine speculation. His uncanny ability to spot the phony side of pietistic conformity made him a force to be reckoned with. But he could lose all balance and proportion; Oslo and Emerson's Concord alike became caricatures in his energetic hands — which could be as grasping as those of the capitalists or college professors he so repeatedly condemned.

A shift took place with the publication of *Pan* (1894) and *Victoria* (1898). The Nordic love story replaced politics, social satire, autobiography. For the first time his fiction offered intricate situations; he constructed complex, active figures, set them against a nature newly influential in his imaginative life: the mysterious forests, the bleak, rain-drenched countryside and the sea — its dangerous beauty, its constant temptation to a people who need its fish for survival. The Nobel Prize came to him in 1920, by which time he was increasingly conservative politically. (During World War II he became involved with the Nazis — a terribly sad ending to his life.)

Farrar, Straus & Giroux have been commissioning, one by one, translations of Hamsun's major novels, each rendered carefully, indeed. The latest is *Wayfarers*; it has a special place in a Hamsun chronology — and in a literature that might be described as Norwegian-American. The author was 67 when the book appeared in 1927; it was a tour de force — demonstrating new, unsuspected literary power in an old man seemingly ready to rest on his laurels. Hamsun returns to his earlier interest in America as a dubious haven for Scandinavia's poor, harassed and disenchanted. He draws on his knowledge and experience of Norway's fishing villages, constructs a vigorous yet melancholy romance, and uses the novel form, once again, but ever so subtly, to warn his countrymen of the dangers — the moral malaise, the craven self-centeredness — that can accompany industrial "progress."

James McFarlane, who gave us *Pan* in English a few years ago, is wonderful with Hamsun's lyrical prose. This is a long novel, for Hamsun, and full of ocean storms, desperately hard-working fishermen, fearful coastal villagers who know well the jeopardy of their lives. Through it all, there is the noble but increasingly tormented figure of Edevart, the protagonist — a personification, arguably, of Norway's peasant and seafaring yeomanry, which Hamsun saw to be bedeviled, ultimately, by the blandishments of both European and American secular materialism.

Edevart is, of course, the outcast and wanderer; the traveler whose journey becomes a pilgrimage — thereby enabling the novelist to view a given social scene. But Hamsun's prose never turns into a polemic; his images, his humor and sense of irony are the best ever. He is tighter than usual with his scenes. He is relaxed and gentle one minute, appropriately bitter or sad the next. We are offered a gruesome death (a roguish skipper enticed into a muddy bog), a number of sea interludes, such as a herring catch, a tenderly wrought love affair, and a good deal of mercantile trickery, all set against an austere, dramatically compelling Nordland landscape — fjords of provincial narrowness, but also of exalted dreams and touching, everyday reveries.

If Hamsun wrote in English or French he'd be much better known in this country. This novel, ironically, first appeared in English the same year, 1927, that gave us O. E. Rölvaag's comparatively familiar *Giants in the Earth*. They both mine a similar historical experience; but Rölvaag's emphasis is on the American prairie as a place of hope, for all the sacrifices exacted by fate, whereas Hamsun (unlike other Norwegian poets, Bjornson, Kieland, Jonas Lie, for instance, and the renowned Ibsen) portrayed our country as, ultimately, a kind of fantasy.

Wayfarers shows a proud, beaten people seeking through immigration an impossible release from the sinful constraints of this life, symbolized by the inscrutable, untamed Norwegian landscape. The hero Edevart is to cross the Atlantic, but the reader has been persuaded to expect little in consequence, and even an eventual return to Norway. *Wayfarers* also tells us that every hope and lust and ambition will, in time, meet a sly antagonist in fate, in accidents, in unyielding circumstance. Hamsun in this novel suggests an America of hardship and loneliness, best evoked visually by the South Dakota artist Harvey Dunn — not to mention Edvard Munch with his unnerving version of modern "psychological man." An initially picaresque story ends in fear, unrest, uncertainty — the "dread" so much 20th-century fiction aims to evoke.

The New York Times Book Review, 1980

24

FREUD AND GOD

Relatively unknown, and resident of a strongly Catholic city, Freud dared take on belief in God at a meeting in early March 1907 of the Vienna Psychoanalytical Society. He presented a paper with the title "Obsessive Actions and Religious Practices." Most of the observations were clinical — the work of a brilliant physician connecting instances from his practice into a narrative presentation meant to convey a theoretical point of view. But at the end, when Freud mentions "the sphere of religious life," a morally argumentative strain begins to appear. The reader is told that "complete backslidings into Sin are more common among pious people than among neurotics," an incautious generalization even then (despite the inhibitions Freud had noticed among "his" neurotics) and a quaintly unsupportable one now.

When Freud approaches "religious practices," he is intelligent and helpful to the kind of scholar who is not interested in debunking, but rather in understanding man's church-going history. The "petty ceremonials" of a given religion can, he points out, become tyrannical; they manage to "push aside the underlying thoughts." He sug-

gests that historically various "reforms" have been intended to re-
dress "the original balance" — rescue beliefs from arid pietism. But
in his concluding paragraphs Freud again makes a sweeping generalization, tries to join an analysis of psychopathology to social criticism. "One might venture to regard obsessional neurosis as a
pathological formation of a religion, and to describe that neurosis as
an individual religiosity and religion as a universal obsessional neurosis."

This is a kind of naïve and gratuitous reductionism we have seen
relentlessly pursued, these days, in the name of psychoanalysis.
Freud himself was often more careful. In the well-known essay
"Dostoievski and Patricide" he acknowledged the futility of a psychoanalytic "explanation" of a writer's talent, as opposed to any psychological difficulties he or she may happen to share with millions of
other human beings. When he risked social and political speculation
(in the exchange of letters with Einstein or in *The New Introductory
Lectures*), he could be guarded about using his ideas to interpret culture. Sometimes, even when writing about religious matters, as in
Totem and Taboo or *Moses and Monotheism*, he was frank about being
conjectural. In his first draft, completed in 1934, a book on the origins of monotheism was titled *The Man Moses, a Historical Novel*.

But religion clearly excited him to truculence, nowhere more evi-
dently than in *The Future of an Illusion* (1927). He starts out warning
himself to be objective, to summon a long-range historical view, to
be modest, restrained. Yet he quickly connects religious ideas to
man's obvious helplessness in the face of life's mysteries. He then
connects *that* condition to the child's predicament — "an infantile
prototype." After pointing out that there is no conclusive "proof," in
the word's modern scientific sense, of God's existence, he refers to
"the fairy tales of religion," and indicates with a rising vehemence
that religion is a mere illusion, "derived from human wishes." His
tone here is distinctly different from his other sociological writing.
He contrasts his line of argument ("correct thinking") to another
("lame excuse"). "Ignorance is ignorance," he reminds us, and adds
immediately, "no right to believe anything can be derived from it."
And then: "In other matters [than religion] no sensible person will
behave so irresponsibly or rest content with such feeble grounds for
his opinions." He declares that "the effect of religious thinking may

be likened to that of a narcotic," and that religion, "like the obsessional neurosis" he had described so vividly years earlier, "arose out of the Oedipus complex, out of the relation to the father."

To his great credit, he then pulls back, and acknowledges that "the pathology of the individual" does not provide a fully accurate analogy to the nature of religious faith, but he is soon referring to faith as "the consolation of religious illusion," and expressing the hope that in some future, when human beings have been "sensibly brought up," they will not have this "neurosis" — will "need no intoxicant to deaden it." Then, at the end, he embraces "our God, Logos," insists yet again that "religion is comparable to a childhood neurosis," and makes an invidious distinction between his stoic adherence to science, and those who look with faith to God: "My illusions are not, like religious ones, incapable of correction. They have not the character of delusion."

Philip Rieff, whose essays and books have been among the most learned and suggestive responses to Freud's writings, has been harsh about *The Future of an Illusion* and the kindred writing which preceded it. Rieff refers to Freud's "genetic disparagements of the religious spirit," and finds his reasoning tautological: "he will admit as religious only feelings of submission and dependence; others are dismissed as intellectual dilutions or displacements of the primary infantile sentiment." It is, Rieff says, "scientific name-calling," though in the service of a sincerely held modern rationalism.

Freudian psychologists have seldom challenged Freud's views as Rieff has done. But in 1979 Ana-Maria Rizzuto, who teaches at the Psychoanalytic Institute of New England, published a major study of the relation between psychiatry and faith, *The Birth of the Living God*. "The cultural stance of contemporary psychoanalysis," she begins, "is that of Freud: religion is a neurosis based on wishes. Freud has been quoted over and over again without considering his statements in a critical light." Examining her own experience as a psychoanalyst, she finds herself rejecting Freud's assertion that "God really *is* the father"; she also rejects his insistence that religion is a kind of oedipal offshoot — a "sublimation," a means by which erotic and aggressive feelings toward a particular man, the father, are given expression. Such an explanation, she argues, takes an extremely complicated and still continuing emotional and intellectual process and "reduces it to a representational fossil, freezing it at one exclusive level of development." And it incidentally denies mothers, grandparents, brothers, and sisters any substantial involvement in the emotional events that affect religious belief. Extremely preoccupied with "the father-son relationship" in his analysis of the psychology of religion, "Freud does not concern himself with religion or God in women."

The English psychoanalysts D. W. Winnicott, Charles Rycroft, and Harry Guntrip have obviously influenced this American psychoanalyst. Like them, she puts strong emphasis on the texture of "object relations": the mind as constantly responding to and reflecting involvements with a range of human beings, rather than the mind as a battlefield in which certain "agencies" fight things out with various maneuvers — in the hands of some psychoanalytic theorists, a kind of solipsism.

She seems especially influenced by Winnicott's revisions of Freud as a result of his work as a pediatrician and child psychoanalyst. He emphasized the significance of early months and years, when babies begin to distinguish *themselves* — the mother is there, and I am here — and when babies begin to show the distinctively human characteristic of symbolization. The first instance of that lifelong habit is known to all parents — those so-called "transitional objects" which mean so much to young children: a part of a blanket, a teddy bear, a doll, a spoon, an article of clothing, and later on, a certain song or story or scene. To be sure, even in the nursery, history, culture, class, and caste determine what "materials" are available; but Winnicott's work with infants casts a new light on their mental complexity and variability. Anywhere, any time, infants discover their very own world of word and thought, symbol and memory.

Winnicott did not find that adult ideas or inclinations were similar to a baby's mental stratagems. His point is that, early on, all children learn to carry with themselves ideas and feelings connected to persons, places, things — and these mental "representations" attest to nothing less or more than powerful human capacities. It would be foolish to *equate* a baby's attachment to a part of a blanket with a poet's use of synecdoche or a supplicant's attachment to Rosary beads, but there *is* a connection — as in that between incipient and full-fledged humanity rather than early and later psychopathology.

What analysts such as Winnicott or Rizzuto aim to document is a beginning effort at self-definition — through our thoughts and interests, likes and dislikes, fantasies and dreams, affections and involvements.

Dr. Rizzuto calls *one* of these efforts "God representation," referring to the notion about God that most of us in the West acquire early in life from what we hear at home, at school, in church, in the neighborhood playing lots. Even agnostics or atheists, she finds, have had ideas about God, given Him some private form — a mental picture, some words, a sound. In the lives of children, as parents know in one way, child psychiatrists in another, God joins company with all sorts of kings, generals, superheroes, witches, monsters, demons, friends, brothers and sisters, parents, teachers, policemen, firemen, and on and on. Dr. Rizzuto offers histories of His presence in the minds of people who firmly call themselves nonbelievers. She points out that God may be someone rejected, denied, ridiculed as well as embraced, relied upon constantly — and that each of those psychological attitudes can be connected to the constraints and opportunities (and good luck and bad luck) of a given life. Her interests, in this regard, are not clinical or categorically judgmental. She is writing as a phenomenological psychologist.

II

Freud continually returned to the idea of God; he wrote about His origin in the minds of others, devoted numerous articles and three books to Him. Why? Not necessarily to work out a "problem." As did Winnicott, Rizzuto sees religious ideas as part of our cultural life — like music, art, literature, or for that matter, formal intellectual reasoning and scientific speculation. They are all connected to our endless effort to place ourselves in space and time, to figure out where we come from and what we are and where we're going. In a touching statement at the end of her book she arrives at the point where her "departure from Freud is inevitable." Great as her daily professional loyalty and obligation are to him, she writes:

> Freud considers God and religion a wishful childish illusion. He wrote asking mankind to renounce it. I must disagree. Reality and

illusion are not contradictory terms. Psychic reality — whose depth Freud so brilliantly unveiled — cannot occur without that specifically human transitional space for play and illusion . . . Asking a mature, functioning individual to renounce his God would be like asking Freud to renounce his own creation, psychoanalysis, and the 'illusory' promise of what scientific knowledge can do. This is, in fact, the point. Men cannot be men without illusions. The type of illusion we select — science, religion, or something else — reveals our personal history — the transitional space each of us has created between his objects and himself to find a 'resting place' to live in.

In her view it is in the nature of human beings, from early childhood until the last breath, to sift and sort, and to play, first with toys and games and teddy bears and animals, then with ideas and words and images and sounds and notions. We never stop trying to touch base with significant others, to settle upon some satisfying idea of who and what we ourselves are, to build a world that is ours — with blocks or bricks or iron, with money and signatures of ownership, with acts of affirmation and loyalty and affiliation, with outbursts of meanness and rancor, with mental images, and not least, with theories saying the life we live should go one way or another.* Dr. Rizzuto should be clearer about how we ought to analyze and evaluate the different "illusions" she refers to. The history of science is in large part the demonstration of illusion; and if "reality and illusion are not contradictory terms," they are not the same, either. And, of course, some of us are willing and able to be more skeptical of the beliefs in which we've invested our hopes and wishes. With respect to the activities or beliefs in which we invest hope or feeling, we differ in the degree of skeptical scrutiny we may be willing or able to apply to them. Nevertheless, this book, one assumes, will not be

---

*The political implications of that mental activity are obviously enormous. Even elementary school children use presidents and prime ministers and kings and dictators, and not least, the flag, in a continuing effort to establish loyalties, preferences, a sense of place, affiliation and purpose. And, of course, our political leaders reciprocate — try to connect themselves (their names, faces, messages and slogans) with the personal as well as material aspirations of as many people as possible.

smugly classified as evidence of someone's "psychopathology," a practice that has been all too much a part of the contemporary, bourgeois Western world, for which psychoanalysis itself has been so useful in establishing, interestingly enough, a version of the saved and the damned.

A psychoanalyst has wanted to demonstrate the universality of an element of mental function. She need not at all have summoned the polarity of "reality" as against "illusion"; and did so, actually, because Freud had repeatedly thrown that either/or gauntlet down to his readers and followers. What she means she states better when she refers to a "capacity" each of us has and indulges — "to symbolize, fantasize and create super-human beings"; or when she describes the role that fantasy has in the lives of people: a means by which they (meaning, again, every single one of us) "moderate their longings for objects, their fears, their poignant disappointment with their limitations." A baby uses its eyes with the "longings" Dr. Rizzuto mentions, and we adults, babes in the woods of a universe whose enormity and mystery and frustrations are only too obvious, do likewise. The word "theory" is derived from *Oewpía*, which refers to the act of looking and seeing — as in the spectator at a religious ceremonial, or as in examining portents, or as in scanning the sky to figure out what is going on, what will happen next. Theorists assemble facts to help us look with a little less anguish at enigmas often enough impenetrable. Not because we are sick, or uneducated, or naïve, but in response to our nature as human beings, we elaborate upon factuality: "The objects we so indispensably need are never themselves alone, they combine the mystery of their reality and our fantasy."

What does Dr. Rizzuto mean by that crucial statement? She is saying, in the tradition of Winnicott and others, that facts may be stated independently, as in a chemical equation, a physics formula, a finding by a psychologist about rat behavior on a maze, an observation by a psychoanalyst that people who do X have had, to a significant degree, a Y kind of childhood — but the matter doesn't rest there. Skinner takes his behaviorist laboratory findings and constructs of them stories, recommendations on child rearing, utopian suggestions — notions of how to live a life. And Steven Weinberg, in a lovely book, *The First Three Minutes,* uses his work in theoretical physics to give us "a modern view of the origin of the universe."

Wonderfully, he starts with an old Norse myth about that "origin," yet ends up with his own candid surmise, his own effort to deal with the "uncertainties" he keeps on mentioning. "It is almost irresistible," he tells us, "for humans to believe that we have some special relation to the universe, that human life is not just a more-or-less farcical outcome of a chain of accidents reaching back to the first three minutes" [when this universe may have begun, so his *facts* have prompted him to *speculate* or *fantasize,* the latter verb used nonpejoratively]. A little later on he observes that "the more the universe seems comprehensible, the more it also seems pointless."

Dr. Rizzuto knows, from her work with children, that they, too, struggle with just such a sense of things — and can be heard saying so again and again. Witches emerge from the desire of boys and girls to understand life's cruel arbitrariness. Witches are discarded for Satan — and yes, for notions such as a "drive" called "aggression," or what Freud called Thanatos. It is not necessarily "neurotic" for a child to talk of witches, nor is it necessarily "immature" or, again, "neurotic" for an adult religious person to summon Satan, or for Freud to talk of a "primal horde" or a "totem" or of Thanatos — examples of *his* move from fact-finding to the kind of rumination Dr. Rizzuto refers to: an exploratory play of the mind characteristic of all of us, though of course it varies in symbolic complexity and content, or too, in clarity or pretentiousness. (Freud himself once referred to his "mythological theory of instincts.") From Plato's *Timaeus* to Professor Weinberg's essay, from Egyptian stories to the modern day notion of "black holes," man's cosmological yearnings have found in various facts, or in ancient geometry or contemporary physics, a means for — what? Not illusion, maybe, strictly defined, but a little help in knowing what this life is about, or as Winnicott and Rizzuto would have it, a little help in gaining a sense of greater proximity to the heart of the matter, namely, the particular "objects," or symbols of them, which we have learned to regard, with good reason, as literally life-giving, then life supporting. The issue is not, though, a "regressive" tendency; the issue is the nature of our human predicament, no matter our age — *and* the way our mind deals with that predicament, from the earliest years (child analysts have observed) to the final breath.

That is why it is particularly ironic and dismaying to find both Freudian and Marxist thought so arrogantly abusive when the subject of religion comes up. True, religious thought, like everything else, has lent itself to tyranny and exploitation. But so has Marxist thought, Freudian thought. The clarity of Marx the economist and historian (the facts, or speculations tied closely to them) become the futurist "fantasies" of a supposedly (one day) "withering" entity called "the dictatorship of the proletariat." Talk about opium — and ingested not by gullible peasants but by all too theoretical advocates of "dialectical materialism." The clarity of Freud the clinician and historian of lives became the "movement" called psychoanalysis, with special rings given to a few anointed ones, with sectarian argument, with "schools" and splits and expulsions, with references by analysts themselves to "punitive orthodoxy." A century that has seen Lenin's Mausoleum, pictures of Karl Marx waved before the leaders of the Gulag, Freud fainting in the arms of Jung, and postponing for years a trip to Rome, even as he immersed himself in accounts of Hannibal's life, and turned heatedly on this, then that colleague, cannot be considered a stranger to what Dr. Rizzuto has described: among the most brilliant and decent of individuals, those most determined to explore "reality," one or another fantasy, if not illusion, will take deep root, often getting worked into something called a theory.

III

Dr. Rizzuto's understanding of Freud's battle with religion is not quite that of the contemporary Catholic theologian, Hans Kung. In his recent Terry lectures at Yale, published as *Freud and the Problem of God* (1979), Father Kung deals with Freud's religious preoccupations rather more gingerly than Dr. Rizzuto has done. He takes pains to acknowledge the Catholic anti-Semitism Freud had to contend with, and he spells out what he calls "ecclesiogenic neuroses" — the result of a prudish, overbearing Church. "Over the centuries," he acknowledges, "the churches have acted like a superego: dominating souls in the name of God, exploiting the dependence and immaturity of poor sinners, requiring submission to the taboos of untested authority, continually repressing sexuality and displaying contempt for women (in the law of celibacy, in excluding women from church ministries)." His is a sweeping denunciation of Catholic rigidity rendered in the name of a late 20th-century (second Vatican Council) Catholic humanism. (This part of his book recalls his *On Being a Christian,* in which some of the same points were made at substantially greater length.)

At times Kung sounds like Freud. He describes the religion of many people as "a return to infantile structure," or "a regression to childish wishing"; further, he calls attention to "the Churches' misuse of power." As a social and cultural critic, Freud was often right, Kung says: "How abundant are the examples of arrogance or power and misuse of power in the history of the churches: intolerance and cruelty toward deviationists, crusades, inquisition, extermination of heretics, obsession with witches, struggle against theological research, oppression of their own theologians — right up to the present time."

Such thoughts are sweet music to the ear of many critics of the church, and they are not often heard from Catholic theologians. He thanks Freud for the very real help psychoanalysis offers ministers and priests in their daily work, is grateful to Jung, who deigned to grant us a "religious need," and who generously declared God "psychologically existent"; and to Adler, who, seeing God as a handy ally in a theoretical battle with Freud, wrote:

> The idea of God and its immense significance for mankind can be understood and appreciated from the viewpoint of Individual Psychology as concretization and interpretation of the human recognition of greatness and perfection, and as commitment of the individual as well as of society to a goal which rests in man's future and which in the present heightens the driving force by enhancing the feelings and emotions.

The fuzzy and inspirational tone here — the opposite of Freud's scientific pessimism — is shared by other psychologists. Kung summons as witness Erich Fromm, for instance, who reassures us that "the attitude — religious in the widest sense of the term — of wonder, of rapture, and of becoming one with the universe, is found also in psychoanalysis." The psychoanalytic process, Fromm writes, is one "of breaking through the barriers of the conscious ego and of contact with the hitherto-excluded unconscious, advancing toward a surrender to a framework of orientation which transcends the individual, to an unconditional assent to life."

We not only have a "religious need"; we have, again, a "need" to invest our observations, as did Jung his, with our various hopes and fears, with our mind's associative and symbolic nature, its daily insistence upon our moment-by-moment trains of thought — and by night, our dreams. Kung calls upon psychoanalysis to help him criticize Catholic history, Catholic religious reality — forgetting that much of what he finds unacceptable in Rome was to be found not only in Freud's Viennese world but Jung's Zurich world: rigidity, arrogance, pettiness, or legalistic fractiousness. And when Kung starts using normative judgments ("maturity" or "childish wishing"), he is on dangerously thin ice. For just the reasons Dr. Rizzuto has made clear, it is sadly inappropriate for a Catholic theologian to use psychoanalysis as a means of name calling. And we may have a clue, here, about what is now going on between Rome and Kung. He doesn't like some of the meditative fantasies (again, absolutely no pejorative implication intended) that the Pope, the Cardinals, and millions of Catholics find congenial, and they don't like his way of seeing things — regarding what they believe. In all such shared reveries or "beliefs" (political, scientific, religious) there are felt limits by those involved. At a certain point, for instance, it is possible for a psychoanalyst to shift thinking to such a degree (from, say, notions of "id" or "super-ego," to those of "drive" and "conditioning and learning"), to the point that colleagues, as well as men of power in professional societies, begin to wonder about a particular intellectual commitment, and *especially* if a newly embraced terminology gets used invidiously — as in the phrase King uses: "childish wishing." Needless to say, the point is not that Kung or anyone else ought to abstain from taking a tough critical look at the Vatican, its past and present shortcomings, its moral vulnerability — as well documented, actually, in this century, by such grave Catholic writers as Georges Bernanos and François Mauriac. But Kung is so busy criticizing the psychological development of his religious brethren, he seems to have lost sight of the feisty, theoretical possessiveness, narrowness or truculence that Marxists or Freudians, in *their* humanity, have demonstrated.

From Fromm, Kung learned that there are two kinds of psychoanalysts — some "adjustment advisors," but also another kind: "for them the primary goal is the 'cure of the soul,' that is, the optimal development of a person's potentialities, the realization of his individuality and of his moral and intellectual integrity in the unfolding of a fruitful affirmation of life and of love." Such talk is not, alas, meant (by Fromm or Kung) in any sardonic, or even ironic sense. One can sense the glee in the Curia — *this* is what we have to gain from these secular liberal movements! Nor is Kung more convincing when he describes how "an authentic regression," supposedly to "infantile" behavior or thinking, can be facilitated by faith. "A regression rightly understood, with the aid of certain religious practices (prayer, worship, examination of conscience, confession), can be supremely helpful for a healthy person and can smooth the path to progression and maturity, inasmuch, that is, as he reexperiences, positively assimilates, and reintegrates into his self-identification what has been forgotten or repressed."

Kung is offering what Flannery O'Connor called a "stomach full of liberal religion." Dr. Rizzuto, in contrast, wants to make it clear that hers "is not a book on religion." The sociologist Peter Berger in his recent book *The Social Reality of Religion* similarly excludes "questions of the ultimate truth or illusion of religious propositions about the world." They seem to be saying that psychological and sociological analyses are not meant to tell us whether or not God exists; are not meant to serve as arbiters on the nature of faith, grace, and transcendence. Everyone's ideas and beliefs have a psychological and sociological history: the liberal's, the conservative's, the radical's, the agnostic's, the atheist's, the convinced mystic's, the half-believing, half-doubting churchgoer's. To explore that history is one thing; to use the exploration as a means of insisting on philosophical, theological, or moral conclusions is quite another matter. Every psychoanalyst would presumably accept that there is a psychological explanation of his or her choice of vocation (voyeurism, narcissism, and on and on), as well as sociological ones — membership in one or another family, class, ethnic group. But what analyst would allow such explanations wholly to determine a judgment on the essential nature, meaning, and worth of his or her work?

Both Winnicott and Rizzuto connect our religious thinking to the kind of thinking we do, from the time of childhood to the time of old age, as the aware creature who hungers for an answer to the well-known question: what is the meaning of life? The history of philosophy and theology is, to a significant degree, the history of proposed answers to that question — even as psychoanalysts observe the nature of one person's, then another person's fantasies, connected to the "objects" that were once "incorporated" as enduring "representations" to which, directly or indirectly (symbolically), we continually appeal for reassurance.

IV

In a recent book, *The God of the Philosophers* (1979), Anthony Kenny shows how certain ideas "propounded by scholastic theologians and rationalist philosophers" don't fit the demands of logic — omniscience and omnipotence, for instance:

> If God is to be omniscient, I have argued, then he cannot be immutable. If God is to have infallible knowledge of future human actions, then determinism must be true. If God is to escape responsibility for human wickedness, then determinism must be false. Hence in the notion of a God who foresees all sins but is the author of none, there lurks a contradiction. Omnipotence may perhaps be capable in isolation, of receiving a coherent formulation; but omnipotence, while capable of accounting for some historic doctrines of predestination, is inadequate as a foundation for divine foreknowledge of undetermined human conduct. There cannot, if our argument has been sound, be a timeless, immutable, omniscient, omnipotent, all-good being.

But no matter what other religious philosophers would say, in reply, Dr. Rizzuto would simply point out that the attribution of those qualities (omniscience and omnipotence) is, obviously, something human beings have always done, in order to gain just the kind of mental and physical mastery those two words omniscience and omnipotence suggest. But we do so not necessarily because we are "superstitious" or in need of a psychiatrist. We do so as Steven Weinberg did, as Freud did, and yes, as plenty of ordinary human beings do all the time: "I'll be standing there on that assembly line, and my mind will wander, and I'll be asking myself why, a thousand why's, about the reason things happen, and what the future has in store, and just about everything. I remember asking my mother and father how we got here in the first place, and damn if my kids don't ask me, and I don't know — but I still ask myself. I even picture my mother and dad sitting near our old Philco radio, and I'm talking with them; and then I'll be out in our yard with my kids, and we're talking — and meanwhile I keep up with that conveyer belt! I add my 25¢ to the Ford Motor Company!"

Ultimately (even for theoretical physicists or psychoanalysts or proponents of dialectical materialism), what Kenny and others before him have called "The God of Reason" merges, *in one way or another*, with an imaginative, symbolic, fantasying life that becomes a kind of upheld "faith"; and the "reason" for *that* outcome is connected, as Kenny states, to our *situation*, rather than our personal "problems":

> There is no reason why someone who is in doubt about the existence of God should not pray for help and guidance on this topic as in other matters. Some find something comic in the idea of an agnostic praying to a God whose existence he doubts. It is surely no more unreasonable than the act of a man adrift in the ocean, trapped in a cave, or stranded on a mountainside, who cries for help though he may never be heard or fires a signal which may never be seen.
>
> Such prayer seems rational whether or not there is a God; whether, if there is a God, it is pleasing to him or conducive to salvation is quite another question.

To which Winnicott and Rizzuto, not to mention the philosophical novelist Walker Percy, would add something like this: we are the creatures who recognize ourselves as "adrift" or as "trapped" or as "stranded," or as in some precarious relationship to this world; and as users of language, we are the ones who not only take in the world's "objects" but build them up in our mind, and use them (through thoughts and fantasies) to keep from feeling alone, and to use Kenny's imagery, to gain for ourselves a sense of where we came from and where we are and where we're going, lest we feel rudderless, at a dead end, or hopelessly out of touch.*

Kung deplores "Protestant biblicism and Catholic traditionalism" for their attitudes toward science. He admires Freud's "critical rationality." He wants "dialogic cooperation" with 20th-century empirical minds. In case we want specific warnings, he offers this broadside:

> For we can see in connection with Pascal, Jansenism, Kierkegaard, and Barth how often Christians and theologians have been in danger of devaluing the conclusions of reason, in order to revalue faith — a specific form of hostility to reason which does not seem in any way to be required by Christian faith. Must we cease to be philosophers and scholars in order truly to believe in God? Did not Pascal, Kierkegaard, and Barth allow faith to overwhelm reason in this way?

It is something of an irony that Dr. Rizzuto, a psychoanalyst who for the most part protests loyalty to Freud, has understood better how to criticize Freud's view of religion than a theologian who expresses great admiration for what various psychoanalytic theorists insist on telling us about God. As for Kierkegaard, one could wish that Kung would confront his reasoning in the electrifying essay on "The Difference Between a Genius and an Apostle." It is a "differ-

---

*Simone Weil struggled long and hard with her own mind's considerable capacity to speculate about the world. The sections on "Illusions," "Idolatry" and "Decreation," in *Gravity and Grace* show her shrewdly aware of how anxious we are to use reverie and fancy in order to catch hold of meaning — and not only, she insisted, the uneducated or the overly emotional. Her fierce espousal of "decreation," awesomely severe and frightening even to many of those who love her ideas, can be regarded as an all but impossible attempt to remove what she felt to be the barriers of the imagination from her contemplation of God. She is, in contrast, much more relaxed about her (and everyone else's) imagination when she writes about science and its connection to our fantasy life — in, for instance, "Classical Science and After."

ence" that Dr. Rizzuto and Professors Berger and Kenny know well. It is a difference that has to do with the use and limitations of the intellect.

Kierkegaard says that a genius and an apostle are "qualitatively different." The former is pursuing an intellectual or aesthetic inquiry with the greatest of distinction. The latter is on an errand: "No genius has an *in order that:* the Apostle has absolutely and paradoxically, an *in order that*." Those last words of the essay (italics Kierkegaard's) have to do with faith of the kind Kenny describes — faith connected to a perceived situation or predicament, whether localized at sea, in a cave, up a mountain. In matters of the meaning of life and death, some gather the best facts available — if with the imaginative elaborations mentioned earlier; others turn explicitly to prayer and stop talking about ideas or theories. Here is Kierkegaard saying it his way:

> That is how the errors of science and learning have confused Christianity. The confusion has spread from learning to the religious discourse, with the result that one not infrequently hears priests, bona fide, in all learned simplicity, prostituting Christianity. They talk in exalted terms of St. Paul's brilliance and profundity, of his beautiful similes and so on — that is mere aestheticism. If St. Paul is to be regarded as a genius, then things look black for him, and only clerical ignorance would ever dream of praising him in terms of aesthetics, because it has no standard, but argues that all is well so long as one says something good about him.

For Kierkegaard, the God of Faith is not available to us through factual analysis or presentation, however gifted the genius making the attempt. For Rizzuto, the "difference" Kierkegaard mentions is not so absolute; we successfully see larger and larger elements of the world (by means of rationality, logic, the work of various "geniuses"); but we also embark on quite other (subjective, existential, teleologically or cosmologically speculative) lines of mental activity. In any event, speaking of "aestheticism," one can imagine the contempt Kierkegaard would feel for some of the stupid talk, the dreary banalities that have become the proud property of 20th-century "psychological man" — a contempt, one imagines, not unlike Philip

Rieff's, and perhaps a contempt Freud himself would feel, were he to be given a chance to take a look at what has happened in his name.

Barth, also, was not one to need a defense. Like Kung, he visited America to give university lectures, in 1962, and thereafter put them into a book, *Evangelical Theology,* at the beginning of which he made the following observation — not to dethrone reason, but simply to describe what happens time and again, and may even happen to the work of Hans Kung:

> Ever since the fading of its illusory splendour as a leading academic power during the Middle Ages, theology has taken too many pains to justify its own existence. It has tried too hard, especially in the nineteenth century, to secure for itself at least a small but honorable place in the throne room of general science. This attempt at self-justification has been no help to its own work. The fact is that it has made theology, to a great extent, hesitant and halfhearted; moreover, this uncertainty has earned theology no more respect for its achievements than a very modest tip of the hat.

Pascal, the physicist and mathematician, struggled hard and knowingly with the issue of science and religion. Freud's *The Future of an Illusion* can be read as a footnote to his *Pensées* and *Provincial Letters,* and it is a scandal that Kung doesn't choose to recognize the power of Pascal's analysis of religious faith. What Kierkegaard and Barth knew, what Pascal, before them, made preeminently clear, is the difference between a consideration of man and nature (scientific inquiry), and a consideration of God: intellectually through theology, but also through the various mental motions of a life — not just the awareness of prayers or the commitment of energy to rituals of church attendance, but a day-to-day attentiveness (including the fantasies and reveries, the symbolic *work* Rizzuto and Winnicott describe) that touches all spheres of activity, and is best characterized, with regard to its nature, by the Latin phrase *sub specie aeternitatis.* Pascal puts it this matter-of-fact way: "Therefore, those to whom God has imparted religion by intuition are very fortunate, and justly convinced. But to those who do not have it, we can give it only by reasoning, waiting for God to give them spiritual insight, without which faith is only human, and useless for salvation."

Such a comment, part of the 282nd pensée, is a recognition that for some men and women there comes a point at which the issue is not knowledge, not even asserted and analyzed belief, but really, what Pascal calls "spiritual insight," a quite distinct kind of psychology, put in the service of a particular exertion of love; maybe in Dr. Rizzuto's words, a love for "a living God" — for, that is, a particular "representation" which (Who) rescues us, so we fervently hope and pray, from our otherwise absurd condition. For Hans Kung, one assumes, that God was the one who entered history, Jesus of Nazareth. For Hans Kung, one assumes, the earthly institution, for all its flaws, entrusted to give that love a continuing setting, so to speak, is the Holy Roman Catholic Church. It is a Church for whose thousands of priests and nuns it comes surely as no great surprise that we all work facts into our imaginative constructions; that reason can turn to faith, be it religious or secular; and that part of our love life is a cosmological passion connected to no small measure of felt (existential) desperation. Dr. Rizzuto, one suspects, would find Pascal's *Pensées* more congenial than Kung seems to; they would be, for her, yet additional examples of the kind of rapt and suggestive contemplation she has seen so repeatedly in the lives she has studied — lives that belong to particular boys and girls, men and women, who are all on a decidedly perplexing journey, and who, as they plunge on, are trying to figure and sort out, the way Pascal tried to do, the various requirements of the head and heart.

The Virginia Quarterly Review, 1981

25

HARRY STACK SULLIVAN

In the course of an important lecture delivered at the New York Psychoanalytic Institute on April 16, 1968 ("Difficulties in the Path of Psychoanalysis"), Anna Freud commented on the "personalities" of those men and women "who, by self-selection became the first generation of psychoanalysts." She described such individuals, with her usual mixture of tact and directness, as "the unconventional ones, the doubters, those who were dissatisfied with the limitations imposed on knowledge." Then she added further particulars: "Also among them were the odd ones, the dreamers, and those who knew neurotic suffering from their own experience." Surely Harry Stack Sullivan, who would be 90 were he alive today, belongs in the above-mentioned company, as his biographer Helen Swick Perry is quick to indicate in this substantial, readable account [*Psychiatrist of America*] of an exceptionally gifted American psychiatrist's life.

Without question, Sullivan was a controversial figure in Washington and New York in the late 1920's and 1930's. He was forever pushing the limits of his profession, and so doing, he acquired both followers and opponents. He was also forever revealing contradictory inclinations or points of view. He wanted his colleagues to be less connected with the rich, the powerful; yet he was himself a man of expensive tastes, and he had some extremely influential and well-heeled patients. (He also went bankrupt during the Great Depression, partly because he was careless about money and was at times a spendthrift.) He emphasized the importance of dependable, trustworthy friendships in human affairs, yet was himself so often a guarded, distant figure. He saw early on that the psychoanalytic "movement" had a political and religious character — the sectarian strife, the dogmatism that, for a while, caused so much pain and suspicion among so many psychiatrists. Yet he was not above lobbying his colleagues, helping to build alternative institutions (such as the Washington School of Psychiatry) and waging a good old-fashioned professional fight. He was, finally, an uncanny if not unnerving mix of the humble and the charismatic.

As Mrs. Perry makes clear, Sullivan to the very end of his life involved himself in America's social conflicts and political struggles. He was one of the first psychoanalysts to pay serious attention to the ordeal of blacks in both the South and our northern metropolitan areas. He went South in the late 1930's to observe life there, on both sides of the color line. He treated life there, on both sides of the color line. He treated black patients, among them the dancer Katherine Dunham. In 1936 he gave a job (file clerk and receptionist at his office in Manhattan, where he then practiced) to the young Ralph Ellison, newly arrived from Alabama's Tuskegee Institute. Sullivan was one psychiatrist who knew that poverty and injustice could undo even fairly solid minds; could make decent, honorable and conscientious men and women become apprehensive, doubtful of their worth; could prompt aberrant, mean-spirited, even criminal behavior. And after Hiroshima he was quick to see what the stakes were: an end to world wars, such as this century has twice witnessed, or the likely end of countless millions of lives. He died in Europe (of a stroke) in 1949, working feverishly on behalf of a kind of human understanding and solidarity that would transcend nationalist constraints; he was talking to psychiatrists all over the Continent in a prophetic effort to enlist their opposition to any further use of nuclear bombs.

Mrs. Perry worked with Sullivan in his last years, when he had become recognized the world over as a brilliant clinician, especially for his knowledge of the mental life of schizophrenics. She helped Sullivan edit *Psychiatry,* long regarded as a haven of sorts for restless social scientists — anthropologists, sociologists, psychologists and psychiatrists, who have dared to territoriality and who have wanted to address a general as well as a professional audience with a reasonable level of literary accomplishment. In her introductory remarks, she does exactly what Sullivan would have suggested: declare frankly the nature of their collegial work, then indicate the social and cultural influences they shared — a New York state, rural, working-class background. Here is Mrs. Perry, not yet 10 paragraphs into her prologue, writing about a trip she took during her research for the book: "Near evening, after a drafty, cheerless day, I scribbled on a piece of paper I found in my pocketbook: 'Evening falls like a Hardy novel — sad, with brave little lights. This is mid-April, the farms of central New York. This train might be fifty years ago — it has gone backward. I feel this loneliness through me, but it is real and edgy and existence.' "

She was at the time trying to find out whether Sullivan had experienced psychiatric hospitalization, and if so, where and when. The answer seems to be yes, but otherwise we get few specifics. One of Sullivan's traits was a fearful secretiveness, the other side of his disarming, sometimes truculent candor. He covered the tracks of his youthful psychiatric turmoil rather well. Mrs. Perry also made a conscientious effort to figure out the nature of Sullivan's sexual life. She handles that subject gingerly, maybe too much so. She tells us he never married and notes his sexual shyness with women. But a previous (and quite admiring) biographer, the psychiatrist A. H. Chapman, with far less research under his belt, felt it important to discuss openly Sullivan's episodic homosexuality.

Many psychiatrists have wondered about Sullivan's relative anonymity in a culture excessively preoccupied with psychiatrists and what they have to say. Mrs. Perry herself speculates on this strange anomaly: "A psychiatrist [Leston Havens] of another generation who never knew Sullivan personally has defined Sullivan as secretly dominating much of clinical psychiatry as it existed in

America in 1970: 'Nothing is more ludicrous about modern American psychiatric writing than our ability to use Sullivan's observation, ideas, and techniques without even mentioning his name. He would have felt like a bastard at the family reunion.' " Perhaps that "family" is composed of secular bourgeois Americans for whom "normal" has the standing of Heaven, and "abnormal" of Hell. If so, a doctor who has experienced both craziness and queerness would be a distinct embarrassment, a kind of fallen priest, no matter what Miss Freud had to say, and no matter what the extraordinary breadth and depth of Sullivan's insights for a generation of therapists.

Sullivan was bold and resourceful. He took on the hardest, most forlorn people — the young and seriously deteriorated schizophrenics — and paid them the closest heed, often becoming, he dared admit, thoroughly immersed in what amounted to the collective madness of back ward hospital life. Doctors such as himself, he came to realize (and nurses, attendants and all others who work with psychotic patients) will not get very far as aloof diagnosticians, or as austere if zealous practitioners of one or another "therapeutic approach." Doctors are, he stressed, "participant observers," wittingly and willingly or not. The issue is how openly they come first to understand their position as what he called a "significant other," then to use it. These days, needless to say, those expressions have become thoroughly familiar, even elements of a cultural banality, as has been the case with many of Freud's phrases and ideas. But in the 1920's, when Sullivan was working at St. Elizabeth's Hospital in Washington and then at The Sheppard and Enoch Pratt Hospital not far away in Maryland, comparatively little was understood about the ways severely agitated people manage, day in and day out, with the various people they happen to meet.

Moreover, the direction of psychoanalytic theory had always been inward, so to speak — deeper and deeper into the unconscious. Freud had a keen sense of history and could be shrewd about social and cultural matters. But the thrust of his work, both as a theorist and a clinician, made for a kind of isolation — the patient on the couch, with even the analyst out of sight, and with all those "associations" carrying both speaker and listener further and further back in time, away from the here and now. Even the strong feelings generated by psychoanalysis are predominantly seen (on the part of both analyst and analysand) as phantoms — the consequence of earlier attachments and experiences given a new lease on life.

Sullivan, an early member of the Washington psychoanalytic community, did not take issue with this view of mental life or of what happens in the course of psychoanalysis. His work with psychotic men and women showed him every day how influential the unconscious was, how persuasive our early memories are, over the long haul of his life, and how inclined we are to merge in our minds those we get to know as adults with earlier figures in our life. What he struggled to achieve, however, for and with his highly disturbed patients was some manner of not only understanding but control, which had to be earned gradually — through healing exchanges with doctors, yes, but also with a whole world of people, events, activities. The mental hospital had to become a community whose guiding notion was that "therapy" was not something obtained only in an hour, but all through a person's stay in a given setting.

Sullivan's language was not inspired and was sometimes terribly murky. He talked and wrote of "interpersonal relationships," of "security operations," of "self-systems." He lacked Freud's (and Anna Freud's) talent for rendering an uncluttered convincing narrative prose. But he was a passionate phenomenologist, anxious at all times to observe actual human behavior. He pictured us as not only besieged by "drives" or "instincts," but also exceedingly anxious to placate or win over our fellow creatures. He assumed that even utterly loony behavior made complete sense — as an effort to appease some shadowy yet compelling "other" who may be long dead, yet alive in dreams or brief reveries, quickly forgotten. He showed that psychoanalysis had something to offer psychotics as well as neurotics.

His insistence upon human particularity and complexity, his refusal to settle for psychological determinism, his emphasis on the unpredictable, his effort to find hidden reservoirs of ability and promise in even the most disturbed and seemingly hopeless of patients earned him deep respect from those — Frieda Fromm Reichmann, for example — who knew how hard and long the treatment of psychotics can be. He anticipated the importance of much that achieved widespread recognition many years after his death — for example, the notion of paying attention not only to the learned symptoms of a child or an adult, but to the ways an entire family manages. He was also a genius of the symbolic detail — the habit, the interest, the preferred article of clothing, the favored expression, the gesture or mannerism that can both conceal and reveal so much about a person's life. His case histories are full of scrupulously observed incidents that reveal a novelist's sensibility. He appreciated the drama of plain, ordinary living; he applauded the everyday as the best approach to an under-standing of the larger questions about human nature that continue to puzzle us.

He also had a strong interest in the social sciences and was a close friend of Edward Sapir, Harold Lasswell, Erich Fromm, Ruth Bene-dict. He dreamed of a time when he could work full time with such individuals and learn from them what he knew he needed to learn about the way human beings get along. On the other hand, he was ever the critic. He saw all research studies as a kind of activism — with the researcher as someone who changes his or her observed world — and he ridiculed the notion of, say, an anthropologist's col-lecting "data" in a village, supremely indifferent to the thoughts and questions he or she prompts in "them," located in that mysterious site called the "field."

Sullivan's life, so long nervously ignored or the subject of gossip, is rescued in this touching portrayal, at once appreciative and, when necessary, dispassionate. Mrs. Perry does well to make much of his American rural heritage. His family unfortunately learned gradually to shed their Irish Catholicism, to embrace the fierce, hardworking, ornery stoicism of the American Protestant yeomanry — including its irregular lineaments, best evoked by Theodore Dreiser, Sher-wood Anderson and Willa Cather. The Sullivan family could easily have lived in Winesburg, Ohio. But there was another side to this son of New York's Chenango County, its bleak hardscrabble landscape a part of the Appalachian foothills. He was an American psychiatrist in the tradition of our mythic exceptionalism — everyone supposedly by rights different, if not a loner before God and/or nature. His ma-jor intellectual ancestor was Emerson, with his determined opti-mism; another spiritual kinsman was certainly John Dewey.

Sullivan was his own kind of American adventurer. He was constantly exploring lives, discovering the importance of this, then that academic discipline. His eyes saw a frontier of hurt people waiting to be helped. Surely they could be, they would be helped — in this New World where, after all, everyone is supposed to have or get his or her chance. Helped toward what ultimate purpose, or toward whom? Sullivan was not one for such questions — which obsessed Freud (his declared atheism not withstanding, hence his nagging, argumentative skepticism and his ambitious discourses on such diverse moralists as Moses, Dostoyevsky and Woodrow Wilson). In an ironic way, the supposedly materialist Freudian canon is in the tradition of the brooding, metaphysical speculations of Hawthorne and Melville, the doubtful side of our national consciousness that contrasts with Emerson's seemingly unlimited confidence in human beings. As this century, so dominated by both America and psychology, comes to an end, it is well that yet another American life has offered us a chance to address the continuing split in our soul: Sullivan's man-centered hope as against Freud's misgivings about our purely human possibilities.

The New York Times Book Review, 1982

26

FREUD, THE SECULAR

MORALIST

I have recently been reading a book by Jeffrey Abramson on Freud's moral and political thinking (*Liberation and Its Limits*). Once again I've been reminded of how significantly that particular genius shaped our (bourgeois, Western) view of ourselves in this century. Freud was not only a physician, a psychiatrist, but a tough polemicist, a gifted essayist, and a compelling storyteller.

In *The Future of an Illusion* he yields not an inch to his religious adversaries as he carries the banner of science in a steady (and sometimes impatient, sometimes fiery) confrontation with their ideas and ideals — overlooking, alas, his own illusions with respect to science and its possibilities, and revealing a sadly distorted notion of what religion can end up being in various lives. Still, the book is a major tract, all too convincing to all too many.

His *New Introductory Lectures on Psychoanalysis* is a brilliantly clear-headed, persuasive exposition of a complex subject — a model of precise, yet relaxed writing unequaled, surely, by any social scientist. His *Totem and Taboo* and *Moses and Monotheism* are provocative exercises of speculative fiction (the latter was originally titled *The Man Moses: A Novel*).

Then, there is Freud the ambitious social and political theorist — as in *Group Psychology and the Analysis of the Ego,* or the exchange with Albert Einstein, titled "Why War?" This Freud is anxious to understand the way individuals respond to the press of crowds, if not mobs, and the way nations deal with other nations. If the early Freud was a radical challenge to the medical establishment, and eventually, the proper bourgeoisie of the West, the later Freud comes across as skeptical, cautious, and socially and politically conservative — and no wonder, given his own declining health and the steady rise of fascism in the period between the two World Wars. Moreover, the psychoanalytic view of human motivation is necessarily inclined to doubt and suspicion. What appears to be may be a deceptive cover for what ("underneath") truly is — hence Freud's scorn for certain Victorian pretensions, *and* his distrust of the avowals and promises uttered by various social reformers, whether the ones he knew as fellow psychoanalysts (Reich, Ferenczi) or those who operated full-time in the world of politics.

Of course all politics has to do with the manner in which people get along. A political philosopher (from Plato and Aristotle through Hobbes and Locke) is bound to be a psychologist as well — uphold a particular notion of what people are like, what they want or fear, what their limits often are, what their possibilities might well be. Many political thinkers turn to Freud's later (social) essays for such help, only to find obvious encouragement for any gloom they may feel, and little support for their more idealistic energies.

Few scholars have done what the political scientist Jeffrey Abramson does in his book: dare direct concentrated attention at Freud's clinical findings (the absolute essence of his work, and the part of it that still stands solid and immensely suggestive, nearly a century after it was offered the world). What Abramson's *Liberation and Its Limits* provides is a closely reasoned analysis of the social implications of psychoanalytic psychology — the message Freud's look at childhood and family life has for those who want to speculate on how far politics can go in shaping human nature, and indeed, how much the individual, even at his best, has to offer politics.

At no point does Abramson try to fit psychoanalysis into a particular political ideology. He realizes that a view of the mind that aims to be accurate and representative will have to acknowledge freely the paradoxes, inconsistencies, and contradictions which make us all what we are — a mix of so many apparently irreconcilable inclinations and urges. Instead, he seeks to understand, rather as psychoanalysts do, the reasons for that outcome; the result, perhaps unintended, is an excellent exposition of Freudian developmental psychology — detailed, coherent, accurate in all respects, with nothing taken for granted. Apart from its merits as a reflective essay on our political potentialities as human beings, this not very long book could serve as a first-rate introduction to psychoanalysis for the general reader or for college and graduate students.

But Abramson does not fail to make use of his own special talents as a political philosopher — for whom Freud's study of the earliest events in a child's life (the complex involvement with the mothering person) has an obvious lifelong significance not only in everyone's personal existence, but in that larger realm that gets called a community, a nation's life. All too often psychoanalytic theorists plumb the nature of "mind" in a social vacuum — and by "social" one means not only the society at large, *its* impact upon our thoughts and desires, but the smaller world of particular others we all grow to know, and from whom we take countless important cues throughout our lives. Even an infant, Abramson keeps reminding us, is already well on its way to becoming a social and political creature. Babies know well what loyalty is (that of their parents, that of their own responsive selves), and they know, too, what power is — the struggles waged with respect to food intake, sleeping schedules, and increasingly, the body's various functions, the mind's desires.

Abramson stresses this "intersubjective" side of childhood — the experience of connectedness we all (one hopes and prays) start having immediately on being born. His social theory, his notion of what politics might become — were it to be respectful of human possibility and of certain decent moral standards — harkens back to this "I — Thou" aspect of our lives: the so-called dyadic rhythms of mothering and fathering that prepare us, in later years, for friendships, membership in a neighborhood, and commitment to a nation's expectations. Words such as "solidarity" or "citizenship," phrases such as "civic duties" or "community involvement," ought not be ignored by psychoanalytic psychologists who want to understand what in childhood paves the way for the character of adult life. In this book those words and phrases take on powerful meaning as we see what enables them to have more than an abstract life in textbooks.

Here, for instance, is Abramson talking about not only an "objects-relation" theory of child psychoanalysis, but of so much that happens in any doctor's office, among other places: "This 'intersubjective' feature of therapy has important implications for politics. It suggests that self-understanding is completed only in communities of a certain sort — communities in which friends and fellow citizens, and not just professional analysts, know me well enough to help me know myself." Such an interpretation is "existential," of course, in the tradition of moral philosophers the author doesn't mention: Gabriel Marcel or Jaspers.

No question the author is a friendly reader of Freud's. Still, this is no slavish exegesis — a not rare phenomenon when someone outside of psychoanalysis begins to realize how seminal psychoanalytic ideas have been to the 20th-century cultural thought. Abramson picks and chooses his way through the canon, spotting and discarding the unsatisfactory, the narrow or confining, the thoroughly outdated — and reaching always for the broadly illuminating, as in the theory of narcissism, so much discussed these days.

In this regard he is an original, knowing, trenchant interpreter — and manages to take on not only many within psychoanalysis, but some of its best known (and valuable) friends from other disciplines. We are, for example, given this summary of one prominent viewpoint: "These narcissistic underpinnings of identification (we love our own image as perceived in the other) are considered in Rieff's account as further evidence of 'the duplicity of erotic sentiment'; all love is partly but a 'devious means of self-love.'" But at a certain point such a critique loses proportion and balance: "Freud's wide-ranging study of narcissism cannot be reduced to a moralism about human duplicity without also reducing psychoanalysis to a caricature of itself." Alternatively, the author insists that "the common image of narcissism as self-insulation" ignores the meaning others have to us. Our narcissism can, indeed, cut us off — but can also help us reach out to others, bring others, so to speak, deep within ourselves:

"To love the other in whom one sees oneself is, in this sense, to affirm the indispensability of the other to who one is. Freud did not always carry through with this vision of the essential connectedness of narcissism."

Like the works of many great novelists, Freud's writings lend themselves to all kinds of interpretative forays — to "all sorts and conditions" of social theorists. Pessimists quarry certain texts; optimists find others appealing — and similarly with liberals and conservatives. Jeffrey Abramson is obviously a reasonably hopeful proponent of the Western tradition of political and social democracy. He is willing to take into consideration Freud's dour and even grim side, but is alert to the ever energetic "conquistador," who took for granted in himself and others a measure of free will, no matter the determinism he so repeatedly discovered at work in human affairs.

The author does not, however, examine in any detail a number of Freud's moral and political preoccupations — his interest in, yet skepticism about the possibilities of socialism; his long-standing fascination with charismatic, prophetic military or social reformers; and his complex sense of himself as a Hebrew prophet of sorts. Nor does this book try to examine the spiritual and moral hunger that set the stage for the triumph of psychoanalysis among secular, agnostic, and well-to-do people of this country. The man who told us that religion is an "illusion" ended up, ironically, supplying a faith of sorts to many thousands. Moreover, Freud was a moralist who, also ironically, shirked the kind of self-analysis that would have revealed his messianic dreams and aspirations — a kind of deliverance from instinctuality.

But once so rescued, where do we go, and with what purposes in mind? Such questions are spiritual — and Freud offers little help with them, though he might have, had he been not only a cultural Jew but a religious one in the tradition of Isaiah, Jeremiah, and Amos, for whom the moral life may inspire the conflicts Freud knew to describe, but is, finally, a God-given possibility we dare not cease trying to achieve.

New Oxford Review, 1985

27

A DOCTOR'S ODYSSEY

Side by side, at the very beginning of her new book, Sara Lawrence Lightfoot, a sociologist and professor of education at Harvard, chooses to offer the reader more than a hint of what is to come — with words from a lamentation of Jeremiah and from an old Negro spiritual. Both make reference to "balm in Gilead," which is her book's title. (That balm was an ancient aromatic resin used for medicinal purposes in biblical times.) In a touching way, before a word of her own is offered the reader, the author connects the longtime suffering of the Jews and the blacks, and their similar search for healing. *Balm in Gilead* is about such healing; it is a personal portrait (a word the author favors in her teaching and research) of one of the world's first psycho-analytically trained black child psychiatrists, Margaret Lawrence, who also happens to be the mother of the author.

It is not rare for psychiatrists to have vivid memories of pain and suffering. Dr. Margaret Lawrence's life may take its place in that tradition. She grew up an only child in a family that E. Franklin Frazier would have firmly labeled a part of the "black bourgeoisie." Her father was an Episcopal minister, her mother a schoolteacher. An older brother, known as Candy Man, died at the age of one; and a picture of him, with his "white skin and blond curls," haunted his family: "Each time they moved, Candy Man's picture would be hung in the central spot in the living room over the couch." Eventually his darker-skinned younger sister would connect her medical aspirations and her interest in children to that tragedy — a resolve to struggle on behalf of others like Candy Man, and a desire to help those who have lost children, and, so doing, have lost themselves beyond the power of time and talk and tears to heal. Hence the need of Gilead's special substance, the equivalent in this modern day of a career in pediatrics and psychiatry.

Sara Lightfoot is an exceedingly graceful narrative writer, and this is a delightfully affectionate rendering of a woman of great personal poise and professional achievement. But no effort is made to spare the reader the most demanding possible moments — a tough, candid analysis of what has happened to black people who have tried to better themselves during the 20th century. Lawrence grew up with "painful memories of family struggles." Her mother was subject to prolonged spells of melancholy. For days she withdrew to her room. The girl's father was a minister who moved the family from town to town — eventually to Vicksburg, Mississippi, where a certain stability descended upon this threesome. But always there was the fear and the anxiety that went with being black in the rural South during the 1920s and 1930s. Lawrence, reminiscing for her daughter, reminds us of our country's recent past: "I can remember walking back from town with my mother on Jackson Street near First North [in Vicksburg]. Suddenly she [her mother] grabbed me and shoved me off the sidewalk and onto the grass because a white man was approaching from the other direction. She was frightened of staying on the sidewalk."

Even more confusing and degrading, perhaps, was an intense color consciousness among black people — a constant kind of self-scrutiny based on the degree to which one did or did not resemble white people. The pride and the arrogance of light-skinned blacks, and the disdain they showed others who were darker, has been noted by any number of writers and social scientists. This book conveys the sad consequences of our nation's prolonged racial strife in an especially gripping manner: through the recalled experiences, the stories, of one family as they have been relayed from mother to daughter, and now to us. As I read these accounts of self-hatred, I remembered the words of a black woman in Georgia who had no education at all, yet knew enough to tell my wife that "as bad as the whites are with us, we're worse with each other." When my wife asked why it is that victims become their own persecutors, the 30-year-old scrubwoman and mother answered tersely: "You be scared, you copycat the ones who scare you, and try to do them one better, and that way you can catch a taste of the boss man's life!" The subtleties of such a psychological inclination are each family's secret, of course, as the future psychoanalyst Margaret Lawrence well knew by the time she ventured north (at only 14) to fulfill her dream of becoming a physician.

Even as we know the facts of Southern segregation — it was a caste system that obtained for generations and only began to end a quarter century ago — we also know that the North for a long time was only a relatively better place for black people. The chapters that tell of Lawrence's situation as "the only black undergraduate on the arts and sciences campus" of Cornell, of her similar experience as a medical student at Columbia's College of Physicians and Surgeons, and of her lonely, tense, even tearful time as the sole black psychoanalytic candidate at one of New York City's institutes provide a devastating glimpse of an aspect of upper-class intellectual life that all too frequently goes unnoticed. "I listen, disbelieving," Lightfoot remarks, as she compares her mother's "solitary arrival at Cornell in the fall of 1932" with her own Swarthmore life of three decades later.

The great virtue of this book is its preference for storytelling rather than abstract argument or theoretical assertion. The reader is enraged, surely, at the injustices that took place in Ithaca or New York City, in those high-and-mighty university settings. But he or she is also immersed in the details of particular incidents, and so, soon enough, made to feel as Margaret Lawrence did, utterly and arbitrarily and relentlessly wronged. Put differently, before we learn that the Cornell student Margaret Lawrence could not even live on campus ("No blacks were allowed in the dormitory, of course"), we hear her asking, upon arrival at the Ithaca train station, "My Lord, where is this?" We also see her: "Margaret was wearing a suit that had been made for the occasion by her mother's seamstress in Vicksburg: steel gray, with shoulder pads and a fitted waist. She carried a black purse, with matching shoes, but did not wear the gray gloves that would have completed the outfit. Her thick black braids, gleaming almost blue in the bright afternoon sun, were wrapped into buns on either side of her head, a concession to the adult image she was trying out."

At moments the author-daughter finds it hard to comprehend the responses of her mother, who is also the "subject" of her presentation. She has just been told by Lawrence that "if I walked across the campus, people would stop talking, turn their heads, and ask 'Who is that?'" She has also been told this:

> One Sunday a white woman from one of the local churches invited Margaret to come and speak about her experiences in Mississippi. The Vicksburg girl responded with style and grace as she told the Ithaca folks about her life in the Deep South. We can only imagine it was not the exotic tale or the rags-to-riches story that they had anticipated. Perhaps disappointed by the girl's sophistication, or perhaps unknowingly resenting it, the woman who had invited Margaret approached her after her talk. Her smile was sugary sweet as she took Margaret's hand. "I am so pleased you came," she gushed thankfully. Then, without skipping a beat: "You remind me so much of a maid I had. The only problem she had was that she would steal."

Such a memory is told "with lightness and humor" — and the author remarks upon her "shock and anger at the humiliation that my mother does not seem to be feeling."

The reader begins to realize that Lawrence's life was constantly visited with outrages, small and large. She was rejected by Cornell Medical School for no reason but her race. She became an excellent medical student, but for similar reasons was turned down for a pediatric residency at New York's Babies Hospital. Even her psychiatric and psychoanalytic training was marred by rebuffs, insults, brushoffs. Black patients were remanded for "supportive therapy," she heard, "because they can't use anything deeper." Similarly with black doctors interested in psychiatry and psychoanalysis. This book presents a discouraging yet revealing glimpse of a little known matter — the condescensions and worse, the outright racism that blacks experienced in the course of their postgraduate medical and psychiatric education. Just before her certificate of psychoanalytic training was to be awarded, Dr. Lawrence was suddenly told she needed a further evaluation. She had dared express reservations about the ways some of her psychoanalytic teachers regarded black people — their problems and burdens. She had dared have misgivings about Abram Kardiner's *The Mark Of Oppression*, a book that many social scientists, black and white alike, have come to regard as inadequate in its portrayal of black life in America — all too preoccupied with psychopathology.

She is still, obviously, offended by such past memories: even today "for Margaret, the feeling of being in the elevator of the Columbia Presbyterian Hospital opens up the old wound of self-consciousness." Yet she never really wavered. She had acquired a necessary forbearance and a determination to prevail. She married a strong, decent, bright, and able man, Charles Lawrence, a sociologist. She became a distinguished clinician, researcher, educator, writer. She worked for years in Harlem with troubled children, and with the distinguished psychologists Kenneth and Mamie Phipps Clark tried to help hard-pressed parents to do better by their sons and daughters. In a sense, she was redeeming her own childhood difficulties — doing an about-face on her mother's legacy of dejection and episodic withdrawal from life. In her interviews with her daughter, she comes across as her own mother's opposite, as a lively, outgoing, delightfully engaging person and doctor. Most of all, Margaret Lawrence's career has been in the pastoral tradition of doctoring — years and years spent with her patients, black and white, adults and children, the well-to-do and the poor.

I first heard of Margaret Lawrence from a number of civil rights activists whom she had taught or treated. I heard of her, too, from her white colleagues, who by the 1960s were beginning to make her concerns theirs. This book, in that regard, is especially interesting for the complex professional issues it raises. During her psychiatric and psychoanalytic training a talented, energetic, empathic, and resourceful trainee learned to keep silent about certain matters dear to her, to wait until she graduated. In a fascinating comment, Lightfoot tells this about her mother's way of holding on to her religious convictions during a trying period: "Her faith endured even the inhospitable environment of the Psychoanalytic Clinic. Throughout her analytic training, she simply kept her contrary theology quiet, continued to go to church every Sunday at St. Martin's in Harlem, continued to 'be in touch with the Spirit,' and continued to rehearse the words of her father's favorite psalm, 'The Lord is my light and salvation.'" Such quiet spells have not only been the habit of black candidates of religious sensibility in psychiatric or psychoanalytic training, as any number of us will testify. There can be an unfortunately ideological quality to such training; vulnerable young doctors learn to keep their mouths shut with respect to certain matters, to bide their time.

Balm in Gilead is a daughter's loving witness to a mother's important healing life. Margaret Lawrence is obviously Sara Lightfoot's heroine — and black or white, we need such heroines. But *Balm in Gilead* is something else, too: an attempt to demonstrate by example what a humane and clear-headed kind of social science might offer us, were it more a presence in our social and intellectual life.

The New Republic, 1989

III

CREATIVITY,

LEADERSHIP, AND

"PSYCHOHISTORY"

Before I began a psychiatric residency I had been interested in and studied "history and literature," one of those university "departments" which hope judiciously to combine related elements of two separate "fields." I do not believe the essays in this section are merely of tangential relation to my work as a psychiatrist. Novelists and poets, and not a few historians, have a lot of good judgment, if not rare wisdom, to offer social scientists; the artist's or historian's angle of vision frequently helps us in psychiatry become less narrowly deterministic, less forgetful of those ironies and ambiguities which no zealous outpouring of theoretical formulation will quite banish. And then there are those psychiatric and psychoanalytic efforts to play seer with respect to the efforts of various writers, artists, or statesmen. Despite Freud's self-admonitions on the matter of "creativity," he himself was drawn to hazardous and sometimes unfortunate speculation: on what prompted the emergence and policies of a certain public figure, Woodrow Wilson, for example. I look rather skeptically, I fear, at such efforts. At the same time I have wanted to indicate the contribution a novelist, poet, or playwright can offer us in the way of psychological acuity and complexity. If the essays on Giuseppe Berto, Strindberg, Cormac McCarthy, Raymond Carver, William Styron, and Walker Percy are "literary," I think they also attempt to indicate how much we in psychiatry might learn from such men and women, as opposed to the common practice on our part of "applying" our knowledge, gratuitously and even arrogantly, to the remarks or the paintings, even the life work, of various gifted individuals.

28

ANALYSIS ITALIAN STYLE

At noon on Monday, September 2, 1901, Freud arrived in Rome, there to spend twelve almost ecstatic days. It was a very significant and long delayed moment in his life. For several years he had been taking trips to northern Italy, always with the capital city as an eventual goal. He was European and Viennese; like Browning, Goethe and Heine he saw Italy as a place of warmth and reigning beauty, a refuge from the excesses of that single-minded devotion to "cold reason" or "pure thought" so common north of the Alps. He was also drawn to the Italy (and particularly the Rome) of ancient history. Memories, whether of an individual or of an entire people, were his great and consistent interest.

Yet psychoanalysis as a cultural or institutional force has not taken hold in either the Italy or Greece that Freud found so compelling. In 1965, at the Twenty-fourth Congress of the International Psychoanalytical Association held in Amsterdam, two hundred and thirty-nine Americans and fifty Englishmen provided the obvious, predominant majority of registered members. There were ten Italians and no one from Greece. Although some analysts so define their work that social

and cultural "factors" (as they are called) not to mention historical
or political ones, count for little in psychoanalytic theory or treatment, the everyday vicissitudes of the world and of history have
given the psychoanalytic profession no corresponding immunity.
Americans have taken to the couch, among other reasons, because
they *are* Americans, of a certain kind. Italians have stayed away, and
often enough for reasons having nothing to do with "health" or
"sickness." It is not their style to take man so seriously, or to dwell on
his thinking so interminably.

Of course in the United States we seldom dance in the street or
close our shops to take afternoon naps. We are much too serious,
much too self-conscious for that. Is it any wonder, then, that no
American novelist has really been able (or willing) to come to terms
with psychoanalysis in the relaxed and smiling way Italo Svevo did
with *Confessions of Zeno* (1923) and Giuseppe Berto has done again
with *Incubus?* While we have produced a culture (and, God help us, a
literary criticism) saturated with caricatures of both the principles
and practice of psychoanalysis, our writers (or the best of them)
have withdrawn from that culture into strictly regional movements,
exiled coteries, or a kind of intensely private world that would certainly want to resist the presence of the all-time busybody that the
conscientious analyst quite properly has to be. What is left, as far as
literary treatment of psychoanalysis goes, is the vulgar snake-pit
novels, the absurd, syrupy doctors who practice in movies, television, or what passes for the theatre, and, finally, the excellent stories
of Lillian Ross.

In *Incubus,* published two years ago as *Il Male Oscuro,* just now
translated (and very well) by William Weaver, a distinguished Italian
novelist has managed to portray in words the almost impossible combination of the ironic, the comic, the almost unbearably sad, that together characterize both a patient's life and his analyst's work. The
incubus is an elusive, hard-to-describe malady that afflicts the name-
less writer whose thoughts, feelings, and experiences are, in sum, the
content of the book — which is, thus, a fictional autobiography. Periods, commas, paragraphs are largely absent in this book. Every effort is made to bring alive a worried (and literate) man's mind as it
works by itself or considers other people, and with those particular
other people, a succession of psychiatrists.

The book is one long funny and woeful circle, from the beginning when the author starts telling about his struggles with his father, to the end when he is presumably in the midst of writing what the reader has just finished reading. We gradually learn about the man's petit-bourgeois social background, his schooling, his participation in Mussolini's vainglorious military escapades, and his career as a film script-writer. In early middle age, with his father's illness and death, he becomes increasingly upset, confused, and plagued by nondescript aches and pains, ominous dreams, premonitions and forebodings of one sort or another, and a spreading, worsening, finally crippling mixture of anxiety and fear.

His sisters nag at him, his father in his last days can be as inattentive, cold and cruel as the son remembers he used to be. The past intrudes on the present as the guilty, angry, remorseful son visits the dying father, and wishes him (an easy, painless) death. Upon that death the son starts worrying about baldness and his own body's decay. The tug of childhood becomes stronger, as does the self-absorption that goes first with illness, then with analysis of illness. We learn more and more about the writer's (and patient's) fantasies, guilts, and dreams as his doctors try to show him how his past "vicissitudes" live on to influence his everyday malaise and despair.

The book is filled with an extraordinary, subtle kind of knowledge about the mind's function. It is a pleasure to be spared all those simpleminded terms and phrases that some psychiatrists as well as laymen call upon to "explain" life's complexities — by arbitrarily isolating them into convenient categories. If the doctor occasionally has to do so in his office because both he and his patients have so little time, he should know enough to look elsewhere (and more broadly) when he leaves that office. Certainly the novelist, if he is something more than a wordy clinician-manqué, will demand of himself and his readers the willingness to see how many truths can be gleaned from any experience or problem; even from the most discrete and "obvious" dream. Throughout this book *that* truth stands out, and it does so despite the inevitable abundance of lesser if flashier truths produced by all forms of introspection, including a novelist's kind that is fashioned to resemble an analyst's.

Marvelous scenes come one after another as we are rushed back and forth through the author's life. There are doctors, operations, bills, and many women. There is his *angst,* his search for greatness, his near enjoyment of worry and fear, his exhaustion, and always, his phobias, well-known to his doctors and friends. He resolves, and then procrastinates. He speculates tirelessly on his loss of energy. He dwells on death, posterity, fame, love and money. There are pills to be taken and shock treatments threatened. Feverish periods of poor health alternate with the hilarious, demeaning scriptwriting he must do for money. He is convinced that his final purpose is to write a masterpiece, perhaps the book we are now reading.

In the end he is "better"; that is, he has fought his illness to a standstill: the symptoms go, but there remains a certain fatalistic sense of being cheated and hurt in spirit. He knows the nature of his "compulsive" malady. He admits reluctantly that he can manage without further treatment, and eventually he decides to leave his wife (they have had a stormy time of it) and daughter to seek peace and a final, uninhibited confrontation with the father of his youth.

He gets older and more wrinkled; he lives a peasant's life near the sea and opposite the Sicily he heard his father mention to him as a child. He feels closer to his father, to his ancestors; he is resigned and somehow shed of vanity. The writing he dreamed he would do and the ambitions he wanted fulfilled mean nothing to him. He works at the land and does his daily chores, almost ascetically. No cure can mean anything unless it leads to a certain rhythm of life. At the end of this book we realize that somehow the setting for its beginning has been established. Out of a bleak childhood almost fiercely met, and for a while relived, will come the willful perspective that the artist at work possesses. I suppose that is what psychoanalysis at its best can sometimes do, help people live intimately enough with their past to learn to use its power, not simply know its details.

The New Republic, 1966

29

A BULLITT TO WILSON

For about him at the very end
were still
Those he had studied, the nervous
and the nights,
And shades that still waited to enter
The bright circle of his recognition
Turned elsewhere with their disappointment. . . .

Auden's tribute captures the hungry impatience of Freud's mind, even in the final, weary years of a ninth decade of life. He wrote steadily despite the constant pain of cancer, and if anything, much of his writing became more pointed, self-critical and ironic. He repeated in his essay on Dostoevski (1928) what he had said earlier (1910) in his ill-fated analysis of Leonardo da Vinci: "Before the problem of the creative artist, analysis must, alas, lay down its arms." In his public exchange of letters with Einstein (1932) he referred to "our mythological theory of instincts," and toward the end of his attempt to discuss the causes of war he had this to say: "The result, as you see, is not very fruitful when an unworldly theoretician is called in to advise on an urgent practical problem."

Freud possessed the modesty of one who never for a moment doubted the essential and unique significance of his lifework. Perhaps it was such inner confidence that enabled him to present even his most complicated ideas in strong and unpretentious prose, the apparently effortless outpourings of a rich and candid mind. In *Moses and Monotheism,* one of his most speculative and I think least substantial works, he talks about "the labored, poor, and patchy attempts at explanation which are the best we can produce." He insists that the reader know how many "enigmas" have not been solved by psychoanalysis, and he characterizes his own efforts as "a simple contribution." Whether he was pursuing a biblical figure like Moses, artists like Leonardo or Michelangelo, or a writer like Dostoevski, he was careful to be a courteous observer. Writing of "the trivial peculiarities and riddles" of Leonardo da Vinci's nature Freud said:

> We respect him by learning from him. It does no injury to his greatness to study the sacrifices which his development from the child must have entailed. . . . Let us expressly emphasize that we have never considered Leonardo as a neurotic or as a 'nervous person' in the sense of this awkward term. . . . We no longer believe that health and disease, normal and nervous are sharply distinguished from one another. . . . We know today that neurotic symptoms are substitutive formations for certain repressive acts . . . that we all produce such substitutive formations, and that only the amount, interests and distribution of these substitutive formations justify the practical conception of illness. . . .

It must be admitted that not all psychiatrists have read and understood the man who wrote those words — in 1914. Certainly an idolatrous American public has found in psychiatry a suitably pagan and pleasantly self-centered form of religion, with all kinds of hazy and swell virtues — things like "maturity" or "mental health" — pitted against an expanding array of vices like "acting out" or "hostility," many of them turned into the purest of epithets even by so-called professionals. Yet Freud had no such outcome in mind for his work, though it is clear from passages like the one just quoted that he knew as always how much stupidity and malice one could safely take for granted — among one's admiring colleagues as well as elsewhere. A man in constant pursuit of reason, he never allowed what he found to make him self-important or indeed very hopeful about finding a way to end man's mental suffering.

It seems now that we all will have to look once again at both Freud's ideas and the way he gave expression to them. Twenty-eight years after his death a book has been published under his name. With the former diplomat William C. Bullitt he is listed as coauthor of a "psychological study" of Woodrow Wilson. According to Bullitt each of them "criticized, amended or rewrote the other's draft until the whole became an amalgam" for which both of them are responsible. Apparently they did not have an easy time of it ("both Freud and I were stubborn, and our beliefs were dissimilar"), so that in 1932 when their collaboration had resulted in a manuscript they could not come to terms with one another. ("After general arguments we decided to forget the book for three weeks and to attempt then to agree. When we met, we continued to disagree.")

Six years later, Bullitt, then America's ambassador to France, met Freud in Paris on his way into exile from the Nazis. It was an exile Bullitt had very much helped to arrange, and one for which Freud had every reason to be grateful. Relatives of his would soon be marched to gas ovens. In Bullitt's words: "I met him at the railroad station . . . and suggested that we might discuss our book once more after he was settled in London." To the ambassador's (surprised?) delight Freud agreed to take out various sections he had written. It was agreed that the "study" would be published after Wilson's widow died — with the guarantee that Freud's name would command for it widespread attention.

The book can either be considered a mischievous and preposterous joke, a sort of caricature of the worst that has come from psychoanalytic ideologues, or else an awful and unrelenting slander upon a remarkably gifted American President. I fear it is meant to be the latter, a serious, vindictive effort that unhesitatingly takes the complicated life of a very unusual man and reduces it to a few "explanations" — which in fact tell us much less about Wilson than the man or men who wrote this book. I would add right here that in my opinion it is overwhelmingly Bullitt's work: the style, the use of words, the content, the tone, everything is unfamiliar. If this is Freud, it is a thoroughly new and different Freud — certainly not the gifted writer and compassionate man hailed on his eightieth birthday by Thomas Mann's essay, "Freud and the Future."

Only a few pages are Freud's alone, and they contain a revealing introduction in which the European doctor (whose country lost to America and her allies in 1918) frankly admits the distrust he and his countrymen felt toward Wilson. Yet he claims to have lost some of that feeling during the study: "A measure of sympathy developed; but sympathy of a special sort mixed with pity . . . so overwhelming that it conquered every other emotion." He pointedly asks the reader not to dismiss the book as "a product of prejudice," and goes on to say that his initial feelings against Wilson were eventually put under "thorough subjugation." He then, for some reason, has to promise the same for Bullitt, justifying at least on this occasion another line from the poem Auden wrote after Freud's death:

> If often he was wrong and at times absurd,
> To us he is no more a person
> Now but a whole climate of opinion.

This book certainly adds drizzle to that "climate." It is appallingly easy to summarize: Wilson had a very strong and affectionate father, to whom he was unusually close, so that his entire life was dominated by the reenactment again and again of that complicated and intense relationship. Wilson's friends, his marriage, his career, and his behavior in the course of that career must be examined under that one light — generated by a son's particularly strong love for his father, his secret hate for him, and his endless loyalty to both of those feelings. If only the Princeton faculty, Colonel House, the Kaiser, Senator Lodge, Lloyd George, Clemenceau, Orlando, and many others could have been told how utterly irrelevant they or the causes they represented were to President Wilson, who throughout this "objective" study is called Tommy or "little Tommy."

That is the message of the book, though the way it is presented requires an amused or disgusted look, depending I suppose on how seriously you take the whole business. In Bullitt's "digest of data" (supposedly prepared for Freud's enlightenment) Wilson is called "a prig, but a prime prig." We are told that "Tommy Wilson never had a fistfight in his life." Later on, when Wilson's marriage comes up, Bullitt says: "He could rest on her shoulder with as complete confidence as ever he had had as an infant sleeping on the breast of his mother." When his wife died he had to marry again because "he could not do without a woman on whose breast he could rest." Moreover, at college he sang and debated, and later became a gifted orator, as a result of which Bullitt concludes: "His pleasures were all connected with the use of his mouth."

Then comes the study proper, to which Freud's name is attached. There is talk of libido charging psychic "apparatus," and we find that "libido begins to charge three accumulators: narcissism, masculinity and femininity." A few pages later we hear about "a dam of repression" that builds up until it is "too strong for the insulator." Lest we get the idea that Wilson is the only subject fit for this kind of psychoanalytic study the following is stated: "Unsatisfied desires of the libido sublimated produce all art and literature. Human society itself is held together by sublimated libido, the passivity of the boy to his father transforming itself into love of his fellow men and desire to serve mankind." (Those who up to now thought talent had something to do with writing or painting, and social, political and economic institutions with making up and keeping together a society, will realize how naive they have been.)

Since Woodrow Wilson's father was a minister, then of course "Tommy Wilson found his supreme expression in sermons from a pulpit which was the White House." (Wilson also had a mother, but she could only cause the same old trouble: "He, like all other men, had a mother identification and through it a portion of his passivity to his father found outlet.") Since Wilson loved and venerated his father, it follows that he "established this father-God as his Super Ego" and then "identified himself with the Only Begotten Son of God." It also follows that the Wilson who didn't fight as a child and who fancied himself as Christ could not later take on the British and French at Versailles, though he saw the result of his effort at that conference as successful because he had "to remain in his own belief the Savior of the World." There was an un-Christian fight with the French President, Poincaré, but that can easily be explained: "The libido insulated in his reaction-formation against his passivity to his father had been without outlet and had reached such a pitch of intensity that it had to break out against someone." When Wilson and Poincaré settled their differences here is why: "Then in the end Wilson submitted to Poincaré, and the charge of mingled libido and Death Instinct was again without outlet and remained repressed, awaiting Lodge."

That is about enough; if 307 pages of such talk seem inviting, the book awaits you. Like a Greek Chorus there are periodic chants containing words like "libido," "outlet," "passivity," "cannibalistic identification," "conduit." ("We have seen that submission to God and unconscious identification with Christ were the only two large conduits for his passivity to his father through which his libido was still able to run freely.") Perhaps the manuscript will be of interest to hydraulic engineers.

Meanwhile those of us who every day fall back upon Freud's observations, who know from clinical experience what and how much he discovered, have to face the harm this book will do. The many who keep looking for excuses to condemn psychoanalysis will have good cause for excitement. Historians and political scientists will be made nervous or freshly skeptical; they know that somehow the private lives and problems of leaders do indeed influence world events, but they will certainly wonder whether they need the kind of vitriol, the pitiless and sinister character assassination this book provides. Nor will the more narrow and cliquish elements in psychiatry and psychoanalysis be jolted out of their tiresome and pedantic arrogance by this demonstration of what can be done when a man's life, his social background, his religious faith, his values and ideals are ripped out of context and subordinated to the workings of a single-minded, mechanistic, conceptual scheme — and one that all too many use as a weapon of cheap gossip or sly innuendo.

I suppose that a while back the kind of "data" Bullitt prepared on Wilson frightened a generation of intellectuals into submissive enthusiasm. Today it is likely that this book will be greeted by laughs or indifference, though I hope it will in addition evoke a respectful second look at what the best of psychoanalysis has recently been able to accomplish. A theory of psychopathology has been converted by analysts like Anna Freud into a flexible body of knowledge that increasingly concerns itself with normal growth and development and does so by relying on direct observation rather than metapsychological speculation. A number of leading analysts have stopped looking for those categorical childhood analogues that once were mobilized at the sight of everything done by anyone over five; instead, emphasis is put upon the mind's (non-neurotic or "conflict-free") intellectual development, as well as the social and cultural influences that constantly shape our thoughts and feelings. Years before the recent civil rights struggle analysts like Viola Bernard worked with Negroes and wrote sensitively and with proper ambiguity of the challenge they present to white psychiatrists. There is, finally, the psychoanalytic work of Erik Erikson, far too rich and extensive to be summarized in a passing comment, but all of it particularly alert to the relationship between gifted men and the moment of history they in various ways dominate. In *Young Man Luther,* subtitled "a study of psychoanalysis and history," Erikson showed how the clinician can enlarge his own vision and make extremely suggestive contributions to historians — if he will only immerse himself in the times as well as the life of the particular person he is studying.

All this has to be said and emphasized because this book on Wilson — with its meanness and antique thinking — is in a class by itself; and should be so judged. If, as Goethe said, "The greatest man is always linked to his own century through some weakness," then the weakness of Freud that makes him today a man of the nineteenth century was the uncritical faith he put in the uses and imagery of science. Perhaps he also trusted some of his friends too much — because it can be argued that William Bullitt's twisted vendetta against Woodrow Wilson may actually be an underhanded assault on psychoanalysis and Sigmund Freud.

The New Republic, 1967

30

VAN GOGH:

THE FEVER OF GENIUS

We have had recent cause to shudder at what a certain kind of psychoanalytic biography can do; the study of Woodrow Wilson's purported hang-ups, a disastrous exercise full of simpleminded, arrogant and spiteful comments mixed with awkward, ostensibly humorous formulations; the long and unfortunate book about Whittaker Chambers and Alger Hiss, whose text again and again demonstrated how psychoanalytic interpretations, like any other sort, can be used in a partisan, moralistic, antagonistic way. And from year to year for those of us willing to read them, the articles continue to appear — telling how Kafka never got over the bad time he had with his father, or how Emily Dickinson didn't quite succeed in overcoming one or another "psychotic process."

Such thinking fails to distinguish between universal human conflicts and the distinctive craft of the writer or the artist, or for that matter, the doctor, the lawyer, the businessman. Millions of people have directly or obscurely fought with their fathers. Millions of men and women have felt "ambivalent" toward their mothers, have suffered "sibling rivalry" — as van Gogh did. Yet, what made Vincent van Gogh, or Kafka? What separates one person from another? A *person* is more than a bundle of neurotic problems, or as one prominent psychiatrist put it, "a series of structural systems in conflict." A person is a particular man or woman who either has or has not put to use the various endowments, experiences and possibilities that go into each life. Nor can a person, especially a genius like van Gogh, be confused with what makes him a bit, or more than a bit odd. Put differently, Freud generally knew the limits of his own "view," or way of looking at man; and he never claimed that the particular experiences he as a clinician wanted to study were *all* the experiences that existed.

It can be said that some of Freud's self-proclaimed followers have done with his ideas exactly what they are so eager to do with the books or canvases of other great men. That is, Freud's complicated, rich notions, hard-won and meant to be tentative, are given sweeping, uncritical authority. The dead artists and writers whose "problems" are "analyzed" at length suffer the insult of narrow-minded, idiotic caricature, and so does the ghost of Freud.

Significantly, two of the most thoughtful recent psychoanalytic essays have been prompted by the lives of Leonardo da Vinci and van Gogh. Kurt Eissler, one of the most respected and learned of the older group of American analysts, has written a long and interesting if overly apologetic book on Leonardo. He is least successful in his effort to defend Freud's study of Leonardo against attacks on it by art historians and critics. Toward the end of the book, however, one stumbles upon a rather surprising train of thought. Many geniuses like Leonardo (or van Gogh) are also very troubled men: "The question, however, has not been answered, what connection exists between the genius's psychopathology and his achievements. Psychopathology, in general, is looked upon as defect. . . . Observation of the genius, however, suggests the possibility that psychopathology is indispensable to the highest achievements of certain kinds." If that is so, if a certain genius demonstrates psychopathology which may be "indispensable to his geniushood," then Dr. Eissler is up against a real problem. Unlike most analysts, he is willing to face it:

Consequently if what we observed in the genius struck us as neurotic or psychotic or perverse or even criminal, we would then have to reconsider our classification under these accustomed headings. If, for example, an apparently obsessional symptom were observed and it turned out that symptom was indispensable to geniushood . . . there would be no sense in calling it a neurotic symptom. Whatever the essence of neurosis may be, the concept of neurosis makes sense only when it is correlated with a deficit.

Just before he wrote *Werther*, Goethe repeatedly attempted suicide. Here is how such "morbidity" strikes Dr. Eissler:

> This behavior pattern (and particularly Goethe's rationalization of the choice of method . . .) is under ordinary circumstances characteristic of a deep-seated disturbance and may even announce the onset of a malignant psychosis. Goethe, however, shortly thereafter wrote his famous novel *Werther* in which the hero ends his life by shooting himself. . . . The biographical evidence compels us to connect Goethe's "neurotic symptom" with his subsequent successful writing of the novel. It can be safely said that only somebody who had repeatedly gone through the throes of preparing for suicide could have presented it so overwhelmingly as Goethe. . . . Here, then, we have a conspicuous example of undeniable pathological behavior that was one of the indispensable prerequisites for the writing of one of the greatest novels. If we continue to call such behavior an indication of a neurosis or psychosis, we make such categories meaningless.

I am not sure that Eissler is right, that *only* someone who has attempted suicide can write about it convincingly. I am, however, struck by his dangerous "special-interest group," the genius. Once the floodgates are open, any of us may find ourselves carried along by the current. Men like Eichmann have, after all, been called "sane," and thereby that particular "category" has also been made a bit senseless. White people (certainly including upper-middle-class psychiatric "practitioners") have been told they can neither understand black men nor apply to them white standards and measurements. Eissler is struggling valiantly but perhaps hopelessly with the built-in rigidities of a conceptual system that was originally meant to clarify only certain actions of particular individuals — members of Vienna's turn-of-the-century bourgeoisie. By largely ignoring such bothersome problems as the relationship between a patient's problems and his race, class, values, it is possible for a psychoanalyst to bear down on certain "psychological" developments, developments that some analysts resolutely call "internal," as relentless and universal as life itself. Eventually, though, issues of "health," "creativity," "normality" or "sickness" arise in most analyses. Who decides which "inner process," which sort of psychological "adjustment" is valuable and which is to be frowned upon? Who is the arbiter, who is to call one man a madman and another a valuable eccentric? Is the psychoanalyst really "objective," or really free of social constraints and common values? How does the mental doctor — who obviously is *not* doing the same kind of thing as his medical colleagues — make his decision? Where does he get his standards, his "criteria"? These are vexing questions, and right now we haven't enough knowledge to answer them satisfactorily. We are fools if we think we do. Dr. Eissler is a first-rate scholar, not a fool. He knows irony when he sees it, and knows when to stop applying knowledge to others and look inward in order to ask exactly what is known about whom. Perhaps his good sense — in some respects it is common sense — will filter through to the provinces.

Humberto Nagera's recent "psychological study" of Vincent van Gogh follows the same line of reasoning that Eissler suggests. He also makes an important avowal: "Though one can identify the early origins of the feelings expressed on the canvas, the means by which van Gogh succeeded in expressing them, in embodying them on the canvas, in conveying them to the casual observer, remains to this day the secret of his genius and the testimony of it." That is very good, and should be put at the beginning of the book, rather than at the end of a middle chapter.

Dr. Nagera's study begins with one of those lovely gems that occasionally grace a significant psychoanalytic work, a foreword by Anna Freud. She speaks of "the sincerity of feeling, the force of expression and the depth of human suffering" that van Gogh's letters and canvases demonstrate. She compliments her colleague on his ability to summon a "striking image of a high-minded individual's struggles against the pressures within himself," and she reminds us that "even the highly prized and universally envied gift of creative energy" won't always work to keep in check an artist's particularly ruinous disposition.

Dr. Nagera has not tried to "interpret" van Gogh's *paintings* or "explain" why he was an artist, but to show through his prolific correspondence (mostly with his brother Theo) how a particular mind came to terms with the burden of its past and the contrasting daily hope implicit in extraordinary artistic sensibility. Perhaps just because he set himself that kind of task, Dr. Nagera has written a clear, tactful and poignant account of van Gogh's life — an account impressively free of psychoanalytic jargon and overwrought, abstract formulations. As Miss Freud points out, Dr. Nagera does indeed rely heavily on van Gogh's letters, themselves an awesome work of art. But he also becomes, without ostentatious effort, a decent, sensitive and shrewd biographer — who wants to look without envy at the entire span of a great life rather than bear down exclusively and relentlessly on its pitfalls.

Vincent Willem van Gogh was born in Zundert, near the Belgian frontier. Unlike Rembrandt, who came from a family of sturdy, pious burghers, van Gogh's ancestors included a number of very well-educated and rich men. His maternal grandfather studied theology at the University of Leiden; one uncle was a vice admiral, and three others were art dealers, one in Rotterdam and later Brussels, one in Amsterdam, one in The Hague and then Paris. The latter uncle had no children of his own and for a while viewed his nephew as successor and heir. As for the painter's immediate family, his father was a minister of a moderate sect of the Dutch Reformed Church; his mother was the daughter of a famous bookbinder, her family also being connected to the world of art through the marriage of her niece to the well-known Dutch painter A. Mauve.

Detailing these matters, Dr. Nagera gives us a sense of those family, social and cultural circumstances which would have a decisive bearing on the future painter's life. He also places great emphasis on the fact that van Gogh was born exactly one year to the day after an older brother, scarcely delivered, suddenly died. He also had been named Vincent. "The replacement of a dead child by another has been a subject of study by a number of psychoanalysts," says Dr.

Nagera. He spares the reader a review of the "literature," and is content to suggest that a mother who has recently lost a son may still be grieving when she gives birth to another. She may even be desperate about the possibility of losing her new child, which thus becomes both a sign of redemption and a source of apprehension; and as the child himself grows up he may acquire "a conviction of his inadequacy and vulnerability in a world of constant unpredictable dangers." Dr. Nagera keeps coming back to this theme, particularly when he is discussing van Gogh's obvious vulnerability at the end of his life, when he was a broken and haunted man, prey to delusions, hallucinations and suicidal urges. We are also reminded that the painter's mother never really appreciated her son's abilities: "When she moved away from Nuenen, a year after her husband's death, Vincent's paintings were packed in cases and totally forgotten, with the result that the carpenter at Bredo in whose care they were left sold everything after several years to a junk dealer!"

Interestingly enough, the author finds it harder to formulate what he nevertheless (to his great credit) keeps on recording — the evidence from van Gogh's early childhood that he was *not* a lunatic who quite inexplicably could paint. He may have had a "rejecting mother" as some categorical and simpleminded doctors put it — thereby themselves rejecting the subtleties and ambiguities of a particular life. Nevertheless, the mother who herself liked to paint was also one whose son was doing watercolors and drawings at the age of eight. A few of them, along with some of the mother's, can be found reproduced in *The Complete Letters of Vincent van Gogh,* published about a decade ago by the New York Graphic Society. At twelve he was still painting, not all the time, nor brilliantly, but with obvious talent and perseverance. In 1864, for his father's birthday he made a drawing entitled *Farm and Wagon-Shed* — which somehow his mother kept through the years, however "unaware" she was of her son's genius.

In any event, when Vincent was sixteen he was sent to The Hague to join his uncle's firm of art dealers. As a child he had been described as self-willed, and as a young man he would be found exactly that. For a while he was a willing apprentice, first in Holland and later in the London branch of the company. His younger brother, Theo, also became an apprentice in the firm (in Brussels, then in

Paris) and it was at this point in their lives that they started a continuous, outspoken, intimate correspondence which would be ended only by Vincent's death. Theo is the steady, earnest, sympathetic one, in contrast to Vincent's passionate, moody, searching and argumentative nature. In The Hague Vincent seems confident, satisfied with his young manhood, but in London he sounds not only lonely and homesick but a little too strongly nostalgic for the past, at twenty the very recent past of childhood.

In London van Gogh fell in love with his landlady's daughter but was rebuffed. He became more and more religious, reading the Bible and praying in long stretches. Intensely on his own, he seemed without joy. In 1875 he was transferred to Paris, and soon dismissed because he showed no interest in his work. He had actually liked England, for all his sadness there, and in 1876, at twenty-three, he returned, now to teach. He spoke both English and French fluently, and rather enjoyed working with children. He also did some drawings and continued his study of the Bible, which soon became his chief interest. Returning to Holland, he secured a job as a bookseller in Dordrecht, but it was *the* Book that absorbed his time and energy. Deciding to become a minister, like his father, he moved to Amsterdam, where he lived with his uncle, the commander of a naval base. He studied Latin and Greek and became increasingly ascetic, denying himself a bed, and eating frugally. Abandoning formal theology, he decided to go among the poor as an evangelist. Living among Belgian miners, he read to them from the Bible, taught and cared for their children, visited their sick. He slept on the floor of an old shack and gave everything he had to those desperately poor and hard-working people.

But van Gogh was considered a "sick" man. His religious superiors found him "overzealous" and eventually dismissed him. Van Gogh was one of those troubled, foolish men who tried to live up to Christ's spirit — in the belief that God's Will had to do with righting the concrete wrongs of the immediate world. His religious superiors wanted him to ask the workers for submission, for unquestioning faith, but instead, after witnessing a dreadful mine accident, van Gogh became disenchanted with organized religion and began to wander through France, Belgium and Holland. He met a prostitute and decided to live with her, to redeem or save her — and at this point he begins to sound in his letters very much like the Dostoevski of *Crime and Punishment*. He also started to draw in earnest, and for the first time to paint. For a while he stayed in Drenthe, a bleak, rain-drenched section of northern Holland where the great task is simply to stay alive. Then he abruptly returned home — shortly before his father's sudden death.

He was gravely upset, but at the same time was able to paint with more energy and conviction than ever before — all of which, according to Dr. Nagera, is no coincidence at all. Now the aspiring young artist went to Antwerp and was quickly expelled from the Academy as a wild, childish man of no talent. Moving to Paris, he studied and worked on his own and met other painters. Finally he left for the South, the "glorious South," settling in Arles on the Rhone. The sunshine was everywhere, orchards were in bloom. When he was not alone he was with "plain people" who did not clutter his mind with pompous talk, self-centered, distracting, faddish theories which both succeed and betray one another. He enjoyed his neighbors and his work. The paintings poured forth: *The Sunflowers, The Yellow House, The Harvest, The Drawbridge, The Boats on the Beach.*

On October 20, 1888, Gauguin came. Dr. Nagera describes his mind as "cold and calculating"; like van Gogh he was stubborn, proud, eccentric, fiercely independent. They fought — and eventually van Gogh inflicted on himself the well-known injury that marked the beginning of a serious psychological disturbance. For the remaining two years of his life he was in and out of hospitals, with and without medical care. Nevertheless, he did one remarkable painting after another: *The Cypresses, The Olive Trees,* and dozens of pictures of the skies, the fields, and particularly human beings. In addition he wrote to his beloved brother Theo, letters that were sad and tormented but also joyful and beautifully expressive. His last work was almost tranquil. The brushwork becomes broader, the forms less distorted; things seem hopeful, even buoyant. Unaccountably, then, on July 27, 1890, he took to the fields, shot himself, and died two days afterward. Half a year later on January 25, 1891, his brother Theo, long sick with nephritis, was also dead. They are buried side by side.

I suppose in this century it has to be noted that their love was tinged with "ambivalence." Dr. Nagera finds in their letters evidence of strain and tension, and he made his case with tact and intelligence. Still, much more went on in Vincent van Gogh, and between him and his brother, than any "psychological study," no matter how well-intentioned or comprehensive, can even convey, let alone explain.

In his last six years, from age thirty-one to thirty-seven, van Gogh produced seven hundred and eighty drawings and five hundred oils. At the end he was seized by the fever of genius, and he submitted to it, letting it drive and inspire him, draw from him the sweat of work, of achievement. As death approached he grew resigned, as had Rembrandt. The two have many resemblances. Neither was scientific or exact. Both worked intuitively. Both were interested in people, in what is called "character" or "expression," and favored the emotional, the mysterious. To a homely sitter Rembrandt would give a plumed hat, a turban, a "look" that made the exotic or the profound mere extensions of the commonplace. Both were deeply religious — but not in a remote or abstract way. Rembrandt never painted super-human or symbolic religious protagonists, and van Gogh's open, honest, religious feeling came through in almost every one of his letters. Even formally the two men are akin. At first Rembrandt's brushwork was tight and restrained; toward the end he loosened up, turned to rich colors and painted as if he foresaw what direction another Dutchman would take much later on.

The New Republic, 1968

31

ON PSYCHOHISTORY

In a letter dated October 9, 1898, Freud made mention of Leonardo da Vinci: he was "perhaps the most famous left-handed individual," and he "is not known to have had any love affairs." The letter was one of many addressed to Wilhelm Fliess. As Freud step by step began to formulate what we know today as psychoanalysis, he turned to his friend to present his thoughts openly and with some passion, as if he needed to ask whether all those ideas made any sense or were hopelessly out of kilter — useless notions prompted by the disturbed minds a psychiatrist sees, not to mention his own dreams and fantasies, which he had relied upon rather significantly in *The Interpretation of Dreams*.

That book, published in 1900, was unquestionably Freud's masterpiece; rich with years of clinical observations, written in a forceful style, it is by no means out of date now, nor will it ever be. A writer had sensed something important about human experience and found for himself an original language — a means by which his ideas might take hold of the reader's imagination. Soon after its publication Freud broke with Fliess. Why write letters about ideas when they are already set down in a book? Why discuss possible discoveries when they have been made, and are even attracting a limited but impressively brilliant cadre of admirers? Anyway, if Freud had once overestimated Fliess extravagantly, soon enough the latter's distinct limitations became apparent, and that was that — no awful scene, just a moment or two of recognition that became much more only as time passed.

Leonardo da Vinci was harder for Freud to put aside. Though by 1907 he was caught up in psychoanalytic work (by then the Vienna Psychoanalytical Society had been established), there is evidence that the achievements and the spirit of one genius were very much on the mind of another. Freud was reading a study of Leonardo that year, and called it one of his favorite books. On December 11, 1907, he spoke at some length about the general subject of psychoanalytic biography. Two years later he again referred to Leonardo, this time in a letter to Jung dated October 17, 1909: a patient under treatment had the same "constitution," the same psychological makeup, as the famous artist, but not his genius. He also told Jung that he was hoping to obtain a book, published in Italy, on Leonardo's youth.

In early December of 1909 Freud spoke to his Vienna colleagues at the Psychoanalytical Society about Leonardo, not the first time, incidentally, that such a presentation had been made. Isidor Sadger, one of the earlier members of the society (he joined in 1906, the same year Rank did), had studied the lives and writings of Heinrich von Kleist and C. F. Meyer. A short story of Meyer's, "Die Richterim," had also interested Freud; he once wrote to Fliess about that, too, remarking how Meyer's own life seemed to come across in the fiction he wrote.

By 1910 Freud was engaged in more than a casual inquiry; he went through every book on Leonardo he could lay his hands on, and he started writing one of those inviting, even charming essays of his that have a way of stirring up far more controversy than they seem meant to. In America the essay was translated by A. A. Brill and published as *Leonardo da Vinci: A Study in Psychosexuality*. More recently Alan Tyson has made another translation that is more faithful to the German at points, yet reads much better in English: *Leonardo da Vinci and a Memory of His Childhood*. In 1957, nine years before the surprise publication of *Thomas Woodrow Wilson*, supposedly a collaborative "study" by Freud and William Bullitt, the editors of the Standard Edition of the *Complete Psychological Works of Sigmund Freud* described the short book on Leonardo as "not only the first but the last of Freud's large-scale excursions into the field of biography."

It is an excursion well worth looking at today. What Freud tried to do over a half century ago still is being done, sometimes under the name of "psychohistory." Moreover, both his successes and his difficulties as an analyst of a long-dead historical figure's mental life are being experienced by others in our time. The Leonardo book stirred up an immediate reaction of disapproval — "more than the usual amount," we are told.[1] In 1910 everything Freud wrote was met with incredulity or anger by his colleagues. With the appearance of this new book many could find him guilty of an additional crime: not content with declaring the behavior of his patients to be the result of sexual tensions deviously expressed, he was now implicating one of the greatest artists of all time.

In fact Freud took pains to express his admiration for Leonardo. He was not writing an exposé. He had no intention of hurting the reputation of a great man. He was writing of "one who is among the greatest of the human race," and doing so because he firmly believed that "there is no one so great as to be disgraced by being subject to the laws which govern both normal and pathological activity with equal cogency."

Freud was intent on finding at all costs a way of looking at the human mind. He had started doing so with a few patients, then had the courage and honesty to include himself in their company, and around the time of the Leonardo study was ready to look elsewhere: at ordinary men and women who have no symptoms and never see psychiatrists; at patients with disorders other than those he would be likely to see in his office; and in this instance, at a historical figure whose life in certain respects seemed to lend itself to the kind of investigation Vienna's psychoanalysts were making with (as they saw it) astonishing success.

The point was to move from the given clinical case to the broader statement, from the specific to the universal — the "laws" Freud

---

[1] Volume XI of *Complete Psychological Works of Sigmund Freud* (Macmillan, 1964).

mentions. He wanted to move from the apparent, the readily observable, to "deeper layers" — to those unconscious forces he was convinced control just about every aspect of our lives. He wanted to leave the psychiatrist's office and find in the life of a man who was never a patient further evidence that it is correct for analysts to deny that "health and disease, normal and nervous, are sharply distinguished from each other, and that neurotic traits must be considered proofs of a general inferiority." And finally, he wanted to go back far in time, find in the remains, so to speak, of a man of great historical importance — his words, remarks attributed to him, his sketches and paintings — evidence that explains some of the contradictions and ambiguities of his life.

Freud acknowledges that not much is known about Leonardo's childhood. He refers to "the obscurity" of the artist's boyhood. Still, in his scientific notebook Leonardo did mention a childhood memory:

> It seems that I was always destined to be so deeply concerned with vultures; for I recall as one of my very earliest memories that while I was in my cradle a vulture came down to me and opened my mouth with its tail, and struck me many times with its tail against my lips.

When mentioning the bird Leonardo used the word *nibio*, which in the modern Italian form *nibbio* refers to a kite, not a vulture. Freud keeps on using the German word *geier*, meaning vulture. He was misled by several German translations.

There is no doubt that this memory of Leonardo's stirred Freud's imagination. He argues his case not only forcefully but elegantly. He does indeed make the sexual interpretations that by now are unsurprising to those who have experienced psychoanalysis firsthand. The vulture is the mother, yet Leonardo, strangely, has "succeeded in endowing precisely this bird which is a mother with the distinguishing mark of masculinity." Such a paradox is explained, and soon (if we are disposed to go along) a man's memory is made the clue to his later psychological characteristics.

Nor does Freud stop there. Immensely learned, and especially so about the various ancient cultures, he makes what Alan Tyson calls "the Egyptian connection." Leonardo was not alone, and may well have known so, Freud suggests, because the hieroglyph for the Egyptian word for "mother" also happens to represent a vulture. Moreover, Freud's friend Oskar Pfister came up with another notion, and in 1919 Freud added it as a footnote to his book's argument: in Leonardo's *St. Anne with Two Others*, at the Louvre, Mary's "curiously arranged and rather confining drapery" turns out to have the "outline of a vulture." Pfister called it an "unconscious picture-puzzle," and by the time he was through with his analysis one part of the drapery is "a bird's outspread tail, whose righthand end, exactly as in Leonardo's fateful childhood dream, leads to the mouth of the child, i.e., of Leonardo himself."

It is easy to scoff at all this. Freud was not altogether won over to Pfister's imaginative vision, as it could be called; but apart from Pfister's contribution Freud had constructed his own elaborate interpretation on what turned out to be, in retrospect, rather shaky ground. Still, the immediate response to his book had nothing to do with the details of the argument, but rather was moral: how dare these psychoanalysts, their minds always so grimly centered on pathology, most of it sexual, take on a much revered man, dead several hundred years, and saddle him with a host of psychiatric complexes and disorders? No matter how generous Freud was to Leonardo's genius, no matter how carefully and incisively he tried to connect the artist to every single one of us, the anger and mockery continued; nor were they without effect.

Irrational rejection breeds even in the best of men disappointment and sadness. Freud often reassured his colleagues that some day the world would take seriously their various formulations and conjectures — and one measure of his genius was just that self-assurance. On the other hand, under constant assault he and his coworkers became victims of their effort to defend themselves. Wrongly dismissed, they in turn dismissed others, however well intentioned such skepticism and misgivings were. Well-educated and cultivated men, they couldn't help becoming cliquish, even parochial, and highly self-protective. The next step, alas, was a kind of arrogance that demolishes all criticism as "irrational," or treats such criticism with a barrage of unnecessarily self-justifying counterargument — for example Kurt Eissler's effort to challenge the more cautious and justifiable criticism of Freud's Leonardo study.

Eissler's *Leonardo da Vinci* is a long book, in comparison to which Freud's own seems a mere monograph. Much of Eissler's argument is set forth, far less polemically and legalistically, by the four editors (James and Alix Strachey, Anna Freud, and Alan Tyson) in their introduction to Mr. Tyson's translations of Freud's book. They grant that certain "arguments and conclusions are invalidated by careful analysis of Freud's assumptions." (A kite is not a vulture.) Still, assuming a certain psychoanalytic sensibility in their readers, the editors quite justifiably refuse to give way completely. Leonardo's memory or fantasy or daydream (who can ever know exactly which?) seems justifiably of psychological interest, as does the "interesting problem" of how it came about that the Egyptians linked the ideas of "vulture" and "mother." Egyptologists attribute the connection to chance: a phonetic coincidence. Psychoanalysts have a right to speculate otherwise, though not at Leonardo's or anyone else's expense, unless with some evidence.

Most important, for all his ambitiousness and speculative ingenuity, Freud never lost the guardedness that clinical work demands. "The aim of our work," he said at the end of his study, "has been to explain the inhibitions in Leonardo's sexual life and in his artistic activity." To a degree he succeeded. Leonardo's hopes and his fears make a good deal of sense to the receptive reader by the time he has read the various interpretations offered by a writer who had more than a touch of the novelist in him: the text is clean and direct, its narrative power hard to resist. Very important, there are discussions that amount to a separate contribution; Leonardo's life stimulated Freud to think about a number of psychoanalytic issues he had not before dealt with very seriously, and for the first time he broached the subject of "narcissism." Later on that aspect of human development would prompt in him and other analysts no end of concern.

On the other hand, he ran into difficulties, some of them not unforeseen. Leonardo had himself in his own language admitted to the "sexual inhibitions" Freud calls to our attention repeatedly, so he was not in the position of making a case that may well be false. Perhaps on that account the writing at times is so relaxed and satisfactory: we are not being nervously grabbed by the collar and told to ignore all existing documents and legends in favor of a premise that can never be proved, only believed.

However, quite another tone appears when the second part of the author's "aim" is being fulfilled. We are warned that some critics, and even more significantly some of Leonardo's contemporaries, simply didn't look upon his "artistic activity" as "inhibited" — not that they were likely to use such a word. Instead, they offered excuses for his failure to finish much of his work, or were frankly puzzled by it, or felt prompted to remember that others (like Michelangelo) also worked slowly, even enigmatically. They also have insisted that Leonardo was a man of the very widest interests; when he was not painting he was occupying himself with an astonishing range of scientific investigations and forecasts, often wedded to his artistic capabilities through intricate sketches or drawings.

Such efforts to look at Leonardo as a thoroughly successful and productive artist and scientist, entitled to make his own decisions about what to work on and for how long at a time, are to Freud "excuses," admittedly "valid" but not sufficient. Whereas he freely admits that little is known about Leonardo's childhood and youth, he is less willing to stress what is nevertheless true: that absolutely nothing is known about any thoughts or "associations" Leonardo may have had about his decision to pursue careers as an artist and a scientist, and to do so at his own speed. His problems as a child and later as a man who feared sexual relations with women and sought out intense relationships with men are treated sensitively by Freud, and in such a way as slowly to produce a plausible picture: against considerable odds a particular man struggled hard to find the best kind of life he could, given impediments he simply could not shake off.

In contrast, when Freud considers Leonardo the man of Western scientific and cultural history, a rather different approach becomes evident. Things are not so much clarified and furnished a perspective as made the subject of all too fixed and unqualified interpretations. Leonardo's interest in how birds fly, his prophecies that man may one day do the same, move Freud to ask: "But why do so many people dream of being able to fly?" The answer: the wish to be able to fly is nothing else than a "longing to be capable of sexual performance." Leonardo's career as a sharp naturalistic observer is explained this way: "His rebellion against his father was the infantile determinant of what was perhaps an equally sublime achievement in the field of scientific research." True, the *Mona Lisa* is a portrait, the product of observation and imagination, but the artist found his model's smile so powerful and unforgettable "for the reason that it awoke something in him which had for long lain dormant in his mind — probably an old memory."

The memory, of course, had to do with his mother, and her influence on Leonardo's later life is put this way: "For his mother's tenderness was fateful for him; it determined his destiny and the privations that were in store for him." Elsewhere Freud is more restrained; Leonardo's mother is connected only to *part* of his destiny — as a celibate and lonely man. But at the end, after pointing out modestly that "psychoanalysis does not throw light on Leonardo's artistic powers," Freud feels he has to insist that both the "manifestations" and "limitations" of those "powers" are indeed made "intelligible" to us by psychoanalytic inquiry — and then he goes on to make this claim:

> It seems at any rate as if only a man who had had Leonardo's childhood experiences could have painted the Mona Lisa and the St. Anne . . . have embarked on such an astonishing career as a natural scientist, as if the key to all his achievements and misfortunes lay hidden in the childhood phantasy of the vulture.

That last phrase is, of course, not at all substantiated, nor has the fate of any psychoanalyst ever since been to find such a "key" to anyone's career, however "astonishing." It can be argued that the same holds for anyone's life, even that of a terribly hurt and suffering mental patient who can barely stay quiet long enough to read a book or look at a painting with any concentration. Ironically and without prejudice one might observe that it is a key dream of the author's that is revealed in such a comment: somewhere a person's creativity — his or her "astonishing career," all the achievements that get recorded in history — can be located and then exposed.

Yet the study throughout works against such a conclusion. Again and again Freud connected Leonardo's presumed childhood experiences and his later psychological characteristics to those that millions of other people have. Health and illness, he emphasized, are not so "sharply distinguished from each other," nor are the so-called normal from those referred to as "neurotic." Insofar as each of us is a "civilized human being," he points out, we are susceptible to one or another neurotic tendency; the repressive function of the mind, so constantly in operation, guarantees such an outcome. Leonardo was indeed "obsessional," but so are millions of other people. The real question, of course, is what Leonardo did with his life; not just with neurosis, but with his remarkable energy — his emerging intelligence, his perceptiveness, his sensitivity, his imagination, his resourcefulness of spirit, his artistic sensibility, his capacity to take note of how all sorts of things (including the body's muscles and joints) work.

These are not words or phrases Freud uses. He more or less takes for granted Leonardo's genius. He mentions it but does not "analyze" it. That is not the kind of analysis he is up to. Mostly he is willing to admit that as a psychoanalyst he will never be able to make such an analytic attempt. He calls his study a "pathographical review" and defends it as such against those who would call it "a piece of useless impertinence." Such people, he insists with some truculence, really want utterly untarnished heroes. Such people go about idealizing certain gifted historical figures and for that reason "find all pathography unpalatable." Still, he puts in the mouths of such people an argument that he never answers, intent as he is on analyzing their "real" (worshipful) intent. The argument is that a psychoanalytic study of a great man "never results in an understanding of his importance and his achievements," so there is no point in making "a study of things in him that could just as easily be found in the first person one came across."

As one reads Freud carefully in this important psychoanalytic biography his dilemma becomes apparent. He wants to comprehend an elusive and gifted man. He has a limited amount of information to go on. He is not interested in undercutting his subject, turning him into some perverse eccentric whom everyone without his talents can pity. He is a man of discrimination and refinement. He wants to learn — from his own frailties, as they come across in dreams, slips of the tongue, fantasies, as well as from Leonardo's life, in so far as it can be discerned.

On the other hand he is in his own way as insatiably curious as Leonardo was; he wants answers — and not just to small questions. He once likened himself to a conquistador, but like all conquistadors, there was just so much territory he could conquer. He had at his disposal a nineteenth-century mechanistic view of nature, a cause-and-effect mentality that scientists of his day found helpful in the course of their work. This produces that. One thing brings about another. X lies at the root of Y. And if it doesn't *seem* that way, if there are many other forces at work and all of them make for a murky atmosphere, then the greater the challenge. With more knowledge comes increased specificity — and that is the direction a scientist travels. So, back and forth he goes, even from paragraph to paragraph. One moment he says he is trying to fathom Leonardo's "trivial peculiarities" and the "riddles of his nature" so as to discover "what determined his mental and intellectual development." The word "determined" stands out, especially when it is used in connection with Leonardo's *intellectual* development. No wonder, a page or two on, we encounter quite another line of thinking:

> In Leonardo's case we have had to maintain the view that the accident of his illegitimate birth and the excessive tenderness of his mother had the most decisive influence on the formation of his character and on his later fortune, since the sexual repression which set in after this phase of childhood caused him to sublimate his libido into the urge we know, and established his sexual inactivity for the whole of his later life. But this repression after the first erotic satisfactions of childhood need not necessarily have taken place; in someone else it might perhaps not have taken place or might have assumed much less extensive proportions.
>
> We must recognize here a degree of freedom which cannot be resolved any further by psychoanalytic means. Equally, one has no right to claim that the consequence of this wave of repression was the only possible one. It is probable that another person would not have succeeded in withdrawing the major portion of his libido from repression by sublimating it into a craving for knowledge; under the same influences he would have sustained a permanent injury to his intellectual activity or have acquired an insurmountable disposition to obsessional neurosis.
>
> We are left, then, with these two characteristics of Leonardo which are inexplicable by the efforts of psychoanalysis; his quite special tendency towards instinctual repressions, and his extraordinary capacity for sublimating the primitive instincts.

One can try to pin a life down, but only so far. There is that "degree of freedom" — frustrating to a scientist who wants to have every possible "variable" tracked down and fitted right in its place. Even more vexing, that "quite special tendency" and that "extraordinary capacity" were by no means only Leonardo's, nor are they only the property of a few geniuses. Those tendencies or capacities are widespread. Many talented people respond to thousands of different childhood experiences through their own unique blend of repressions and sublimations. Anyway, as Freud goes on to say, there is a biological element in all this that defies our comprehension — even now, decades later. He writes of "the organic foundations of character on which the mental structure is only afterwards erected."

His language here is as vague as the state of knowledge warranted. What I suppose he might have said, were he less of a hopeful, ambitious scientist and of a more philosophical nature, would go something like this: we can understand some of this man's psychological troubles, but his gifts as an artist and a scientist are beyond anyone's ken; they are God-given or part of Nature's mysterious design, though maybe someday, centuries later, we'll know more — and meanwhile let's not try to do the impossible with the valuable but thoroughly limited tools available. If he sometimes approaches saying that, he also backs into quite another corner: *only* a man with Leonardo's kind of childhood could have painted the *Mona Lisa*.

The difficulties Freud faced and candidly admitted in his study of Leonardo have persisted, despite the efforts of psychoanalytically sophisticated biographers. Nor have all of Freud's successors been as fair and self-critical as he was when he wrote about Leonardo. In the name of "applied psychoanalysis" the lives of an assortment of political leaders, generals, artists, and writers, not to mention characters in novels, short stories, and plays, have been examined; and as one goes through those attempts, dozens and dozens of them, one keeps coming back to the Leonardo study — and to Freud's superior quality as a thinker and a writer.

He may not have been able to transcend the limits of his own historical era. He may have made mistakes of fact, even at times of judgment. He may have tried unsuccessfully to harness language to a number of ambitions. As a scientist searching for tangible discoveries, but also as a man of artistic temperament, especially sensitive to the opportunities and hazards that words present, he was not unlike Leonardo, caught between opposing directions of his own making. But Freud did not in frustration, resentment, and envy turn on the man he was trying to learn more about. Words like "oral" or "anal" or "phallic" are not fastened upon Leonardo. His ideas about religion are discussed in the context of the fifteenth and sixteenth centuries in which he lived.

If Freud shows pride and more than a dash of the messianic explorer, determined at fifty-three to find an intellectual New Jerusalem, he is also able to be tentative, and frankly so. Almost inadvertently, and ironically just at the point when he becomes categorical, we are given a chance to see the confines of his own thinking. When we are told that psychoanalysis finds "inexplicable" Leonardo's particular bent for repression and his remarkable powers of sublimation we are confronted with the author's own impasse. Freud can describe Leonardo in new ways but in the end that impasse remains: a man's various gifts defy the imagery of pathography. If I am able to play tennis all day and score quite well at it, too, I do so not because tennis has a symbolic meaning to me, based on a "problem," or because I lack various diseases or handle certain physiological stresses in a way that differs from that of many others, who find that their symbolic sense of what tennis "means," based on their past or still present "problems" and their physiological makeup, however like mine, do not get translated into my kind of game.

To put it differently, infirmities, or the thoughts they prompt, or even the absence of infirmities don't explain the presence of assets. Here words and phrases come to mind that Freud for his own reasons learned to distrust: will, determination, ingenuity, spirit, ambitions — dreams of a broader kind than he tended to analyze. He had found it necessary to move away from those ways of speaking (and looking at the world) because many of his first patients had for years been slapped on the back or kicked somewhere and told to find willpower, shape up, and get better. The more he listened to his patients the less respect he had for the moralistic pieties of Victorian consciousness. He wanted to expose all that for the sham it was. Anyway, he was not a fuzzy or abstract philosopher, certainly not a theologian, but a neurophysiologist become psychiatrist become a new kind of scientist, a psychoanalyst, so he did not wish to talk about Leonardo's willful spirit, which at times had given way to indifference or apparent apathy.

In a sense, then, Freud's study was a dramatic standoff. There was Leonardo, across the centuries, a man whose obvious capacities and achievements could not be taken for granted or buried under an avalanche of terminology developed in response to the plight of seriously disturbed patients. And there was Freud, anxious to extend his observations to include people like Leonardo, but smart enough to hold back, or venture out only for so long on thin ice.

The best psychoanalytic theorists, first Freud himself, then his daughter Anna, and Heinz Hartmann, have tried to find concepts that would make it easier for them to consider not only Leonardo but those many people who may have their moments of tension, but who in general live useful and untroubled lives. The ego has been emphasized; its capacities have been described in detail. The id may exert its pressures, but we have those various "mechanisms of defense" to call upon. Moreover, the ego is not only in the position of reacting to demands or outright assaults made upon it. The ego has its own energy, some of it "conflict free." When we mobilize our intelligence, use the mind's power of logic and analysis, we are summoning "conflict-free" energy.

The expression "conflict free," used so often by Heinz Hartmann, is a revealing one; with respect to man's everyday work, his various successes as a competent and resourceful creature, it is as far as psychoanalysis can go conceptually, given its history, its concerns, and not least, the nature of its imagery. Hartmann, like Freud, was a man of vast knowledge, and sensitive to the respect and good manners, if not admiration, that novelists or artists, like other human beings, have the right to assume from those who study them. The same can be said for Ernst Kris, a colleague of Hartmann's who had a special interest in artists and the sources of their creativity; and for Anthony Storr; whose recent book[2] shows that such an interest continues to preoccupy certain analysts. Kris worked hard at distinguishing between the paintings or drawings of hospitalized psychotics and those

---

[2] *The Dynamics of Creation* (Atheneum, 1972).

done by artists, and Storr emphasizes the difference between what he calls "pornographic images" and "great art."

But one wonders whether there is any need for psychoanalysts to bother themselves with such distinctions, however well intended. Critics, maybe even ordinary viewers, are quite able to do so on their own. No doubt both of those analysts were angered by and ashamed of what some of their colleagues have done in the name of psychoanalytic "interpretation" of writers, artists, political leaders. Yet at a certain point, all these psychological efforts at biography, literary criticism, or the "analysis" of artistic production come upon the very stumbling blocks Freud had the good sense to discuss openly in his Leonardo book. Here, for example, is Dr. Storr, writing about "creativity" over half a century after that book was published:

> Man is a creature inescapably, and often unhappily divided; and the divisions within him recurrently impel the use of his imagination to make new syntheses. The creative consequences of his imaginative striving may never make him whole; but they constitute his deepest consolations and his greatest glories.

Always it is trouble, problems, conflicts, "divisions" that generate novels and paintings, or for that matter, the efforts of history's gifted leaders. A phrase like "impel the use of his imagination" may be an attractive way of putting it, but the cause-and-effect assertion is both utterly clear and utterly unsubstantiated — and the use of such a phrase only serves to show that those of us who are trained to dwell upon psychopathology, to think of people as variants of one or another "psychiatric model" (the anal or oral or phallic "character,") are also "impelled" to use our imaginations for certain reasons.

To his credit Kurt Eissler has furthered discussion of this issue substantially, as I mentioned in a previous essay:

> The question, however, has not been answered, what connection exists between the genius's psychopathology and his achievements. Psychopathology, in general, is looked upon as defect . . . Observation of the genius, however, suggests the possibility that psychopathology is indispensable to the highest achievements of certain kinds.

He then takes the next logical step:

> Consequently if what we observed in the genius struck us as neurotic or psychotic or perverse or even criminal, we would then have to reconsider our classification under these accustomed headings. If, for example, an apparently obsessional symptom was indispensable to geniushood . . . there would be no sense in calling it a neurotic symptom. Whatever the essence of neurosis may be, the concept of neurosis makes sense only when it is correlated with a deficit.

Needless to say, what goes for the genius goes for the near-genius and on down. One has a right to ask the broader question: What connection is there between an ordinary human being's daily achievements and his psychopathology, or between a psychiatrist's, a lawyer's, a politician's accomplishments and the various emotional upsets he as a human being is bound to have? Open-minded on this issue as Eissler is, he can't give up the conviction that psychopathology of some kind is a *sine qua non* of genius. In fact, psychopathology is a *sine qua non* of life — as Freud among others (Job, Isaiah, Saint Paul, not to mention some of those geniuses Eissler mentions) has made quite clear. Why is its presence in anyone, gifted or not, an occasion for surprise, and more than that, aggrandizement — the insistence that other elements in a person's life are tied to, or are expressions of, or are causatively linked with "deficits" or neurotic developments in childhood or "mechanisms of defense," such as sublimation?

For some reason it has been psychoanalysts, among psychological theorists, who have been most anxious to study the lives of creative men and women, or of historical figures. Piaget, whose studies of intelligence as it develops over the years might be considered particularly well suited to such studies, has avoided them, perhaps because his speculations always follow from what he has watched and heard, even as Anna Freud has in recent years insisted that "direct observation" ought to precede theoretical formulation and elaboration. Perhaps a scientist like Piaget knows full well that the "variables" that make up a man's creative life — be it a writer's or a political leader's or a psychoanalyst's — defy the language and concepts of any particular psychological theory.

Anna Freud once referred to "the universally envied gift of creative energy."[3] There is no point in turning that gift into an unap-
proachable mystery. Scientists have a right to move closer toward
any "phenomenon" they happen to find interesting. Nor need such
an approach be insulting, abusive, or destructive. The issue is one of
evidence — is there enough of it? — but also of motives, as Miss
Freud has mentioned; and envy is only one of them. Theorists, like
the presidents and dictators they study, can be overcome by ambition
and a kind of intellectual aggressiveness that has to be checked by the
prudent skepticism of critics.

In this regard, some of Freud's most valuable discoveries — the
nature of "resistance" and the workings of "transference" and
"countertransference" in psychoanalytic therapy — have become
ironic instruments in the most narrow kind of ideological self-
justification. Doubts or misgivings are chalked up to a lack of psychoanalytic experience or sophistication, if not to outright
"hostility" or "ambivalence" of one or another kind. This *ad
hominem* tendency obviously undercuts the possibility of any rational argument, except of the kind sanctioned by those who do the
thinly disguised name calling.

Even friends can get caught in such intellectual warfare, where
sides are taken and one is considered either a friend or a foe. Referring to an interesting and suggestive biography, *Woodrow Wilson and
Colonel House,* the editor of a collection of essays called *Psychoanalysis and History* makes an interpretation of sorts: "Brodie's
review-essay of the Georges' book about Wilson points up the
overtly psychoanalytic aspects of their work, which they felt con-
strained to conceal in a footnote."[4] The editor himself notes a few
sentences later that the book's subtitle is "A Personality Study." Furthermore, in an author's note at the very beginning, even before the
table of contents, Alexander and Juliette George acknowledge forth-
rightly the influence Harold Lasswell and Nathan Leites had on their
study of Wilson's relationship to his longtime principal adviser. A

---

[3]Foreword to *Vincent Van Gogh: A Psychological Study* by Humberto Nagera (International
Universities Press, 1968).
[4]*Psychoanalysis and History,* edited by Bruce Mazlish (Grosset & Dunlap, 1971).

special "Research Note" discusses that influence for six pages — before the section called "Notes and Bibliography" even begins.

What have they concealed — or rather, why are they described as concealing anything? True, they write as historians. That is to say, they want to examine the psychological quality of a particular president's involvement with one of his aides, but they also want to move from one point in time to another, and carry their readers with them. In other words, their interests are chronological and narrative as well as psychological. They have a broad view of American political life to present and, just as important, to document convincingly — in a way that will make the reader understand what he is reading and feel satisfied that a sincere effort has been made to start with facts, assemble them into a point of view, and present the latter as that and only that, not as the answer to a "problem."

No doubt about it, psychoanalytic terminology is avoided by the Georges. We are not told, as we are in *Thomas Woodrow Wilson: A Psychological Study* by William Bullitt and Sigmund Freud, that "the libido insulated in his [Wilson's] reaction-formation against his passivity to his father had been without outlet and had reached such a pitch of intensity that it had to break out against someone." We are told much about Wilson and his father, considerably less but nevertheless much about Colonel House. The President and his aide found in each other a fateful dovetailing of psychological qualities. Certainly they worked out "neurotic needs" through one another, as we all do, and eventually (when things were going downhill on other accounts) at each other's expense. But the Georges can't seem to forget that the involvement of the two men has to be viewed from other directions: the nature of the presidency, the social and cultural characteristics of a given moment in American history, the particular stresses that wars, accidents, unexpected tragedies (the death of Wilson's first wife) can bring upon a man's character and personality, whatever the determinants of childhood that bear down on him, on all of us.

I doubt very much that even the most eager proponent of "applied psychoanalysis," or one of its contemporary equivalents or closely related "areas" of inquiry, "psychohistory," would want to change the perspective the Georges have given us. How might they have made their debt to psychoanalysis more explicit? As other historians and essayists have done over the centuries, they have drawn upon knowledge that is available, traditional modes of study or reflection and new modes, and made of it all an exercise in exposition, explanation, and comment.

If they conceal anything from the reader it is any temptation they may have felt to fix static labels on the men they were studying or to come up with sweeping, unqualified statements such as this: "In fact, psychoanalytic theory fully accounts for the observation that no known charismatic leader can be described as a genuine genital character."[5] Or, "The personality of the charismatic leader can be characterized briefly, since we already indicated that his behavior must conform to childish fantasies about how omnipotent adults behave."[6] Or, with regard to Robespierre: "Unfortunately, the implacable superego coupled with the released sadism and the projective paranoid mechanisms common to the Leader and the masses created the need for further human sacrifices, and thus the Revolution in a truly cannibalistic way devoured its own children."[7]

Nor is Robespierre unique: "The psychological truth expressed in this last speech of the doomed leader exceeds his singular case and applies to every revolutionary leader and to every dictator."[8] In this century the love they give us, the good and decent intentions they possess and offer to us as something to imitate and make our own, the cultural heritage they hand down — so many facts, so many assumptions, so much that has to do with proficiency and self-assurance and comprehension of the world — all of that somehow is either taken for granted or overlooked in favor of "complexes" of various kinds.

There is, further, a pejorative streak in the language of psychopathology that not only demeans the "object" of description but the writer doing it and his or her "discipline." There is also a stingi-

---

[5]"Charismatic Leadership in Crisis" by George Devereux, in *Psychoanalysis and the Social Sciences,* edited by Warner Muensterberger and Sidney Axelrad (International Universities Press, 1955).
[6]Ibid.
[7]"Dictatorship and Paranoia" by Gustav Bychowski, ibid.
[8]Ibid.

ness of spirit in some of the descriptions psychiatrists and psychologists (and those who follow their lead in other disciplines) give to individuals of the most obvious attainments. Which contemporary historians or critics advocate unthinking, reflexive sentiment or glorification? These days the danger comes from quite another direction: will the application of psychological "insight" to history or the arts be done in such a way as to produce caricatures of human beings — and those only to be turned into proof of some larger generalization about the "laws" that govern the human mind?

Or will one kind of knowledge be called "superficial" simply because it possesses its own richness and complexity of vision — in contrast to another kind of knowledge that somebody else happens to find congenial or happens to be trained to call upon? Or will a book's manner of organization and language be pushed into intellectual arguments or vendettas that really have nothing to do with what an author has intended?

In the case of the Georges' book on Wilson, two historians have nicely drawn upon psychoanalytic principles without in any way doing an injustice to their own responsibilities. To imply that they are hiding something out of fear is to be less than fair not only to their profession but to their scholarship. No one would deny that some historians, like some doctors or lawyers or writers, have no use for *any* effort to look at historical figures from a psychoanalytic perspective — overtly or otherwise. Still, it is absurd at this time for analysts and those interested in "applying" psychoanalysis or developing a "field" called "psychohistory" to imagine themselves embattled, scorned outcasts, neglected on all fronts — rather as Freud and his first followers were.

Psychoanalysis and its various "applications" have been embraced all too ardently by the American public — and not only by its so-called "lay" segment. Sometimes that enthusiasm was for the bad: it is astonishing, for example, how many writers submitted willingly to the brutal, stupid lashings an analyst like Edmund Bergler gave them in his books supposedly meant to "explain" writers and their "personality structure." But sometimes much of value came of this enthusiasm: it is remarkable how openly and generously many important American medical schools welcomed analysts during the

1930s and 1940s, often to good effect so far as the education of young doctors goes. In any event, to this day a historian or political scientist, not to mention a psychoanalyst, who writes a biography or discusses some contemporary issue, or one connected with the remote past, from a psychological point of view stands at the very least an excellent chance of getting the public's attention.

Walter Langer's "secret wartime report," now become *The Mind of Adolf Hitler*, has hardly been ignored. In view of the substantial scholarship on the Nazis that has gone relatively unnoticed — the work of historians, economists, political scientists — one has to look not only at the book itself but at the reasons for its appeal. Nor has Bruce Mazlish's "psychohistorical inquiry" into Richard Nixon's life been ignored — any more than will the portentously named *The Kennedy Neurosis: A Psychological Portrait of an American Dynasty*. Each of them is yet another variant of the kind of inquiry Freud began long ago: harnessing psychology to an understanding of certain people who have taken a significant part in history.

To start with the worst, the book on the Kennedy family is, alas, an exercise in nastiness, and an instructive lesson in how psychological words and phrases, presented as a means of scientific exposition, can become in certain hands instruments of moral condemnation, and even malicious abuse. The author of *The Kennedy Neurosis*, Nancy Clinch, refers to her "study of the Kennedys' characterology" as a "form of psychohistory"; it is even "psychohumanism." People have what she calls "self-actualizing needs." There are "parental patterns" and a "specific cultural milieu," and they, of course, affect a "hierarchy of needs." When things go wrong a neurosis develops: "a self-defeating defense pattern of feeling and behaving." Something called a "pseudo-self" comes into being. There is "basic anxiety" and it keeps generating "unconscious hostility." After we learn about all that, we are told where we are going:

> It is my purpose to analyze what the historical record seems to reveal: that the Kennedy drive to power was largely neurotic in origin and thus largely neurotic in goal; and that when power was obtained, the Kennedys were severely limited in the use of their authority for positive aims because of emotional conflicts and ambivalences.

Note the word "because": assertive, unthreatened by any modifiers, anxious to make its connection. There is no point in looking at the structure of our government, let alone at our society. Those political scientists and journalists who try to figure out what presidents can and cannot do, those historians who try to apprehend the subtleties of America's development as a democracy, the regional tensions, the push and pull of economic and social forces — they have been seduced by complexity, ambiguity, even uncertainty. The author says we need "autonomy, self-direction, and freedom." Those observers and scholars of American history need the freedom to use the word "because" more boldly — though one can drop the word and get the same startling result:

> The Kennedys, like American scientists, achieved the "impossible" through teamwork in their election triumphs. But once elected, they seemed to "fall under a fairyland spell" that kept them from accomplishing any significant part of their professed aims.

The "spell" is next defined: "neurotic conflict." It seems that Mr. and Mrs. Joseph P. Kennedy (called "Joe and Rose") made "excessive demands for perfection and social success" on their sons and daughters. The result: a need on the part of those children for their own "frustration, punishment and even destruction":

> I do not see the Kennedy failures in performance as caused mainly by bad luck or by the vagaries of politics and human nature. Rather, the factual failures were largely the result of psychohistorical circumstances that existed for the Kennedy sons even before they were born and that strongly affected the shaping of their individual characters.

So much for "bad luck" or the "vagaries of politics and human nature" — the stuff of novelists or playwrights, the passing fancy of newspapermen, the preoccupation of old-fashioned, overly scrupulous scholars or essayists, who may be aware of "unconscious emotional conflicts," but who get sidetracked by their search for facts, their insistence on maintaining detachment as well as respect for those they study.

Perhaps this book has its place; some day social historians will want to study its by no means unique mixture of Nichols and May psychology, non sequiturs, simpleminded social commentary, and dizzying historical overstatement. For example, Mr. Joseph P. Kennedy is singled out from the rest of us parents for "unconsciously" projecting "his needs and longings onto his sons." Even though the author admits that some of the book's points "may seem strained, and even cruel," she persists, in the interest of truth. Thus, "Jack, Bobby, and Teddy" (as they are called by this expert on their lives who has never even met them) "would all take up cigar smoking, the Freudian symbol of potency and power."

Then there was President Kennedy. Here is what his White House staff was all about:

> Thus Kennedy was not only in close and constant touch with his family, but he also created a new family of staff retainers who seem to have served partly as substitute parent images daily filling the old dual role of nursemaids and slave drivers.

One of them was Kennedy's secretary, Mrs. Lincoln. He may have liked her, but his general attitude toward women, along with a few other things, is summarized in the following four sentences:

> Kennedy essentially disliked and distrusted women. Therefore his strong emotional need for support and approval led him to follow the counsel of male authority figures. Unfortunately, a large number of these authority figures — such as McNamara, Rusk, Acheson, Taylor, Bundy, and Rostow — were as confused and misguided as Kennedy about national values and priorities. The 1971 publication of the Pentagon Papers clearly revealed this about their Vietnam policy.

There it is: from sexism to Vietnam in less than a paragraph. Not that the author forgets other parts of the world. She says the President had "an emotional fixation" on Castro, who was "Kennedy's alter-ego: the bold leader Kennedy longed to be but could not bring himself to become." Why could he not? "Making laws may arouse unconscious resistance in the lawmaker who has suffered much in his own life from rigid legalisms."

As for the President's brother and trusted adviser, he was similarly "neurotic." Did he have compassion for the poor and vulnerable in this nation? Yes, but "this is understandable in view of his 'underdog' position in the family and the emotional insecurity he never lost." Did he like athletics and inspire young people to follow suit? True, but there was a reason:

> Here we can see a belief in the masculine mystique of physical toughness, and also a probable need for reassurance and affection through physical contact with other males that was more difficult to express directly. Football for the Kennedy sons — and especially Robert, who even kept a football in his Attorney General's office and often tossed it around with his staff — carried deep psychological undertones of emotional need and gratification.

Finally, the author, who can toss a few passes of her own, reserves the longest throws for the book's last paragraphs: "Yet the Kennedy mystique can also be seen as essentially the outcome of some four thousand years of the Graeco-Judeo-Christian ethos which has directed and energized Western civilization, and which has now spread over the world." There is cause for hope, though: "By studying the lives of national leaders, such as the Kennedys, we can find reflections of our own search for identity and confirmation, and help change both ourselves and our nation toward maturity and health rather than neurosis."

There are other reasons to study the lives of important men of history. As Walter C. Langer makes clear in his book on Hitler, the Office of Strategic Services was interested in winning the war; "maturity" and all the rest could come to Germany (and America) later. Colonel William J. ("Wild Bill") Donovan knew Dr. Langer, then a Boston psychoanalyst, and asked him to put together a psychological appraisal of Hitler, including an estimate of what he might do if things should go badly for him, as they already were going in 1943 when Langer began his hurried job. Yet, for all the rush, this book is decidedly better than the one on the Kennedys. Langer's portrait of

Hitler is far more thoughtful and sensitive than Miss Clinch's caricatures of the Kennedy family.

Langer avoids psychiatric name calling.[9] He emphasizes Hitler's strengths, his abilities, his obvious capacity to mesmerize and lead a nation. There are mistakes of judgment or emphasis, but these are usually owing to false information which was supplied to the relatively uninformed analyst and his quickly assembled staff. The prose is clear, a clue to the author's essential modesty and common sense. Once in a while there is an utterly fatuous remark, but it is usually delivered in a way that makes one less angry than regretful:

> I may be naïve in diplomatic matters, but I like to believe that if such a study of Hitler had been made years earlier, under less tension, and with more opportunity to gather first-hand information, there might not have been a Munich; a similar study of Stalin might have produced a different Yalta; one of Castro might have prevented the Cuban situation; and one of President Diem might have avoided our deep involvement in Vietnam. Studies of this type cannot solve our international problems. That would be too much to expect.

At only one point does the author reveal the smugness and arrogance that are all too common in such efforts, and even then they derive from a remark of one of Langer's colleagues: "Now I know what his [Hitler's] perversion is." Not that anyone *knows*. We are never given any hard, concrete evidence — only guesses and secondhand speculations, some from highly reliable sources, as the historian Robert B. L. Waite makes clear in his useful afterword. "It just came to me out of my clinical experience," the surprised Dr. Langer

---

[9]We are spared the absurd generalities of Gustav Bychowski's study a few years later on the same man (*Dictators and Disciples: A Psychoanalytic Interpretation of History,* International Universities Press, 1948).

The repressions of his psycho-sexual development did not permit the proper integration and sublimation of his aggressive-sadistic drives, which, to begin with, were not utilized for the construction of normal erotic aggression. The intended identification with his father was not even psychically successful, and instead of the expected masculinity, the constantly competing passive, female attitude appeared.

heard when he asked his colleague how she had come to that conclusion. Fortunately, it was Dr. Langer and not his colleague who tried to figure out the personality of a man whom he had never met and about whom he had only the most shadowy and suspect of information. Professor Waite says that such an attempt is justified: "Basically, he is convinced the perversion existed because he knows as an experienced analyst widely read in the literature of abnormal psychology that many patients with the same patterns of behavior as Hitler have exhibited a penchant for the same perversion."

Once again we are back to the same problem. Clearly those "patterns of behavior" Hitler had (shiftlessness for a while, anxiety, phobias, sexual inhibitions) have been and are shared by millions of people. *Some* of them may end up, as conjecture about Hitler would have it, lying on the floor and pleading with women to empty themselves (the nearer the better, and all over, if possible), but some may choose other ways to find pleasure, and by no means do all those with Hitler's "patterns of behavior," or anyone else's, share his supposed "penchant." A million prior interviews with disturbed men and women would not enable anyone to know the facts of a particular person's private life. Nor does Dr. Langer's prediction that Hitler would probably commit suicide when and if he were cornered constitute "dramatic and convincing evidence of the validity of his approach to an understanding of Hitler's personality." But Dr. Langer mentions several other possibilities, and is unwilling to pin himself down — a refreshing trait, in view of the certainties that other writers are drawn to.

Hitler himself repeatedly mentioned his intention; he would go down to death on his own rather than surrender, bringing all of Germany with him, if he had the choice. Clearly Dr. Langer was right in suggesting suicide as "the most plausible outcome," though he lists insanity and death in battle as other possibilities. But then, my ninth-grade Latin teacher made a similar prediction — he was more unequivocal — in class around the same year, when we were reading Caesar's *Gallic Wars;* and so did the journalist Dorothy Thompson, who mentioned the very same likelihood several times in her syndicated columns during the 1940s. I would imagine that thousands of people thought about Hitler as a probable suicide when they read their newspapers and saw how desperate his situation had suddenly become.

With Langer's study of Hitler we face once more the nagging questions other "psychohistorical" inquiries pose; and Dr. Langer can no more settle those questions for us than could Freud in the case of Leonardo. How did a wretched, deeply troubled, at times pathetic youth — the "neurotic psychopath" of this book — end up Führer of the Third Reich, a man not only possessed of authority and power but believed and heeded by millions? If not Hitler, might it have been someone else? If only Hitler, then surely it was not his "perversion" or his disordered mind (the province of the psychoanalyst) that accounts for his successes.

Hitler's life, like many other lives, presents several purely psychological mysteries, apart from the "psychohistorical" one of his particular rise to power. After the First World War, this nondescript, pitiable ne'er-do-well suddenly turned into a remarkably persistent and adept politician, then into a charismatic leader, finally the Führer of most of Europe. Langer refers to a "transformation of character," as well he might. But how to account for it? We are told that there is an explantation: the weak and panicky Hitler, "in order to quiet his fears," suddenly "imagined himself as a person who far surpassed his enemies in all the 'virile' qualities." We are given the name for such a psychological maneuver, "identification with the aggressor," and its importance is described in language not unlike that used by Freud in connection with Leonardo: "This is the key to an understanding of Hitler's actions since the beginning of his political activities to the present time."

Presumably Hitler was thereby freed to become what he eventually did become. If only that maneuver worked as well for thousands of other nobodies, who have tried desperately to convert their vulnerability and self-hate into something they can use on others. The Weimar Republic was full of such people; America has its share: people who "identify" with various "aggressors" — and, having done so, get nowhere. As for psychological recovery or "transformation," psychiatrists can spend long, intimate months, if not years, with patients and not know why at a particular moment a person is suddenly, it seems, "better." *In retrospect,* we come up with formulations, explanations: such and such was "interpreted." We are less likely to mention the many times we have offered similar "insights" to other patients, even to the same patient, all to no avail.

Langer was no doubt right about the turn of mind Hitler experienced. But he goes way beyond the bounds of logic — and his own profession's knowledge — when he makes that commonly indulged-in "mechanism" the "key" to an understanding of Hitler's "recovery," let alone all the subsequent "actions" of that satanic genius. Nor is the "messiah complex," also cited by him, very helpful — as any psychiatrist knows who works with the severely disturbed and utterly ineffectual "paranoid schizophrenics" who inhabit our state hospitals, insisting every day that they could save the world, if they were only heeded.

No one wants to circumscribe the continuing attempt of psychologists and psychiatrists to make sense of the irrational and bizarre, the seemingly normal but in fact pathological. It is when a more polemical, even aggrandizing tone enters the discussion that the possibility of a rational distinction between different objectives becomes hard to maintain. In this regard, Kurt Eissler is at least candid in his book on Leonardo. The first section of the book is frankly called "Polemics," and in a chapter called "The Historian vs. the Psychoanalyst" Eissler makes no bones about what he believes and, moreover, expects of those who disagree with him:

> There can, of course, be no doubt that the psychoanalyst has to know the results of historical and iconographic research; but what he does with that knowledge in order to reach psychological conclusions will more frequently than not strike the historian as far-fetched and inconclusive. [Meyer] Schapiro dismisses us with the admonition that the analyst should inform himself better about Leonardo's life and art and the culture of his time before applying his science to the psychological study of that life. Wohl and Trosman, with their little understanding of the subtleness of the genius, believe the problem could have been solved if Freud had "allowed his manuscript to be scrutinized" by an expert in history. These writers bypass the essential question that is at issue between the historical sciences and psychoanalysis and that cannot be resolved as long as the historian and philologist do not acquire full insight into psychoanalysis and are restrained by the bias of our

time from obtaining maximum knowledge of the structure of the human mind by consistent and long-lasting clinical work.[10]

No doubt somewhere there is a historian prepared to insist that any psychoanalyst who wants to write about history take a full graduate course and spend a few years doing "proper" historical research. But some scholars have to some degree combined the two disciplines — the historian Bruce Mazlish, for example, or the political scientist E. Victor Wolfenstein. Both men have psychoanalytic knowledge — of an order Dr. Eissler would doubtless find acceptable — as well as training in their professions.

Professor Mazlish has been an especially active proponent of what he and others (Robert Jay Lifton, Joel Kovel, John Demos) call "psychohistory." Each of these men has his own particular way of working with historical materials from a psychological (more precisely, psychoanalytic) point of view. They share a common interest in drawing upon several disciplines in the hope of seeing human experience more broadly, and escaping the rigidities and biases inherent in any particular psychoanalytic activity:

> Consider the impact on the assessment of an individual's psychological functioning if the limiting social postulate were changed from that of the "average expectable environment" to that of a "systematically fluctuating or a turbulent environment"; compare a campus in unrest set within a world in turmoil. That is, the simplifying assumptions made for its purposes by behavioral science, if *looked at as variables* as they are in another behavioral science which makes them its central subject matter, would influence the explanations arrived at in important ways.[11]

---

[10]One wants to read Eissler with respect and detachment but his persistent arrogance and rudeness make it hard to do so. We have reason to be grateful to Meyer Schapiro for the first-rate critical essays in which, without rancor, and with great sensitivity, he showed how Freud had erred. Eissler's book on Leonardo was largely prompted by Schapiro's observations, particularly his essay "Leonardo and Freud: An Art-Historical Study," first published in the *Journal of the History of Ideas*, Spring, 1956, and reprinted in *Renaissance Essays*, edited by P. Kristeller and P. Wiener (Harper & Row, 1968), and in *Ideas in Cultural Perspective*, edited by P. Wiener and A. Noland (Rutgers University Press, 1962).

[11]*The Psychoanalytic Forum*, Vol. 4 (International Universities Press, 1972).

Yet as one goes through Mazlish's *In Search of Nixon: A Psychohistorical Inquiry* or Wolfenstein's *The Revolutionary Personality: Lenin, Trotsky, Gandhi,* it seems clear that both scholars have as many dangers to avoid as opportunities to grasp. In both books we are warned that psychoanalytic "reductionism" is offensive and perhaps a thing of the past. Nevertheless, Nixon is called "oral" and "anal" at various points, as are Lenin, Trotsky, and Gandhi. Ambivalences are discussed, problems with mothers and fathers are described at length.

In the case of Mazlish's book an interesting dialectic of sorts takes place. First the President is described or typed. ("Orality is an important element in Nixon's character.") Then the reader is informed that such a description merely makes Richard Nixon a human being. If he has used a "genital metaphor and an anal one," then "others frequently use similar metaphors." After we have read two-thirds of his book, in which words or phrases like "passivity," "death anxiety," and "survivor guilt" are pervasive, Mazlish makes this statement: "What we have been discussing up to now may be thought of as the psychological banalities of Nixon's character." One wonders, at this point, why the author has bothered to write this book at all, especially since the rest of the book offers nothing else about the President's "character," only an extensive justification of the value of "psychohistory" as "science."

Understandably, Professor Mazlish has singled out Nixon, who has, after all, singled himself out. This "search" for Nixon ends with the discovery of "three traits," which he characterizes as "role identification," "ambivalence," and "denial." We have already been informed that any of us can possess these qualities. But Nixon apparently has more of them: "ambivalence, of course, is in all of us. Yet as a scholar I have never dealt with a public figure as ambivalent as Nixon." Exactly how does one qualify "ambivalence"? Has Mazlish studied other public figures? If so, which ones, and on what basis has he made his judgment? How are we to compare Nixon's "ambivalence" with, say, Wilson's? How does a psychiatrist distinguish among the degrees of ambivalence he finds in his various ambivalent patients? If the "degrees" of those three traits are at issue, one can find many patients who qualify as intensely ambivalent and who are also inclined to "deny" and resort to "role identification."

Nor do such patients become, on that account, hard to "know," as the President is claimed to be: "The three traits have made Nixon one of the most difficult political figures to analyze." Maybe the problem lies elsewhere; maybe the tools of psychoanalysis are inappropriate to the task at hand. In contrast, intelligent political journalists like Jules Witcover or Garry Wills, whose mind has been disciplined by the Jesuits, can "analyze" Nixon suggestively. Wills has evoked brilliantly those aspects of America's social reality that President Nixon has, one suspects, never overlooked or failed to understand. Wills understands the power of a certain kind of religious piety, even when it has become thoroughly secularized.

Richard Nixon's career — assisted, one should not forget, by Lee Harvey Oswald and Sirhan Sirhan — can be seen as the discerning response of an able and ambitious man to currents in American life he fully appreciates, and even manages to evoke with some credibility, in spite of the widespread distrust he also generates. When Wills analyzes our country's conflicting ideals and assumptions he gets as close to the "real" Nixon as any of us may find possible or desirable.

It is sad to find toward the end of Mazlish's book this remark: "Earlier we acknowledged that many people are wary of applying psychoanalysis to historical figures (and usually distrust therapy as well, a problem with which we cannot deal here)." It may be that many clinicians, who every day trust "therapy" enough to show up in an office and try hard to work with other human beings, have good reason to be wary: to repeat, so much that goes on in "treatment" is mysterious, intangible, elusive; one hesitates to apply to politics concepts already of very circumscribed or indeterminate value. Perhaps some of those wary clinicians would want to say what the psychoanalyst Leslie Farber did in response to the way human beings, from great men of history to ordinary workers and citizens, continue to be treated by members of his profession:

> Without examining these normative statements in detail, the reader can see why psychiatry is so often charged with being reductive. For while the creatures described above may bear some resemblance to animals or to steam engines or robots or electronic brains, they do not sound like people. They are in fact constructs of theory, more humanoid than humans; and whether they are

based on the libido theory or on one of the new interpersonal theories of relationships, it is just those qualities most distinctively human which seem to have been omitted. It is a matter of some irony, if one turns from psychology to one of Dostoyevsky's novels, to find that no matter how wretched, how puerile, or how dilapidated his characters may be, they all possess more humanity than the ideal man who lives in the pages of psychiatry.[12]

True, psychiatric jargon can be defended: it is a kind of shorthand for busy doctors who are not interested in describing "life," as novelists like Dostoevski are, but in understanding and "curing" patients. Even assuming that such a way of thinking and speaking about people helps clinical understanding and doesn't itself affect "treatment" — an assumption I would certainly not want to make — one has to insist on the obvious, so far as men like Leonardo or Nixon go: they are not "patients" in treatment by "psychohistorians" and so nothing absolves us of the responsibility to measure up to the standards Dr. Farber suggests.

When the theoretical intent of the writing Farber describes becomes more ambitious, as it does in Wolfenstein's book, among others — when we are after the roots of genius or the specific "drives" or "psychohistorical contexts" that make for a gifted artist or writer or politician, we are likely to find the same sorry results. Generalizations are heaped on one another and they turn out to be mirages, deceptively intriguing, but ultimately susceptible to being dismissed on the most elementary logical grounds. Lenin, Trotsky, and Gandhi, we are told, "each had an unusually ambivalent relationship with his father." Even the word "unusually" does not deprive those men of the company of thousands and thousands of others. Because those men were "ambivalent" they couldn't take orders. But they must be singled out even further, the author knows:

> . . . the inability to be a follower, of course, does not account for the ability to be a leader. For this something more is needed, namely a firm identification with parental authority, an underlying

---

[12]"Martin Buber and Psychiatry," *Psychiatry, A Journal for the Study of Interpersonal Processes,* XIX (1956), p. 110.

feeling of connection with the moral standards and behavior of one parent or another.

Does that formulation work, though? Are those leaders thereby distinguished from many men and women who have become "doctors, lawyers, Indian chiefs," factory workers and white-collar workers, maybe even psychiatrists and historians?

No discussion of "psychohistory" can even begin without mention of Erik Erikson, yet I come to him toward the end of this essay. Most of the "psychohistorians" I have mentioned refer to him constantly. His influence rivals Freud's; on those historians and political scientists I have discussed, I think it is fair to say his influence surpasses Freud's. Philosophers and theologians, also, have been especially indebted to him. "Religion," he writes in *Young Man Luther,* "elaborates on what feels profoundly true even though it is not demonstrable: it translates into significant words, images, and codes the exceeding darkness which surrounds man's existence, and the light which pervades it beyond all desert or comprehension."

One can look at such a sentence and be grateful for the subtlety of its content and expression. One can note the absence of heavy-handed "interpretations"; it is clear the writer does not intend to denigrate religion as an "illusion"; to "get" Luther, "explain" him, "expose" him, use him to prove a theory of his own — but rather to write a biography, an imaginative response to a series of facts about a particular person's life. Those facts are assembled to tell a story, to interest and maybe bestir the reader, to allow a writer with, say, psychological or philosophical interests (and how many writers are without such interests?) a medium for self-expression through another's life.

But there are obligations: to the letter and to the spirit of the subject's life. Though *Young Man Luther* has been widely praised, it has also been subject to serious criticism. Roland H. Bainton, Professor of Ecclesiastical History at Yale Divinity School, and an authority on Luther, has taken strong issue with a number of Erikson's assumptions. He has emphasized how vague, ambiguous, and sometimes severely distorted are those "sources" which even the best of Luther scholars ultimately have had to rely upon.

Bainton is not opposed to psychological speculation — with regard to Luther or anyone else. He mentions in what respects *Young*

Man Luther was helpful to him, even suggests further issues Erikson might have profitably explored. But he insists that much of Erikson's thesis necessarily has to depend on his translation of remarks by Luther, and on the validity of various statements attributed to Luther, often at second-, third- and fourthhand. He takes issue with several of Erikson's translations. He also points out that sometimes there is contradictory information about Luther — so much so that several different yet plausible conclusions can be drawn, depending on which sources, letters, anecdotes are cited.[13]

Even so, in spite of such hazards Erikson's book provides opportunities: to connect the past with the present, to show with discretion how the application of a particular discipline, psychoanalysis, developed in the twentieth century, makes more intelligible to us events that had a different kind of coherence for others who lived long ago. It is not enough to call Erikson a gifted writer or an unusually sensitive psychoanalyst. He is more than these. He has dared to bring up subjects like "virtue"; not just "conflict-free" or "neutralized" energy or "ego-strengths," but various ethical strivings. He has insisted that those who would write about historical figures openly examine what their own prejudices might be, what their purposes are in studying a particular "life" or historical issue.

Erikson's prose is the product of careful struggle because he knows the damage that has been done, particularly in psychology and the social sciences, by the use of "becauses," "contexts," and "interrelationships." Erikson talks about "trust" and "initiative" and "industry," plain and risky words that bring us closer to life and imply judgments on human experience. By doing so, he is also choosing not to rely on an evasive technical vocabulary. "Conflicts" there are; but also resolutions to them — and beyond that, affirmations that have their own authority, momentum, and, yes, psychohistory: a thoughtful father here, a kind-spirited mother there, a friend who helped, a husband or wife who helped even more, a time that begged for something from someone.

In Wolfenstein's book we are told that Lenin lacked "trust" in comparison to Trotsky and Gandhi, and all three went through an

---

[13]"Psychiatry and History: An Examination of Erikson's *Young Man Luther,*" *Religion in Life,* Winter, 1971.

"exceptionally stormy" adolescence, which, we are told, is "the period of the 'crisis of identity.' " Here a phrase of Erikson's has been turned into a new label. His ability to pull together in a single formulation many observations or ideas can be a mixed blessing. What is meant to inspire in others one kind of response (does this way of putting things fit? is it helpful? or ought I look elsewhere, perhaps use my own words, or simply keep looking and listening?) gets quite another response (that is the answer, or what I want to prove, or what I had better well prove, since everyone else these days is doing so).

In December of 1871, the first book of George Eliot's *Middlemarch* was published; within a year the eight sections of that long and demanding novel had appeared. She had spent years preparing for the writing, and as an unashamed moralist, she wanted not only to tell a story but to instruct. She hoped in *Middlemarch* to show how certain individuals live — and thereby to raise the old philosophical questions that some of us in psychiatry claim to have new ways of approaching: Who am I? What makes me behave as I do?

Middlemarch is "about" life in the English provinces from 1829 to 1832; it offers a detailed picture of a nation on the brink of political reform, social upheaval, economic change, and it also offers an astonishing breadth of sociological "data": dialects, customs, beliefs, prejudices. A novel of manners, a philosophical novel, a psychological novel, a Victorian novel, a novel which, as Henry James said, "sets a limit" to what "the old-fashioned English novel" can be — it is all of those, but it is also in a class by itself.

George Eliot combed through the available medical literature to prepare for her study of Dr. Lydgate. She knew English provincial life from personal experience, but she read newspapers, books, articles to supplement her knowledge. She paid especially close attention to historical sources; like Tolstoy in *War and Peace* she was writing about a generation that immediately preceded her own, and she was aware that sometimes it is harder to be accurate about the recent past than about a more distant time. She knew theology and religious archaeology, and as a result Casaubon is unforgettable; he draws our sympathy as well as our scorn. She had a thorough grasp of the workings of the unconscious mind, so that Bulstrode's agonizing struggle with himself is presented with a keen eye for psychological nuance.

As she wrote she kept a notebook, published some time ago as *Quarry for Middlemarch*. All the facts in it, all the information she had gleaned, all her ideas and theories about human nature, all the historical veins she had tapped somehow came together in a story, in her characters. She condensed an era into a book. She transformed psychological characteristics into people — men and women who are not mechanisms or bundles of reflexes or drives or "needs." In *Middlemarch* history lives through the individuals whose lives, large and small, go to make up history.

I suppose we could call Eliot a psychological novelist, or a novelist interested in how social forces mold individual "behavior" or how particular men and women respond to the demands of a given era. Certainly she knew how to "integrate" her "perspectives." She meticulously fitted her knowledge into the novel, as Jerome Beatty in "History by Indirection: the Era of Reform in *Middlemarch*," (*Victorian Studies*, December, 1957) and Asa Briggs in "*Middlemarch* and the Doctors" (*Cambridge Journal*, pp. 749–762) have shown. It might be useful for some of us today to study how she went about her work, rather than to try to figure out her "personality." Maybe she was just a woman of broad sensibility who had taste and diligence and an extraordinary capacity to evoke the human complexity she saw about her.

In the same way, when one reads C. Vann Woodward's *Tom Watson* or Isaac Deutscher's three-volume biography of Leon Trotsky, one gets a notion of how that impoverished Georgia youth or that Russian student, so fiercely determined and so high-minded, slowly came to terms with themselves — and with the historical currents of their times. We are not given the "mind" of Tom Watson or Leon Trotsky; rather their lives, their concrete struggles, their disappointments, their blind spots, their inevitable pride. Eventually we come to know them well, as well as we can know anyone we have not met or spent time with.

True, not all scholars can glimpse as much as C. Vann Woodward; few can give biography the power and drama of a novel, while providing the most vivid and searching kind of history. We certainly need more psychologically sophisticated historians — and more psychiatrists with a sense of history. But will that need be met by creating yet another "field" called "psychohistory"? One suspects that

good historians like Woodward have no need of old or new psychological terminology or "perspectives," even as an analyst like Erikson calls upon history naturally and wisely because he is an intelligent and learned man — possessing a quality of mind which no college degree, and maybe no course of study, necessarily provides.

Meanwhile Bruce Mazlish may well have offered us an "objective" when he described the historian William L. Langer's suggestion that historians take a greater interest in psychology as an appeal for such an attempt on "a rather low level of theory." That would do — along with plain old thoughtfulness, tact, and the hope that a measure of grace, so mysterious in origin, so impossible to define, so evident and satisfying when present, will somehow come to inform what is written.

The New York Review of Books, 1973

32

HELL ON EARTH

August Strindberg was a strange, brooding, difficult writer, whose novels, essays, short stories, plays, journalism, and polemical tracts struck his nineteenth-century readers with the vehemence of lightning. They turned away from him in fear, anger, or bewilderment: surely he belonged to another age. That age is ours; Strindberg's obsessions are both the familiar and the "new" preoccupations of the West's twentieth-century middle class.

He worried about class and caste, power and freedom. He knew the virtues of a quiet rural life but also the narrowness and meanness that clear skies and virgin forests and the cleanest air do not diminish. He scoffed at organized religions yet immersed himself in Kierkegaard, drew upon the mystical ideas of his fellow-countryman Emanuel Swedenborg, and, in the end, made his own peace with God. He looked down upon the weak, the inefficient, the not especially knowing or competent. Like Nietzsche, with whom he corresponded, and whom he admired and at times very much resembled as a man and as a writer, he insisted upon the rights and privileges of his kind — the specially gifted artist. Yet he wrote the boldest and most evangelical of Socialist pamphlets, in favor of equality for all and privileges for none. And he could demonstrate an intense interest in life's earthy, practical side, then turn to a highly symbolic and perplexing spirituality that celebrated the ineffable.

Getting Married (Viking), an excellent translation by Mary Sandbach of thirty of Strindberg's short stories written when he was thirty-five and already a famous exile from his native Sweden, is proof of his many conflicting attitudes toward women. He has acquired — and, to a degree, earned — a reputation as a misogynist; in these stories, as in such plays as *Marauders, The Father, Miss Julie,* and *Creditors,* he stresses the tensions between husbands and wives — those who court and those who are courted. For him, women who are made to feel they must await the attention of men merely await the chance to exact vengeance for all the anxiety and uncertainty they have experienced. Strindberg did not have in mind social or political legislation to alter the way men and women get along. He had contempt for reformers, among them Ibsen, though he admired Ibsen's dramatic craftsmanship. For him, "the Woman Question," as he calls it in his argumentative preface to this book, is something that no laws can change: "The present attempt to liberate woman is a revolt against nature."

Not that he was incapable of urging sweeping changes. In the preface he says also that women have a "right to the same education as men"; that boys and girls ought to go to the same schools, so they will get to know each other better; that women should be allowed to "run wild," live where and with whom they please; that "there shall be complete equality between the sexes, which will do away with that revolting form of hypocrisy called gallantry, or politeness to ladies"; that women should have the vote, be eligible for *all* occupations, and not be bound by the vows of marriage: "Man and wife will conclude a contract, verbal or written, for a union of any length they may decide, which they will have the right to dissolve when they please, without reference to law or gospel." Every woman should keep her own name and have a separate bedroom. Moreover, she should receive no presents "for which she has to say thank you," and she should have the right to pay for herself when she is away from home with her husband; being "treated" was for Strindberg a form of condescension. All that from a man called a woman-hater.

For Strindberg, there are fundamental psychological differences between men and women, handed down by "nature" — biological givens. Women are accepting, peaceful, hopeful, affirming; men are moody, unsure, on the verge of irritability or restlessness. Women either are mothers or are totally frustrated; men should provide for mothers and their children. If women don't become mothers, or if they are unsatisfied with themselves as mothers, they become truculent, unpredictable, crafty — and sometimes out-and-out amazons. If Strindberg was in fact a misogynist, he was also a misanthrope: men are stupid, gullible, arrogant, insensitive; women beg for a condition of dependency, whatever they profess, and men are accordingly seduced into the arrogant assertiveness they assume to be their right. If women are to be pitied, as Ibsen urged, because they are treated as children, men are also to be pitied: the tyrant is a child, too — vain, out of control, as demanding and petulant as a baby.

Strindberg acknowledged his inconsistencies. His active mind was prone to outbursts that were sometimes ranting or merely absurd, but his stories are more restrained than the preface, and more penetrable than some of his plays. Among the best of his brief descriptions of men and women struggling to love one another, experiencing ups and downs, not quite succeeding but also not failing, is "The Reward of Virtue," a delicate, psychologically sophisticated story in the naturalistic tradition of Zola, who for a while exerted a strong influence on Strindberg. Young Theodore loses his mother, a kind and decent woman — a friend as well as a parent — when he is thirteen. Her life was dedicated to her children. She wanted no recognition or applause. The father, an enormously respected scientist, is ambitious, brainy, in command of himself. His dying wife was but an instrument of his greed. She was an asset to him even in her illness: the world will pity this great scholar burdened by a cruel and unjust fate. He appeared "an admirable and exemplary husband," but there was a "sordid selfishness" in him — as both scientist and human being. He had tricked himself into believing that his work was "for humanity." For a moment he saw this, but insight is often not redemptive — something Strindberg knew long before twentieth-century psychiatrists were puzzled by the failure of interpretations to "take hold" and change lives. Theodore, an adolescent torn between natural impulses and a conformist society bent on exacting propriety, tries to make sense of life. The more vulnerable the youth, the more difficult (and potentially more damaging) the conflict, and for Theodore religious preoccupations became an only partial means of resolution. From the temptations of the flesh he turns to God and His commandments, but at a cost. At first, Strindberg withholds judgment, but the artist eventually loses to the ideologue; the story is not allowed to conclude with a young man in an agony compellingly presented. There has to be a lesson, and we are bludgeoned with it: Theodore grows up, turns more and more ascetic, studies for the ministry, becomes tired and sickly. At the very end of his short life, he marries a strong, earthy woman, who, however, can bear him only a rickety son. Theodore soon dies; his wife marries twice more, has eight healthy children, and writes about overpopulation and immorality. His oldest brother, a lusty army lieutenant who never could comprehend all those hours and hours of prayer and penitence, marries, too, fathers six children, and lives "happily to the end of his days."

Maybe a novel could have sustained Strindberg's moralistic simplifications as he turned finely wrought character analysis and social satire into propaganda. But propaganda for what? It is never easy to know what Strindberg wants, for men or for women. He even caricatures a position he himself often takes: Theodore's wife, at last free of her puritan husband, is called by one brother-in-law "a damnable woman who killed her husbands." But she met Theodore only when he was dying, a victim (the author more than implies) of years of self-denial. Death is "the reward of virtue" that the author had in mind. Here he wryly goes after those (himself included) who blame women for what a social and cultural tradition demands of young men like Theodore. On the other hand, in many of the stories men are well-intentioned and innocent but are soon enough manipulated, deceived, teased, or brutalized by women, who gain affection only to destroy it — an all too transparent effort to further the author's polemics. But most of the stories have considerable merit, for all the stridency and uncertainty. (Strindberg seems to be writing in order to find out what he does believe.) In "Just to Be Married," husband and wife are in a dilemma of neither's making. The first line gives her point of view: "There was good reason to say that they literally threw her into his arms." She felt let down and angry. Was she a self-respecting person only because she wore a wedding ring, and had a husband? He also felt betrayed; her reservations about him became his own questions. What is marriage? How should husband and wife get along? As master and servant? As equals? Somewhere in between? They move apart. Then comes a child — for Strindberg, often the way to resolve a crisis. The new mother is happy, fulfilled. The father is pleased but feels lonely and rebuffed. Still, he has been arrogant, heavy-handed, and wrapped up in himself. We are asked to pity him, but nevertheless judge him to be lacking in character. If his wife married for the sake of being a wife, he proposed simply because he had decided to stop being a bachelor, and he expected his wife to be glad forever after that he had rescued her from spinsterhood. He even has to struggle to keep himself from beating her: she is and ought to be as obliging as a slave. Eventually, his arrogance is exposed: his loneliness comes not so much from his wife's withdrawal — the child means everything, he very little — as from an unwillingness to get along with a woman except on his own terms. And in the tense and unsettling "For Payment," the heroine, Helène, is an early version of Miss Julie: a bold, skittish, independent young lady who trusts no one, including herself, and manages to intimidate everyone. Helène is an interesting and believable character; she has lived a solitary life, and her inability to get along with people is accounted for subtly — no psychological interpretations, simply character portrayal by a novelist who knows what he is doing. But toward the end Strindberg loses control; Helène becomes a frenzied, taunting shrew, like a number of his other women characters. Strindberg begins as a naturalistic observer whose aim is to describe objectively a person, a scene, a set of circumstances, and then he examines the intense and tortured subjective life of a woman become virtually mad. He cannot sustain one attitude toward women, and when he shifts his point of view he does so wildly.

Strindberg insisted that he could not live alone, and he married three times, though he was obsessed by the tensions he saw in every marriage — tensions inescapably rooted in the flesh — and by "the Woman Question," and by new ideas, suggestions, proposals for dealing with it. For a while, he thought that socialism would change things: men would be less insecure, women and their potential as workers less a threat to the economy. Then he turned to God: the day would come when divine interference would rectify what divine will had no doubt brought about in the Garden of Eden, when a reasonably content and immortal Adam suddenly found Eve's joyful company — but with it a tragic temptation.

In these stories, as in his essays and plays, Strindberg is occasionally seized by the sharpest and most vexing of intuitions. Women for him are utterly enviable. They can have children — and what is a story or a play compared to a child! Man is the pitiable giant, possessed of so many exclusive rights yet a rather silly and flabby creature, with his bluster and self-importance, and his nervous insistence on the reins of power lest the slightest surrender set in motion his dissolution. Those of us who want women freed from a whole range of irrational traditional constraints will find that a century ago a most extraordinary writer agreed wholeheartedly: one half of the species has branded the other half unfairly, and exacted a high price for "protection." Strindberg was also convinced that the price paid by women as the objects of that kind of imperialism has been higher than many of them can bear to realize — smoldering resentment that obtains a life of its own, exemplified by the outright harridan, or the slyly demure or coquettish woman whose strategy appears only when the trap has been sprung. Strindberg is murky, ill-tempered, unjustifiably taken with the significance of psychopathology — as if a man or a woman gone berserk were to be considered a mirror for all of us. Moreover, his instability makes it hard to deal with him critically — and, not incidentally, made it impossible for him (and his three wives) to have an easier time of it. It may be, though, that the apparent disorder of his mind, its refusal to be tamed, its near-anarchy at times, represented a considered judgment. We are here on earth for a brief while, he kept reminding his readers, and the attraction between men and women is an essential for our survival, rather than a potential source of energy for the City of God. For Strindberg, as for his mentor Kierkegaard, the ultimate irresponsibility, the real madness, is to forget that distinction, and to expect from one another — from any society — the transcendent love that Christ and His disciples tell us we shall not possess this side of Heaven.

The New Yorker, 1973

33

THE STRANGER

Nothing about man's psychological nature amazes us these days, for our novels explore ruthlessly or gleefully all the passions, ordinary or peculiar. We take pride in being "liberated"; we bear down hard on matters people once shunned examining or had no knowledge of. Centuries ago, too, a few writers may have examined incest, fratricide, sexual perversions, violence, but not with our own fearless attentiveness. Sophocles is almost casual in his presentation of Oedipus, an outcast whose very name is a source of horror, but who is not regarded as someone whose actions (we would now say "behavior") had understandable causes. What was once awesome or inexplicable is now ours to call grotesque, bizarre, clinically significant, and then to analyze.

Cormac McCarthy is a forty-year-old American novelist who lives in the high country of Tennessee. His first and second novels, *The Orchard Keeper* and *Outer Dark*, earned him awards and fellowships. His *Child of God* (Random House) will further enhance his reputation. The "Child" is Lester Ballard, aged twenty-seven, "small, unclean, unshaven," a stranger to everyone, including himself, and of "Saxon and Celtic bloods." His activities will surprise no one interested in contemporary fiction: he lusts, he hates, he has voyeuristic and necrophilic tendencies. He is capable of violence; he is a mass murderer. Mr. McCarthy might easily have obtained a fortune with this novel, but he was not intent upon a psychiatrist's bestseller, and one begins to wonder whether he must reach many Americans through the long, circuitous route Faulkner took: a limited recognition here, increasing response from Europeans to his strange and brooding novels, and only later the broader acknowledgment of his own countrymen.

McCarthy's territory is the hill country of Appalachia; this novel is set in solidly Republican, somewhat impoverished eastern Tennessee, and it chronicles Lester Ballard's descent into isolation, loneliness, and a craven, frenzied self-sufficiency that is extraordinary even for the region's country people, who believe in fending for oneself. He has been living in an abandoned farmhouse, apparently content to keep his own grouchy, suspicious company. But the place is being auctioned. Ballard, ignorant of law, confused by the assault upon his privacy and stability, and resentful of those who would dispossess him, raises his rifle toward the auctioneer and is clubbed down. "Lester Ballard never could hold his head right after that. It must of thowed his neck out someway or another. I didn't see Buster hit him but I seen him layin on the ground. I was with the sheriff. He was layin flat on the ground lookin up at everybody with his eyes crossed and this awful pumpknot on his head. He just laid there and he was bleedin at the ears. Buster was still standin there holdin the axe."

But the author is not beginning yet another novel about the corruption of society; Ballard is not an innocent whom "the system" ultimately drives to madness. He was on his own by the time he was nine; his father had committed suicide and his mother abandoned him. "I don't know," a schoolmate remarks. "They say he never was right after his daddy killed hisself. . . . He come in the store and told it like you'd tell it was rainin out." And McCarthy has little more than that to say about his principal character's childhood. The author seems not to wish our twentieth-century psychological sensibility to influence his work. Ballard's madness is simply acknowledged, and he ends up in a mental hospital. But his state of mind is not the subject of inquiry. His motives are not examined, his behavior is not sorted out, labeled. Ballard comes upon a parked car, two lovers within, and remains to watch. Later, he comes upon other cars, other lovers, and each time suffers the loneliness and despair of a man who can taste life only at a remove. "On buckling knees the watcher watched. The mockingbird began." Then, on a hunting expedition, he encounters a car with two dead lovers in it. He pulls the girl out, so that he can take her back to his cabin. Birds sing. A wind rises, falls. The squirrels he has shot weigh heavily on his belt. "A crazed gymnast laboring over a cold corpse." But we never learn why he is "crazed," nor are we asked to feel compassion or contempt.

The author is not indifferent to our curiosity; he simply cannot, for reasons of his own as a novelist, oblige us. When he tries to (maybe one should say when he is tempted to), the result is a fleeting moment of sentiment that discomforts the reader. Falsely accused of rape, Ballard spends nine days in jail, talks with a black man in the opposite cell, and, prodded by this neighbor's unashamed introspection, tries to be good company. Nigger John admits to being "a fugitive from the ways of this world. I'd be a fugitive from my mind if I had me some snow." He swears, rails against the white world. He is trying to explain his life, its trials and misdeeds. Ballard finally tries to account for *his* life: "All the trouble I ever was in," he begins, "was caused by whiskey or women or both." The author quickly adds, "He'd often heard men say as much."

The storyteller seemingly has gone as far as he wants to go. Ballard isn't really of a mind to talk about himself, and he has no very original "insight" into his condition. He is alone, but not really lonely. He is attentive to himself; he makes do, in spite of poverty and the suspiciousness or outright hostility his eccentric manner generates. But he does not wonder who he is and why he has come to live as he does. He drifts. The author moves him relentlessly through the Appalachian countryside, offering us the language and habits of fiercely proud yeomen who still struggle against the influence of the industrial life beyond their hills. A country fair is held. Men and women come to a store, exchange news. When Ballard is with them there he is alternately surly and compliant, clever and disarmingly innocent and then vulnerable. His meanness and eccentric manner diminish as others reveal themselves to be cranky, narrow, calculating. Yet we are not persuaded to feel any special pity for him. He moves toward his fate, and others have theirs to contend with.

Ballard has no "relationship" with any of these people, who, though they demonstrate, briefly, a capacity for humor, are mostly self-preoccupied. So it is with animals: "The hounds crossed the snow on the slope of the ridge in a thin dark line. Far below them the boar they trailed was tilting along with his curious stifflegged lope, highbacked and very black against the winter's landscape. The hounds' voices in that vast and pale blue void echoed like the cries of demon yodelers." And so it is with him: "Ballard has come in from the dark dragging sheaves of snow-clogged bracken and he has fallen to crushing up handfuls of this dried or frozen stuff and cramming it into the fireplace. The lamp in the floor gutters in the wind and wind moans in the flue. The cracks in the wall lie printed slantwise over the floorboards in threads of drifted snow and wind is shucking the cardboard windowpanes. And Ballard has come with an armload of beanpoles purloined from the barnloft and he is at breaking them and laying them on."

Lester Ballard destroys and is destroyed, but we have not a clue as to why. It is as if the author thinks his character is beyond scrutiny — possessed of a nature and a destiny that lead to the impersonal collisions of the Oresteia, rather than the exchanges and confrontations of our contemporary theater; it is as if only when we learn to accept the mysterious and the terrible judgment of the gods do we come close to what wisdom is allowed us. Ballard is the child of only one God; he is a desperate man set down among professed Christians who claim to know more about life than he does: that it is a pilgrimage toward a destination, Heaven, rather than a brief span of time filled with absurd moments and events. The high sheriff who keeps Ballard under surveillance for a long time and then arrests him has not only the law but a larger moral vision to uphold.

Cormac McCarthy resembles the ancient Greek dramatists and medieval moralists — a strange, incompatible mixture: Ballard blind to himself and driven by forces outside his control, and Ballard the desperately wayward one whose vagrant life is one day to be judged by God. Strangers like Ballard, errant outsiders who bewilder and sometimes brutally assault a community, remind those who shun them that a "child of God" can inexplicably become, in the imagery of ancient Greece, an instrument of the gods. Cormac McCarthy does not know why some men are haunted Ballards, while others live easily with kin and neighbors. He simply writes novels that tell us we cannot comprehend the riddles of human idiosyncrasy, the influence of the merely contingent or incidental upon our lives. He is a novelist of religious feeling who appears to subscribe to no creed but who cannot stop wondering in the most passionate and honest way what gives life meaning. His characters are by explicit designation children of Whoever or Whatever it is that we fall back upon when we want to evoke the vastness and the mystery of this universe, and our comparative ignorance and uncertainty. His task is ambitious and enormously difficult — to tell his readers that we are not as knowing or in control of our lives as we assume. He cannot yet affirm with confidence life's possibilities. From the isolated highlands of Tennessee he sends us original stories that show how mysterious or confusing the world is. Moreover, his mordant wit, his stubborn refusal to bend his writing to the literary and intellectual demands of our era, conspire at times to make him seem mysterious and confusing — a writer whose fate is to be relatively unknown and often misinterpreted. But both Greek playwrights and Christian theologians have been aware that such may be the fate of anyone, of even the most talented and sensitive of human beings.

The New Yorker, 1974

34

ON KAFKA'S

"METAMORPHOSIS"

Of all Kafka's stories, *Metamorphosis* is certainly the best known; perhaps more people have read it than his three novels — *The Trial, The Castle,* and *Amerika.* Certainly this story reveals a particular author well on the way to achieving a masterly style — the direct lucidity of presentation which unnerves readers as, disarmed and eager, they struggle with provocative, if not overwhelming, mysteries. Though Kafka was dead at 41, in 1924, his writing — at once plain and earthy, yet quite suggestively metaphysical, even religious — has become a major literary presence throughout the twentieth century. Long before "existentialism" became a faddish way of indicating a concern with some of this century's widespread and dangerous moral, cultural, or psychological conflicts, Franz Kafka, who made no claim to being a philosopher, a psychiatrist, a social critic, had taken the measure of many of our contemporary lives and figured out a way of rendering what ails and torments us.

There is no point trying to figure out *the* explanation for this startling, elusive, powerfully affecting story. Numerous scholars have studied *Metamorphosis,* tried to get at its heart and soul, only to be followed by others, similarly dedicated and agile, yet anxious to recommend a quite different angle of approach. The story is a Rorschach card of sorts. As the reader thinks about Gregor Samsa, who "found himself transformed in his bed into a gigantic insect," a moment or two of self-recognition may ensue. The story opens with a *fait accompli* (the sentence just quoted), and nowhere in the pages that follow are we told what in the character's life prompted this impossible (though, thanks to Kafka, quite imaginable) transformation. Nor, for that matter, is the exact nature of the transformation specified. Gregor Samsa, we do learn, has become a kind of insect, a bug or a beetle, but by no means are we told how such an event took place, and for that matter, with what authorial purpose in mind. Our surmise about these matters, even our carefully argued analytic interpretations of them, may well bring us closer to ourselves (our way of seeing the world) than to Kafka's intent as a shrewdly evasive storyteller.

We do know, however, on the author's say, that Gregor — as he is called throughout the story, no matter what his strange fate — "awoke one morning from a troubled dream" and immediately realized what had befallen him. That information is the one piece of evidence (a clue?) granted us, and we may choose to ignore it and proceed to deal with *Metamorphosis* as a description of what happens to someone who is somehow, and for some impossible-to-know reason, stripped of his humanity; or we may characterize that restless sleep, that nightmare, as portentous in the extreme — a psychological prefiguration. In the latter instance we approach *Metamorphosis* as a brilliant psychiatric parable — an evocation of severe mental illness and, too, a reminder that when such a tragedy takes place, not only the patient suffers (and is changed) but also those who belong to his or her family. For instance, Gregor's sister Grete (the similarity of their names is no accident, surely, even as Samsa is not all that unlike Kafka in form) becomes deeply affected by this bizarre visitation upon a given household; and some readers have wondered whether the story's title doesn't describe marked alterations in her character as much as in that of her brother.

It can be argued that in Gregor's tragedy Kafka has tried to portray what gets called "dehumanization" by people in my profession of psychoanalytic psychiatry. Not rarely, in fact, clinicians hear seriously disturbed patients describe themselves as utterly lost, to the point that they feel themselves to be animal-like rather than men or women. Alas, in mental hospitals an occasional patient can be heard barking, or trying to imitate the purring or the wild cry of a cat, a wolf, a coyote. A colleague of mine once told me of an especially eerie experience in his hospital work — a young patient, recently graduated from college, had declared himself to be a cockroach. Moreover, he gave himself a curious sanction for so doing: he had read *Metamorphosis,* written a paper on it, and concluded (as a biology major) that "the monstrous kind of vermin" Kafka describes is, in fact, the cockroach, and that the story is about the hallucinatory experience of psychosis.

The young man had gone through a schizophrenic episode while in college, and now, a would-be graduate student in biochemistry, had become agitated, withdrawn, depressed, severely anxious. To his doctor he kept repeating incoherent phrases. Alternatively, there were spells of unyielding silence — and bodily contortions. Eventually, the patient told a nurse to go find and read every book of Kafka's, so that she would then be able to understand him! The nurse rather astutely asked the patient to narrow the selection of Kafka down a bit, and was told that *Metamorphosis* would suffice. She and the doctor working with the young man felt that they had, indeed, been given a message — a statement of pain and radical isolation made through resort to a literary reference. Kafka, a master ironist, would no doubt appreciate such a moment — a strange story's strange usefulness!

Of course, in our century "dehumanization," and even madness, have been declared social commonplaces — everyone's problems in the so-called "civilized world," where people by the millions feel useless and isolated from one another, or go to war and die in wars that so often are as senseless as they are (on a grand scale) life-consuming. Dorothy Day and Peter Maurin, co-founders of the Catholic Worker Movement, a religious and social effort, were each steeped in the existentialist tradition and both could be heard saying, years ago, how harsh this twentieth century urban, industrial life can be — to the point, Miss Day once observed, that "we become ants."

She would not then have claimed any originality for such a comparison. She knew how bewildered and vulnerable many people feel, and indeed once described that condition in words Kafka might have appreciated: "We are lonely and hurt, millions of us, and we wonder what we are meant to do, to *be*. We are cut off from one another. Is there any difference between us and the creatures we stare at when we go to the zoo?" I heard her make those remarks, ask that question, as an introduction to a personal statement of faith, of Catholic conviction, but she knew that many conclude their contemporary expressions of perplexity, if not despair, with no such devotional assurance. On the contrary, like Gregor in *Metamorphosis* they feel themselves to be in a limbo; they are morally drifting, spiritually and psychologically at loose ends.

Kafka does not hesitate to give us a good deal of information, social and economic, about Gregor and his family. Gregor, we learn, is a commercial traveller, a salesman — though the exact nature of his wares is not disclosed. His job kept him on the move "day in, day out." He was far from independent. His parents had taken a loan from his company's boss, and his work was helping pay off that loan. When he fails to appear for work, the boss sends his subordinate, the General Manager, to visit the Samsa home, find out what is wrong. The General Manager is solicitous, but also ominously pointed in a skepticism which he attributes to another: "The chief did hint to me early this morning a possible explanation for your disappearance — with reference to the cash payments that were entrusted to you recently — but I almost pledged my solemn word of honor that this could not be so."

With the word "almost" the author conveys an entire subjective world: the fear and doubt so many working men and women must endure, the personal jeopardy that goes hand in hand with one's all too uncertain economic situation, the dog-eat-dog atmosphere of our twentieth century industrial society. Kafka makes much of Gregor's time-consciousness, the alarm he feels as he watches the clock move, yet cannot leap from bed to get to the office at the usual early hour. Such punctuality is no mere idiosyncrasy — but rather a measure of what we become if we are to survive (just barely, often enough) in a given social order. "Sometimes I think I'm an animal completely owned and run by a clock inside my head," I was once told by a factory worker who had never heard of Kafka, never mind his stories or novels. I think it can be safely assumed that Kafka had a substantial awareness how such a man's sensibility had developed — the nervously prompt exertions so many of us feel to be utterly necessary lest we become penniless, homeless.

Not that psychosis and social malaise exhaust the interpretative possibilities *Metamorphosis* can prompt in us. Gregor may well have awakened from his "troubled dream" only to fall back asleep and have another one — the story. Kafka needed no psychiatrist to inform him of the workings of the unconscious. His fable is well stocked with the kind of psychological conflict our age takes for granted, maybe dotes on excessively. Gregor's attachment to his sister is obvious, as are his frustrated longing for his mother and his abiding fear, distrust, dislike of his father. The scene that has the father running after the son, in circles, throwing apples at him, trying to kill him, once and for all, is at the same time sad and hilarious — as if Kafka was already (twelve years after Freud's *The Interpretation of Dreams* was published) able to appreciate our present-day psychoanalytic mentality, and even to mock its future banality.

Moreover, the story shows a remarkable integration of psychology and sociology: an author's awareness that a twentieth-century Oedipus, namely each of us, has to work — and so is confronted with emotional conflicts which are not confined to the family. Gregor's travail with his boss is as powerfully compelling in its impact as his resentment of his father. Kafka, like one of our family therapists, insists that we carry home the tensions generated at work, even as we bring to work worries and fears of our childhood years. Gregor, after all, upon finding himself so drastically altered, has to come to terms with his employer, his sister, his parents, their lodgers, and, not least, himself — an entire social spectrum.

Kafka had a strong and subtle religious side. Both *The Trial* and *The Castle* lend themselves to theological and philosophical analysis. So does *Metamorphosis* — with its references to both the "Heavenly Father" and the Devil, not to mention the apple which figures prominently in Genesis. Gregor may appear to be "an insect," but the reader never fails to regard him as a *person* — someone who thinks, observes, struggles long and hard to understand the world, to be understood by others in it. A mind and soul lose a given body, yet persist (for a while, at least) in their earthly journey.

Kafka is not intent on anthropomorphism; he has no interest in attributing human qualities to the natural world. Rather, through a marvellously ambiguous story, he invites an examination of this life's purposes. Ought we surrender, be conventional burghers — harassed, intimidated, obliging with respect to the *status quo*? Ought we try to break free, to take on various "principalities and powers," hence become feared outcasts, soon enough killed? Gregor is hardly an Old Testament prophet, or a Redeemer for pre-World War I Prague, but his metamorphosis turns him into a hurt, suffering, intently observant outsider, who experiences the callous rebuff, and worse, of just about everyone. The emotional and moral suggestiveness, both, are surely Biblical in nature.

The story ends not with Gregor's demise but his sister Grete's eerie ascendance; she is lovely, flowering. A bizarre, dislocating event, carefully portrayed in its impact upon a series of individuals, yields to an idyllic termination. A brother's death is followed by a sister's birth — her sexual emergence. Were they all too close, those two? Has one, accordingly, had to pay the price, be punished as severely as possible? Dare any of us reach out to others, except fearfully, as children with demanding parents, workers with overbearing bosses? The psychological implications are obvious, and so the reassurance at the end is, as always with Kafka, minimal.

This Samsa family as a whole is meant to remind us that not only workers, but their kin, suffer the "alienation" that Marx, Jaspers, and Gabriel Marcel (or in literature, Camus and Walker Percy) have evoked in various ways. Gregor's sacrifice oddly nourishes (? redeems) others in the Samsa family — a statement of costs "alienation" can exact. This story is, after all, an early and profound assertion of a theme now familiar: "the death of a salesman." Gregor's fierce solipsism (erotic and intellectual) is a consequence, one suspects, of more than a particular family's private disorders. Kafka saw how wretchedly some of us treat others (parents and bosses as against children and employees). He saw the result — the betrayal of life, the strong feeding upon the weak. His *Metamorphosis* asks us to consider not only Gregor's deadly transformation but our own continuing experience as survivors. Do we profit handily from the human degradation of others? Is our comfort earned at the expense of a terrible suffering? If so, what happens to us, what "metamorphosis" falls upon us? Kafka's story is of immense and continuing moral significance — a means by which each of us can take a demanding look at what we are and, yes, what we might become.

The Limited Editions Club, 1984

35

SHADOWING BINX

In late 1956 I was a psychiatric resident at the Massachusetts General Hospital in Boston — and wondering why, not to mention whither. I had stumbled into psychiatry out of frustration, innocence, inadequacy. Indeed, I'd stumbled into medical school for somewhat confused if not inappropriate reasons. As an undergraduate I'd become much taken with the poems and short stories and novels of William Carlos Williams, had been encouraged by Perry Miller, my advisor (and hero) at Harvard, to write my thesis on the first book of *Paterson,* and thereby had come to correspond with, then get to know, Dr. Williams, who was at the time in good health but who would soon enough be struggling with several illnesses. His writing life was my intellectual concern, but I became interested in the uncanny and (I thought then, and still do) exemplary intensity of his personal commitment to his medical practice — to his working-class patients, actually — for all the headaches involved. Such passionate attentiveness to hurt and ailing men, women, children struck me as an edifying contrast to — well, my own late adolescent self-centeredness. Moreover, I was beginning to wonder what the devil I'd be doing with this uncertain stretch of time given each of us, called a life to live. In that regard, I seemed by my junior year badly adrift. Others I knew were headed in one or another direction — and their determination was often in those years after the Second World War a reasonable response to their past experiences as veterans. But I was younger, and my battles were, it seemed, taking place in my head.

Once, while seeing Dr. Williams work with his patients (he was an old-fashioned doc who regularly visited the tenements of northern New Jersey, and made no fortune doing so), I told him I was at loose ends and wished there were a doctor like him to attend my dreary ills. He laughed, even as I was half-joking. We then got a bit serious, and when he asked me my "interests," I answered theology and moral philosophy and American literature, all of which, in a way, I was studying with the brilliant and inspiring Perry Miller. Perhaps I could pursue that line of study, connect literature and history with theology in some fashion; but to do so meant going to graduate school, and I had no real inclination in that direction. Instead, I talked of finding a job, any job, and in my spare time reading and thinking about what gets called one's "future."

Dr. Williams's response was characteristically quick, sharp, concrete, specific, and yes, impatient: "Try medicine, why don't you! Lots to keep you busy, and lots to make you think. The great thing is — you get to forget yourself a lot of the time."

I was properly reprimanded, and prompted to get going — somehow, down some road. And I did. I took the chemistry, the biology, the physics, applied to some schools, and with the help of one very patient, kindly (and I now realize, properly puzzled) interviewer at Columbia's College of Physicians and Surgeons, the biochemist Philip Miller, I got into medical school.

Once there I continued to flounder badly. I had trouble working in the labs; I had trouble dissecting the cadaver. I would go visit old Doc Williams and tell him I was wasting my time. He said no; he said "stick it out"; he said in the long run I'd be glad I ended up knowing how to use a stethoscope and a neurological hammer and an ophthalmoscope. I argued with him, but was convinced. I got by — but I read lots of novels, and took courses at Union Theological Seminary, and got myself signed up to work in a small hospital in rural India. I was searching for ascetic indulgence, an obligation nurtured in my head by my idealistic mother, who would always tell me how I must "give unto others," and so on and so on — until, at times, as a child hearing that talk, I would want to run and buy a Cadillac or a gold watch, anything to show how independent or immune I was.

I tried pediatrics after medical school and had trouble with the children: they'd cry bloody murder when I approached them with a syringe needle or an otoscope. I'd say soothing things; and correctly, they'd not believe me, and I began to realize I hadn't the iron in me to be the best friend a sick child needs — an effective, able physician who gets done what has to be done, so that a diagnosis is set, treatment begun. It was at this point (in 1955) that my friend Dr. Williams suggested psychiatry — a proffered solution that meant, I feared, his complete loss of respect for me. So I signed up for the psychiatric residency, and kept reading: more and more novels, and lots of poetry, and magazines, all sorts of them — for example, the fall issue (1956) of the *Partisan Review*, in which I found a piece called "The Man on the Train."

I was drawn to the title, and at one point in reading the essay, I remember checking to see who the author was: someone named Walker Percy. I remember saving that issue, then throwing it away, having cut out the Percy essay. I showed it to my friends. One of them, a Catholic doctor training in surgery, returned the favor a year or so later with two issues of *Commonweal* featuring articles by the same Walker Percy, who carefully identified himself as a physician but *not* a psychiatrist, even though he had titled those articles "The Coming Crisis of Psychiatry." The essays were a tonic, and I glowed: all the dreary, smug tautological reasoning of the social sciences pointedly exposed — all the secular, agnostic obsessions of self-preoccupied people for whom the mind was the latest fad, if not the last refuge and hope. And a knowing, appreciative critique: Percy respected Freud's contributions to human knowledge, yet saw in the reductionist labelling, in the arrogant, condescending postures, the overwrought generalizations, the messianic promises of a certain species of experts, a certain category of American doctors — well, a sign of what we had all become in mid-twentieth-century America, namely, terribly afraid and alone, dangerously adrift, cut loose from our spiritual moorings.

In 1958 I found myself in the United States Air Force under the auspices of the Doctors' Draft, which fingered all of us physicians at that time. I was sent to Keesler Air Force Base in Biloxi, Mississippi, and put in charge of a large military neuropsychiatric unit — forty beds, a substantial out-patient evaluation service. I was now, at twenty-seven, a psychiatrist; I had even taken my further specialty training in child psychiatry. I had a sports car. I was a captain, and with the help of my uniform, which turned potentially hostile Mississippi policemen into smiling onlookers, I could speed along on Route 90, along the beaches of the Gulf of Mexico, past the lovely ocean-front homes of Pass Christian, over the Bay St. Louis Bridge, over smaller bridges, traversing bayous, then Gentilly, the suburban outskirts of New Orleans, "The City That Care Forgot." Finally the sign: Elysian Fields, which can connect with Desire, and the low-slung buildings, columned or with elaborate grillwork and high, high windows, and bars open all day and all night, and jukeboxes with lots of Louis Armstrong, and restaurants with fine, fine food, and soon, Preservation Hall and its jazz, and The River, and its levees, and those enormous tropical plants and tall and wide (and enveloping) trees and azaleas everywhere and plenty of attractive women who in January or February, often enough, needed no coats to hide, to mar the lines of their bodies, and after a while a doctor to visit, one of those shrinks, we were calling them then, too — who examines heads gone awry.

"Captain Coles," said the colonel in charge of the big Biloxi hospital, "why do you need to go see a psychiatrist in New Orleans when *you're* one, and in charge of four others? Are you looking for excuses to visit that city?"

The charming innocence, I thought — but he was a tough, cynical man: No, the captain avers: depression, that's it, low spirits, down in the dumps, moodiness that won't go away.

"Hell," says the boss, "we all get like that sometimes, and it's not a 'problem,' it's part of life!"

I remember looking at him closely at that minute, saying to myself: the smart old bastard, he may be right, and I might save a few dollars and lots of time if I dared give his way of seeing things a chance. But no, I was in trouble, I definitely was — all those movies!

The movies: I'd been going to them more and more — so much that I couldn't find enough to see for the first time on any given day. (This was not New York, or Cambridge, where in fact I'd not gone much at all, but "La.–Miss.," as the combined two-state abbreviation was often rendered on advertisements.) I'd go to see my analyst every afternoon, and I'd go to a movie afterwards, then there'd be a girl friend, a long ride in the car, a jazz bar — and, too commonly, memories of the movie intruding in my mind as I talked with the young lady, or as I made hospital rounds the next morning, and talked with all those tough, strong, brave SAC pilots who were defending us against anyone and everyone and flying incredible speeds in incredible planes — and breaking down in fear and in tears, unaccountably it always seemed.

"Doc, what in hell does this life mean?" one hot-shot jet pilot kept asking me, and some scene out of some movie would come to mind — *Purple Noon,* for example, which I saw five times, and wherein the hero (Alain Delon) gets away with everything (money, love, adventure) and sails into the warm, Mediterranean sun: *that's* the meaning of life!

"Why do you keep seeing *Purple Noon?*" my Prytania Street doctor asked. "Why do you see those James Dean movies over and over — what do they, what does he, *mean* to you?"

"Dunno." Then, on my back, my face turned toward the wall, I would see a scene in *East of Eden* or *Rebel without a Cause,* or one or another John Wayne movie, or Billy Holden in *Sunset Boulevard,* a movie I'd not seen when it came out (1950, I believe) but saw three times in three days in New Orleans in 1960.

The Moviegoer was published on May 15, 1961. I read it in the fall of that year — an obscure novel, headed for extinction, a few hundred copies sold, mostly in New Orleans.

"He lives here, in Covington, across the Lake" (Pontchartrain) I was told by the clerk in Doubleday's bookstore on Canal Street, when I seemed to be clutching at the book, afraid to let it go, so he could (all he wanted!) see the price.

I missed my movie that afternoon and evening. I phoned "a certain someone," as the author of *The Moviegoer* puts it, to claim illness. I finished the novel around midnight. I took a slug or two of bourbon: who *is* this Walker Percy?

"But the real question," said the Prytania Street analyst the next day, "is who are you?"

"What do you mean?"

"You're always asking questions in response to my questions."

"What do you mean?"

"There you go again."

"Well, I'm now seeing that movie *Purple Noon* again — the sky, the water, the boat speeding away."

"You are?"

"Yes." Long silence.

It is, I fear, a psychological banality of our time that biographers have their personal reasons when they happen upon their subject, someone's life and work. For me Walker Percy's writing has offered a continuing intensity of awareness and, I suppose, self-recognition. His writing has made me feel less lonely, more in touch with this world: his has been a voice in the wilderness, to use a phrase, and a voice that makes one's own high-pitched raspy drone seem less peculiar and, yes, not quite so loony. To my mind Binx was, for all too long I fear, myself writ large — put into a book, rendered for others.

"You seem to be shadowing Binx," the New Orleans doctor said.

I was delighted: Binx had become real enough for *him*, so that he had stopped addressing him (disdainfully, I thought) as "this fictional character in *The Moviegoer*, Binx Bolling." But doctor, thinks the snotty analysand, of course a character in a novel is "fictional"! (Best not to tell him what just came into the head; he'll be offended.)

"Are you thinking of something now?" asks the doctor, aware of a restless pause.

"Oh hell, I was just being a jerk in my mind again."

Then — well, not a vision of *Purple Noon* but this question, wondered aloud to the listening alienist: did Walker Percy ever see a psychoanalyst?

"How would I know?"

Yet another long lull. Years later I would get to ask the question in person.

I found out in 1973 that the answer is yes. In 1966, actually, I had begun to suspect so — having read *The Last Gentleman*. Will Barrett was a Binx up North, Binx moving across America, Binx still on "the search" — mentioned in *The Moviegoer*, enacted in *The Last Gentleman*. And "the search" is what the *New Yorker* editors called the profile I did of Dr. Percy, published in 1978.

For me the act of asking the *New Yorker* whether I might write about Walker Percy's essays and novels, the act of getting in touch with him to say that such a project was feasible were — I suppose the characterizing word is "existential." Percy's essays and novels are efforts to explore the moral and spiritual dimensions of the twentieth-century middle-class life so many of us live in America — our god Mammon, materialist culture and its artifacts, the mind and the promise of science, including the so-called social sciences. Percy is in the tradition of novelists such as Dostoevsky, Kafka, Sartre, and Camus — a contemporary American mind at work connecting European existentialist reflections to storytelling and essay writing. For me, a profile in a magazine about him and his writing, a later book about the same, were chances to address some preoccupations I'd long possessed (been possessed by!). Moreover, Percy's humor is obvious, highly developed, important to his work — and I found it from the first acquaintance I made of it especially intriguing and powerful. That wry, modest, pointedly ironic humor is very much a hovering presence — the eyes ever aware, the faint smile, the head slightly tilted: hey, what's next to see, to hear, as the clock ticks and the human parade continues?

In person, Percy is intelligent, hospitable, gracious, informative, alert, willing to be friendly, generous with information about his life, his ideas, his questions and the answers he's tried to find for himself. Existentialism emphasizes the meeting of people, the so-called encounter, the "fidelity" (Gabriel Marcel's term) that we seek for each other — of ourselves as would-be spiritual kin of others. For me, Percy has been that, a spiritual kinsman — if I dare presume a substantial moral and intellectual connection to him as a physician, a writer, a person anxious to ask lots of questions about the nature of things, and willing, also, to be unhappy with lots of all too readily accepted, influential answers.

I never had any intention of trying to bring my psychiatric training into this personal effort — this friendship with an interesting, thoughtful, enjoyable, and relaxing friend. I was doing an *intellectual* biography, to be somewhat self-important about the task. The result was a lot of reading, some of it damn difficult for me: Heidegger and Merleau-Ponty and Husserl, not to mention the relatively more accessible, if no less weighty and suggestive philosophers Buber, Marcel, Jaspers. Percy himself is a learned man indeed. His humor, his storytelling gifts, mask a penetrating, wide-ranging, eager intellect. For years before he wrote his essays, never mind novels, he studied philosophy, ethics, theology — read and read in the New Orleans home he occupied with his wife Bunt in the early years of their marriage. His deep knowledge of Kierkegaard is a real challenge to those of us who want to know what he is really about. I've read *The Moviegoer* four times, and each time see more of that difficult, provocative, unnerving Danish essayist and theologian in the story of Binx and his struggle to figure out how (and with whom) to live a life. Since I've continued to teach Percy's writing, fiction and non-fiction, both to college students and medical students, I sometimes find myself rather disappointed with my own interpretations, as rendered in the profile I did, the book I wrote. A particular student does much better, or yes, prodded by the requirements of leading a seminar, giving a lecture, responding to the questions of individual students during office hours, I find myself a much better reader and critic of, say, "The Message in the Bottle" (an essay of his I especially love) or *Love in the Ruins* (a novel my medical students find compelling) than I'd once been as the anxiously knowing and assertive writer intent on examining a particular philosophical novelist's work.

My own lack of interest in applying psychoanalytic metaphors to the lives of men and women such as Walker Percy and Flannery O'Connor (did not Freud himself give us permission to abandon the idea when he tried to confront the genius of Dostoevsky?) may have, at times, been an unnecessary obstacle in comprehending Percy's literary life. He himself observed, after reading an early version of my profile, that his father's suicide was a given and not by any means a secret. He had no objection to the mention of that important event in his life and those of his two younger brothers. I had not wanted to conceal the fact, yet I feared not so much the busybodies of the world as the fools — among whom, these days, are those obsessed by psychology, as in the "Living" pages of all our newspapers, and regrettably, as in a substantial segment of our intellectual life: psycho-social and psycho-historical and psycho-political, world without end, it seems. To be sure, a father's self-imposed death, a mother's accidental death two years later, can be, *were*, an enormous ordeal for a young teenager, and surely his even younger brothers. They were adopted by their cousin, the distinguished lawyer and poet and essayist William Alexander Percy, and he was a wonderfully thoughtful, kind, decent, and generous person. But pain there was, sadness and disappointment — and yet Walker Percy the novelist is not at all to be *explained* by such unlucky personal circumstances, else we'd have hundreds of thousands of others, remarkably gifted because remarkably injured by all sorts of tragedies which children all over the world suffer.

True, the issue is *themes,* one can argue — the relationship between a kind of suffering and a topical continuity in a given writer's life. But do one scene in *The Last Gentleman* (the recollected suicide of Will's father) and one scene in *The Second Coming* (Will's potentially suicidal descent into a cave) constitute a preoccupation? And even if existentialism itself, arguably, can be deemed a mode of philosophical inquiry characterized by speculation as to the meaning of life, the meaning of death — with despair a constant threat and challenge — we still must wonder whether each of those men and women taken by that line of reflection is to be declared morbid, neurotic, endlessly compelled by obscure or all too apparent childhood injuries to ruminative speculation.

Needless to say, a knowing summons of psychoanalytic theory as an instrument of biographical inquiry requires the constant reminder that conflict is in everyone, that we are all neurotics, that even craziness lurks in each mind, though most of us fight it back successfully, and that (very important) there is no straight line between any particular trauma any of us experiences and any future interest, capacity, predilection, or antipathy we happen to end up having. How we love the *this equals that* way of thinking, as if the salt of our lives is a constant matter of adding Na to Cl, and voilà! The texture of any life is, in the end, a mystery — or if that word scares or embarrasses the twentieth-century reader, then at the least he or she has to settle for an astonishing degree of complexity, the result of irony and contingency and paradox and inconsistency and chance or luck (good and bad) all doing their exceedingly intricate work, so that one's fate, so often regarded as linear by us in the convenience (and ambition) of retrospect, has in actuality been a matter of personal circumstances gradually emerging, with a turn here, a setback there, a leap forward now, a stretch of consolidation then. The correct model, of course, is George Eliot's vision in *Middlemarch*, or Tolstoy's in *War and Peace*, wherein even those large-scale events, war and political reform, exert their chief encouraging or disabling influences on the particular lives of human beings. Hence history both public and private has been an intensely shaping force on the development of personality, character, talent. I wonder whether Percy's essays, or indeed, his novels, especially *Love in the Ruins* and *Lancelot*, can be illuminated by reference not only to Percy the existentialist, or the physician, or indeed the physician whose parents died when he was relatively young and who fell dangerously sick himself with tuberculosis when in his twenties, but to Percy the American who watched the world go utterly mad, murderously so, in the late 1930s and early 1940s.

For me, writing about Percy's work was a way of learning what I believed — how I saw and comprehended this world. I had, long ago it now seems, "shadowed Binx," as many of us have — lucky and comfortable heirs of Western civilization who nevertheless are quizzical, at loose ends often enough, not sure what really matters, even as we go about our appointed rounds, accumulating certifications and cash and nods and having our "relationships." Now older, I see Binx still, in my students and my patients, in my sons growing up, and still in myself as I catch myself up to his (my) old tricks; and I think of Binx while walking and noticing, driving and forgetting, stopping and all of a sudden — yes, feeling that one, by god, *is:* that elusive *being* of those high-and-mighty existential philosophers. In a sense, then, doing a certain kind of biography of Percy has in this instance meant not so much dealing with this or that challenge, so far as the "subject" goes, as coming to terms with one's subjectivity.

To repeat the old question: who is this Walker Percy? He is, a biographer finds out, not only a doctor, an essayist, a novelist, but a rather thoughtful and humorous and unpretentious human being. I think of him, again, as a friend, a person of wisdom, still there — with whom to correspond, to whom one turns for a now-and-then conversation, a drink or two of bourbon. Is "friendship" fair game as a "variable," to be discussed as an "aspect" of the "relationship" which develops between "biographer" and "subject"? Is a "good and decent example" another "variable"? Ought we mention the pleasure we've obtained — the fortunate and delightful encounter with a wry, quiet, but strong and lively intelligence? We are all (in one or another way or moment) lonely, as those existentialists Walker Percy knows so well have insisted again and again. Still, their own tradition is sturdy and growing and, not least, a real and mighty help to us. Each of them is a presence for many of us (and a book can be a persuasive companion), and so we may often feel less lonely. Sometimes I will look at my Percy shelf, think of statements I've heard him make, of time spent chewing the fat with him (and dissolving it in a good, strong amber fluid), and incline, just then at least, a little more toward yes, in respect to this life rather than toward *no* or *maybe;* a consequence, for one soul, of "doing work on," "doing a biography of" — oh, getting to know another soul.

Literature and Medicine, 1985

36

A WRITER'S MELANCHOLY:

A Review of William Styron's

Darkness Visible

One of America's most sensitive and thoughtful novelists, William Styron has recently given all us physicians pause with a brief, unnerving exercise in nonfiction — a long essay meant to discuss his own serious bout of depression. In a sense his title addresses not only the "darkness" that for a while became all too "visible" for a particular writer, his family, and friends, but the grim, melancholy moods millions of others the world over experience and struggle to comprehend. A writer who has for years tried to help us understand through stories other kinds of "darkness" (the consequences for various individuals of war and racism, for example) has now told us part of his own personal story — what happened to a man over sixty, who fell apart emotionally, found himself at loose ends, then at wits' end, as a debilitating episode of depression drove him to the point of suicide.

As with so many illnesses and disasters that come upon us, Styron's depression seemed to come out of nowhere. He does mention a declining bodily capacity for alcohol before the onset of his depression — this in a man long a fairly serious drinker — but the seeming revolt against booze of his physiological makeup did not, in itself, set him into a tailspin. Rather, he went about his ways as an honored writer — and indeed, he starts his narrative of psychiatric decline with an account of a visit to Paris on the occasion of a literary award presented to him. It was then that he became incapacitated — unable to get through the ordinary challenges of a rather pleasant day. He became disorganized, panicky, fearful, and in no time, it seemed, paralyzed by a mood of hopelessness, by a conviction of his own uselessness. Soon enough, he was taking (or being told to take) pills to go to sleep, pills to keep his spirits up. He mentions, in that regard, Halcion and Ludiomil and Nardil. At one point he also mentions electroconvulsive therapy — he began to get better just as that most serious, if not drastic, measure was being considered a possibility for him.

We are also brought face to face with Styron's psychiatrist, whom he calls Dr. Gold. The doctor does not come off well in his patient's memoir — but rather as patronizing, smug, even simpleminded. Styron talks of "platitudes" offered — even as some of us who have worked with severely depressed patients know how hard it can be to say anything that is of use to them, however brilliantly and cogently stated, given the manner in which their mood determines their judgment with respect to what they hear. Perhaps Styron's physician was, indeed, yet another inadequate or foolish doctor who failed miserably to understand and communicate with his patient. But depression notoriously clouds the judgment of those who suffer its consequences, and so one wonders what this pseudonymous physician might have to tell us, were he of the writing kind.

For the general reading public, Styron has no doubt rendered a great service: he tells his thousands of readers what a clinical depression can come to mean — a grave threat to life itself. For physicians his short memoir, of sorts, is a puzzle, even a cautionary tale. He never does figure out why he got so depressed — or for that matter, why (or how) he got better. He was hospitalized, and for sure, that outcome was significant — helped him gather together what strength was left him, and too, helped him share the company of others, similarly distressed. Still, he has no good words for much that happened in the hospital. He mocks some of the efforts of art therapists, group therapists, ward personnel who attempted to be of help to him; and while one sympathizes to a degree with his sardonic ear (his sense of the banality and worse that can masquerade as a "therapeutic milieu"), one also has to consider, yet again, how mischievously distorting a spell of the blues can be even for some of us who never have and never will become as "sick" as Styron was — the way everything heard and seen seems so futile and stupid when we are badly down in the dumps. Perhaps the real failure of Styron's relationship with his physician was just that — not enough trust and affection between the two of them for this distinguished patient to realize that depression not only impairs mood, but judgment, even retrospective judgment.

As I read Styron's indictment of his doctor, I remembered a remark Anna Freud once made — her recall of what a depressed adolescent had once said to her: "You're lucky you're my *second* analyst! I was so unhappy a while back, no one had a chance with me!" Miss Freud went on to say this: "We [who practice psychoanalysis] ought to think of 'luck' every once in a while: not only the lucky patients (so we think!) who see certain analysts, but the lucky analysts who get to see them at just the right time — or the unlucky ones who may sometimes be fated never to make much progress with certain patients!"

No question, Styron himself was lucky; he was, at one point, actively considering suicide — but he survived. We are not privy to the reasons for that psychological triumph — presumably the former patient himself doesn't know how to render such an account, because he seemed to recover on his own. He gives us (gives himself through the reflection of this essay) only some hints of what in his life might have made him especially vulnerable to depression: his mother died when he was a youth — and he recalls her singing the beautiful, haunting Brahms' *Alto Rhapsody*, even as he heard that extraordinarily evocative and touching piece of music at his lowest ebb, as he prepared to make an end of himself: "I do know that in those last hours before I rescued myself, when I listened to the passage from the *Alto Rhapsody* — which I'd heard her sing — she had been very much on my mind" (p. 81).

Her return, as it were, to him through music now serves the interests of a powerful, compelling story-teller, and surely hints at the kind of drama psychoanalysis has for a century pressed upon our sensibilities, be we doctors, mental health professionals, or members of the laity. Surely those of us more inclined to see things neurochemically will take note that Styron himself is exceedingly tentative with his psychological observations; not at all tempted, as some psychiatric theorists might be, to proclaim them as definitive explorations. We are left, then, with what another Southern writer, Flannery O'Connor, has lyrically called "mystery and manners" — the essential mystery, so far as we can know, of the cause of Styron's spell of "darkness," and the powerful and telling "manners" he offers us: the concrete details, wonderfully rendered, of how it went for him through a terribly trying, even life-threatening spell. We are also left with this impressively suggestive and poignant book; and it may tell us more than the author credits it for doing: a splendid essay as itself the elusive cure the author once so desperately sought — the depression as a prelude to, an occasion for, a talented writer's journey within himself.

For the rest of us, however, such a literary outcome is not possible — and so, perhaps, we try to find our own manner of narrative exposition (psychotherapy) and whatever psychopharmacological assistance will be of help.

Journal of Child and Adolescent
Psychopharmacology, 1990/1991

37

TEACHING RAYMOND CARVER

During the past decade I have been calling upon novelists, short-story writers, poets, in the teaching I do at Harvard University. I am a physician, trained in pediatrics, child psychiatry, psychoanalysis. For twenty years my wife and I, with our children, lived as wandering "field workers" — an effort to understand how children of various backgrounds grow up: black and white, Southern and Northern, those who live on Indian reservations, or in the Eskimo villages of Alaska, or up the hollows of Appalachia, or indeed, nowhere and everywhere, as boys and girls whose parents are migrant farm workers. Eventually, we worked with children abroad, in the *favelas* of Brazil, the various townships of South Africa, and the strife-ridden neighborhoods of Belfast, for example — in hopes of learning how young people caught in third world poverty, or in a kind of racial or religious conflict that dominates a country's political life, manage to figure out their loyalties, their aspirations, their values and ideals.

More recently, for about ten years, I have made a major commitment to teaching, a real pleasure and challenge. When I came back from the South to Boston (in 1966), after an eight-year spell of studying school desegregation and working in the sit-in movement, I studied with Erik H. Erikson, who had in his late-middle age begun teaching at Harvard College. Erikson asked me to be one of his teaching assistants, and I gladly accepted the offer. He was interested in the relationship between psychoanalysis (his profession) and history — how our thoughts and interests are shaped not only by our early experiences but by the world we happen to inherit: our class and race and nationality, and not least, the time in which we live. He used much of his own writing, and that of other social scientists; but he did assign Ralph Ellison's *Invisible Man* and he did allow each of us who taught the course's sections to come up with a book or two of our own as something for the students to read and discuss.

I still remember some of those sections, the way a story by Flannery O'Connor, say, or William Carlos Williams, caught the attention of the young readers, prompted in them a kind of discussion all its own: less attention, by far, to generalizations with respect to the psychology of "human development" or "psychohistory," and much time given to a contemplation of life's ironies, complexities, ambiguities, inconsistencies, paradoxes — the terrain of fiction, with its modest interest in rendering the concrete as faithfully and suggestively as possible. I still remember the braking influence of those stories on our conceptual energies, our desire to tuck into this or that generalization all we could grab in our hands. "The task of the novelist," Miss O'Connor had told us, "is to deepen mystery," and thereupon she added, pointedly: "But mystery is a great embarrassment to the modern mind." An embarrassment, for sure, to some of us eager, ambitious social and psychological theorists: as in "The Artificial Nigger," whose character, Mr. Head, is quite readily able to betray his own grandson for the pettiest of reasons (so much for all of our heady, self-important lives); and as in "The Lame Shall Enter First," which offers a psychologist of sorts who can't see how hurt and vulnerable his own son is, even as he seeks to work with a youth who has no use for him. In such stories the old adage that "pride goeth before the fall" gets worked into a narrative that turned out to be disturbing, indeed, to those late-twentieth-century secular students, many of whom had never laid eyes on the Bible, even as they knew a lot about psychology and sociology not only through courses taken, but as one student told me, a memorable moment: "My folks brought us up on psychoanalysis and politics — that's what they believe in: you should have your head shrunk and you should try to change the world!" I was obviously not one to disagree — and yet: after the hundreds of analytic hours, and the various legislative victories (or the struggles on the streets that preceded and enabled them) there remains our rock-bottom humanity, with all the warts and larger that make us, always, less than perfect in the way we present ourselves to others.

By the early 1970s Erik H. Erikson had retired, and my wife and three sons and I were living in New Mexico, where I was talking with Spanish speaking children and with children who lived on the Pueblo reservations north of Albuquerque. In 1975 we returned to New England, and it was then that I was offered a job at Harvard by the President, Derek Bok — to teach, as he put it in a letter to me, "what you want, where [in the university] you want." I knew I did not want to teach psychoanalytic psychiatry, no matter my respect for what it can offer particular individuals (in the right physician's hands, one wants to add, immediately). I knew, actually, that I wanted to use fiction and poetry in my work with medical students and young doctors learning to be pediatricians or child psychiatrists; and I knew, too, that I wanted to teach undergraduates. Soon enough, then, I was offering a college lecture course, a freshman seminar, a "medicine and literature" course, and "supervisory seminars," as they are called, to psychiatric and pediatric residents. Across the board, I called upon William Carlos Williams: I had written my college thesis on the first two books of *Paterson*, had come to know him, and respect him, and seek his advice — and yes, follow his example by choosing a career in medicine. I called upon Chekhov and Tolstoy, old loves, and Tillie Olsen, whose stories meant a lot to me, and Flannery O'Connor, who had done so well as a disturber of the peace when I had taught for Professor Erikson. I called upon Walker Percy and Ralph Ellison and Zora Neale Hurston (then, in the mid-seventies, far less well known than she is today). I called upon *Middlemarch* and *Great Expectations* and *Jude the Obscure* — and Simone Weil and Dorothy Day and James Agee and George Orwell; and I often added a poem of Phillip Levine, whose work I have long much admired, a "son," in certain respects, of Dr. Williams — a big, generous heart that has been notably responsive to the lives of "ordinary" (so-called working-class) American people.

I've tried hard not to grow old with those authors alone, those books alone. I've tried to meet others, get close to their writing, feel able to teach their stories, their poems — most recently, the work of Raymond Carver, who has been a mainstay of my teaching life, now, for over five years, to the point that I don't frankly know how I did without him back in the seventies. I had read an occasional story of Carver's on my own, but I was introduced to his full range and power by a former student of mine, Jay Woodruff, who went on to attend the Iowa Writer's Workshop, become a short story writer, and also (for four years) work with me, help teach (and run) my college course. Jay knew how much time I'd spent talking with factory workers, with men and women who barely get by, who are nurses or automobile mechanics, who work in restaurants or hotels, who are struggling hard and long to pay their bills, to hold on to what they have, no matter the odds against them. He brought to my attention one Carver story after another, and soon I was exploring every square mile of Carver country, and eager to take with me my students.

I began by connecting Carver to one of his own heroes, William Carlos Williams. I asked students in my college lecture course to read Williams's "Doctor Stories" and his novel *White Mule,* then read Carver's stories such as "Cathedral," "Vitamins," "What's in Alaska," "Fat." The students really took to those stories — asked a lot of questions not only about them, but their author. We have about twenty-five sections (each with twenty members) in the course and we who teach found ourselves in our weekly discussions spending more and more time on Carver — on the way Carver gets so much going among all of us who read him. He became more than yet another author for us; he became the heart and soul of the course — an important writer, indeed, for a number of students and their section leaders (not to mention me, who gives two lectures a week). When I read passages from the stories, in a lecture, or read from the personal essays, such as "My Father's Life," or "On Writing," or "Fires," I sometimes hear my voice crack; and I learn, afterwards, that a number of students had teared up, or had gone back to their rooms and read those passages again and again — and had wanted to talk and talk about them with their roommates and friends, or in the sections which they attended. When I visit those sections (and I do so throughout the term) Carver is more on the minds of many of these young men and women than the other writers: he touches them, gives them pause, stays with them in a powerful way.

Moreover, he prompts those youths (so many of them lucky all their lives, at least with respect to the money and social position they can take for granted, or in hopes, soon enough, of being lucky) to stop and think about others, and not only a distant "them," living in another city, but men and women and children who live only a few blocks from important university buildings — indeed, even nearer than that, as one student reminded himself in an essay he wrote, and later, me, in a discussion we held during my office hours: "The people who keep this place running — they're out of Carver's stories. I worked a summer for 'buildings and grounds,' and we'd be raking or sweeping, and I'd hear them talk, and I realized, after a while, that they were really on the edge, those guys. They were, up to their ears in debt, and there'd always be some trouble, it seemed — something that was about to pull the rug out from under them. There I was, making a few bucks for the summer, in between my sophomore and junior year at Harvard; and there they were, fighting disaster all the time, or just 'keeping even.' There was a guy who kept knocking on wood, any time he talked about his life, his family and himself, and if there wasn't any wood nearby, he'd go walk, to find it — and he kept saying 'things are OK,' and 'we're keeping even, so far,' and he'd knock on wood, and I could see in his eyes that he was glad, but he didn't know how long his luck would hold out, and he was always expecting the worst. I kept thinking of him when I read Carver's stories — and when I'd see him, sometimes, I felt a little closer to him. I mean, he wasn't this stranger, who seemed to be a big worrier — that's how I first saw him. He was a guy I understood a little now: he was trying to steer clear of trouble, but he sure didn't have much leverage on life, and so he was running scared!"

Somehow, for that student, as for others, Carver's stories enabled a leap out of one world, into another — not an immersion, but a sense of how it goes, walking in other shoes as a result of such conversations. I decided three years ago to offer a freshman seminar devoted to Carver alone, so far as reading goes. I titled the seminar "American Light," with this subtitle: "Raymond Carver's writing and Edward Hopper's paintings." I gave this description of what we'd try to do: "Members of the seminar will examine those [books and paintings] separately and together as a means of thinking about the lives of America's twentieth-century, working-class people. All of Carver's fiction and essays, and much of his poetry, will be read. The seminar will look closely at selected Hopper paintings and drawings. Members of the seminar will discuss contemporary American working-class culture, its characteristics and its values, as narrated by a master American storyteller and as glimpsed by a master American artist. The tradition of documentary observation and research will be discussed to provide a context for the lessons Carver and Hopper offer with respect to the lives of ordinary working-class Americans — their routines and habits, their goals and aspirations, their values, the moral complexities and ambiguities of their lives."

Such flat, stilted academic language notwithstanding, the ten or so students and I have had quite a time each autumn, once a week for several hours, reading those stories, talking about them, sharing with one another what they have caused us to think about, remember, notice, ask of ourselves and others. I'm no great one for "deconstruction" — I share Carver's bold suggestion that it may be a kind of lunacy. But I love reading him carefully, closely — noticing moments, scenes, images, words I'd missed the first or second time around. I love imagining the people he has created — their looks, their surroundings. In my thoughts, I start with Carver's descriptions, then amplify, sometimes out of clear memories I have of others: people I've got to know doing my "field-work" — meaning fellow human beings I've visited in their homes, sat with, the television on, now and then my tape-recorder also on, or people I've heard talking in offices or stories or factories or hotels or bars, people who have spoken of how it goes for them in this life. (When such "field-work" ends and "life" begins might be described in the pompous literature of social science as a "methodological issue"!) So with the students — I encourage them to make friends with Carver's stories, read them for pleasure, for the education about the world to be had, for the wisdom they offer. I encourage them to meet his longtime companion, Tess Gallagher, to read her poems and stories, and to meet his two friends, Richard Ford and Tobias Wolff, to read their stories. I encourage them to learn to be as watchful as Carver was, and to enjoy his plain yet magically suggestive language. I encourage them to let his cast of mind inform what used to be called their "sensibility" — the shrewd and knowing clarity of vision that helps us comprehend the confusions, the mix-ups, the perplexities that present themselves to us during this time spent here called "life." I encourage them to stick fast to those stories, to take them on as companions or friends, as warnings, as reminders, as teachers. Needless to say, what I urge of them, I try hard to keep in mind for myself. I know we are all getting someplace when a student will say (it keeps happening, repeatedly, each year): "This Carver, he's really something." What follows is not an outburst of cleverness, a "text" analyzed, words and more words devoted to big-deal abstractions, but silence, and the nods of us who have also begun to know just that, and to talk in moments as this guy who has become a presence of sorts in our lives used to talk, and maybe even, to think as he used to think.

I've gone elsewhere with Carver — to medical students at Harvard and at Dartmouth medical schools. In those places I teach something called "medical humanities"; that is, my old hero and friend Doc Williams, and Tillie Olsen and Tolstoy and Walker Percy and Carver's hero Chekhov, and Carver himself: "A Small Good Thing," obviously, and "Errand" and "Cathedral," and his last poems, such as "What the Doctor Said" and "Gravy" and "After-Glow" and "No Need," but also some others, such as "Poem for Hemingway and W. C. Williams" (I love it) and "The Mailman as Cancer Patient," and "Alcohol," and "Your Dog Dies" — as many of them as I can work into the time I have. I get excited, really turned on, trying to figure out how to introduce a particular poem, how to bring it to those soon-to-be doctors in such a way that the language, the sights and sounds, will stick fast and long to minds filled to the brim with the fearful or foreboding factuality of those big fat medical textbooks.

So many of Carver's stories tell of the trouble people have in understanding one another: remarks that are heard the wrong way; silences that won't yield to a reasonably pleasant exchange; outright battles that are, really, in their sum, the last straw, the final goodbye for people supposedly so close by virtue of blood, or the past intimacy of sex, or marriage. Again and again, misunderstandings are evoked, small and large, and we become sad, or we shudder, aware that we run our own risks along similar lines. Doctors, especially, in their work, struggle to make themselves clear — and so often, fail miserably, out of their own fear and anxiety, out of callousness, out of simple human error, out of the limitations imposed by their inevitably flawed humanity.

Still, we ought keep trying to reach out, to connect with those others who get called patients in such a way that we have a good idea what we intend to convey, and then offer our words in a manner that enables the person addressed to get our intended message. If the immediately foregoing is a bit didactic or hectoring, the reason may have to do with the precariousness of a doctor's situation, not to mention that of patients: they are desperately seeking clues, not to mention reassurance, hope, and they will, often enough, take what they've heard and tailor it to their urgent needs, their craving, even as some of us physicians are tempted to appease at all costs those we fear to disappoint, or too, tempted to hide from them with inscrutable phrases, or the inscrutability of our manner, our mien. Our arrogance can measure fear of the apprehension of a coming defeat, even as a patient's pleadings, become importunate demands, can measure a hunch that soon it may well be over for good — all of which Carver knew to work into some of his poems and stories: a wonderfully thought-provoking gift to a profession he, alas, like Chekhov, came to know too well, as a patient, far too early in life. Speaking of Chekhov, my medical students find "Errand" especially stirring — and some wonder whether a glass of champagne might be exactly what certain patients and their close kin need to share with their physicians at a certain point in time — even as those students, too, wonder how they, as future doctors, might somehow become the kind of baker who sat with the heart-broken father and mother in "A Small Good Thing," fed them, helped drain their anger, their bitterness, their rage: a communion, a taking of "bread and wine."

I've brought Carver to other students, to a class I gave, one spring, at Duke University's Center for Documentary Studies — those stories, again, as a way of seeing the world, taking note of dozens and dozens of social variations: the subtleties of class and region that inform our lives, given shape by someone with a keen ear for language, a wide-eyed responsiveness to a broad segment of America's people. I've brought Carver, also, to the psychiatric and pediatric residents I get to teach — in separate seminars, each calling upon the reading of stories as a means of moral and personal reflection. Sometimes, as I listen to them talking about their patients, I ask them to read one of Carver's stories, such as "What We Talk About When We Talk About Love," or "Elephant," or "Neighbors," or "Why Don't You Dance" — and we have quite a time of it. These young psychiatrists or pediatricians, occasionally, are all too condescending, at first: how "intuitive" the writer is, I hear them say to one another, to me — as if he has almost approached *their* level of psychological or medical savvy. After a while, though, such gratuitous compliments (a masquerade for a put-down) yield to a growing respect, and in turn, a sense of awe, of enormous admiration. I have sat with these psychiatrists, these pediatricians, at moments, in a hushed silence, watched them as they shake their heads: an acknowledgement of a particular writer's extraordinary grasp of the mind's life — its capacity for aspiration, for survival, and its more than occasional moments of self-deception, meanness, despair.

Not rarely I work with graduate students, some of whom teach in my course. I ask them (I ask myself) to pick up "The Student's Wife" now and then, reflect upon all it has to say. When I read it, I remember Doc Williams giving me lectures on the distinction between "big shot learning," as he put it, and "our daily conduct." Throughout *Paterson* he reminds us (sometimes confessionally) that one can be learned, indeed, gifted with the muse, a great success, and not necessarily a kind and thoughtful person. That story of Carver's, for me, belongs with Chekhov's "Anyuta," with his "Two Tragedies," with Williams's moments of Augustinian self-scrutiny in *Paterson*, with Tolstoy's *Confession,* with Walker Percy's observations in *Lost in the Cosmos,* as well as *The Moviegoer* and *The Last Gentleman* — to read Rilke, yet to be unable to meet the challenge a marriage presents, is to be one more bright failure, and so it can go for any of us.

Teaching Raymond Carver, for me, has meant calling upon a great storyteller in order to bestir both my students and myself: that we look inward and outward, both; that we try to extend the range of

our social vision, but also, our moral empathy; that we try to understand how pitiable any of us can be, how isolated and lonely (as in
many of Hopper's paintings — such a strange congruence, their vision and Carver's), but that we also remember those daily, unher-
alded breakthroughs which, finally, give us human beings what
dignity we can achieve, as in those closing moments of "Cathedral,"
moments worth textbooks of psychology and philosophy. Teaching
Raymond Carver has meant, I now realize, learning about how to
teach, and yes, how to be: we all, so often, as in "Cathedral," are the
blind leading the blind, yet we can and do enable sight, even elicit the
visionary in one another — our only hope, one another. Teaching
Raymond Carver has meant glimpsing lots of flaws in myself; yet
feeling stronger for partaking of the wonderful feast this exceptionally talented twentieth-century writer has left us: a large and great
thing, his books, their astonishing, compelling wisdom as it slowly,
modestly unfolds, nourishes and sustains and inspires us fragile,
thirsty, hungry, ever so needy readers.

American Poetry Review, 1993

IV

LECTURES

ঽ๏ *This section requires no introduction, only an explanation of how the first two essays came to be written. I was asked by the San Francisco Psychoanalytic Institute to give their thirteenth annual Sophia Mirviss Lecture for 1971. It has obviously been an occasion for a psychoanalytic statement, and I tried hard to live up to the tradition with "The Inner and Outer World," since printed as a monograph, and as a chapter in a book,* The Infant at Risk. *The second essay was delivered as the fifteenth T. B. Davie Memorial Lecture at a formal convocation of the University of Cape Town, South Africa, in August of 1974, and later published in* The New York Review of Books. *The Davie Lecture commemorates a brave university official's struggle against one kind of "political authority," apartheid. I have never been so moved as on the occasion of that lecture — an entire university in nonviolent protest against a government's arrogant and cruel policies. I only hope that these two lectures help indicate what it is that such political, economic and social activities on the part of various levels of a government ultimately end up doing to the minds of children. The third essay was prompted by an invitation (1992) to speak to a group of psychoanalytic psychiatrists in New Orleans, where so much of my work with children was done during the early years of the Civil Rights movement. By then, those children were all grown, even as I was still trying to make sense of what they (and I, with them as an observer) had experienced.*

38

THE INNER AND OUTER WORLD

When Sigmund Freud began to study the anxious and fearful men and women he saw as a young doctor in the final years of the nineteenth century he did so in a way which singled him out. His patients were people apart, people looked down upon, people who annoyed and even enraged their doctors, let alone everyone else in Vienna's middle-class world. Indeed, I do not think it is an exaggeration to represent those patients of Freud's as scorned, humiliated, even brutalized men and women; their complaints were either ignored, laughed at, or perhaps worst of all, manipulated forcefully by the stern, contemptuous and moralistic men physicians upon occasion can often be. In contrast Freud wanted to understand and heal. He treated those "neurotics" with a revolutionary kind of respect. He listened to them. He watched them. He held off judging them, or labeling them, unlike his colleagues, who seemed to feel that if only we can classify people into categories, we have done our job as scientists. Eventually he began to feel that he had some idea what was going on in the minds of those "outcasts" he was spending his time with; and with that achievement secured, he could perhaps go on to do the most doctors can do — be of some limited help to them.

Meanwhile the medical and psychiatric world of Vienna, the powers and principalities Freud well knew about, took notice — and in an especially vindictive way employed by the powerful, not in Freud's day alone. Even when he had become a world figure Freud was virtually ignored in Vienna. Worst of all, his patients had to live with the knowledge that a handful of psychoanalysts might be on their side, but most doctors held stubbornly to the old ways, the old prejudices. For Freud all that was to be expected; he knew from the beginning that his particular intellectual struggle was going to be challenging. Those wrought-up, desperately confused "hysterics" he saw in hospitals and clinics and in his office were, unquestionably, members of an oppressed minority. For various reasons they did not think like others, and most important, did not act like others. By the time each one of them had come to Freud they had exhausted just about every avenue of "treatment" available, and in so doing aroused against them all the wrath a notably conformist and self-consciously "proper" society could mobilize. And if Freud continued to work with such people, even became an advocate of theirs, in the sense that he insisted that they were not all *that* different from everyone else, he must have also had his second thoughts — especially when for six years (from 1900 to 1906) only 351 copies of his masterpiece, *The Interpretation of Dreams*, were purchased, and the leading medical and psychiatric journals chose to ignore it.

Later Freud would take note unashamedly of his ability and willingness to stand removed from the dominant majority; he referred to the fact that he was a Jew in a Gentile world, and an iconoclastic thinker in a thoroughly conservative profession. There are advantages to being an outsider, he seemed to be saying — though he also realized that there can be a stiff price to pay. Rather obviously, had Freud been less courageous or more vulnerable he easily could have made his accommodations, thrown in his lot with those he viewed as narrow, blind, impossibly biased men — and accordingly been treated better. Instead he never stopped being denied, even oppressed, throughout his professional life. If he did not as a result become pathologically suspicious and bitter and envious, it was because he did indeed have a superior cast of mind; he found for himself a means of self-affirmation and self-respect which made bearable, at times even satisfying, a situation of professional exile which he knew to be unjust.

Neither middle-class children nor ghetto children can take much comfort from Freud's example; an extraordinary man, he tends to command awe rather than emulation these days from those in our middle-class suburbs — and, of course, in Harlem or Chicago's Southside or Cleveland's Hough section or San Francisco's Fillmore district he is largely unknown. Nor can it be said that we in psychiatry and psychoanalysis have chosen in recent years to remind ourselves excessively how embattled this man was, how brazen and unfettered his thinking turned out to be, how much of a threat and a source of confusion he became for so many people. To be sure, we say he was unpopular; and sometimes when we have trouble getting our ideas across to others we remind ourselves that it is our fate, also, to be misunderstood or "resisted." Most of us in this country do not lead the lives of suspect, feared, or hated men and women. Psychoanalysis now has a history of its own, whose length exactly corresponds to this century's. The original struggle has become transformed into a worldwide network of institutions and programs. The new generation need not seek out the old struggles, and the sort of pioneer drawn to an ostracized "movement" is likely to differ from the professional who wants to treat patients and learn psychiatry under circumstances that carry little or no social or economic risk. Freud had to endure not only social rejection but constant economic insecurity over a significant stretch of his life. At various points in his life he might have changed things, or so we are, again, tempted to think; that is to say, he could have become just another neurologist and psychiatrist, or one of those smooth, uncontroversial doctors who know how to mix rhetoric, suggestion and conventional pieties in such a way as to "comfort" their rich, vain, but altogether susceptible patients — whose loss of religious faith in our time has benefited all sorts of secular authorities. Could he ever really have done so, though? Here one is up against a dilemma as old as man himself. How "free" are we to be what others are like? How bound are we by a certain fate we have: the quality of our mind; the psychological experiences we have had while growing up, and for that matter, the color of our skin or the social and economic "background" our parents gave to us as a birthright?

In Freud's case it was clear even in the 1890s that nothing would stop him from at least trying to assert his ideas and convictions. Still, something had to be done in the way of self-protection against the worst of the risks he was prepared to assume. Such a man had to make sure that he could in fact over the long haul face the concrete and exhausting difficulties which can overwhelm even the best-intentioned and most spirited of nonconformists. He developed a way of speaking about the very special events he was spending his life looking at and thinking about. He found himself keeping company with certain other colleagues who were interested in the same things he was interested in and who in general shared his determination to uphold a certain point of view at all costs. He sought consolation and self-justification in the face of the criticism and outright rejection he had to contend with; and in doing so he often turned his mind both back into the past and toward the future. Other pioneers had been lonely exiles in the midst of their own countrymen, only to triumph eventually. Other prophets had been tested and tried by adversity, and not without reason either — because people are afraid to grow, to widen their horizons, to be confronted with their darker side. The point was to continue, and look to the future. Someday a grateful world would come to its senses and realize what it had been denying — and why. Meanwhile Freud created a language of his own, a community of men and women who shared his fate, and a philosophical viewpoint meant to nourish him and his colleagues, and protect them from the psychological hazards which inevitably bear down upon a small and somewhat persecuted minority. What mattered was survival, and if upon occasion the small group of outsiders became grandiose, or excessively tight-knit, or suspicious to an extreme about anyone and everyone — still, the "enemy" was real and not a fantasied one. Those early psychoanalysts were vulnerable and fallible human beings for all the power and brilliance of their minds.

I do not wish to belabor a comparison which has only a limited value, but I think there is a good deal in the history of psychoanalytic psychiatry that ought to make us especially sensitive to the ways children who belong to our so-called "minority groups" grow up and come to feel about the world they so often have to take on against great odds. Furthermore, it is not only a certain history that ought dispose us to such understanding. We are dedicated to the study of particular lives, as they are lived in all their complexity and ambiguity — and so we want to know how a given infant, born on such-and-such a day of such-and-such a year in such-and-such a place and under certain (medical, social, psychological) circumstances becomes, week by week, a particular baby, child, boy or girl, youth, and grown man or woman. To say that is to say we want to know how bodies, in need of food and urged along by physiological and biochemical rhythms and forces we as yet only partially comprehend, become over time individuals who think and act in ways that distinguish them from millions and millions of other individuals within their own country, let alone in other nations or continents. In the case of the black and white children I have been working with these past years such a study in certain respects has been a study of *outsiders*, which is why I have drawn these parallels with Freud's experience. How does an outsider deal with a world he both lives in and feels separated from? How does an outsider keep his head up, go on from day to day, even feel hopeful, sometimes specially chosen, all in the face of the explicit unfriendliness or even unrestrained hatred of those many "others" who constitute the majority of citizens? Alternatively, what happens when the going gets rough, when an outsider loses faith in himself and in his "future," when nothing seems to work and nobody seems to care?

Those questions are not new or surprising. All of us ask them every day — and since it can even be said we are all to some extent "outsiders," we ask them of one another, however "fortunate" we are with respect to our race or our social and educational background. Still, for black children or Chicano children or Indian children or white children who are to be found up the hollows of West Virginia and Kentucky or in the streets of cities like Dayton and Cincinnati and Chicago (where Appalachian families have moved by the thousands) such questions are not of only casual interest. Certainly they are not asked rhetorically or philosophically, any more than Freud was indulging himself or being frivolous when he established the Psychological Wednesday Society, a prelude to the Vienna Psychoanalytic Society, and took pains to estimate from time to time how far along toward acceptance and respectability psychoanalysis had come. Needless to say, in the course of what we call "childhood," boys and girls of whatever class or region worry about how readily accepted they are, how worthy others find them. But again, some boys and girls, like some men and women, worry more than others; and, of course, the way they talk about those worries or preoccupations tells us not only what is on "top" of their minds, but at the very bottom — "at the heart of their being," as an existentialist philosopher might want to say.

Here is what I once heard from a black boy of eight who at the time lived in a town called Roundaway, Mississippi — and what he said on one occasion he repeated in various ways on various other occasions, as our patients so often do, and indeed as our intellectual parents and predecessors, so to speak, like Freud, also did: "I've been told to watch out for white people. They don't like us, so we have to be careful. My daddy says there will come a time when they'll realize their sins, and change their minds about us, but it'll take time, because people are stubborn, you know. I do the best I can. I try to keep learning all the time in school, and I try to keep my spirits up, like our minister says we should. Sometimes I get discouraged. I get to worrying. I feel bad. I think it's unfair, the way the world is. I start complaining, I guess. But you mustn't feel sorry for yourself. Besides, I have my friends. We don't have to spend *all* our time with *them*, the white folks. We go off in the field over yonder and we are away, thank God. 'Get away and be by yourselves,' my grandmother always tells us. She works up there for the boss man's wife, so she knows. She says there's just so much you can take of their mean tongues and their bad habits, their sinful ways. That's what she says, and she's right. When we go playing, my friends and me, we're free of white people, all of them. We have a club, you know. We're the Eagles. I dream of flying a lot. I dream we all have wings, and we go way up to the sky and have the best time rising and falling and then rising again. Sometimes I wake up when I'm falling, and it doesn't seem I'm going to pull out of it and I might crash, but I don't believe I ever do crash, and the next time, when I have the next dream, I'm up over the clouds again. If I had my choice, I'd be a pilot. They can go where they want to go, and get there without a lot of people being in their way, like on the roads with cars. And a plane is big and strong and fast as can be. Don't be in a rush, they'll tell you in church or in school. But try to do the best you can, as quick as you can, my daddy always says.

"A lot of the time I sit out under the tree there. We've taken in all the crops we can for the day. I'm thirsty. I see the chipmunks poking around; they'll be hungry and thirsty — just like me. They're scared of me, the little animals are, just like when I see the boss man I want to go and hide in a hole and wait until he's gone. I'm sure he gets scared, though — that boss man of ours. You can bet your life on this: the white people hereabouts are plenty scared. My mother hears them talking while she's serving them. That's why I say we're doing all right, even if the white people make a lot of trouble for us. To them we're bears, maybe. Sometimes I'll look at them and I'll figure they are snakes, or maybe alligators. They're slippery and danger-ous, but if you keep yourself on guard and know what to expect of them, you can outfox them.

"I'd like it to be different; I mean, if people were nicer to each other, we'd all feel better. Most days I feel all right, but some days I don't like the way I'm spoken to by them. They'll kick us around, my daddy says. You're a nigger and don't you forget it, so long as you're with them — my daddy tells us that. But the day will come that they'll feel bad for what they've done, according to our minister. They might even come and ask for our help (he says) and we could teach them to be nicer people (he says); but I'm not so sure he's right. I think a lot about those white people. My friends and I (in the club) talk over what they're like. I think the Negro man is smart if he is careful. No sooner do you raise your hopes than you're disap-pointed. My aunt says God must have had His reasons for making all the trouble He did for us, but I can't believe she's right. I think the bad outnumber the good, and the only way the Negro can stay alive is to stick together. In our club we have hideouts. We have secret places, and no one knows where they are, not even our families. I've spent the night and longer with my friends out there in the woods near the field. It hurts, when you're cold in the middle of the night and your stomach is growling on you, and there's nothing around to eat; but if it hurts it hurts, and better a little pain than the sheriff's gun or the jailhouse they have. (The sheriff is mean: he'd as soon kill you as not. I hear he's scared of his wife. She shouts at him, then he leaves the house scratching his head and sweating bad and red as can be, and he'll hit a white kid, even. Stay clear of him, the minister says.) We have a harmonica and we take turns using it. We know a lot of songs. We can each tell our stories. My friends tell me I tell good stories. My mother used to say that we should dream all we can, even in the daytime when we get a chance, because there's no white man can come along and stop you from doing that, so long as you be careful and don't' let them catch you. Just pretend you're doing something, anything, when you have your dreams there out in those cotton fields. That's my mother's advice to us.

"The other thing we do is play games. We have a baseball. We have fishing lines and we know where the worms are and we can catch fish better than the white man can. They come and pay us to help them. They're not so smart that they know all they tell you they know. There will be times when they'll admit they can't do one thing, or something else, and they'll say they're glad we're around — the niggers they'll say, right to your face. Help me kid, they'll say. How do you know as much as you do about worms and fish, they'll ask you. They're smart, those nigger kids are, if you take the time to find out, I've heard them say about us. It goes to show you: they don't always remember what they've said a few minutes earlier. They'll be swearing and cussing us and they won't have a good word for us; but then they will go and reverse themselves and admit they're wrong. I guess if they're having a bad day, they turn on us, and if they're out to have a good time fishing, they can be nice to us. In our club we swap stories — about what we heard them say at different times. The white people don't know it, but we're keeping track of them!"

That black child might be called "culturally disadvantaged" and "culturally deprived"; in the less pretentious language of former times, he no doubt would have been called poor, to some extent sick in body and plain unlucky. Nor do I wish to deny that he faces formidable hurdles, to the extent that his future is as bleak as any American child's can possibly be, and he knows it. His parents are virtually penniless. Even in the early 1970s they are also virtual peons: in return for the barest minimum of food and shelter they work and work and work. Sure, they can all escape from their locality and go to

Chicago, where hundreds of thousands of their fellow blacks have arrived with high hopes indeed. But the boy I have just quoted knows what our most learned sociologists and political scientists and economists know; he knows that there is no real escape possible, not even "for pretense." Yes, he once told me that it is possible for black people to leave Mississippi, and years ago that might have truly been the wise thing to do. But things have changed: "Now it's the same all over for us, and if you're out for pretense, then you can fool yourself up in some city, but we have people come back here, and they say it's bad here and bad up there and there are good things about living here and good things about being up there (you're away from those gun-toting sheriffs) and so it's no big difference where you are, because there's the Negro and there's the white man, and that doesn't change in any part of the United States of America, no sir."

Now when one goes over his remarks, pulled together from several conversations and put into "our" (grammatical, if often less expressive) language, certain qualities of thinking and feeling can be seen to come across. The boy has his mood swings. He has his doubts and misgivings one moment, but the next he can be heard asserting himself almost fiercely. He insists upon his God-given right not only to exist, but to find whatever destiny a child's imagination and will-fulness can conceive of. At times he is even an adventurer of sorts; he will soar, he will fly and fly, gain a view from a great height, and not least, escape from a dark forest. Then, he can become allegorical, or if you will, metaphoric — and almost, upon occasion, metaphysical. His mind struggles with its desire to understand an exceedingly hard-to-fathom world, and as a means of doing so he calls upon symbols — for instance, the imagery animals suggest to him. Nor does he let himself be carried away by his own mind's achievements. He is aware that he is trying to make sense of the world, but he is not about to become an ideologue or a dogmatist. He acknowledges openly the inconsistencies of those he observes: sometimes those white people act one way, sometimes they contradict their way of acting. Ordinarily so self-assured and powerful, sometimes they almost plaintively call for help from him and others like him, who know so much about worms and bait and fishing holes. He goes a step further, too; he takes note of the link between stated values and beliefs and the emotional life of the person who declares them. Those big, confident, bragging sheriffs are at times afraid and uncertain and frustrated. They talk a lot but can be seen scratching their heads, flushing up in anger, perspiring heavily, and turning upon their very own kind. Their greedy, resentful side is not only the black man's curse, so to speak, but a larger, less specific part of their lives — as human beings. All of which makes him at times fatalistic and stoical, at times cheerful and optimistic in the way a canny and clear-sighted boy can be when he takes stock of his assets and liabilities — and proceeds to size up people and the world they go to make up.

By himself he broods; now and then he dares hope. But he also goes off and joins others. Together they discuss what they have experienced; they share ideas, and just as important, they affirm one another — rather as Freud and his colleagues did for so many years in their Psychological Wednesday Society. Again, I know comparisons can be overdone; but I wonder how far removed the young black children I have just mentioned are from the spirit an observer might have noticed had he been able to watch unobserved that Psychological Wednesday Society. Freud had few illusions, and those boys from Mississippi's Delta also have few illusions. Freud had his gloomy side and his more hopeful side, even as those boys do. Freud needed friends to meet with and exchange ideas with, even as those boys do. Freud resorted to metapsychology in a stubborn effort to find in abstractions a certain coherence, even as those boys call upon animals and their various qualities to lend force to conversations held in a rural Southern setting. And finally, Freud knew his history, just as the black boy for all his poor education, knows his race's past rather well. I suppose those who challenge prevailing orthodoxies (be they professional, social, political or economic) have to keep their wits about them and search in the past for whatever instruction, sustenance and consolation they can find.

If there are certain parallels between Freud's experience as an outsider and the experience of the black child I have just mentioned, can one go even further and say that Freud's psychoanalytic ideas, like the lessons of history, can offer someone who works with such children a degree of instruction and sustenance and maybe even a little consolation? I would like to answer that question by indicating some of the challenges that black child and others like him have presented to me over the years; perhaps as I do so my indebtedness to the richness and complexity of psychoanalytic theory will become apparent. For one thing, the boy himself has always taken pains to let me know how many-sided his life (and mind) is — notwithstanding all the tidy formulations I was tempted to make about him and his kind. In his own way he would tell me that he was not only someone who has thoughts or ideas, but someone who feels (and feels strongly) about people and about a whole range of subjects. He also would tell me that he doesn't jump to anyone's command (or bell or buzzer or even offer of reward, let alone suggestion of punishment) as quickly or automatically as I might think. Indeed, he knows at age eight how subtle and rewarding and tortuous and frustrating and enabling it is even when two loving people — he and his mother, he and his father, he and his brother, he and his sister — try to get along with each other. I would even be willing to say that he senses about himself what we psychiatrists might explicitly be aware of, were we to observe him all the time: that he is pushed forward from year to year by his body's growth — its need for food, its increasing assertiveness — and by his mind's ambitions and strivings, the things he likes to do and wants to do and every single day does do.

But before I go on talking about him, making an analysis of his life and his mind's activity, and speaking *for* him, I had best stop and let him once again speak for himself: "I help on the land. I can do almost all that my father can do, but not everything, because I'm little and he's big. I start when he does, with the sun coming up. I stop when he does, with the sun going down. A lot of the time I'd like to sit and play with my friends, and sometimes I do, but only when I've done a good job of picking the crops or doing errands for the boss man's wife. School is no good; they shout at us all the time. The teachers call us niggers, and they're niggers themselves. I wouldn't mind never going back to that place, that school. I like it when my daddy tells me what is right and what is wrong (well, sometimes I confess I don't like it) and I don't mind the minister jumping on all of us, come Sunday, but that Miss Johnson, she hates us. She said so once; and she looks as if she does every morning when she comes into the room — and before she even finds out what we're doing, she'll start being mean and sour.

"I get in fights. There are the older kids. They want to run everyone. You have to fight back. You can't fight with the white people, because they outnumber us and they like to kill — yes, sir, they like to kill us, the colored people. So, I try to keep clear of them. I know parts of the county where no white man has ever been, I'll bet; at least I've never seen any. There I can walk and spot the different kinds of birds, and pick some flowers. My mother tells each one of us to keep our eyes open — and if we see some wild flowers, pick them and bring them home. Then we can look at them on the table while we eat our supper. I have a cousin up in Chicago, and I'll bet he's never seen any of the flowers we have growing hereabouts. Of course my friend says they have a lot of good food on their tables up North, so they have no room for flowers. But I've seen the boss man's television; and on the programs the colored people up North are always pictured in trouble: sometimes they'll be marching to tell people what's wrong, or they'll be beaten up by the police, or else they'll be talking on the televisions — saying they wouldn't mind being back South, if they could get a job. They might not like my daddy's job, but he says he's happy being here and not up there.

"There will be times I get scared. I wonder if God was being so good, when He made us colored and turned the white man against us. The minister says He knew what He was doing, and maybe I'll be sorry if I disagree, but I can't help myself every once in a while; I mean, I think to myself that God made a mistake, He really did, and who can prove He didn't — is what I say. It's true, He may come up with some trick to prove He was right all along in what He was do-ing, but I doubt He will. At school the teachers and the principal will tell you that God made the colored people one way and the white people different, and it's no one's business but His, and if the white people are the big people and the colored people have to be afraid all the time of the white people, then God must want it to be like that, or He'd change His mind, and when He changes His mind then the people down here will go and do what He tells them to do. I laugh to myself when they talk like that — because it goes to show that our teachers are dumber than our ministers! The teachers call us dumb about ten times a day, but we trick them twenty times a day. My teacher will come up to me and shove a book in front of me and tell me to read, read. I say I can't. She says go ahead, anyway. I pretend I can't. She shouts that I'm a 'dumb, lazy nigger.' I nod, I even say 'Yes, ma'am.' That pleases her, to be yessed. My daddy has taught me how to get around the white man, so a nigger like our teacher is not hard to fool.

"When I grow up I hope the State of Mississippi will be a better state. I think it would be a better state if they let the white kids and the colored kids be together, and if they gave us all good jobs when we get older. I think I know how the white people think. They are winning the game, and they don't want to see us come along and take away all they've won for themselves. But we can't always be way on the bottom. Like my daddy says, there's got to be more sharing in this world, especially since the colored have nothing to share, and the whites have almost everything that's worth much money. Someone came here from a college, from a big city, and he said we've got to turn the state of Mississippi around. We've got to change everything, so that the white people stop being so bad. Afterwards I had a dream and there was the boss man and some of his friends in it, and they were afraid of us, instead of us being afraid of them, and they were running and talking to us at the same time. My daddy was chasing them. He said he was going to let them off easy, easier than he does us, his own children. He said there are too many white people to punish, so let's start fresh, and we'll all be good to each other. That's what the minister says he hopes will happen one day: white people and colored people will all be brothers. I'm pretty sure, though, it was my father who spoke like that in the dream.

"A while back I dreamed that the whites were trying to burn down our cabin; but my daddy told me to go find a hose, and I did, and we put the fire out, and turned the hoses on them, and they all fell down, the boss man and the sheriff. They came to see us get burned, and instead they did. I told my mother what I'd dreamed the next day, and she said maybe that was a sign that trouble is coming. She told my daddy, and he said maybe, but even so, we have no choice but to stay right where we are. My mother has a brother who went up to Detroit, and he got sick. He had trouble breathing. Then he lost his head, and they had to put him in a hospital. My mother says he was seeing God, and there's no one supposed to see Him. (I sure wouldn't want to lay my eyes on Him!) That's why my daddy always reminds my mother, when she talks about going North, how dangerous it can be. There are people all crowded together, worse than in our school, and the buildings fall in on them sometimes. It's real bad. I'm sure I'd be in trouble if I went to Detroit, but I could get by. I can tell what people are thinking a lot of the time, so I can be ready for them. My daddy says he can read the white man's mind. He says if you're colored, you have to — otherwise you'll be caught off your guard, and the next thing you know, you'll be locked up. And when a colored man gets locked up in jail, he's there for good. They never let us out, once they catch us. They have prisoners working the plantations up and down the state, my daddy says."

That child may scarcely know how to read and write, may never really learn how, but he has keen eyes and ears and already a well-developed sense of himself — of his obligations and responsibilities, his likely difficulties, his possible future achievements, and most of all, his particular tasks as one who comes from a particular race, and place, and time. As I have listened to him (as well as to others whose parents have taken them North to our ghettoes) I have again and again had to notice that what some categorical minds would want to call the "outer world" (the child's environment) and "the inner world" (or the child's conscious and unconscious mind) are in a great many respects one world, so far as the concrete, everyday life of such children goes. Mississippi's segregationist "boss men" live in his mind, in his daydreams and nightmares. Likewise, the state's social and economic and political reality is, among other things, his psychological reality. What racist laws say, he heeds, and what racist customs demand, he obeys, and what racist men live out, he in the private corners of his mind also lives out.

I know that we have to make distinctions between various kinds of "reality" in this world, but if in daily fact those distinctions are not so clear-cut and precise, but rather thoroughly blurred, then that, too, ought to be emphasized. What Mississippi's segregationist governor talks about on a television program can quickly become part of a child's unconscious life — and not only in such a way that the governor is transformed into a "symbol" of someone else, a stand-in for a father or an uncle or an older brother, a representative of the child's growing conscience, a means by which the child's mind expresses its conflicts. All of that holds; the mind can use anyone and anything for its own private purposes, as any clinician knows.

Still, one has to listen to a child talking about the experience he had watching a governor speak, and the dream he had, and the

thoughts he has had as a consequence of that dream — and in so doing let the child tell *us* something, even as we have our own ideas
about what he was and is going through: "I went to the boss man's
house, and his wife told me I should come in and listen to the governor of the State of Mississippi. She said he was my governor, as
much as hers, and I should listen to him. So I said yes ma'am, and I
stood and listened. She didn't ask me to sit down, but once she got up
and told me she had to sit in the other chair, because it was softer and
better. The governor kept on talking about the rest of the country,
and how down here we're good, but in other states, they're bad. He
must have repeated himself, saying so, a hundred times.

"The governor doesn't like colored people. He said we should
stay in one place, and the whites should live in another place and
send their children to their own schools, like they mostly do anyway.
He said the white people of the state are not going to be pushed
around by anyone, no matter who he be. I came home and told my
mother that I'd heard the governor. She asked who he is, and I said I
don't know, but he has three names and they told them to you before
he spoke. She asked what he said, and I said he said he was worried
that people are being unfair to the white people, and wanting to push
them all over. What people, my mother asked, and then she said it
couldn't be us, because we're pushed, not pushing. Try and get sassy
with a white man, and he'll have the sheriff pick you up and keep you
locked up until he cools off and tells the sheriff to let you out. That's
how it is.

"I had a long dream, and I couldn't recall a lot of it, except that my
brother says I woke him up and he heard me say 'the governor, the
governor.' I think I can remember something: the governor was
telling me that I'd better not try to sit in any chair that belongs to a
white man. He said white people have their chairs, and the colored
had better watch out and not get greedy eyes."

There was no more, he assured me. There was no more, he was
sorry to say. Well, maybe he did dream more, but all he could remember was that, and he could make no sense of anything — except
that perhaps he had the dream because he'd gone "up to the house"
to do some errands for "the lady" and she had asked him to keep her
company while she looked at that big color television set, which endlessly fascinated him. He had never expected to hear a governor talk;

nor had he expected to hear him talk about racial matters so bluntly. Not that he or his hostess had been made uncomfortable by the program. She had offered him a chocolate after the governor finished, and he told her that he thought the governor was an important man. Yes, he was, she had agreed; then she added that the governor knew what is best for everyone in the state, a statement the boy could only agree with to her face by nodding his head. Then she had gone on to tell him that her husband is an old friend of the governor's, and a political ally as well. The boy had nodded at that piece of news, too.

So goes the drama (if not the psychopathology) of everyday life in what surely must qualify as the deepest part of the so-called deep South. It is well to keep in mind that in 1970, after decades of migration North, 52 percent of this nation's black people still lived in the South. Many who have gone North, of course, have also had experiences not unlike the one just described. I marvel at the way sociologists and political scientists and psychiatrists can take such "scenes," such constantly occurring encounters, and somehow transform them into exemplars of the class and caste system; political microcosms of a state or society; oedipal tragicomedies. But surely at some "level" of theoretical elaboration it is possible for us to set aside the complexities of abstract thinking and our own intellectual self-esteem, and merely retain, intact, the reality of a child's experience as it can be observed or heard recounted.

For the boy whom I've been calling upon for help in this essay, there are no such things as "society" and "political system" and "unconscious." Instead, he leads a daily life in which elements *we* happen to subsume under those "entities" constantly mingle with one another, blend into one another, confront one another, even turn into one another. Here language may become inadequate, because life's flow (its continuity as well as its sudden shifts of direction) so often defies our effort to stop things, put them in order, label them, and thereby gain control over them. For that boy, however, it is all rather simple, and of course, infinitely complicated. He must indeed learn about "the society"; he must come to know how to behave "appropriately" in dozens and dozens of ways — and for doing so he gets no certificate, no recognition of intellectual achievement. By the same token, in order to survive he has to acquire a thorough knowledge of America's legal system and its political structure; that is, he must know who holds the power and who doesn't, as well as what can be done and what is absolutely forbidden, on penalty of severe punishment. For learning all this his "mind" is not credited with any great accomplishment; yet he has to pull things together for himself, make sense of what he has observed and come to know; and he has to do so in such a way that he can live with what he has learned, live with his feelings, his sense of disappointment, his heartsickness, his envy and greed and fierce anger and confusion and bewilderment. He will, in fact, learn to live as opposed to exist — for liveliness and sly humor and rhythmic joy are very much his cultural inheritance, somehow to be "acquired" and "integrated" into what people in far-off universities call his "personality."

Those of us who want to understand children like him, Northern children or Southern children, will often find ourselves compelled to think twice about our own assumptions, maybe even the very nature of our kind of living. For instance, I must insist in these pages that I am not romanticizing either the boy from Mississippi or the plantation owner's wife when I insist that despite the barriers of class and caste a lot has gone on between those two human beings — a lot of learning has taken place, a lot of affection has been exchanged, and a lot of sadness and loneliness and frustration has been shared. Here is the woman who owns that color television set talking about "the colored children" she occasionally entertains: "I like them, the colored. They are good people. Of course, they can be used, you know, by the Communists we've had coming down here all during the sixties. But I think it's still a fact that forty percent of our people in this state are colored and they are fine people. They know better than going North! I try to spend some time with our colored. I worry over them. Their children are shy and quiet when you first meet them, but they warm up. I have some colored children up here from time to time. I give them cookies and milk or juice. Lord, they gobble up food fast. I like to spend a half hour or so with one of them alone. Then we can talk. They are good listeners.

"My husband is away so much, and when he comes home he nurses those bourbons of his, one after the other. He scarcely even watches television. He's worrying about the price of cotton and he's worrying about his cattle. But he's a good man. Sometimes he'll ask me which nigger child I had up here today, and I'll tell him. He knows that they do a lot of errands for me. I need them as much as I need our maid and cook. I have my clubs and charities, so I'm busy, and need the help. I miss my children, but they grow up and leave you and that is that. One of the colored boys reminds me of my own son; he's so lively and curious, and yet he's so well-behaved. I know it's because he's here with me, the colored boy, that he's so quick and polite and intelligent-acting, but I can't help but think he carries those qualities around with him wherever he goes. You can't just pretend; I mean, even if you *are* pretending or putting on, you're behaving in a certain way, and that's part of you, don't you think?"

I believe it is necessary for us child psychiatrists to look more carefully at what goes on between women like her and children like those she openly and warmly (and smugly with condescension) seeks out. Rather obviously I am not suggesting the plantations of the rural South as the only places where we might travel in order to look and try to learn — though we must never forget what Ralph Ellison keeps on reminding us: areas like Mississippi's Delta go to make up the black man's homeland, and what went on there for generations lives on today (at least to an extent) in the minds of millions who now call themselves New Yorkers or Chicagoans or residents of Los Angeles. Among ghetto children (nearer our psychiatric offices than Mississippi's plantations) I hear of moments spent watching this person, hearing that one, exchanging a comment or two with *"them."* I have in mind a whole range of interactions we psychiatrists (or sociologists and anthropologists) might ordinarily not recognize as having significance for the psychological development of ghetto children. As I observe those children, look at their drawings, read their compositions, and most important, listen to them talk with one another, I come across fragments of human contact which have become absorbed into each child's mind — and very important, made something of by that child. Bus drivers, storekeepers, schoolteachers, janitors, garbage collectors, ministers, taxi drivers, poolroom owners, prostitutes, drug addicts, alcoholics, rent collectors, policemen, firemen, community organizers, local politicians, insurance collectors, traveling salesmen — they are all part of the lives many city children live. They all speak, sometimes scream and shout. Every day boys and girls take notice of them; and over time, as clinicians know, children's minds take in what they notice and in various ways turn what has been witnessed and overheard into their own vision of the world, their own voice.

It is true, within the families of the poor — poor blacks, poor Chicanos, poor white folk — there is much disorder and early sorrow. Fathers are often absent, or when present are not infrequently angry, sullen, dazed, inert — beaten by life at the point when their children need from them a different kind of example. Mothers are commonly sad, tired, harassed, given to fits of crying or outbursts of rage, or perhaps worst of all, a kind of unyielding moroseness — again, at the most vulnerable moments in the lives of their children. Drugs are in evidence, and alcohol, and the numbers man and his promise of a lightning stroke of good luck that will put an end to all that is tiring and frustrating. Promiscuity is not rare; desperate men and women reach out, give themselves to one another, seek a moment of pleasure which somehow (but only somewhat) pushes aside all of the other moments — the hours and hours that go to make up life's dreary, brutish side.

Still, it is simply not enough for us to realize how awful life can be for so many of our fellow citizens; and I say that not only because we risk denying them their successes and victories, achieved against such high odds, but also because we ourselves pay a high price for the apparent sympathy and near-despair we demonstrate. We run the risk of becoming self-satisfied and opinionated rather than genuinely concerned and aware, and thereby we do both others and ourselves a grave injustice. For the fact is that a man like Malcolm X was both a leader, hence to some extent extraordinary, but also a representative man. His early childhood must make those of us who specialize in "child development" wonder how he ever grew up at all, let alone became the man he was when his life was so tragically cut down. He lived in suffering and hate and poverty — his father killed, his mother driven mad; and yet, he could become in his thirties a political leader, and even more valuable, a man of genuine spirituality, a man of forgiveness and charity. No doubt thousands of worried and frightened and near-frantic boys and girls in our ghettoes will never approach his success but thousands do, every day, in their own various ways. They struggle hard to find work. They establish islands of order and even beauty in the midst of the chaos they can't eradicate. Yes, beauty; in ghettoes I have seen the equivalent of those wild flowers the black boy from Mississippi makes mention of: a water glass with a dandelion or two in it, placed in the one spot sun can be found; or a picture of Christ (or Dr. King or John and Robert Kennedy) hung on a wall and dusted frequently (unlike our expensive paintings and woodcuts) and mentioned and looked at and paid attention to. Then, there are television programs, and not only *Sesame Street*. Out of what we call soap operas and domestic comedy shows a mother can extract a lesson, find a moment of encouragement, build a day's foundation of confidence and tenacity and inventiveness.

I have said nothing that today's psychiatrists ought to find very surprising or original. Freud's view of the mind still clearly dominates our way of looking at man's psychological development for the very good reason that he never saw us as fixed and static, as all *this* or all *that*. His genius was for the most difficult of tasks — to appreciate and try to convey in words and theoretical constructs the mind's energy, its incessant activity, its never-ending struggles and conflicts, its depth and breadth, the range of its involvements and attachments, the power it possesses, the diversity of responses and urges and affiliations and loyalties and lusts and resentments and outright hates it can contain. Tugged and pulled, driven and propelled, we also look and listen, and out of a world that never stops being (for *any* of us) troublesome and perplexing and frustrating as well as (for *some* of us) thoroughly satisfying and rewarding we try to pull things together, figure things out, achieve for ourselves whatever "sense and sensibility" we can manage. Certainly the poorest of our poor, the most "disorganized" of our "disadvantaged" cannot be denied the life of the mind — with its attendant possibilities for the good and the bad. It would be ironic indeed if people who have helped build America — harvested our crops, labored to provide us with the raw materials that have clothed and housed us, provided us with elements of our cultural tradition (in jazz, spirituals, work songs, styles of speech, ways of cooking and dancing, wearing clothes, playing sports, singing and praying), were now to discover that even though things are getting slowly but surely better in this country, there is in fact no hope for them — because a host of experts, self-assured if nothing else, have said so, or implied so by the pervading tone of their remarks.

In any event, even were such hope to be denied, I fear that the tragedy will be ours and not the ghetto child's. "We've taken a lot since we've been in America, and we'll take more, and we won't drown, we'll kick and float and swim, and one day we'll find a place to rest and grow in peace." At eight this child was no fool. He was preparing for a lifetime he could only describe tentatively and warily. Nevertheless, he had about him the kind of courage and capacity for endurance writers like William Faulkner and Richard Wright and Ralph Ellison have in their various ways tried to represent and characterize. I believe it is that ambiguity, that contrapuntal quality in such a child's psychological existence, we must keep in mind and attempt to understand as clinicians — all of which ought to make us guarded and cautious indeed, but also persistent and at the very least undespairing.

From *The Infant at Risk*, edited by
Daniel Bergsma, 1973

39

CHILDREN AND POLITICAL

AUTHORITY

In her long essay "The Great Beast," written in 1939, Simone Weil tried to understand what she called "the permanence and variability of national characteristics." She was intent on showing that Hitlerism was indeed different from many other kinds of nationalist imperialism; but was by no means something new in the world's history. She insisted that Rome, a long-standing *bête noire* of hers, had anticipated the Nazis, and in fact was far more successful as a conqueror: a relatively large number of people subdued absolutely for a much longer time. Yet, she was quick to point out that nations change, often unaccountably. She judged medieval Romans "completely unlike" the ancient Romans. The latter had, in her eyes, perfected a ruthless military machine, harnessed to "a centralized state." The former were "incapable of unity, order, or administration"; the various city-states to which they owed allegiance squabbled, but not in a vengeful, or even, it seems, murderous way. Machiavelli mentions that in one of Florence's campaigns not a single soldier was killed. As for Mlle. Weil's native land, she scoffs at the expression "eternal France"; sometimes it has had more than a touch of Roman hauteur ("the state as sole fount of authority and object of devotion") and sometimes it has been ruled quite differently. She considered Napoleon another of history's Roman consuls; whereas upon occasion France has been among the more peaceful nations.

How does a nation maintain a certain notion of itself over a given span of time — so that policies pursued by one government with or without the consent of a particular citizenry, become policies believed in, accepted quite eagerly or casually by succeeding generations of men and women? With respect to Rome's lengthy tenure of military and political supremacy, Simone Weil observes, in partial explanation: "It is only from the conviction that she is chosen from all eternity for sovereign mastery over others that a nation can draw the force to behave in this way." She knows that a sustained "conviction" has to be passed down from parents to children. Myths are developed, and one way or another they become transmitted; in the remote past by word of mouth, more recently through books, and in our time over radio and television as well. The Nazis had their explicit propaganda, aimed at "public enlightenment"; for Mlle. Weil the renowned Virgil was not much more than a Goebbels who could write narrative poetry. She declares his "Thou, Roman, bethink thee to rule the people imperially" to be "the best formulation" of an empire's need for a myth of "universal dominion." Successive generations of Romans heard those words, and others like them; and soon enough were willing to help out in practice the vicious, senseless, arbitrary practices Weil documents at considerable length in her essay — which is meant to show that Hitler was not a barbarian: "Would to heaven he were!" she exclaims. The distinction she draws between the assaults of barbarians and those of Hitler is an interesting one, and deserves quotation:

> There was always a limit to the harm done by the ravages of barbarians. Their destructiveness was like a natural disaster, which stimulated the spirit by its reminder of the uncertainty of human fate; their cruelty and perfidy, mixed with acts of loyalty and generosity and mitigated by inconstancy and caprice, represented no danger to any real values in those who survived their onslaught. It requires an extremely civilized State, but a basely civilized one, so to speak, such as Rome, to infect all those it threatens and all those

it conquers with moral corruption, and thus not only to destroy in advance all hope of effective resistance but also to disrupt, brutally and finally, the continuity of spiritual life, which is then replaced by a bad imitation of undistinguished conquerors. For only a highly organized State is able to paralyze its adversaries' reactions by overpowering their imagination with its pitiless mechanism, a mechanism for seizing every advantage undeterred by human weakness or human virtue and equally able to pursue this aim by lies or the truth, by simulated respect for convention or open contempt for it. Our situation in Europe is not that of civilized men fighting a barbarian, but the much more difficult and dangerous one of independent countries threatened with colonization.

The "mechanism" she mentions is something more than a mix of propaganda and sustained, ruthless military action. Rome's leading families, and those associated with them, had to believe quite strongly in their mission, and continue to do so not only in the midst of war, when passions on behalf of the motherland or fatherland are readily ignited, but in the years of apparent triumph. And though Rome ultimately did crumble, it took a long time to happen. Weil acknowledges the devilish genius of a certain kind of imperial rule: the slightest evidence of unrest was regarded as a life-and-death threat; indeed, turmoil was imagined, was conjured up — hence the arbitrary, agitated, senseless punitiveness of the *pax Romana*, best described by Tacitus himself, no enemy of Rome's, when he has a British chieftain, an "uncivilized native" of his time, observe in connection with the Roman empire's generals and soldiers that "you cannot escape their insolence by submission and self-restraint."

Not that Rome's well-to-do, influential people had Tacitus's or Weil's image of themselves. Nor is the "conviction" Weil refers to a matter of mere rationalization and self-deception — the clever use of slogans or excuses to justify greed. In any empire there is always plenty of cynical exploitativeness — whether of the old territorial kind, or the more recent, thinly disguised version, in which a leading nation settles gladly for control of raw materials, leaving the day-to-day problems of the so-called under-developed nations to themselves, so long as they understand where the line of *ne plus ultra* is drawn. But for staying power political authority needs to become an object of belief, if not faith — especially among those who live closest to the center of things. In the outlying provinces or territories, in the remote corners of an empire, the *legatus* and his cohorts took care of any eruptions, threatened or actual. These days, a show of force through jets and, maybe, a number of vessels called a "fleet" accomplish the same purpose. In the event of out-and-out war there is usually little need anywhere for elaborate persuasion of a population, only the waving of the flag. If, however, those who over the years live, so to speak, near the heart of an empire, and are nourished by it constantly and enormously, begin to have doubts or suspicions about its authority, its legitimacy, then all may well soon be lost, no matter how many legions, or atomic bombs, are available to those called *dux,* chairman, prime minister or president. Simone Weil put her finger on the problem this way: "Since the sons of the great Roman families were trained for government by the spectacle of gladiatorial games and by commanding thousands or tens of thousands of slaves, it would have needed a miracle for the provinces to be governed with any humanity."

She is referring to a process others (her own writing had a strong literary bent) would call "political socialization":

> Only since the 1950s has a generic label — "political socialization" — become attached to the process of initiation into politics and have scholars started with some frequency to bemoan that "we know next to nothing about 'political socialization.' " The recency of systematic attention to political socialization can be traced to the slow process by which political science established itself as an academic discipline and liberated itself from its origins in departments of law, philosophy, and history, and to disciplinary compartmentalizations which assigned the study of children to psychologists and sociologists.

As the man who wrote those words, Fred Greenstein, acknowledges in his suggestive and thoughtful book, *Children and Politics,* there is nothing new about the notion that children ought to be systematically educated politically. Plato was what we would call a "psychologically oriented" political philosopher, well aware of the need each society has for the transmission of values and assumptions — and of political loyalty. Rousseau's *Émile*, and later on, his *Thoughts about the Polish Government*, published posthumously, take up the matter of political education at great length — as if he knew that at some point a "social contract" lives or dies in the homes and schools where children learn what (and whom) to believe in. Then there was Napoleon; he observed that "as long as children are not taught whether they ought to be Republican or Monarchist, Catholic or irreligious, the State will not form a Nation."

For all the comments one can glean from philosophers and social observers, or anonymous bureaucrats who, in this country as well as the Soviet Union, make quite clear their interest in both explicit and indirect political instruction (or indoctrination), there is, as Professor Greenstein indicates, no enormous literature which would, presumably, tell us when, where, and how, certain children acquire whatever obedience to a given political authority they possess. Greenstein's work, carried out in New Haven during the last years of the Eisenhower administration with children between the ages of nine and thirteen of various backgrounds, indicates how well-disposed elementary school boys and girls are (or more precisely, were then) toward the President, the flag, the government as a whole. They began to learn which party their parents belong to when they were in the third or fourth grade, and well before they knew what the respective parties actually stand for. They tended to be more aware of national politics than state or local politics; the President was apt to be better known than the governor or mayor. If they came from upper class homes, they were likely to be more critical of the political *status quo*, and at an earlier age, than if they came from poor or working class families — though it has to be stressed that the children studied, no matter the neighborhood to which they belonged, by and large were less cynical politically than their parents, however cynical they happened to be. That is, the child starts out with the inclination to idealize important national figures, and more broadly, the country as a whole, its history and its institutions. (Girls given questionnaires and spoken with tended to be less interested in

political matters and less opinionated than the boys.) Studies by
Robert Hess, Judith Torney, David Easton and Jack Dennis,[1] like
Greenstein political scientists, tend to confirm, for the 1950s and
early 1960s at least, a generally conservative quality to the nature of
young children's interest in our political life. True, those observers
note that in adolescence cynicism sets in — not only directed against
the President. But they offer little evidence that such cynicism runs
deep — is part of an overall skepticism about our social and economic institutions. To the contrary, we are told that by the time
youths have become jobholders or parents themselves they have become, by and large, willing if not enthusiastic American citizens —
as a result of a relatively informal but persistent series of experiences
at home, in the neighbourhood, and at school, perhaps best described
in summary form by Greenstein:

> Socialization processes foster the *status quo* through the perpetua-
> tion of class and sex differences in political participation, continu-
> ity between the generations in party preferences, continuation
> (and perhaps even strengthening) of adult assessments of the rela-
> tive importance of political institutions.

So it went over a decade ago, though even the author took pains to
indicate the need for "longitudinal study," as opposed to the usual
cross-sectional research — it being one thing to tap a group of children with standardized questions and another to spend weeks,
months, years with particular families. On the other hand, the more
time one spends with particular children the more complicated and
ambiguous the "findings" — because all the inconsistencies and ambiguities of anyone's life, certainly including a child's, eventually
become apparent to the observer, whereas a series of questions, even

---

[1] See, especially, their research written up in *The Development of Political Attitudes in Children*, by Hess and Torney (Aldine, 1967), and *Children in the Political System*, by Easton and
Dennis (McGraw, 1969). Both books give an account of original research completed several
years earlier. The term "political socialization" was given prominence, if not coined, by
Herbert Hyman, who did not do studies of his own, but wrote a series of theoretical essays
on the subject: *Political Socialization* (Free Press, 1959).

those called open-ended ones, are likely to be felt by many (and *especially* children) as an occasion for quick resolution of those very mixed feelings which, soon after the interviewer is gone, reassert themselves in the given person's mind. All of which is to say that so-called cross-sectional research (the basis of polling) and research based on long-term and close observation are complementary, rather than substitutes for each other.

Any research which aims to study the relationship between individuals, however young, and the world around them requires detachment — the investigator's willingness to look at his or her own social and historical situation and ask certain "methodological" questions. For instance, does the bias toward idealization of the prevailing political order reflect an only temporary or a merely apparent kind of social and economic stability, with an attendant cultural conformity? Even more significantly (so far as any research goes, be it cross-sectional or that of prolonged interviews coupled with direct observation) do many children consciously mouth pieties, while all the while harboring a host of sly, mischievous, and maybe to some minds revolutionary ideas? In a recent, important review of the literature of "political socialization"[2] Richard Merelman worries that many of the studies done "committed the nascent field to a subtly biasing series of theoretical assumptions and methodological decisions based partly upon an atypical period of American politics." Unfortunately his essay fails to discuss the extraordinary work of the Australian social scientist (and literary essayist) Robert Connell, whose *The Child's Construction of Politics* (issued by the Melbourne University Press, and so not easily available here) contains wonderfully rich accounts of how the political world is regarded by particular children, who were watched and listened to patiently, and given a good deal of leeway and reassurance — that what they said would in no way become the property of a given school system. He makes plain the difference between a child's remarks, spoken over a substantial length of time, and the so-called "standardized responses" of survey research, or, even, his own account of those remarks, which contains generalizations based on the theorist's need to formulate:

---

[2]"The Adolescence of Political Socialization," in *Sociology of Education*, 45, Spring, 1972.

We have built up a collective portrait of the group of children and the developments to be seen among them. To do this it has been necessary to summarize and to use short extracts from here and there; but to do *that* is to violate the concrete whole of the interview, to tear statements from their contexts and to present them, in a way, as disembodied types or forms rather than real episodes. To overcome this drift into abstraction it is necessary to see the statement in the context of the full interview — itself a distorted projection of the life and thought of the child on to the plane of interrogation, but the nearest we can come, with these methods, to the actuality of which we wish to speak.

Among his observations, perhaps the most interesting and suggestive is the notion of "intuitive political thinking." Young and not-so-young children, from four or five to nine or ten, say, not only show evidence of "socialization," but of surprisingly outspoken, idiosyncratic, blunt and imaginative political opinions. They can poke fun at the self-important, see through any number of phonies, and wryly take on subjects the rest of us have learned to skirt or get at only indirectly. But gradually something happens:

> After the exuberant half-political fantasy of some of our children at the intuitive stage, the political outlooks become a rehash, sometimes an interesting rehash to be sure, of well-known themes from adult politics. Even the reassertion of personal control over political materials in adolescence is a flattened, rather chastened, control, with little quality of political imagination.

He was interested in going a step beyond the documentation of "attitudes"; the notion that the President is good beyond challenge (which many young school children will say when questioned in a classroom) or that Australia, America or some other country is the best country in the world (which those same children, among others, will also say). Presumably at some point a child begins to develop assumptions about his or her situation as a particular individual: the country beckons, or it doesn't; the political order is just or fearful and harmful or crooked to the core; the people who hold office, near and far, can be counted upon, or are, quite definitely, enemies of

sorts, or at the least, indifferent, if not contemptuous. Race awareness, we know, takes root among preschool children; by three or
four, they not only spot others, who are black or white, or for that
matter (in our American West) Indian or Chicano, but are quick to
come up with various pejorative or congratulatory remarks, tied to
the person recognized as "other."[3] Professor Connell's studies show
certain young Australian children canny indeed about the motives
and purposes of their own and other governments, ours included.
Those same children, incidentally, are quick to distinguish themselves, racially, from the Vietnamese or the Japanese, whom they saw
on television. Why do we so often assume that it takes ten or twenty
years for children to begin to understand exactly what it is that works
for or against them in the world — meaning, more concretely, which
politicians stand for what, and more broadly, how the assumptions of
a given social and political order will quite specifically affect their future lives?

In the South, for years, I heard black children speak of sheriffs
and policemen as "devils," without having sense enough to pick up
the hint they were giving me of attitudes long held. In 1965, in
McComb, Mississippi, I asked a six-year-old child who was President. She said she didn't know, "but they killed President Kennedy
and they killed Medgar Evers." I asked who "they" were. She said,
"the people who don't like us." There is a limit beyond which a guest
begins to feel even ruder and more arrogantly intrusive than he already may have good cause to feel. I may then have felt myself to
have gone too far, because I shut up, and did not pursue the obvious
chain of psychiatric interrogation: *which* people don't like you, and
why don't they, and on and on. Actually, in retrospect, I realize that
then and there I had made a psychological judgment, maybe a discovery: this child knows a great deal about what social scientists call
the subject of "race relations," and I would be foolish, as well as insulting to her, if I persisted in making her spell out not only the obvious, but the exceedingly painful. And too, I probably felt (more than
realized) that she would begin to wonder whether there was any
point in talking about such matters with a white doctor, however

---

[3]See Mary Ellen Goodman's *Race Awareness in Young Children* (Macmillan, 1964).

good he claimed his intentions to be — and not only out of a sense of futility, based on racially connected suspicion. She was fully capable of a firm political assessment: the relatively well-off people don't *themselves* want to be reminded too pointedly how things work in their favor. It is a discomforting accusation.

Eventually, as some of the civil rights workers in rural Alabama and Mississippi turned their attention to the education of children, after dealing with issues like lunch-counter desegregation or voting rights, one heard upon occasion, and almost by chance, astonishing exchanges between schoolchildren and politically conscious and sensitive activists in SNCC and CORE, or, up in the hollows of Kentucky and West Virginia, the Appalachian Volunteers. A young man or woman would enter a home to urge upon parents a certain course of action with respect to school desegregation, or a county official's attitude toward the school budget, and suddenly a child would speak up: "I don't like the teachers; they say bad things to us. They're always calling us names; they make you feel no good. We saw the man on the television, the governor, and he wasn't any good either." It is all too easy to take for granted such remarks, spoken by a ten-year-old boy whose father is a tenant farmer near Belzoni in the Mississippi Delta: black children, badly treated by white *or* black schoolteachers (the latter can sometimes be especially mean to poor children of their own race) will inevitably pick up the rejection and scorn others feel toward them. Yet, when a child of ten links the governor of his state with the schoolteachers who look down upon him in a rural, still all-black elementary school, he is making a significant judgment — one which ought be explored, if we are to understand how and when various political viewpoints begin to take shape.

In the case of that Belzoni boy, there was much more to be heard, not then but at a later time, when nothing was being asked of the family. (Many rural blacks in the South knew all along that those who came to fight on their behalf would soon enough leave; so the apathy and lethargy that confronted the political activists who asked for a signature, a declaration of support, a willingness to march, to picket, to stand up and be counted were, in fact, also expressions of a political judgment.) When asked whether he would one day want to vote, as blacks were then in small numbers beginning to do, the boy had this to say: "Maybe; I don't know. My daddy says what's the use, because even if every one of us voted, the whites would still run Mississippi and still own everything, the whole country. The teacher told us the President is a good man, and he's from the South, and he's trying to do good by the white, and by the colored. To tell the truth, I don't believe her. My sister, she laughed when I told her what the teacher said. My sister said that if I believe everything I hear teachers say, and the governor, and the President — then I'm still a baby, and have a lot of growing up to do. Well, I told her I try on something I hear, to see if it fits, but I know when it doesn't, and I throw it away real fast, because I'll tell you, if you're colored, you'd better learn the difference between a piece of real meat and streak o'lean. My mother cooks them their steaks, up at the boss man's house, and she knows the difference; and she's taught us. And I'll bet it's mostly streak o'lean that they hand out so you, a sheriff or a governor or a President. If they'd be handing out good meat, it would be better. But like my daddy says, there's nothing you can expect to get for the asking from the white people, so it's good the civil rights people are getting the governor mad and worrying the President, even if the teachers say we should obey the law and salute the flag and America isn't second to any country. If you're not white, you're second, and a lot of whites, they're second, too; and my sister says that's the scene, and if you don't know what scene you're watching, you're dumb, dumb, dumb."

He was not especially precocious, for all the implicit sociological and political shrewdness he could muster in an unselfconscious, disarmingly casual way. He never went to high school — and now, a decade after he spoke like that, he works compliantly on a large Delta plantation. When one asks him, a grown man, the father of two young children, what he thinks of the President, or the governor, or Watergate, or any of the important issues that now face America and the world, he shrugs his shoulders and presents a blank look, or else smiles in a way that can only mystify: does he, deep down, have some views, or is he utterly without them? With a drink or two he will speak his mind fully: "It's no good for the black man here, no matter who's up there in Washington as President or down in Jackson as governor. That's all I know. Watergate? They caught a few crooks and liars, I guess. Where are all the rest of them? Still in charge of us, still up to no good."

So it goes: enlightened self-interest. For him there is no point going on and on. No one wire-taps his phone; he has none. But if he so much as speaks out of turn, the consequences are obvious. The black children I have known in our South, or in our northern ghettoes sound — at six, eight, nine, or ten — like certain articulate, politically conscious middle-class white college students. As these children grow older, they tend to become much less candid, though they do not change their opinions. While a number of American youths are becoming more critical politically (even disenchanted with the objects of childhood idealizations) many black youths in the South and mountain youths of Appalachia become less outspoken about what they have, it seems, known for a long time — that their situation in life, the conditions they must continue to face, day in, day out, are in an important way connected to the nation's political leadership. The black man whom I quoted as a child, and whom I have seen every year at least twice since I left Mississippi a decade ago, puts his feelings in perspective all too tersely: "I knew what's going on for us a long time, and I haven't seen a good reason yet to change my mind."

In fact, to return to Simone Weil, as a boy he watched not "the spectacle of gladiatorial games," but this kind of spectacle, no less persuasive: "You remember, when I was a kid I told you about the whippings they gave my daddy for saying he wanted to register to vote. Well, the sheriff did it; and that's the law for you. Now I can go vote, but the same sheriff is there, and even if the bigger politicians watch their language a little better these days, it's no different here. The other day my boy was called 'a little nigger' by the sheriff, just because he didn't say 'yes, sir' when told to stay on the sidewalk until the policeman said it's all right to cross the street. Later he asked me why the governor keeps talking about 'the good people' of the state and the 'bloc vote.' Actually, he's heard me say to my wife that the whites are 'the good people' and we're 'the bloc vote' — bloc instead of black is the way they do it these days!"

A cussing sheriff will do as well as a gladiator or two. The poor or those who belong to the so-called working class always live closer to the law, closer to the whims and fancies of political authority. A nine-year-old boy from Marion County, West Virginia, described the relationship between poor or financially vulnerable people, and those who get elected to office this way: "You make the wrong move, and they'll be on you, telling you off and ready to lock you up, if need be." What gladiator had he seen? What spectacle that "trained' (Mlle. Weil's word) in him a specific attitude toward West Virginia's, America's government? The spectacle of a father's funeral; the man was one of seventy-eight miners killed in an "accident" whose causes, immediate and more distant, his children knew quite well. The boy sat in the church, with many other children; he heard various "powers and principalities" being exposed for their negligence and worse, much worse. He saw on television the Secretary of Labor and the Secretary of the Interior and the governor and the mayor and a host of county officials and the president of the coal company utter their lamentations, apologies and excuses: the litany of self-justifying explanations which miners' wives have a way of hearing as if sounding brass or a tinkling cymbal. In the words of the child, again: "My mother says they can do what they want, the company people; and the sheriff, he listens to them, and that's it, they get their way. Last year there was going to be a strike, and daddy took us and we saw the company people and the sheriff and his people, and they were talking buddy-buddy." Another "spectacle"; and they do not go unnoticed by children whose parents live or die, depending upon how sensitive they are to the implications of such a "spectacle."

In contrast, many upper-middle-class suburban children have quite another view of their nation and its various leaders. A black child of eight, a girl who lives in southern Alabama, just above Mobile, told me in 1968 that she knew one thing for sure about who was going to be President: he'd be a white man; and as for his policies "no matter what he said to be polite', he'd never really stand up for us." Already she knew herself to be a member of "us," as against "them." A few miles away, a white child of nine, a boy, the son of a lawyer and plantation owner, had a rather different perspective on the Presidency: "The man who's elected will be a good man; even if he's not too good before he goes to Washington, he'll probably turn out good. This is the best nation there is, so the leader has to be the best, too." A child with keen ears who picks up exactly his father's mixture of patriotism and not easily acknowledged skepticism? Yes,

but also a child who himself — by the tone of his voice and his earnestness — has come to believe in his nation's destiny, and in the office of the Presidency. How about the governor? "He's better known than most governors," the boy boasts. Then he offers his source: "My daddy says that we have a better governor than they do in Louisiana or in Georgia. (He has cousins in both states.) And he says that our governor makes everyone stop and listen to him, so he's real good. He knows how to win; he won't let us be beaten by the Yankees."

More sectional bombast, absorbed rather too well by a boy who now, a teenager, hasn't had the slightest inclination to develop the "cynicism" a number of students of the process of "political socialization" have repeatedly mentioned as prevalent? Or, more likely, the response of a child who knows what his parents really consider important, really believe in — and fear? "I took my boy over to my daddy's house," the child's father recalls, "and we watched Governor Wallace standing up to those people in Washington; he told the President of the United States that he was wrong." The boy was then four, and no doubt even were he to see a child psychoanalyst for several years he would not at nine, never mind at fifteen, recall the specific event his father and grandfather remember so clearly. But time and again he has heard members of his family stress how precarious they feel, in relationship to Yankee (federal) power, and therefore how loyal they are to a governor who gives the illusion of successfully defending cherished social and political prerogatives.

Up North, in a suburb outside Boston, it is quite another story. At nine a girl speaks of America and its leaders like this: "I haven't been to Europe yet, but my parents came back last year and they were happy to be home." Then, after indicating how happy she was to have them home, she comments on the rest of the world, as opposed to her country: "It's better to be born here. Maybe you can live good in other places, but this is the best country. We have good government. Everyone is good in it — if he's the President, he's ahead of everyone else, and if he's a governor, that means he's also one of the people who decide what the country is going to do. There might be a war, and somebody has to send the troops by planes across the ocean. If there is a lot of trouble someplace, then the government takes care of it. I'm going to Washington next year to see all the buildings. My

brother went two years ago. He really liked the trip. He came back and said he wouldn't mind being in the government; it would be cool to go on that underground railroad the senators have. He said he visited someone's office, and he was given a pencil and a postcard, and he wrote a letter to say thank you, and he got a letter back. His whole class went, and they were taken all over. They went to see some battlefields, too."

She doesn't know which battlefields, however; nor does she know which war was fought on those fields. She is one of those whom Southern children of her age have already learned to identify as "Yankees," even know to fear or envy. There are no equivalents for her, however — no name she is wont to hurl at Southerners, or for that matter, anyone else. True, she learned long ago, at about four or five, that black children, whom she sees on television but has never gone to school with, are "funny" and the single Japanese child she had as a classmate in kindergarten was "strange, because of her eyes"; but such children never come up in her remarks, and when they are brought up in the course of conversation with a visitor, she is quick to change the subject or go firmly silent. Nor is there any great amount of prejudice in her, at least of a kind which she has directly on her mind. Her drawings reveal her to be concerned with flowers, which she likes to help her mother arrange, with horses, which she loves to ride, and with stars, which she is proud to know rather a lot about.

The last interest prompts from her a bit of apologetic explanation: "My brother started being interested in the stars; my daddy gave him a telescope and a book. Then he lost interest. Then I started using the telescope, and my daddy said I shouldn't, because maybe my brother would mind, but he doesn't." And, in fact, her parents do have rather firm ideas about what boys ought to be interested in, what girls ought to find appealing. Men run for political office, she knows. Sometimes women do, but only rarely; anyway, she won't be one of them. In 1971 she thought the President was "a very good man; he has to be — otherwise he wouldn't be President." The same held for the governor and the town officials who make sure that all goes well in her neighborhood. When the Watergate incident began to capture more and more of her parents' attention, she listened and wondered and tried to accommodate her long-standing faith with her new

knowledge: "The President made a mistake. It's too bad. You shouldn't do wrong; if you're President, it's bad for everyone when you go against the law. But the country is good. The President must feel real bad, for the mistake he made." After which she talks about *her* mistakes: she broke a valuable piece of china; she isn't doing as well in school as either her parents or her teachers feel she ought be doing; and not least, she forgets to make her bed a lot of the time, and her mother or the maid have to remind her of that responsibility. Then she briefly returns to the President, this time with a comment not unlike those "intuitive" ones made by Australian children (in New South Wales) to Professor Connell: "A friend of mine said she didn't believe a word the President says, because he himself doesn't believe what he says, so why should we." What did the girl herself believe? "Well, I believe my parents, but I believe my friend, too. Do you think the President's wife believes him? If he doesn't believe himself, what about her?" So much for the ambiguities of childhood, not to mention such legal and psychiatric matters as guilt, knowing deception, the nature of self-serving illusions, and political guile.

As one listens to her and others like her — advantaged children, they might be called — one wonders, again, where Mlle. Weil's gladiators are to be found. Of course, there is nothing very dramatic to catch hold of; unlike black children, or Appalachian children, or even the children of well-to-do Southern white families, the girl I have just quoted has no vivid politically tinged memories of her own, nor any conveyed by her parents to take possession of psychologically — no governor's defiance, no sit-ins or demonstrations, no sheriff's car or a sheriff's voice, no mass funeral after a mine disaster, no experience with a welfare worker, no strike, with the police there to "mediate," no sudden layoff, followed by accusations and recriminations — and drastically curbed family spending. Such unforgettable events in the lives of children very definitely help shape their attitudes toward their nation and its political authority. The black children I have come to know in dfferent parts of this country, even those from relatively well-off homes, say critical things about America and its leaders at an earlier age than white children do — and connect their general observations to specific experiences, vivid moments, really, in their lives. A black child of eight, in rural Mississippi or in a northern ghetto, an Indian or Chicano or Appalachian child, can sound like a disillusioned, old radical: down with the system, because it's a thoroughly unjust one, for all that one hears in school — including, especially, those words quoted from the Declaration of Independence or the Constitution: "all men are created equal, and endowed by their Creator with certain inalienable rights."

The pledge of allegiance to the flag can be an occasion for boredom, at the very least, among some elementary school children; the phrase "with liberty and justice for all" simply rings hollow, or is perceived as an ironic boast meant to be uttered by others elsewhere. Here is what a *white* schoolteacher in Barbour County, Alabama, has observed over the years: "I'm no great fan of the colored; I don't have anything against them, either. I do my work, teaching the colored, and I like the children I teach, because they don't put on airs with you, the way some of our own children do — if their daddy is big and important. The uppity niggers — well, they leave this state. We won't put up with them. The good colored people, they're fine. I grew up with them. I know their children, and I try to teach them as best I can. I understand how they feel; I believe I do. I have a very bright boy, James; he told me that he didn't want to draw a picture of the American flag. I asked him why not. He said that he just wasn't interested. It's hard for them — they don't feel completely part of this country. I had a girl once, she was quite fresh; she told me that she didn't believe a word of that salute to the flag, and she didn't believe a word of what I read to them about our history. I sent her to the principal. I was ready to have her expelled, for good. The principal said she was going to be a civil rights type one day, but by then I'd simmered down. 'To tell the truth,' I said, 'I don't believe most of the colored children think any different than her.' The principal gave me a look and said, 'Yes, I can see what you mean.' A lot of times I skip the salute to the flag; the children start laughing, and they forget the words, and they become restless. It's not a good way to start the day. I'd have to threaten them, if I wanted them to behave while saluting. So, we go right into our arithmetic lessons."

In contrast, among middle-class white children of our Northern suburbs, who have no Confederate flag to divide their loyalties, the morning salute can be occasion for real emotional expression: This I believe! It is all too easy for some of us to be amused at, or more strongly, to scorn such a development in the lives of children: the roots of smug nationalism, if not outright chauvinism. But for thousands of such children, as for their parents, the flag has a great deal of meaning, and the political authority of the federal, state and local governments is not to be impugned in any way. Among many working-class families policemen, firemen, clerks in the post office or city hall are likely to be friends, relatives, neighbors. Among upper-middle-class families, one can observe a strong sense of loyalty to a system which clearly, to them, has been friendly indeed. And the children learn to express what their parents feel and often enough say, loud and clear. "My uncle is a sergeant in the army," the nine-year-old son of a Boston factory worker told me. He went on to remind me that another uncle belongs to the Boston police department. The child has watched parades, been taken to an army base, visited an old warship, climbed the steps of a historic shrine. He has seen the flag in school and in church. He has heard his country prayed for, extolled, defended against all sorts of critics. He said when he was eight, and in the third grade, that he would one day be a policeman. Other friends of his, without relatives on the force, echo the ambition. Now nearer to ten, he speaks of motorcycles and baseball and hockey; and when he goes to a game he sings the national anthem in a strong and sure voice. Our government? It is "the best you can have." Our President? He's "good."

One pushes a little: is the President in any trouble now? Yes, he is, and he might have made some mistakes. Beyond that the child will not easily go. His parents had for the first time voted Republican in 1972, and now are disappointed with, disgusted by, the President's Watergate-related behavior. But they have been reluctant to be too critical of the President in front of their children: "I don't want to make the kids feel that there's anything wrong with the *country*," the father says. There's *plenty* wrong with the President, he admits, and with the way the country is being run — and, he adds, with big business, so greedy all the time, as well as with the universities and those who go to them or teach at them; but America, he believes, is the greatest nation that ever has been — something, one has to remember, every President's speech-writers, Democratic or Republican, liberal or conservative, manage to work into just about every televised address. Only indirectly, through drawings or the use of comic exaggeration or metaphorical flights of fancy (Professor Connell's "intuitive state" in what he calls "the development of political belief") does the boy dare show what he has been making of Watergate, news of which has, of course, come to him primarily through television. Asked to draw a picture of the President, the boy laughs, says he doesn't know how to do so (he had had no such trouble a year earlier) and finally manages to sketch an exceedingly small man, literally half the size of a former portrait by the same artist. Then, as he prepares to hand over the completed project, he has some second thoughts. He adds a blue sky. Then he blackens the sky. He puts earth under the man, but not, as is his usual custom, grass. Then he proceeds to make two big round black circles, with what seem to be pieces of string attached to them. What are they? He is not sure: "Well, either they could be bombs, and someone could light the fuse, and they could explode and he'd get hurt, and people would be sad; or they could be balls and chains — you know, if you're going to jail."

Way across the tracks, out in part of "rich suburbia," as I hear factory workers sometimes refer to certain towns well to the north and west of Boston, there is among adults a slightly different kind of love of country — less outspoken, perhaps, less defensive, but not casual and certainly appreciative. In those towns, too, children respond quite directly and sensitively to the various messages they have learned from their parents — and to a number of low-key "spectacles"; flags out on July Fourth; the deference paid to civil employees; pictures of father in uniform during one or another war; and perhaps most of all, conversations heard at the table. "My father hears bad news on television, and he says 'thank God we're Americans,' " says a girl of eleven. She goes on to register her mother's gentle, thoughtful qualification: "It's lucky we live where we do." Her mother's sister, older and attracted to the cultural life only a city offers, has to live a more nervous life: "My aunt has huge locks on her doors. My mother leaves the keys right in the car." Nevertheless, the United States of America, for the girl's aunt as well as her parents, is nowhere near collapse: "Everything is going to be all right with the country. This is the best place to live in the whole world. That's what my aunt says." The girl pauses. Now is the time to ask her what *she* has to say. But she needs no prodding; immediately she goes on: "No place is perfect. We're in trouble now. The President and his friends, they've been caught doing bad things. It's too bad. My older brother argues with daddy; he told daddy that it's wrong to let the President get away with all he's done, while everyone else has to go to jail; and he told daddy there's a lot of trouble in the country, and no one is doing anything to stop the trouble. The President, I think he's running as fast as he can from the police. I guess I would if I knew I'd done something wrong. But I'd never be able to get to Egypt or Russia, so he's lucky, that President."

It is simply not altogether true, as most studies of "political social-ization" conclude, that she and other children like her *only* tend to "idealize" the President, or give a totally "romanticized" kind of loyalty to the country, on the basis of what they hear, or choose to hear, from their parents or teachers. Many parents do select carefully what they say in front of their children; and children are indeed en-couraged by their teachers, and the books they read, to see presidents and governors and supreme court justices and senators as figures much larger than life. Yet, in no time — at least these days — chil-dren can lay such influences aside, much to the astonishment of even parents who *don't* try to shield their children from "bad news" or "the evils of this world," two ways of putting it one hears again and again. Black children laugh at books given them to read in school, snicker while the teacher recites historical pieties which exclude mention of so very much, and often enough challenge their own par-ents when they understandably try to soften or delay the realization of what it has been like and will continue to be like for black people in America. White children, too, as James Agee noticed in the 1930s, pick up the hypocrisies and banalities about them and connect what they see or hear to a larger vision — a notion of those who have a lot and those who have very little at all.

"The President checks in with the people who own the coal com-pany," a miner's shy son, aged eleven, remarked last spring in Har-lan, Kentucky, where the Duke Power Company was fighting hard to prevent the United Mine Workers from becoming a spokesmen of the workers. The child may well be incorrect; but one suspects that a log of the calls made by the President would show him in contact with people very much like those who are on the board of the Duke Power Company, as opposed to people like the boy's parents. By the same token, when a child whose father happens to be on the board of a utility company, or a lawyer who represents such clients, appears to overlook whatever critical remarks his or her parents have made about the United States and instead emphasizes without exception the nation's virtues, including those of its leaders, by no means is a process of psychological distortion necessarily at work. The child may well have taken the measure of what has been heard (and overheard) and come to a conclusion: this is what his parents really believe. The reason they believe it is to support a whole way of life — the one we are all living. So, it is best for the child to keep certain thoughts (in older people, called "views") to himself, lest there be trouble.

Too complicated and subtle an analysis for a child under ten, or even under fifteen? We who in this century have learned to give children credit for the most astonishing refinements of perception or feeling with respect to the nuances of family life or the ups and downs of neighborhood play, for some reason are less inclined to picture those same children as canny social observers or political analysts. No one teaches children sociology or psychology; yet, they are constantly noticing who gets along with whom, and why. If in school, or even when approached by a visitor with a questionnaire (or more casually, with an all too interested face and manner) those same children tighten up and say little or nothing, or come up with remarks that are platitudes, pure and simple, they may well have applied another of their sophisticated psychological judgments — reserving the expression of any controversial political asides that may have come to mind.

As for some of those children who are a little different, who get called "rebellious" or "aggressive," and sent off to guidance counsellors or psychiatrists, they can occasionally help us know the thoughts of many other, more "normal" children — because someone under stress can under certain circumstances be unusually forthcoming. "My poor father is scared," says the son of a rather well-to-do businessman, the owner of large tracts of Florida's land, employing hundreds of migrant farm workers (who, believe me, are also scared). What frightens the boy's father? His twelve-year-old namesake, who is described by his teachers as fresh and surly, tries hard to provide an answer, almost as if whatever he comes up with will help him as much as his father: "I don't know, but there will be times he's sweating, and he's swearing, and he's saying he gave money to all those politicians, and they'd better do right by the growers, or they'll regret it. Then he says he's tired of living here, and maybe he should go back to Michigan where his granddaddy was born. The other day the sheriff came by and said he didn't know if he could keep those television people out indefinitely. So, daddy got on the phone to our senator, and we're waiting. But it may cost us a lot, and we may lose. Daddy says we will either get machines to replace the migrants, or we'll go broke, what with the trouble they're beginning to cause. But I don't think he really means it. He's always threatening us with trouble ahead, my mother says, but you have to pour salt on what he says."

The same boy scoffs at what he hears his teachers say about American history; one day he blurted out in class that his father had "coolies" working for him. Another time he said we'd had to kill a lot of Indians, because they had the land, and we wanted it, and they wouldn't "bow to us, the way we wanted." His teacher felt that she had witnessed yet another psychiatric outburst, but a number of his classmates did not. One of them, not especially a friend of his, remarked several days later, "He only said what everyone knows. I told my mother what he said, and she said it wasn't so bad, and why did they get so upset? But she told me that sometimes it's best to keep quiet, and not say a lot of things you think." It so happens that the child's mother, when spoken with, and in front of her three sons, and without any evidence of shame or embarrassment, willingly picks up where she left off a day earlier with one of her boys: "Yes, I feel we had to conquer the Indians, or there wouldn't be the America we all know and love today. I tell my children that you ought to keep your eye on the positive, accentuate it, you know, and push aside anything negative about this country. Or else we'll sink into more trouble; and it's been good to us, very good, America has." Her husband is also a grower. Her sons do indeed "idealize" America's political system — but when a classmate begins to stir things up a little with a few blunt comments, there is no great surprise, simply the nod of recognition and agreement. And very important, a boy demonstrated evidence of moral development, a capacity for ethical reflection, even though both at home and at school he has been given scant encouragement to regard either migrants or Indians with compassion. Both Piaget and

Lawrence Kohlberg have indicated that cognitive and moral development in children have their own rhythm, tempo and subtlety. Children ingeniously use every scrap of emotional life available to them in their "psychosexual development," and they do likewise as they try to figure out how (and for whom) the world works. A friend's remarks, a classmate's comments, a statement heard on television can give a child surprising moral perspective and distance on himself and his heritage — though, of course, he is not necessarily thereby "liberated" from the (often countervailing) day-to-day realities of, say, class and race.[4]

What of the Indians those Florida children mentioned? How do, say, Hopi or Pueblo boys or girls in Arizona and New Mexico regard the United States of America, its leaders, its political system and its traditions as a democracy? Listening to those boys and girls it is, more often than not, hard to believe that the scene is the United States of America. There is enormous indifference among the children to the political authority that is vested in Washington or the various state capitals. The Indians in theory have their own nations — but for all practical purposes they live on reservations under the control of the federal government, which runs schools and supposedly provides medical care for, and looks after the "welfare" of, half a million rural people. (Perhaps another half million, it is hard to estimate precisely, live in our cities.) For those who have wanted to work on behalf of, or alongside, the Indians in their various economic and political struggles, the enemy has rather obviously been the federal government which provides schools that have for so long taught children to think little of themselves, thoroughly inadequate medical facilities, often staffed with the rudest and most inconsiderate of doctors and nurses, and administrators, all too willing to

---

[4]Kohlberg's work is especially helpful. Children come across, in his studies, as lively and thoughtful, as inclined to question and make critical moral judgments of various kinds, within limits sets by their developing mental life.

Needless to say, as one Jeb Stuart Magruder has indicated in his public remarks and his recent book (*An American Life*, Atheneum, 1974) the acquisition of moral values is very much connected to the child's moral education, obtained not only within the family (as psychiatrists often emphasize) but in the schools, and not least, informally in neighborhood play. See Kohlberg's "Moral and Religious Education and the Public Schools: A Developmental View" in T. Sizer (Ed.), *Religion and Public Education* (Houghton Mifflin, 1967).

operate arbitrarily, with condescension, and sometimes (in connection with land and water rights) quite exploitatively on behalf of whatever white power or principality happened to exert some influence.

To many Hopi children, however, the presence and power of that government bureau — its agents and teachers and bureaucrats of one kind or another — inspires much less animosity. At first the temptation is to call upon various psychological "traits" (culturally induced, of course) in explanation. The Hopis are "passive," or have trouble expressing directly their "aggressive" feelings, or are afraid to level with themselves, never mind white people, however anxious to be friendly. In a much more sophisticated and subtle vein, both anthropology and psychoanalytic psychology are summoned: the Hopi, who call themselves "the peaceful people," have a "world view" thoroughly different from ours, hence a certain indifference on their part to the white world and all that it holds precious — among other things the authority of the military-industrial nation-state.

I suspect it is not so much indifference as a sly mixture of bemused resignation, and a sense of incredulity. "Do not ask of these children that they reconcile all their feelings," a Hopi mother-teacher once warned me — as if she knew in her bones that any number of us white child psychiatrists forget to observe (among our patients, among our own children) how various and contradictory a child's inclinations and perceptions turn out to be. The woman's own daughter, at twelve both extraordinarily childlike and on the brink of becoming a woman, had this way of saying a striking yes to Simone Weil's essay on Rome: "We are nothing to the white people; we are a few Hopis, but they are Americans, millions of them. My father told me that their leader, whoever he is, ends his speech by saying that God is on their side; and then he shakes his fist and says to all the other nations: you had better pay attention, because we are big, and we will shoot to kill, if you don't watch out. My mother says all the big countries are like that, but I only know this one. We belong to it, that is what the government of the United States says. They come here, the BIA [Bureau of Indian Affairs] people and they give us their orders. This law says . . . another law says . . . and soon there will be a new law. In case we have any objections, they have soldiers, they have planes. We see the jets diving high in the sky. The clouds try to get out of the way, but they don't move fast enough. The water tries to escape to the ocean, but can only go at its own speed.

"Everything, everyone, is the white man's; all he has to do is stake his claim. They claimed us. They claimed our land, our water; now they have turned to other places, and my uncle, who knows the history of our people, and of the United States, says it is a sad time for others; but when my brother began to worry about the others, our uncle sighed, and said: 'At least our turn is over. Don't be afraid to be glad for that.' They are not really through with us, though. They come here — the American police, the red light going around and around on their cars: visitors to our reservation from the great United States of America. 'There they are,' my father always says. He tells us to lower our eyes. I have stared at them and their cars, but I will never say anything, I know that. If their President came here, I would stay home or come to look at him, but not cheer. I have seen on television people cheering the President. In school they show us pictures of white men we should cheer. I never want to. I don't think the teachers expect us to *want* to; just to pretend. So, we do."

Pretense is hardly indifference or withdrawal into self-preoccupation. The Hopis are indeed a quiet, thoughtful people; and they take pains not to offend even those they do not especially get on well with — their neighbors, the nomadic Navahos, and their "protectors" the United States of America. A cousin of that girl's, a boy the same age, told me that white men are just that: "They want to be protectors of everyone, all over the world." Was he making a politically critical remark: the imperialist West, up to its various tricks? Not really, or at least not wholly. He was trying to explain to me how "very strong" white people are, and why: "My father left the reservation; he went to Denver. He said he lived with white people, and he knows them. They are fighters. If they see something, and they want it, they go get it. If anyone is in the way, that is too bad for him. They are very determined. We are not so determined. We stay here; we are determined to remain here. The white people go everywhere, and show how strong, very strong, they are, and soon the people they meet agree, and then the white man is happy and he wants to be of help. That is how the Indians got the protection of the Bureau of Indian Affairs; and maybe the BIA is right: without their protection, we would have troubles we don't have now. The Navahos say: let the BIA stand aside, and we will settle with the Hopi. My father says the Hopi may be a bird that is dying out. The white man will not let himself become that kind of bird. There is a difference between the white man and us."

A rather complicated response, that child's, to the political authority of this nation. He is both detached, yet rather anxious to take notice of a people, a nation, which he can't, in any case, avoid coming to terms with. Rather like the Rome which Simone Weil portrayed, America is for a few thousand Hopis not only an enormous empire, but with respect to the smallest details of everyday life, a constant presence. Sometimes anthropological descriptions of a particular kind of Indian culture (Navaho, Hopi, Pueblo) manage to convey successfully the philosophical and psychological distinctiveness of a given people, as against the ways and assumptions of the "dominant culture," yet fail to account for the inevitable mix of two worlds that comes about — the point, for instance, in a child's mental life where he is not only a Hopi, but a Hopi who lives in the state of Arizona, one of the fifty United States. Unlike their white middle-class counterparts, the Hopi boys I have met don't draw missiles, don't crave airplane models, don't collect scary "horror" statues, luminous Frankensteins, and on and on. They don't even play "war": Hollywood notwithstanding, there are no feathers on their heads, no bow and arrow encounters, no effort to defy invisible cowboys. They do play — a version of hide-and-seek is popular; they also help herd sheep, and they walk and run and climb. They are not averse to teasing and taunting, however "peaceful" they are taught to be; and very important, they learn, thereby, that they are Hopi *and* American, however incongruous the combination.

The result is quiet accommodation, a version of the Hopi's quest for peace — an attitude that has to be contrasted with the intense struggle that black children, say, or poor Appalachian children wage in their minds as they year by year get to see what the future has in store for them. Blacks were brought here forcibly, made slaves, kept tied to the white man's home and place of business. For black children that historical fact has become an occasion for smoldering resentment, often out of necessity somewhat concealed. For poor white children, in the mountains of West Virginia or our city slums and near slums, it is a matter of the injustice of an economic system — and children, sensitive to rights and wrongs, and the discrepancy in power between themselves and various adults, don't fail to notice when their parents are given the brushoff or kicked around by a company like Duke Power, and told to clear out for some other part of the country if they don't like the treatment they're getting. In contrast, Indians sit back on *their* land, go through *their* ceremonial experiences, and seem to express the knowing, introspective confusion they feel with a collective shaking and scratching of the head.

In a Pueblo north of Albuquerque a twelve-year-old boy tried hard to put such a response into words, while aware as he spoke that the effort itself was somewhat alien to him: "I've been living in Albuquerque for a year. The Anglos I've met, they're different. I don't know why. In school I drew a picture of my father's horse. One of the other kids wouldn't believe that it was ours. He said, You don't really own that horse, I said, It's a horse my father rides, and I feed it every morning. He said, How come? I said, My uncle and my father are good riders, and I'm pretty good. He said, I can ride a horse better than you, but I'd rather be a pilot. I told him I never thought of being a pilot.

"Anglo kids, they won't let you get away with anything. Tell them something, and fast as lightning and loud as thunder, they'll say, I'm better than you, so there! My father says it's always been like that. My grandfather remembers the Anglos and their horses; they had them for the soldiers. They'd ride through our reservation. Now they have Air Force bases in New Mexico, all over, and they have their atom bombs stored in the mountains. You go near the places where they do their atomic tests, and they tell you to get away fast. Maybe that Anglo kid will be a pilot, like he says. He asked me if I'd ever been in a plane, and I told him no. He thought I was ashamed, but I wasn't. I told him I'd love to ride our horse as fast as my father does, and never fall off. I told him I hoped I never slouched down, when I got bigger; because then you can't ride too well. But he said he could fly across the country in the time it would take me to ride on a horse from the reservation into Albuquerque. And I told him he could go that way, and I'd stay with our horse Sam, and he said that was a deal; but, you know, he came back and told me not to get the idea it was a tortoise and a hare story. He'd told his older brother, and the brother said: watch out, the slow man can sometimes win. So, I told him no, I knew he'd get in first, but I'd still keep riding our horse, so long as we can feed her all right and take care of her. A horse takes care of you and you take care of the horse. That's what my mother kept telling us when we were learning to ride."

Nolo contendere, I suppose he is trying to tell his white schoolmate, though not because he may feel guilty and want to put himself at the mercy of some court. It is hard, though, to get such a message across to someone who has his own reasons not to hear. A plane is a noisy place, and its pilot has to be self-preoccupied. But then, a man on horseback has to keep alert and attentive, as the Pueblo Indian child knows; if his mind wanders from the demands of riding, he can fall or (just as bad, Indian children are taught) become self-indulgent or careless to others. As for the subject of "political authority," Indian children have no trouble taking stock of this nation. By the time they have reached sixth grade, in what we call our "elementary schools," Hopi and Pueblo children have achieved a rather complex and sensitive vision not only of their future, but the country's future. The Indian child is content to go his own way, and doesn't quite understand why the white child won't let the matter rest there. The Indian child hasn't developed the firm sense of property, of ownership, that his white friend has. The Indian child doesn't worry about time, and seems to regard himself as a mere part of a particular landscape, both human and natural, rather than the master of it. A white child in Albuquerque, not unlike other Anglos who lived in America a century ago, talks of crossing the continent, and the faster the better. His Indian classmate wrinkles his forehead and wonders why the hurry and the greed; the miles of land regarded as a distance to be conquered or done away with, rather than accepted as part of the universe — a territorial presence, a companion almost.

The Indian is not really angry or envious of the white child; maybe in awe of his future power, maybe afraid of it — even as the white child can't help wondering whether somehow, in some way, he has missed out on something, and may possibly end up "losing." I do not believe, however, that the Indian child feels as some of us do — that the white world (its advanced technology, its competitiveness, its acquisitiveness, its absorption in various kinds of swift conquest) is evil, whereas his world is the good one, not merely a contrast, but a total alternative. That boy and his brothers, sisters, and friends have watched supersonic jets, carrying God knows what on practice missions, streak across the clear, vast New Mexico sky, and remarked with astonishment at what others can manage to do. Let those others do as they wish, one hears Indian parents *and* children say: only let us be allowed our rights and privileges, too.

In any event, the Indian boy will learn to bow to America's power, even as his grandfather did: horses are not Sky Hawks and Phantoms, and those noisy, fast-as-lightning planes are yet another version of Simone Weil's "the spectacle of gladiatorial games." The Indian boy will only smile and shrug his shoulders when asked about presidents, congressmen, governors; they exist, he knows, but they belong to others, not him, though he has not the slightest doubt that the decisions those leaders make will affect him. Unlike black children, who can be more reticent, fearful and shy, yet eventually utter their dissatisfaction and rage, the Indian children I have met seem to reserve for themselves, on those "reservations," a notion of psychological independence that assumes both philosophical and political forms: they are they, we are we; their leaders are theirs, ours are ours; yet, of course, we are all part of some larger scheme of things — America.

One must shun the temptation to leap from the child's political awareness to the adult's political behavior. It is true that the cynicism and resentment one hears black children express toward our political system have, in recent years, become quite overtly expressed in the civil rights movement. However, I know from my own work in the South with black children that in the relatively quiescent late 1950s many rural, politically isolated and inert children had strong suspicions of this country, very much like those quoted above; but most of those children were never willing, as they grew up, to become involved with the civil rights activists they met in the middle 1960s. Fear, intense and strong, prevented such involvement — and perhaps most of all a nagging sense that soon enough the protests would subside, the protestors depart for other struggles (or perhaps, to pay attention to the momentum of their own lives). Left behind, as the segregationists of the day kept saying, would be the same old people: sheriffs, businessmen, politicians, and always near at hand, the Mississippi Highway Patrol. On the other hand, the apparently infinite patience of the Hopis, their children's astonishingly high acquies-

cence, in the face of this world's trials and limitations, their continued veneration of so much that is, inevitably, a bulwark to political
quietism, may one day, in a flash, give way to widespread social unrest or protest, even as the Pueblo boy who is reluctant to fight it out
with his white classmate nevertheless makes it clear that, pushed hard
enough, he stands quite definitely on certain ground (literally and
symbolically) and is not averse to self-defense.

Put differently, the attitude that children have toward political authority, toward those who rule them, possess power over them, is but
one element in their developing lives. As the Pueblo boy makes quite
clear, one can at the very least be perplexed by or find oneself alien to
a whole culture, including its political authority, yet be brought up
with enough realism to know what is and is not possible under a
given set of circumstances. We are left, naturally, with the knowledge that *one* element in a growing child's life is his or her political
awareness — some of it, actually, destined to be "forgotten" as the
demands of a given society exert themselves with ever-increasing
urgency. Not everything, though, gets shunted aside into those
"deeper" layers of the mind that psychiatrists study. The poor, the
racially excluded, the long since subdued (who work, "quaintly," on
rugs or jewelry on their reservations), the constantly exploited or
humiliated who live in North America, South America, Europe,
Asia, and certainly, in every part of Africa, have had a way, history
shows, of holding on, as Freud says people do, to their earliest impressions, and treating them, in later years, as important reference
points — a means, actually, of interpreting "reality."

Those of us who want to understand how children grow up to em-
body the political and ideological variations of this planet — revo-
lutionists, loyal soldiers, restive but apparently obliging "natives,"
troubled men of property, confident proponents of one or another
government — would do well to recognize that, like adult sexuality,
a political inclination has a "developmental history." There are, of
course, all too many psychological determinists; one winces at the
thought that "developmental history" will quite soon be read as "developmental imperative." In fact, both clinicians and historians have
reason to know that in the lives of individuals and nations alike there
is simply no way of knowing at what moment an apparently unre-
markable, even unknowable set of feelings or attitudes will suddenly

emerge, to everyone's surprise, as utterly critical and persuasive in the life of a person or community of people. Or, as a Hopi girl of thirteen put it, blending a child's political awareness with a culture's wisdom, and an intelligent citizen's practicality: "The news of Watergate is a dark cloud. The sky was clear, and the hunters ran wild; then dark clouds gathered and rain fell, and the hunters stopped for a while. Will we soon get more hunters, just as greedy? Or will we learn to control greed, so that we don't just pray and pray for bad weather to stop the hunters in their tracks?"

We in America, not to mention others elsewhere, could perhaps profit from such an analysis, made by a "culturally disadvantaged" person, a mere child, who has yet to become as "politically socialized" as her parents, never mind "the people with a long reach," as some Hopis, with only the thinnest of smiles on their faces, refer to a number of our leaders in Washington, D.C. As for those Indian children who fall back upon the tribal imagery they have learned, and represent that political authority in the form of a fierce mountain lion or a nondescript but large, toothy, hungry animal — somewhere in this universe the spirit of Simone Weil, mindful of her essay on imperial Rome with the title "The Great Beast," must be attentive indeed.

The New York Review of Books, 1975

40

PSYCHOANALYSIS AND

MORAL DEVELOPMENT

For 20 years my wife and I have been trying to learn how children manage under a variety of circumstances: racial exclusion and efforts to undo it; extreme poverty or social and cultural marginality; the apparent rootlessness of a migrant life; religious and ethnic confrontation; and, not least, the ironically puzzling, even at times burdensome life that gets called "affluent" or "privileged," among other names. As I look back at this work, I realize that I have had several different angles of vision with respect to it. At first I was interested in stress and its vicissitudes — an early research interest that developed out of medical (as well as psychiatric) responsibilities I had when in training at the Massachusetts General Hospital in Boston. We had an epidemic of polio in the middle 1950s, maybe the last such outbreak this nation will ever see: iron lungs all over a hospital floor. Those people depended upon an electric cord for life itself; in time their minds became distinctively preoccupied with a particular range of worries, fears, and doubts. I regarded my work to entail a certain linear obligation: listen carefully; document the stresses and, in response to them, the defensive responses; write up a report which (one would hope) offers yet additional information on how a threatened, hurt mind deals with its given situation, if not fate.

In time I became more immersed in the overall *lives* of the individuals I was getting to know. I saw it my task to document the distinguishing psychological characteristics, as best I could ascertain them, of certain kinds of childhood — what it means, day in and day out, to be a child alive up in a hollow of Appalachia or "on the road" with migrant farmworker parents. I tried to write stories — factual narratives whose content and import, I hoped, would instruct the reader in the diversity of life, even within one or another region of the country and among this or that segment of its people. Later, I tried making comparisons — the way it goes in a ghetto, say, as against the way it goes in a wealthy urban setting or, indeed, in a foreign community (poor or middle-class or rich).

Now, in retrospect, I have begun to realize that all along my wife had the clearest idea of what we both were up to, starting in the late 1950s and early 1960s as we wandered through a South both confused and challenged by racial conflict. A white teacher had told my wife, also a teacher, how "intensely moral" some of the black children were whom she had begun (for the first time) to teach, in accordance with a federal court order. My wife suggested, at the time, that I explore that matter, try to find out what made such children, so vulnerable in so many ways, behave in a manner that would prompt the curiosity if not the awe of their teachers. I answered quickly: I was already doing that — observing the various "defense mechanisms" which a crisis had been generating in a number of children.

Yet, as Erik H. Erikson has shown us in his studies of Luther and Gandhi, and as any number of clinicians come to realize in the course of their everyday professional lives, neither among the great nor among ordinary people do defense mechanisms quite account for the entirety of psychological life. We all have them, and of course, the particular tone of each life has to do significantly with what defenses we use, with what frequency or emphasis, and on what occasions. But the moral texture of a life is, one suspects, not going to be fully explained by an analysis of how the ego negotiates with the id and the superego. Nor is the ego or the superego, important though they be to an understanding of moral development, quite all we need to know in the face of certain dilemmas — the ethical behavior seemingly "limited," even "backward" people display, not to mention the mischievous, sometimes deceitful, and certainly callous actions which one can find in highly intelligent, well-educated individuals, even those who have had the advantage of receiving rather a lot of psychological knowledge, whether in courses or in treatment.

A well-developed conscience does not translate, necessarily, into a morally courageous life. Nor do well-developed powers of philosophical thinking and moral analysis necessarily translate into an everyday willingness to face down the various evils of this world. I was once helped in the above effort at clarification by a black woman whom I suppose I'd have to call illiterate, if not, God save us, "culturally disadvantaged" and "culturally deprived." She pointed out that "there's a lot of people who talk about doing good, and a lot of people who argue about what's good and what's not good." Then she added that "there are a lot of people who always worry about whether they're doing right or doing wrong." Finally, there are some other folks: "They just put their lives on the line for what's right, and they may not be the ones who talk a lot or argue a lot or worry a lot; they just do a lot!"

Her daughter happened to be Ruby Bridges, one of the black children who, at the age of 6, initiated school desegregation in New Orleans against terrible, fearful odds. For days that turned into weeks and weeks that turned into months, this child had to brave murderously heckling mobs, there in the morning and there in the evening, full of threats and slurs and hysterical denunciations and accusations. Federal marshals took her to school and brought her home. She attended school all by herself for a good part of a school year, due to a total boycott by white families. Her parents, of sharecropper background, had only recently arrived in the great, cosmopolitan port city — yet another poor black family of rural background trying to find a slightly better deal in an urban setting. They were unemployed, though — and, like Ruby, in jeopardy; mobs threatened them, too.

Still, Ruby persisted, and so did her parents. Ruby's teachers, no great integrationists, began to wonder *how come* — about the continuing ability of such a child to bear such adversity, and with few apparent assets as far as her family background was concerned. I reassured those teachers, I regret to say, with the notion that all was not as it seemed. Ruby appeared strong, but she would, soon enough, show signs of psychological wear and tear. Perhaps she was "denying" her fears and anxieties; perhaps her strange calm in the face of such obvious danger represented a "reaction formation." Then there was this bit of information to figure out psychodynamically:

I was standing in the classroom, looking out the window, and I saw Ruby coming down the street, with the federal marshals on both sides of her. The crowd was there, shouting, as usual. A woman spat at Ruby but missed; Ruby smiled at her. A man shook his fist at her; Ruby smiled at him. Then she walked up the stairs, and she stopped and turned and smiled one more time! You know what she told one of the marshals? She told him she prays for those people, the ones in that mob, every night before she goes to sleep!

The words of a white schoolteacher — incredulous and, by that time, quite perplexed. As for me, I'd been interested in knowing how Ruby slept at night (an indicator of her state of apprehension, a measure of how well she was handling things mentally), but I hadn't thought to inquire about what she said or even thought each night before falling off. What to make of such a concern being addressed by such a child? I asked Ruby, after a while, about her prayers — fi rst telling her what I'd heard from the teacher. Ruby was cheerful and matter-of-fact, if terse, in her reply: "Yes, I do pray for them." I wondered why. She said only, "Because." I waited for more, but to no effect. I started over, told her I was curious about why she would want to pray for people who were being so unswervingly nasty to her. She acknowledged the factuality I had described, but reminded me of another element of factuality which I had apparently overlooked or not taken the trouble to consider in any attentive fashion: her churchgoing activities, and their significance to her, to her family, to her friends and their families. "I go to church," she told me, "every Sunday, and we're told to pray for everyone, even the bad people, and so I do." She had no more to say on that score.

When I finally began to take notice of Ruby's churchgoing activities, and those of her parents, I'm afraid I was not very responsive to what I heard and saw. Always I wanted to fit what I was learning into what I had already learned — use what was, after all, a somewhat new "reality" for me, if not "human actuality" (James Agee's phrase), in order to say yes once more to the psychological theory I'd acquired before going South. Ruby was picking up phrases, admonitions, statements ritually expressed, bits and pieces of sermons emotionally delivered, and using all that in a gesture of obedience. She was being psychologically imitative. Her parents told her to pray for her tormentors, even as those parents had been told to do likewise by their minister, and Ruby said yes, of course. She did what she was told, but did she truly understand what she was doing? Was she not, rather, showing herself to be a particular 6-year-old child — scared, vulnerable, not able to read or write, limited cognitively, vulnerable emotionally — holding on for dear life with brave smiles and silence outside the inside school, and with prayers at home?

Was she not, besides, a poor black child in an extremely hostile Southern city neighborhood grasping at whatever straws came her way — hence her brave avowals of prayerful concern for those who, after all, wanted to kill her and had no reluctance to say so again and again? When I did prod the child a bit, I got this evidence of what I then concluded to be fearful piety:

> They keep coming and saying the bad words, but my momma says they'll get tired after a while and then they'll stop coming. They'll stay home. The minister came to our house and he said the same thing, and not to worry, and I don't. The minister said God is watching and He won't forget, because He never does. The minister says if I forgive the people, and smile at them and pray for them, God will keep a good eye on everything and He'll be our protection.

She stopped and seemed positive. I thought I felt some doubt, some uncertainty — hers, of course! I asked her if she believed the minister was on the right track. "Oh, yes," she said; and then came a kind explanation for the benighted, agnostic, Yankee visitor: "I'm sure God knows what's happening. He's got a lot to worry about; but there is bad trouble here, and He can't help but notice. He may not rush to do anything, not right away. But there will come a day, like you hear in church."

She wasn't sure exactly what would happen on that "day." Even the above remarks weren't delivered as a brief sermon, but constitute an assembled collection of terse explications, delivered over the course of an hour or two of talk on a warm, moist spring afternoon in 1961, a terrible time for that American child and, arguably, for her country as well. Was she, with those comments, whistling in the dark? Was she repeating in rote submission the clichés a long-impoverished and persecuted people had learned to rely upon — the analgesic self-deceptions of those who, through no fault of their own, have never quite learned to think rationally, logically, or, as some of us would put it, "maturely"? How well did she really understand what was happening to her city, to her neighborhood, to herself and her family? Set aside her appearance, her pietistic avowals, and her quick smiles, and one would find a terror-struck black child just barely in control of herself — or so I thought; and the same held for her parents, I also believed.

Meanwhile, my wife's skepticism was directed not at Ruby Bridges and her family, but at the kind of inquiry I seemed determined to make, no matter what. Nor would the work we did elsewhere, in Appalachia or among migrants, nor the involvement we had with young civil rights activists, serve to weaken that skepticism. The more I tried to understand the emotional conflicts, the tensions and responses to tensions, the underlying motivations, and the projections and displacements; the more I emphasized the automatic or reflexic behavior of the children we knew, a consequence of their short lives, their lack of education, their limited cognitive development, their inability to handle all sorts of concepts and symbols; the more I read and commented on various developmental points of view, which emphasized stages and phases and periods — and, of course, consigned elementary schoolchildren such as Ruby Bridges to the lower rungs of this or that ladder — the more my wife kept pointing to the *acts* of these boys and girls, the *deeds* they managed.

Soon enough, we had come to know an extraordinary range of children and parents. We had come to know, in fact, a group of poor and poorly educated people who, nevertheless, acquitted themselves impressively in pursuit of significant ethical objectives. I think not only of Dr. King and Ralph Abernathy but of Rosa Parks, a seamstress, whose decision to sit where she pleased on a Montgomery, Alabama, bus in the middle 1950s preceded the emergence of the so-called civil rights movement and of those two ministers as leaders of it. I think of the four college youths who, quietly and without publicity (at first), decided to challenge the segregationist laws of Greensboro, North Carolina, in early February 1960. I think of the many black children my wife and I came to know, in Arkansas and Louisiana and Georgia and Alabama and Mississippi — and of certain white children, too, who braved awful criticism to befriend them: young leaders of a changing South, young *moral* leaders. Whence that moral capacity, that moral spirit, that moral leadership? How are we to make sense of such moral behavior psychodynamically? And how are we, at the same time, to make sense of the well-known involvement of such towering intellectual and moral figures as Heidegger or Jung with Nazism, not to mention the justification of Stalin's vicious, conniving, murderous dictatorship by so many self-styled members of one or another nation's intelligentsia? More broadly, what makes for a moral *life* — for moral *action* — as opposed to moral reflection and analysis and argument? What do we mean, moreover, when we talk about "moral development" and, with the help of psychoanalytic theory as well as the concepts given us by Piaget and Kohlberg, define and declare who is able to reach what "stage" of such "development"?

I think it fair to say that a child such as Ruby was in 1961 (aged 6, black, Southern, of extremely poor background) would not be a likely candidate for the kind of moral accolades some of us secular, agnostic, 20th-century social scientists are likely to hand out. She was not "mature." She was, no doubt, right smack in the middle of an oedipus conflict. She had, without question, the kinds of cognitive inadequacies we have all come to find important to remember — and connect to the general (academic and social) behavior of the young. She was hardly a candidate for the higher level of performance, with respect to moral analysis, that Lawrence Kohlberg requires if he is to call one in possession of "postconventional" or "autonomous" moral thought. Here, by the way, is what Kohlberg tells us about the subject we were and still are trying to understand:

> Moral development is therefore a result of an increasing ability to perceive social reality or to organize and integrate social experience. One necessary — but not sufficient — condition for principled morality is the ability to reason logically (represented by stages of formal operations).
>
> The main experiential determinants of moral development seem to be amount and variety of social experience, the opportunity to take a number of roles and to encounter other perspectives. Thus middle-class and popular children progress further and faster than do lower-class children and social isolates. Similarly, development is slower in the semiliterate village cultures that have been studied.

I suppose Ruby lived in a "village culture" of sorts. Surely she wasn't a member of the middle class. For Kohlberg, she was a "preconventional" or "premoral" lass. Her prayers, her smiles, were, I suppose, mere gestures, not the careful responses of a truly reflective person — a Cambridge theorist, for example. As for many other children we knew in the South, both black and white, I doubt they would fare much better in Kohlberg's scheme of things. I have in mind the first white youth to speak to a black in one of Atlanta's desegregated high schools. He was from a family all too easily called, by the likes of me, "redneck." He was a tough athlete, a poor student, not a well-read boy of 14. God save him, he'd never been up there in Harvard Square, never been presented with all those moral situations freighted with twists and turns, alternatives and possibilities! He'd never been asked to say what he'd do *if*. . . He might have come across then; even now in his adulthood he might still come across, as one of the millions whose fate it has been (according to Kohlberg et al.) that they be "conventional" moral thinkers at best.

Nevertheless, the young man found himself, inexplicably and suddenly, without any forethought (he later had to acknowledge this repeatedly, when asked by me and others), impelled to help out "a nigger" (the words of the helper!). He described the incident (and himself) this way:

> I didn't want any part of them here. They belong with their own, and we belong with our own — that's what we all said. Then those two kids came here, and they had a tough time. They were all by themselves. The school had to get police protection for them. We didn't want them, and they knew it. But we told them so, in case they were slow to get the message. I didn't hold back, no more than anyone else. I said, "Go, nigger, go," with all the others. I meant it. But after a few weeks, I began to see a kid, not a nigger — a guy who knew how to smile when it was rough going, and who walked straight and tall, and was polite. I told my parents, "It's a real shame that someone like him has to pay for the trouble caused by all those federal judges."
>
> Then it happened. I saw a few people cuss at him. "The dirty nigger," they kept on calling him, and soon they were pushing him in a corner, and it looked like trouble, bad trouble. I went over and broke it up. I said, "Hey, cut it out." They all looked at me as if I was crazy, my white buddies and the nigger, too. But my buddies stopped, and the nigger left. Before he left, though, I spoke to him. I didn't mean to, actually! It just came out of my mouth. I was surprised to hear the words myself: "I'm sorry." As soon as he was gone, my friends gave it to me: "What do you mean, 'I'm sorry'!" I didn't know what to say. I was as silent as the nigger they stopped. After a few minutes, we went to basketball practice. That was the strangest moment of my life.

His life had, in fact, changed. In no time, it seemed, he was beginning to talk more consciously (more self-consciously, actually) to the black youth. Soon, he was championing him personally, while still decrying "integration." Finally, he would become a friend of the black youth's and advocate "an end to the whole lousy business of segregation." Meanwhile, it was for me to explain that shift — in an ordinary, 14-year-old boy just starting high school; a boy who, by the way, had to endure lots of scorn himself from the many others who were not as swift as he to show a change in racial attitudes. Press and press that youth, and what does one find? He once told me:

I'd be as I was, I guess, but for being there in school that year and seeing that kid — seeing him behave himself, no matter what we called him, and seeing him being insulted so bad, so real bad. Something in me just drew the line, and something in me began to change, I think.

That youth's tentativeness, his willingness to suggest the complexity of things, contrasts, alas, with the categorical assurance of some theorists who have moral development all figured out, as if life were a matter of neatly arranged academic hurdles, with grades given along the way. Here was a young person with a story George Eliot would have comprehended (as in *Middlemarch*): the *circumstances* that make for such a difference in our lives, the accidents, the incidents that come along out of nowhere, it seems. *Fate* is the word other generations used, and *destiny* — but, of course, to accept what such words imply about this life takes matters out of the hands of those of us who want control, who want to be able to predict all, explain all.

Moral life is not to be confused, one has to keep emphasizing, with tests meant to measure certain kinds of abstract (moral) thinking, or with tests that give people a chance to speculate with hypothetical responses to made-up scenarios. We never quite know what will happen in this life; nor do we know how an event will connect with the various sides of ourselves. It is no secret that we all contend with mental inconsistencies, contradictions — the disparate elements which each of us tries, day in and day out, to forge into a particular life. Meanwhile, there is the world around us, the various social and political and economic issues, the sweep of history even, which together offer us possibilities or, sadly, take them away, deny them. These past years I have seen children such as Ruby, from the most unpromising of backgrounds, emerge brave, thoughtful, compassionate. I have seen youths such as the one quoted immediately above turn away from what seemed to be their quite definite moral selves — assume a new moral life, it can be said, it *has* been said, by them, by their teachers. Novelists know such developments, and so do ordinary men and women the world over. Why not some of us self-styled psychological "experts," for whom words or phrases such as "will," "honor," "moral stamina," and "ethical choice" seem quaint relics of another age?

Ruby had a will and used it to make an ethical choice; she demonstrated moral stamina; she possessed honor, courage. The white youth I mentioned might have turned into yet another, rather too easily labeled "redneck." His family had all the socio-economic credentials for such a human slope to be the one traversed by him — the outspoken segregationist lad we first got to know in 1961, in Atlanta, Georgia. Instead, a series of events — in a nation's life, a city's, a school system's, a neighborhood's — enabled him to show other aspects of himself and his heritage: a mother's hospitable, warm side, a father's personal courtliness, even to a relentlessly poking, New England-descended doctor. When Walker Percy warned us recently, in *The Second Coming*, that it is possible to "get all A's, and flunk life," he had in mind the instructive discrepancy that occasionally develops between the mind's intellectual life and that larger life we all live. By the same token, there are those who never even have a chance to get respectable grades at a good school — yet they may acquit themselves impressively in the course of their time spent on this earth.

Nevertheless, we need not abandon all efforts to figure out theoretically the mind's moral development. As I look back at two decades of work spent in that so-called "field" — ordinary human beings trying to get from day to day, with no pretense to an interpretation of how they do it, and with no claim to great competence, never mind success — I find certain psychoanalytic concepts truly helpful in explaining what I have seen over and over again. Freud's paper "On Narcissism" (1914) is especially helpful. Early on, before the "object-relations" theorists (especially Winnicott) and before the intensification of interest in narcissism which Heinz Kohut and Otto Kernberg have prompted, Freud had essentially sketched out the truly essential particulars of the young child's earliest moral life — the way he or she comes to (judgmental) terms with himself or herself. Mention is made of "the lost narcissim of his [the child's] childhood, in which he was his own ideal." We are, of course, to call upon the book of books, "east of Eden." Once there was that "garden," that innocence, that self-satisfaction, in the nonpejorative sense. Once there was life uncomplicated by language, by wordy speculation and frustration, by "knowledge." Needs were fulfilled. Attention was paid. Death was nowhere to be seen or heard. I suppose our human, developmental analogue to Eden lasts until the child begins to realize that those attentive, nourishing faces (and bottles and breasts), those smiles of eager, persistent approval, have to give way to another kind of concern. The baby starts noticing that the eyes aren't so widely affirming, the voice has an edge to it. Yes gives way to Oh! Oh! Then No arrives; then No! No! Soon it is not only the parents who are offering only qualified love; the child has begun to turn on himself, herself, with the gradually increasing vigor of a ready learner. Language appears — the precise particulars of its (neurophysiological, psychological) appearance still a mystery, for all the explanations. The body's functions become the subject of a struggle. The child who used to lie down and be the subject of grateful, enthusiastic demonstrations of approval is now up and about, caught in a series of negotiations — give and take; and "knows" about all that, to a significant degree, through the exchange of words, messages.

I am hardly breaking new ground here! But I think it important to emphasize the "ego ideal" Freud mentioned in his paper cited above. The ego ideal represents an effort on the part of the child to regain the kind of self-love once enjoyed so freely, relatively speaking. One thinks of a child looking upward, seeing eyes liquid-warm with adoration. One thinks of the child looking upward, hearing the cooing reassurance of all eternity, it must seem — the infinity, almost, of parental space. With the fall comes "development," "progress" — and yearning. The ego ideal is born out of the infant's inevitable entrance into the world of what Paul Tillich kept calling "finitude." Put differently, the ego ideal represents memory as well as desire — a recollection of everyday satisfaction (no matter the gas pains, the unease which culminates in diaper changes) that makes the new vicissitudes of growth seem a bad judgment of sorts.

Of course, we are idealizing somewhat that period when the ego ideal is born; no parent is perfect, so every parent will add a quota of frustrations to those just mentioned which are imposed by nature. The issue is a relative one — the joys of acquiescent, preverbal support, rather constantly offered, as against the hurdles which accompany the child who speaks and understands speech, the child who must lose the breast and worry about cleanliness — indeed, worry about more and more matters, a world without end, it seems. The superego, we know, grows slowly — months and months, years and years, of lessons learned, disappointments severely felt, difficulties endured and not forgotten. It is not only a matter of "right" as against "wrong," of "conscience" in the vernacular sense. The superego has to contend with the disenchantment of self-love, with the child's increasingly critical eye, which responds to the vision of parents, teachers, friends; and with, not least, the self-judgment that naturally follows the experience of change — in Biblical terms, once again, the trek east of Eden. The ego ideal represents our effort to recover the past; we look upward, hoping to see what we once enjoyed so very much, a particular spell of uninterrupted sunshine. The clouds of a later life prompt us to look, to keep looking with hope and anticipation (if with, too, an edge of anxious doubt) for that lost radiance.

Meanwhile, we have to accommodate ourselves to the norms and values of the world we belong to. Not only must we measure up to the hopes generated by an early but increasingly challenged narcissism, to the dreams and values of the best side of our parents, to the grand and noble pieties of a more social nature — national imperatives, ethnic or racial slogans — we must also deal with the hundreds of no's, many intimidating indeed, which gradually make us run for various covers or learn to take (adroitly or truculently) a particular stand. There is wear and tear in this life, and our sense of our worth reflects that inevitable moral strain we feel. Entire modes of existence turn out to be, on close inspection, a response of a "personality" to various internalized psychological injuries: the superego registering its perceptions, and those perceptions calling for a day-to-day (protective) response. (Wilhelm Reich's so-called "character armor," or the so-called "character disorders" one hears discussed rather often these days.)

I am, yet again, coming up with nothing very startling. But let me move from this brief, simply stated reference to some of the "variables" which touch upon our sense of ourselves, our judgment of what we'd like, what we miss, how we ought to behave, to an approach that is less explicitly psychological. In the course of doing work with young black and white people in the South, I heard many a statement of willfulness, determination; many a statement of apprehension, fear, foreboding. Sometimes I heard both kinds of statements worked into one statement. I heard plenty of ideals defined, plenty of goals espoused, plenty of wrongs denounced and rights upheld. I heard a lot of people talk about themselves, their "rockbottom self," their "deep-down self." I heard parents and teachers wonder about children or youth. What did they believe in? Why were they behaving as they were?

Here is a 13-year-old girl talking, in September 1964:

I'm glad we're finally standing up for ourselves. It's been such a long time! We can't be down and out forever! You have to keep your eyes on the goal. Otherwise, you'll get low. Even when those whites say the worst things in the world to you, even when they tell you that your days are numbered and they'll "get" you, even then you have to smile to yourself, whether you smile to them or not, and you have to say to yourself what Dr. King says, and our minister says: "We're headed for the Promised Land, and there's no stopping us now!" There will be days when I close my eyes, and I think of the Promised Land — lots of nice people, and all the food you want, and no one against you, and everyone trying to be of help, and everything where it should be, and no mobs, and lots of candy, especially chocolate bars! But then I remember that first we have to win the battles here, and only later, when we pass on, will we have a long rest. If we can turn around the white folks, the devil will be an easy one to take on! So I try to be good, to do what's right, and I know He's watching, the Good Lord, and in the end He'll call us to Him, and then there will be the bad folks, standing off somewhere, the people who wanted to kill us, and the Klan, and they'll be told by the Lord to wear their robes, whether they want to or not, and they'll be judged and they'll be put where they belong, and if we mind our manners and keep ourselves on the right side, we'll find our place, and it'll be a good rest, and we'll look back and say, *"We did it,* yes, *we did it,"* no matter the sheriff and all his buddies and their guns, and the Mississippi Highway Patrol and their guns.

From a poor family, she had somehow managed to obtain rather a lot: strength to integrate a Southern school; strength to be a young activist in the face of extreme hostility and plenty of danger; strength to believe not only in a particular social and political effort but also in herself as someone able and worthy to take part in it; and strength to maintain her high hopes, to keep her spirits up, no matter the serious obstacles in her way. Whence such strength — in a child whose parents were illiterate, unemployed, with few prospects? For years I have seen such children; they have lots of burdens to overcome, including, often enough, serious educational ones. But over and over I have witnessed their courage and tried to comprehend it — with little luck, as far as psychiatric characterization goes. If I had to offer an explanation, though, I think it would start with the religious tradition of black people, which is of far more significance than many white observers and possibly a few black critics have tended to allow.

In home after home I have seen Christ's teachings, Christ's life, connected to the lives of black children by their parents. Even as Eden was the first Promised Land, and Christ (a second Adam) promised another Eden ("a new heaven and a new earth"), so young children have been taught to regard themselves (have been regarded) as anointed ones, of sorts: those who will lead their people to a better fate, indeed. Such a religious tradition connects with the child's sense of what is important, what matters — the ego ideal. And with the parents' sense, too — as anyone knows who has been in a black church and heard the statements, the hard praying, and seen the look of pain give way to the look of hope in countless faces. At the same time, of course, there is the superego we all mention so often — the scrupulosity of churches, the breast-beating, and the self-lacerating judgments one also hears in many black churches, where an emotional, passionate religion is in no way shunned. Blacks know that the way to heaven is long and difficult; that if one is to gain that final nod of affirmation (the sanction of the ego idea), one has to pass many tests set up by a demanding world (whence the superego).

Such connections are not new to this century. Even as the child quoted above made the obvious leap from her race's struggle to her personal life and showed through her imagery the hopes she holds

for herself, the worries she has about her goodness, her correct conduct, St. John of the Cross, in the 16th century, made an eloquent
analysis of the difficulties in the path of, say, a novice monk, a convert to a religious life:

> It must be known, then, that the soul, after it has been definitely
> converted to the service of God, is, as a rule, spiritually nurtured
> and caressed by God, even as is the tender child by its loving
> mother, who warms it with the heat of her bosom and nurtures it
> with sweet milk and soft and pleasant food, and carries it and ca-
> resses it in her arms; but, as the child grows bigger, the mother
> gradually ceases caressing it, and, hiding her tender love, puts bit-
> ter aloes upon her sweet breast, sets down the child from her arms
> and makes it walk upon its feet, so that it may lose the habits of a
> child and betake itself to more important and substantial occupa-
> tions.

The point is not yet another outburst of 20th-century psychological reductionism. The point is that a wise mystic knew how to draw
upon human experience when considering the moral struggles of his
own kind — and of our kind, too. It is in our nature. St. John of the
Cross knew, and so did the black child just quoted, to hope against
hope, and in doing so, to be reminded of the first such episode —
those strongly felt days, weeks, months, when hope seemed (in
retrospect) so simple, so forthcoming, so free of impediments,
obstacles, impasses, commands, threats, criticism, not to mention
self-criticism. Still, it is our fate to lose those precious days, to harken
back to them in thought and fantasy and desire, to merge such a psychological inclination to look back with the imperatives that push us
on. I believe that the active idealism we see in some of our young
takes place when a beckoning history offers, uncannily, a blend of
memory and desire: a chance to struggle for a new situation which
holds a large promise, while earning along the way the approval of
one's parents, neighbors, friends, and, not least, oneself.

In psychoanalytic language, we might speak of an ego ideal given
a new lease on life and reality, and now in extraordinary harmony
with the often skeptical if not overbearing judgment of the superego.
In the everyday language of our lives, the moral life gets a wonderful

charge of energy: an old dream has become newly sanctioned by a fateful turn of history. No wonder little Ruby, when she was 9, looked back and said, "We inched a little closer to God, and because we did we became a little better ourselves!" A child who knew the subject of moral development cold, or should I say hot? One childhood's "lost narcissism" had become, by the grace of a given social struggle, an element in a *nation's* moral development. It is for others to speak of what, if anything, happens to us after we die. I only know that I don't expect, this side of the grave, to see anything more "transcendent" than the above-stated child's description of a particular kind of moral experience.

INDEX

Index

Index

Narcissism, 86, 88, 93, 94, 111, 112, 403; and narcissistic character disorder, 87
National Association for Mental Health, 67
National Institute of Mental Health, 84
National Institutes of Health, 24, 25
National Socialism, 40. *See also* Nazis and Nazism
Navaho Indians: and politics, 386, 387
Nazis and Nazism, 39, 183, 197, 245, 363, 399; scholarship on, 278; in Vienna, 154
New England Journal of Medicine, xxv
New Introductory Lectures, The (Freud), 200, 224
Newman, Cardinal, 188
New Mexico, 97
New Orleans Psychoanalytic Institute, ix
New Republic, 140
New Yorker, 318, 319
New York Graphic Society, 255
New York Post, 62
New York Psychoanalytic Institute, 217
New York Review of Books, 340
Niebuhr, Reinhold, 11
Nietzsche, Friedrich, 72, 295
Nixon, Richard, 45, 47, 278; Mazlish's study of, 287–89
Normality and Pathology in Childhood (Freud, A.), 158

"Obsessive Actions and Religious Practices" (Freud), 199
O'Connor, Flannery, 96, 210, 320, 327, 330; quoted, 329
Oedipus (Sophocles), 5, 301
Office of Strategic Services, 281
Olsen, Tillie, 330, 334
One Flew Over the Cuckoo's Nest (Kesey), 74
"On Narcissism" (Freud), 92, 403
Original sin, 111
Origins of Intelligence in Children, The (Piaget), 170
Orlando, Vittorio, 246
Orthogenic School (Bettelheim), 183
Orwell, George, 48, 49, 50, 55, 101, 330
Oswald, Lee Harvey, 19, 288
Outline of Psychoanalysis (Freud), 149
Outrageous, 73, 74

Parks, Rosa, 399
Parricide, 42
Partisan Review, xxv, 315
Pascal, Blaise, 193, 213, 216; *Pensées,* 215, 216; *Provincial Letters,* 215; quoted, 215
Paul, Saint, 84, 273
Paxil, xviii

Pax Romana, 364
Peale, Norman Vincent: *Power of Positive Thinking, The,* 193
Peck, Gregory, 74
Peloponnesian War, 93
Penicillin, 59
Pensées (Pascal), 84, 215, 216
Pentagon Papers, 280
Percy, Walker, 96, 212, 237, 311, 315, 320–23; *Lancelot,* 322; *Last Gentleman, The,* 318, 321, 336; *Lost in the Cosmos,* 336; *Love in the Ruins,* 81, 82, 320, 322; *Moviegoer, The,* xxii, 317, 318, 320, 336; *Second Coming, The,* 321
Percy, William Alexander, 321
Perry, Helen Swick, 217, 218, 222; quoted, 219, 220
Pfister, Oskar, 263
Phenomenon of celebrity, 91
Phobic disorders, 59
Piaget, Jean, 3, 167, 171, 172, 173, 273, 383, 399; *Child's Conception of Physical Causality, The,* 170; *Child's Conception of the World, The,* 170; direct observation of children, 169; *Judgment and Reasoning in the Child,* 170; *Language and Thought of the Child, The,* 170; *L'Epistémologie Génétique,* 170; *Moral Judgment of the Child, The,* 170; *Origins of Intelligence in Children,* 170; *Six Psychological Studies,* 168
Placebo effect, xviii
Plato, 225, 366; *Timaeus,* 206
Poincaré, Raymond, 247, 248
Polio, 393
Political activists, 28
Politics, 225; apartheid, 340; children and, 353, 356, 362, 368, 369, 372, 374, 375, 377–91
Populism: racism and, 39–42, 47, 49, 50
Power! (Korda), 89
Power of Positive Thinking, The (Peale), 193
Price, Reynolds, 96
Principles of Intensive Psychotherapy (Fromm-Reichman), 69
Prisons, 33; critique of, 28, 34–36; war resisters in, 25–34
Prozac, xix
Psychiatrists, 3, 174; American acceptance of, 6; black child, 229; child, 67; concentration in Northeast, 62; conformity among, 9; Laing on, 176–80; portrayed in films, 72–74; portrayed in Styron's work, 325